Nick Rider, Harvey Holtom
and John Howell

Buying a property
SPAIN

D0109077

CADOGANguides

Contents

About the authors

Nick Rider is the author of Cadogan Guides' *Yucatan & Mayan Mexico* and *Short Breaks in Northern France*. He writes articles on food, travel, history, music and art, and has been a guest on Radio 5's *Globetrotting*. Having lived in Spain for many years, he is currently based in London.

Harvey Holtom has lived in Madrid for 20 years, where he has worked as a teacher, translator, photographer and writer. He is currently the correspondent for the *Time Out* website, has worked on all five editions of the *Time Out Madrid* guide and has contributed articles on Madrid and other Spanish topics to various publications.

John Howell established John Howell & Co in Sheffield in 1979, and by 1997 it had become one of the largest and most respected law firms in the north of England, employing over 100 lawyers. On moving to London in 1995, John Howell has gone on to specialise in providing legal advice to clients buying property in France, Spain, Italy and Portugal and more recently Turkey and Croatia.

Cadogan Guides
2nd Floor
233 High Holborn
London WC1V 7DN
info@cadoganguides.co.uk
www.cadoganguides.com

The Globe Pequot Press
246 Goose Lane, PO Box 480, Guilford,
Connecticut 06437–0480

Copyright © Cadogan Guides 2002, 2005
"THE SUNDAY TIMES" is a registered trade mark of
Times Newspapers Limited.

Cover photographs: front © Barry Mason/Alamy;
back © Robert Harding Picture Library Ltd/Alamy;
Elizabeth Whiting & Associates/Alamy
Maps © Cadogan Guides, drawn by Maidenhead
Cartographic Services
Cover design: Sarah Rianhard-Gardner
Editor: Linda McQueen
Proofreader: Susannah Wight
Indexing: Isobel McLean

Produced by **Navigator Guides**
www.navigatorguides.com

Printed in Finland by WS Bookwell
A catalogue record for this book is available from
the British Library
ISBN 10: 1-86011-179-3
ISBN 13: 978-1-86011-179-8

The author and publishers have made every effort to ensure the accuracy of the information in this book at the time of going to press. However, they cannot accept any responsibility for any loss, injury or inconvenience resulting from the use of information contained in this guide.

Please help us to keep this guide up to date. We have done our best to ensure that the information in it is correct at the time of going to press. But places are constantly changing, and rules and regulations fluctuate. We would be delighted to receive any comments concerning existing entries or omissions. Authors of the best letters will receive a copy of the Cadogan Guide of their choice.

Introduction

Long before mass tourism, Spain had a magnetic quality for northern European travellers, who found there distinct, inspiring qualities that set it apart. Nineteenth-century travellers and writers visited Spain and wrote enthusiastically about what they saw. 'The most extraordinary vital mass in existence,' wrote the English evangelist George Borrow of 1830s Madrid. Bizet's opera *Carmen* was based on the novel of the same name by Prosper Mérimée, who was enthralled by the sassy, passionate tobacco factory girls he observed. The 20th century gave us Laurie Lee's colourful accounts of a country on the brink of Civil War, and several of Hemingway's novels and stories were based there.

The reason for this fascination was that Spain did indeed have something 'different', owing to its history having developed somewhat outside the European mainstream. The French long believed that Africa started at the Pyrenees, attributing a certain attractive savagery to their neighbour. And the Spanish, aware of this, used it to lure tourists here in the 1960s, with posters claiming 'Spain is Different'. This, perhaps unfortunately, helped create a simplistic and distorted view of Spain in the minds of outsiders, based on a few stereotyped images: the flashing-eyed flamenco dancer, the proud, valiant bullfighter, siesta and fiesta. Spain actually is still quite different in many ways, but in terms of a rich cultural diversity that mass tourism has ignored. Western Europe's second largest country does in fact offer more geographic diversity than any other. This includes snow-capped mountains within an hour's drive of the beach, Norwegian-looking fiords and seemingly endless plains, deserts and green pastures. No fewer than four languages, an immense variety of regional cuisines and a true mosaic of cultures all thrive and coexist, refusing to let themselves be sucked into the melting pot and standardised.

Anyone who is seriously thinking of buying a home in Spain must, at some point, have been enthralled by some aspect of the country's culture. Everyone will have their own reasons for wanting to take the step. Young professionals have been decamping in droves from northern European countries in recent years, looking for a new life in less uptight urban centres without renouncing their careers. Older people, the first of the 'settlers' in Spain, are still among the most regular arrivals, in search of sunny tranquillity in which to live out their well-deserved retirement. Young or old, many love the great outdoors and find Spain's wide-open spaces ideal for hiking, mountaineering and skiing. Enthusiasts of water sports find all their needs catered for at many points around the lengthy coastline. Gastronomes, wine-lovers, bird-watchers, clubbers, rock-climbers, potholers, art buffs, Romanesque and Baroque church enthusiasts and golf aficionados all find their needs and desires more than fulfilled. All that variety, and with sunshine to boot, is probably why so many keep coming to live in Spain.

First Steps and Reasons for Buying

Those who buy a property on the sunnier *costas* or the islands – who make up by far the majority of foreign property-buyers in Spain – do so precisely because the mildness of the climate in winter means that a whole range of activities are 'do-able' most of the year round. The weather allows for lots of golf and other sports, leisurely lunches 'al fresco', sitting in the garden, strolling by the sea or walking in the mountains, and many other outdoor pursuits throughout much of the year. Foreign home-owners (and other visitors) find Spanish people on the whole to be welcoming and hospitable, with a zest for life and living. Life, generally, is much more relaxed and laid-back than in overcrowded, uptight northern European countries.

Now part of the euro zone along with most other EU countries, Spain remains relatively – though no longer massively – inexpensive by comparison with the UK and most northern European countries, since several currencies had gained in value against the old Spanish peseta during the 10 years prior to the euro changeover in 2002. Not the least of them was sterling which, after standing for many years at somewhere around the 200 peseta mark, became ever-stronger in the second half of the 1990s, with the help of a couple of peseta devaluations, often reaching 275 or more pesetas and rarely dropping below 250. As a consequence, the purchasing power of pound-bearing Brits increased, making holidays cheaper than ever and properties rapidly more affordable. Since Spain's conversion to the euro, the popular perception is that prices have taken a considerable hike, particularly for everyday things, which most people spend most of their money on. The peseta–euro conversion rate, until the new currency completely replaced the old one, was a little under 167:1. This meant that, for example, a fixed-price *menú del día* costing 1,000 pesetas, equivalent to about £4 and quite common at the time of the changeover, should have set you back €6. Three years on, you will be lucky to find a lunch for much less than €10. Mathematical genius is not required to see that this represents inflation of around 67 per cent in three years. The same may be said of many of the items found in a typical daily shopping basket.

Why Spain?

Buying property in Spain is, ultimately, pretty similar to buying in Britain or any other country. As everywhere, it's a combination of finding the right place, settling on a price and going through several legal and financial procedures that, while apparently complicated, are logical. When first thinking about buying a property in Spain, though, there are many questions that need to be pondered before making any moves. Your answers will determine where you end up living, how you live and in what type of property.

This section is a brief introduction to the general issues involved; following chapters explain all these issues in more detail. In **Profiles of the Regions** there is an in-depth look at the country region by region; **Selecting a Property** helps you to whittle down your choice of local locations and properties from the many available; **Making the Purchase** takes you through the complex process of buying; **Financial Implications** looks at taxation, investement and other money-related issues; **Settling In** covers aspects of moving to Spain and living there; and **Letting your Property** covers the many considerations for those who will be using their home only part of the time and want to let it for the rest. Finally, a thorough **References** section gives you all the back-up resources and contact information you might need throughout the process.

Before you begin looking, you have to consider what part of Spain you would like to live in and what the real possibility is, within your budget, of finding a home to suit your needs (or dreams). Never forget that Spain is the second-largest country in western Europe. Its huge variety of climates, landscapes and lifestyles will make different areas more or less desirable than others, according to how you want to spend your time. The cost of living, and of properties, can also vary a lot from one region to another, as do relative levels of prosperity and poverty, factors that influence the quality of life for locals and foreign residents alike. Finding the right property can take time, but the more you see, the better idea you will get of the overall market. Most buyers tend to look for a property in an area that they have holidayed in several times and grown to know and like. You certainly will not be able to make an extensive house-buying research tour of the whole country, unless you make it your primary occupation.

You should also think about whether you want to live in a city, a small town, an '*urbanización*' or purpose-built development, in a beach villa, in a village or even amid rural isolation.

City, Town, Coast or Country?

City Life

The big Spanish cities, like Madrid, Barcelona and Valencia, are vibrant places with all sorts of attractions. Cultural life is one: lovers of the performing arts, live music and cinema, museum-goers, fans of spectator sport, night-hawks, ravers, bar-hoppers and foodies alike will find life in a Spanish city full of variety and excitement. For those hoping to work or study, the big cities are always going to offer greater opportunities. There are large communities of other, mostly young foreigners doing the same as you will be, for when you feel a need for some support and to chat about non-Spanish things. The proximity of a whole range of services, such as hospitals, schools, transport and sports centres, may also appeal. Like city life anywhere, though, there is always a down-side. Traffic, pollution and noise can be absolutely maddening: Madrid is officially the noisiest capital in Europe. The services may be overstretched owing to the demands made on them. As in any city today, the pace of life and the cost of living often mean that city-dwellers do not, or cannot, take full advantage of all the entertainment and leisure that is on offer. In city centres, you will need to live in a flat, as houses with gardens are not a traditional feature of Spanish big city living – except in the recently created suburbs that are growing around the major cities, living in which may mean that you miss out on some of those features of Spanish life that attracted you here in the first place.

Provincial Capitals and Small Towns

Living in a provincial capital or a small to medium-sized town has its good and bad points. Property prices are nearly always far lower than in Madrid or Barcelona, and mostly lower than those you'll find in the more fashionable places on the *costas*. Amenities are much closer to hand, the pace of life is slower, out-of-town pursuits are more accessible. Compact cities offer a quality of life that big-city dwellers can only envy. Cultural life cannot match that found in the bigger cities but there are touring performances and many cities host excellent theatre, dance and music festivals. All have their local fiestas, usually spectacular and noisy. All older cities have a *'casco viejo'*, or historic centre, often run-down, at times gorgeously restored, but almost always charming and boasting architectural gems; Granada, Girona and Córdoba, to name but three, are cases in point. On the minus side, provincial cities may not have so many convenient transport options, for getting there and getting away, though the increased number of flights between regional airports in both the UK and Spain has made these places much more accessible. In a small town you are far less likely to find a cosmopolitan atmosphere and the occasional company of other English-speakers than in Madrid or Barcelona.

Villages and Rural Isolation

Away from traffic, pollution, other expats, tourists and the madding crowd in general, a house on a piece of land, maybe with mountain or maybe sea views...what more could you want? Well, more than one or two shops to choose from, schools, medical attention, restaurants, tennis courts, a bit of action perhaps. Make sure you really know what living in rural bliss entails before jumping head-first into it. Life in a village or out in the country implies dependence on a car, which may be okay now, if costly, but what about when you get older? You may, of course, find a rural property that is just divine for a snip of a price. Then again, you may find that renovation and maintenance costs mean that the bargain is not quite such a good deal. Still more than in small towns, in villages you will need to get on with local people. Don't forget that, for many years, much of rural Spain has been increasingly depopulated, and in many places almost abandoned. This does mean lower property prices, but it also means stagnant communities with few young people. If you have children, this is something you will want to bear in mind.

Costa Communities, *Urbanizaciones* and Villas

A huge proportion of foreigners buying homes in Spain choose to live in the holiday areas around Spain's coasts and islands, and very often in purpose-built new estates or *urbanizaciones*. The word *urbanización* simply means a housing development, and these have mushroomed in the last 30 years along nearly every part of the *costas* and islands and, increasingly, around inland Spanish towns and cities as well. They can be big or small, attached to a village or completely self-contained, and made up of apartments, single villas or a mix of both. *Urbanizaciones* often represent the most hassle-free way to buy in Spain – especially if you buy 'off the shelf' from one of the developer's agents – since so many are organised for foreign buyers, and may give you a range of other convenient features, such as communal services, and an on-site caretaker to turn to if you have any problems (for more on *urbanizaciones* in general, *see* pp.103–6). Buying in an *urbanización* will thus usually be a very different process from seeking out an individual house in a village or town. The other side of the coin to this is, predictably, their uniform, housing-estate air. Some *urbanización* villas and apartments are also built quite functionally as holiday homes, designed to allow you to enjoy the local beaches, sun, sports and so on for a few weeks each year in a fairly undemanding way. If you want a home for more than this, you should consider what your house and the surrounding development are going to be like to live in all year round, when you may want a bit more comfort, and whether you are happy that your only neighbours are likely to be a constantly changing string of holiday tenants. Other *urbanizaciones* with a greater number of longer-term residents tend to form into little self-contained communities (as epitomised in the classic failed BBC soap of a few years ago, *Eldorado*) – which is fine as long as you get on with your neighbours, but not if you do not! Many, especially on the most popular tourist *costas* like the Costa del Sol and Costa Blanca, are self-contained to the extent that they are isolated from Spanish life and often from any other nationalities as well – as in the case of the developments that are all-British or all-German – so living in them involves a pretty clear choice as to the kind of life-in-the-sun you want. Other, generally higher-priced villa developments, on the other hand, are much more discreet, more spacious, and make more attractive use of the landscape. And one of the pluses of *urbanizaciones* is that, when located in pleasant areas, they offer a happy medium between urban and rural extremes.

In the same coastal holiday areas there are also plenty of individual villas, or converted farmhouses, as well as villages, generally in the hills a little inland from the *costas*, with a high proportion of foreign-owned houses. More often used as second rather than permanent homes, they allow you to combine the attractions of the coast with more of a get-away-from-it-all feel than the more intensive *costa* developments. They are also, predictably, usually more expensive than villas or apartments in *urbanizaciones* – but not always.

Pitfalls and Things to Remember

Wherever and whatever you decide to buy, one important point to bear in mind is that the Spanish property market is currently a seller's market, though whether, or for how long, it will remain so is currently a subject for debate, as certain factors which have caused the massive increases of the last few years become less relevant. Overbuilding means there are currently around three million unused properties in the country. If a slowdown in economic growth and the reduction of EU funds bring downward pressure on house prices, owners of unoccupied properties may decide to sell, which will increase supply and further depress prices. This, however, remains to be seen.

There are, in any case, lots of properties available, to suit all pockets, but genuine bargains are few and far between, and can get snapped up quickly. If, having found the 'right place', you dither too long, you may find somebody has gazumped you by the time you make up your mind. Nobody is suggesting that you take rushed decisions, but try not to ponder for too long.

Whatever type of home you decide on, there are certain safeguards to make sure your dream purchase does not become a nightmare. Looked at objectively, buying a property in Spain is no more complicated than buying in the UK – unfamiliarity with the language is what complicates matters. Many before you have ended up lost in the unfamiliar terrain and have been ripped off by unscrupulous individuals. Properties with no title deeds, others built without planning permission (and/or with a demolition order hanging over them), or that did not even exist, figure in the extensive literature of Spanish property horror stories. Back taxes owed on the property that are 'inherited' by the purchaser; structural faults; dreadful plumbing and wiring; a new construction on that nice empty space in front of the house a year after moving there; summer noise and bustle not appreciated when buying in winter...the list could go on. Do not be too alarmed; all of these problems can be avoided by careful preparation and Chapters 04 and 05 tell you what to do. Remember, thousands of foreign buyers have successfully completed a purchase and are entirely happy with their home.

The most important thing of all is to have a well-informed, independent legal adviser. This cannot be stressed enough, or you may end up regretting ever getting involved. You can use a UK lawyer who specialises in Spanish property, or a local lawyer. Either, if they are true professionals, will provide you with a reliable service for a fraction of the overall cost. Even if the purchase is straightforward, the simple fact of having a lawyer to count on will save you lots of headaches and justify the cost.

To help you get started, and to help deal with all the formalities, it will also be useful and cost-effective to use the services of another professional of whom you've probably never heard, a *gestor*, who can help you with all sorts of minor bureaucracy that your lawyer may not want to be bothered with (*see* pp.216–17).

Buying as a Second Home

With the ever-greater ease and still-falling cost of getting to Spain, it has never been easier for people from Britain and Ireland to have the pleasure of a second home there, to which they can pop over for holidays, winters or even long weekends. A tremendous industry has built up to meet this demand, especially in the marketing of properties in coastal *urbanizaciones*, many of which are handled by specialist property companies that take care of most of the details (although you are still strongly advised to have your own lawyer to check over everything before you commit). Despite the size of the industry, the range and number of properties on offer in many areas means that it's still possible, despite all the recent rises in Spanish property prices, to find apartments for around £60,000. However, in looking for a second home you need to prioritise. If all you're after is somewhere to sleep for a few weeks each year, during which you expect to be out all day and therefore need only limited cooking facilities, this – in the main tourist centres – is what you might be able to expect to get for this kind of price. If you are after anything more, the price will go up, although by how much varies a good deal according to area. You need to think of how many people you expect to entertain there, how often you expect to go there – in which case proximity to useful transport links may be very important – and how long at a time you plan to stay there.

Even if you have no intention of using your Spanish property as a permanent base, there are issues that should be considered beyond the simple question of whether or not you can afford to buy it. A second home that stands empty for long periods needs looking after when you are not there. Damp, storm damage, flooding, burglary or vandalism can occur when a property is left empty. It is in your interests to arrange for somebody to hold a set of keys and keep an eye on the property the rest of the time. This may be another property-owing expat, or a trustworthy local if your property is in a village or rural area; if you have bought in an apartment block or *urbanización*, there will often be a caretaker or administrator whose duties this will include. This person should be authorised to call in plumbers, electricians or any other type of repair specialist and should keep you informed of all developments.

Your property will also be liable for taxes, whether it's occupied or not. This may be a problem if you are absent, forget to pay and then become liable to pay a fine – or worse. The same applies to electricity, gas and water bills, even if everything has been turned off and there has been no consumption. A standing order from your local bank account takes care of this, and arrangements also need to be made for everything else to be dealt with by proxy while you are absent (*see* **Making the Purchase** and **Settling In**).

Furthermore, an unoccupied property does not generate any income. For the incredibly rich this is not a problem, but probably a majority of owners also consider letting the property as a way of paying for it, or at least as a way of defraying expense. It is dangerous, though, to assume that income from guests will cover all of the mortgage and running costs – this is most unlikely. Many buyers have burnt their fingers, expecting much more income from letting than is actually possible. For more on every aspect of buying to let in Spain, *see* **Letting Your Property**.

Buying as a First Home

Buying a property in Spain to use as your first home implies by definition that you intend to burn your bridges and move there lock, stock and barrel. This means leaving behind a home that may have great emotional significance and fond memories, as well as maybe family, friends and a way of life. If you are able to buy your Spanish property without first selling your home then you are clearly in a good position financially. You have the option of letting out that house and getting some income from it, or of selling it and investing the money gained elsewhere. Either way you will not lose out financially, so long as you take expert advice and proceed carefully. You will also have a 'bolt hole' if living in Spain turns out not to be right for you. If, though, you need to sell up in Britain in order to buy the Spanish property, you are burning even more bridges. For that reason the choice of where and what property, and the issue of financial planning (*see* **Financial Implications**) is even more important than when you are buying a second home. Unless you're a committed gambler, you need to think not just about how 'right' it seems now, but also to think about how it might feel in five, ten or 20 years' time, and how you and your family might fit in once the initial novelty has worn off. On the other hand, no decision is completely final, and **Selecting a Property**, 'What If It Doesn't Work Out? (*see* pp.145–6), considers what might happen if you want to pull out.

Buying as an Investment

Many British people view property as an investment as well as a home, expecting their houses to rise in value, if not year by year, at least over time. In most parts of Spain, in contrast, until recently property has not been seen by the Spanish as a particularly good investment. This was because property prices – generally – increased only slowly, and did not provide significant returns once the costs of refurbishment, legal fees and tax on sales were taken into consideration. This situation, though, has changed enormously. There are still some static property prices in more out-of-the-way rural areas where there is an excess of available properties. But in the more economically active and desirable areas of Spain, such as the main cities and the most popular tourist areas, property prices rose considerably throughout most of the 1990s. In fact, they have increased, on average, by 150 per cent since 1997. As yet they show little sign of slowing down, though the Bank of Spain's view is that properties were overvalued by as much as 35 per cent in 2004 and warns that Spanish household debt, at record levels, could negatively affect the property market. Any slump in house prices would most likely hit the internal market hardest, namely Spanish (and permanent resident) householders – Spain has a 90 per cent owner-occupancy rate – rather than foreign investors as prices are still relatively lower than in, say, the UK so losses would be minimal. And in some tourist areas the growth in prices has been in the region of 10–20 per cent per year: One foreign resident, for example, bought a large apartment in Palma de Mallorca in around 1997 for 8 million pesetas or €48,080, at the time a little over £30,000, and he sold the same apartment in summer 2001 for 24 million pesetas (€144,242), or roughly £96,000. The same property would probably fetch almost half as much again now. The Costa del Sol particularly has experienced rapid property price inflation in the last few years, after a slump in the early 1990s.

There is, of course, no guarantee that property prices will continue to increase at this rate; how much your property returns, simply as an investment, may also depend on its rental potential (*see* pp.293–7). The profile of the average foreign buyer in Spain has also changed noticeably, which has had its effect on the demand for homes. Whereas a decade ago most property-seekers were over 50 and looking for retirement homes, nowadays many 30–40-something professionals and business people who work all over Europe are considering buying homes on the Spanish coast. Relocating somewhere sunnier and with unlimited leisure facilities need not be at all traumatic from the point of view of work, as it's as easy to visit clients in Milan, Zurich or Vienna from Málaga as it is from London. If this trend continues, buying in southern Spain will almost certainly represent a still-better investment should you ever decide to sell up.

Getting There and Around

The ease of getting in and out of the most popular parts of Spain has clearly been a major factor in encouraging the rapid growth of Spanish home-buying by Britons. Most **airports** in mainland Spain are about a 2½-hour flight from most UK airports; the Canaries are more like a 3½-hour flight away, but even this does not deter the islands' fans. The arrival of the no-frills **budget airlines** has greatly increased the number of flights, and knocked down prices: airlines like easyJet, Bmibaby, Monarch, My Travel Lite, Ryanair, First Choice and Excel have opened up entirely new routes to complement those of the established carriers like British Airways and Iberia, making it far less of a trek to get to many parts of the country. Previously little-known destinations, such as Girona, Jerez, Murcia, Almería and even Valladolid, are now on the map, often from UK regional airports. Still operating, too, even if less publicised, are the longer-established flight-only **charter operators**, many of which offer routes to every part of Spain and are also very competitive. Clearly, if you are aiming to travel back and forth several times a year to your new home – and still more if you hope to attract plenty of holiday tenants – its accessibility and the availability of reasonably priced travel to the area needs to be taken fully into account.

Should you wish to travel with your own car to Spain there are several routes for crossing France to get there, and also two **car ferry** services direct to northern Spain that allow you a more leisurely journey, to Bilbao and Santander. If you drive all the way, it's possible, with motorway driving, to get across France in about 17 hours, and then down from the border to the Costa del Sol in another 18. A more leisurely way again is the old method – travelling by **train**. Using Eurostar through the Channel Tunnel and then the luxury French high-speed train TGV network (via Paris), you can expect to get to Madrid or Barcelona and then down to southern Spain in less than two days.

Within Spain, the **road infrastructure** has improved enormously in the last couple of decades. Many major trunk roads that 20 years ago were little more than narrow two-lane highways have been widened, with lanes added for heavy goods vehicles and bypasses built around towns. Road markings and signposts are generally better, too. Motorways, '*autopistas*', indicated with an 'A', do not yet form a complete network, but new stretches are being opened constantly and all major cities will eventually be connected. Motorways are not free but, as in France, there is a system of tolls or *peaje*, and different companies operate different motorways or even different stretches of the same one. **Driving in cities** is best avoided if possible, so whenever you go into town it's generally best to find somewhere to park in the outskirts and continue on the (usually excellent) local public transport system, by metro, taxi or bus.

Spain's **rail network**, nearly all of it operated by RENFE, has also received huge investment since the 1980s and plans have recently been unveiled to make further improvements in the coming decades, including bringing high speed trains to all regional capitals. It still has its idiosyncrasies – especially in Andalucía – and not all services are as punctual as others, but most trains are reliable, clean and comfortable, and the prestige, high-speed services can be superb. Standard trains, meanwhile, provide a more efficient and painless way of getting between main towns and villages than driving. Less comfortably, you can also get to just about everywhere in Spain by **coach** (*autocar*), and virtually all towns have a bus station with a wide range of routes. And Spain also has a very extensive **domestic airline** network, especially connecting the Balearic and Canary islands with a variety of mainland airports. Ticket prices were long kept artificially high, but nowadays there are very good deals to be found.

See **Selecting a Property** for more about transport to and within Spain.

Living in Spain

The countless reasons that make Spain an attractive, and increasingly fashionable, country to live in have been mentioned already. All these apart, another advantage is EU membership. Given the negative spin that's habitually put on anything to do with the EU in the British press, many people are still not aware of just how thoroughgoing the system of mutual rights and obligations between member states has become. When taking up residence in another EU country, provided they are not deemed a health or public order risk, British and Irish citizens enjoy practically the same rights as nationals of that country.

To summarise, residency brings with it the following:

- **The right to take up any kind of paid employment, register as a job-seeker and claim unemployment benefits – if you are entitled to them. This also means the same rights on working conditions, pay, sick leave, holidays, redundancy, trade union membership and access to vocational training. There are exceptions: the armed forces or police are not an option, and certain public posts are excluded. As an EU citizen you can, though, become a public employee in Spain if you are prepared to sit the (often difficult) competitive examinations, known as *oposiciones*. Don't even bother if your Spanish is anything short of near-native level. (*See* more below in 'Working in Spain', and in Settling In, pp.219–29.)**

- **The right to enrol your children in Spanish state schools and, provided you fulfil the entry requirements, also to study at a Spanish university.**

- **The right, without restriction, to open a bank account, move money in and out of the country as nationals do, and apply for mortgages.**

- **The right to vote in municipal and European elections. In the case of elections to the European parliament, if you register to vote where you live you forsake your right to vote in your home country. You may also stand as a candidate in both municipal and European elections. Both voting and standing as a candidate are subject to the same rules as nationals. Do not underestimate the power of your vote: in many towns and villages on the *costas* and in the islands foreign residents make up a substantial minority, and are significant contributors to the public coffers. Politicians are aware of this and in many places actively court the foreign vote.**

Rights, of course, imply obligations. Residents, like nationals, are subject to the law of the land and must pay their taxes (*see* Financial Implications, pp.189ff).

Working in Spain

The bureaucratic procedures required of British, Irish and other EU citizens who wish to work in Spain are fairly straightforward. Since Spain became an EU member, however, the situation has become much more restrictive for anyone from outside the EU.

EU Citizens

All EU citizens theoretically belong to the same huge, continent-wide labour market. A plumber from Málaga, supposedly, can fix U-bends in Manchester just as a Mancunian mechanic can fix cars in Málaga. In Spain, British, Irish and other EU citizens no longer need a work permit. Technically, a residency card is no longer obligatory either, as a Royal Decree, effective as of 1 March 2003, scrapped this obligation for people who work, either as employees or self-employed – though not for the 'economically inactive', such as those living on a non-Spanish pension. In practice, however, you might find it useful to apply for one (*see* 'Permits, Visas and Other Bureaucracy', pp.24–8).

After registering as a job-seeker at the local employment office (*oficina de empleo*) you can compete on theoretically equal conditions with Spanish workers, claim unemployment benefits on losing a job, dependent on contributions made to Spanish Seguridad Social (Social Security), work as a self-employed person (known as *autónomos*) or set up a business. For more details, *see* **Settling In**, 'Working in Spain'. pp.219–29.

The unemployment situation naturally varies from country to country. This makes anyone's real prospects of finding work in their chosen field dependent not so much on the system of rights in place as the practical realities of the labour market at any time. In the case of Spain, those realities may be harsher than you expect. Unemployment is high, acutely so in some regions, though the national average recently dropped to below 10 per cent for the first time in decades. Increasing deregulation of the labour market in recent years has meant that there are ever fewer stable jobs available, and more and more people survive on temporary employment. As much as 30 per cent of the local labour force gets by from one temporary contract to another, known as '*contratos basura*' (rubbish contracts), forming part of what is referred to as the *economía de la precariedad*, the 'precarious economy'. On the plus side, the opening up of the economy brought about by this very deregulation has meant that EU workers can gain access to an increasingly diverse range of jobs, provided they have the skills, the language, a measure of luck and, perhaps, the gift of the gab. In cities like Madrid and, especially, Barcelona, young professionals in particular have been able to move into fields that were previously closed to foreigners; in these cities and on the coast, too, many people also find work in bars, clubs, hotels and so on. But for all this, you need to think before rushing into a Spanish working and living experience: remember, the right to seek work does not guarantee you will find it. On the optimistic side, if you persevere and succeed in finding work, the bureaucratic aspects are far less harrowing than they used to be (*see* 'Permits, Visas and Other Bureaucracy', pp.24–8).

Non-EU citizens

Citizens of non-EU countries can expect more difficulties and do not enjoy the basic right to residency. Depending on the country of origin, requirements can vary but the bottom line is that you need a visa before travelling to Spain, and technically cannot come to seek work. This is not to say that you cannot look for a job while on a holiday visit, but if you are made an offer the employment authorities can refuse you a work permit if there is a suitably qualified Spanish (or EU) person registered at the employment office in the same area. Even with a job offer, you are obliged to get a visa from the nearest Spanish consulate to your home residence, which means a trip home and then back again to take up the job – if the visa is granted. Major door-openers are if you are proposing to set up a business, if you can demonstrate that you have ample funds to bring with you, or if you are recommended by a company as an essential employee.

Issues to Consider and Suggestions

Whether you are a 'privileged' EU passport holder or an 'outsider', there are some issues that affect everybody who plans to work in Spain. Consider your skills, qualifications and experience. Is there a demand for someone with your profile in the part of Spain where you plan to live? Can you get your qualifications recognised? If the answer to either or both of these questions is 'no', are you prepared to lower your expectations and work in a different field? Can you compete with locals who may have similar qualifications and are native speakers of the language(s)? Is your Spanish (or Catalan, Galician or Basque) good enough? Are you prepared to learn it (or them) properly and so overcome the greatest handicap of all, the language barrier?

The fact is, unless you have special, highly prized skills to offer, you may find the job market a hostile place. It may be that, like many British, Irish, US, Canadian and Australian citizens who settle in Spain, you have to start by making your living from the fact of being a native English speaker. Many resident 'anglos' go into the world of TEFL, or teaching English as a foreign language (*see* 'English-teaching', pp.222–4). Fully qualified schoolteachers, as opposed to TEFL-ers, can also find stable work in the burgeoning private bilingual school sector. Others with language skills do a lucrative trade in translating, interpreting and proofreading. Still others get by on freelance travel writing, copy-writing, editing and journalism for English-language publications.

Outside of this mini world, there are all manner of fields where foreigners can and do get on well. If you are, say, a graphic artist or a web designer with a good portfolio of clients, and you work from home anyway, moving abroad may not be very traumatic since, with e-mail, especially if you have a wi-fi connection, you could be on a mountaintop in the Alpujarras for all your customer cares.

For more on all aspects of working in Spain, *see* **Settling In**, pp.219–29.

Self-employment and Starting a Business

The precarious nature of paid employment has increasingly meant – in Spain as elsewhere – that professionals with skills to offer decide to go it alone and take the risks for themselves. Many language teachers, translators, interpreters, journalists, photographers, graphic artists and web designers, to name but a few, choose this option. Self-employed freelancers are called *trabajadores autónomos* (autonomous workers) and, from a legal point of view, are different from the self-employed who engage in entrepreneurial activities as such. The self-employed have unlimited liabilities, and all possessions could be confiscated and auctioned off if large debts are accumulated. Business owners who run limited companies, on the other hand, are only liable for the capital invested in it. Depending on the work you intend to do or the business you aim to establish, you may be required to prove that you are suitably qualified to be allowed to start working. This is not the case for freelance English teachers or translators, but naturally is required of doctors, dentists, veterinary surgeons and lawyers! The processes involved in getting foreign qualifications recognised or *'convalidado'* is one of the areas that has proved most resistant to EU 'harmonisation' plans, and can be a long and convoluted one.

Those with good business sense may wish to try their luck setting up a business. Many have tried and succeeded, running bars, pubs, restaurants, language schools and many other types of business, but it is not easy and there is no guarantee of success. Obviously, setting up a business requires an inspired idea, serious market research, a detailed business plan and sufficient capital. Operating out of a premises also means obtaining licences, being subject to inspections from health and labour authorities and more bureaucracy besides. Many who set up as self-employed workers in their chosen fields avoid all of this. People also often go it alone only after working for a few years in Spain as an employed worker in their field, so that they have contacts, know the sector and therefore have a head start without the overheads.

To register as a self-employed person with the tax authorities, whether you are an EU citizen or not, you must first have an NIE (*see* p.24). In the case of non-EU citizens, a residency card, including permission to work, is also necessary. EU citizens technically do not need a residency card but may not be allowed to register without one (*see* 'Permits, Visas and Other Bureaucracy', pp.24–8). The work permit requirement for non-EU citizens is a Catch-22 situation, since you cannot have a work permit without a job offer. But job offers imply undertaking contracted work (working *de cuenta ajena*) and not self-employment (working *de cuenta propia*). The only real way around this is to get a work permit allowing you to work for a company, and then become self-employed later once you have your foot in the door.

For more information on self-employment and setting up a business, *see* **Settling In**, pp.226–9.

Learning Spanish

'Hola' is the greeting used every day by around 400 million people in the Spanish-speaking world. Spanish, perhaps more correctly and very often referred to by Spaniards as Castilian (*Castellano*), since it started life as the language only of Spain's central region of Castile, is a major world language and is useful not just in Spain but also for travelling in Latin America. For purely practical purposes, such as understanding what you are being told about the state of your bank account, dealing with waiters, shopkeepers, officialdom and everything else, a certain level of proficiency is required. If you want to integrate at all into your local community, this is even more the case. As far as entering into the world of work goes, a good, better-than-working knowledge is essential. Even if you plan to live mainly among expats, it is common courtesy at least to be able to cope with day-to-day situations.

Objectively, Spanish is not a difficult language to learn. It is of the Romance family, like French, Portuguese or Italian, all descendants of Latin. Any contact you have had with these languages will be to your advantage. Pronunciation is relatively straightforward, and the grammar is not too complicated. Learning Spanish, or any other language, need not be traumatic and, with an open mind and a sense of humour, can be a fun-filled, rewarding experience. At some stage in the process everybody puts their foot in it, makes a *faux pas*, upsets somebody or says the opposite of what they mean, but this is all a valuable part of the learning process, and something to laugh about later. More information on learning Spanish in the UK and in Spain is included in **Settling In**, pp.279–82.

Spain's Other Languages

Not everybody is aware that Castilian is only one of four languages spoken officially in Spain. Another aspect of the country's great cultural diversity is linguistic: Castilian Spanish is the official language of the state and enjoys undoubted hegemony, but it shares the country with Basque, Catalan and Galician, known respectively to those who speak them as *Euskera*, *Català* and *Galego*. All three are separate languages, with their own grammar and rules. They suffered greatly during Franco's times but have enjoyed, with varying degrees of success, a great renaissance since the return of democracy in the 1970s. They also enjoy co-official or, as in the case of Catalonia, sometimes primary status within their respective autonomous communities.

For more information on studying all three of these languages, *see* pp.279–82.

Catalan – *Català*

In Catalonia, the Balearics and most parts of the Valencian autonomous region, Catalan and its variant dialects are widely spoken, and it is the official

With Friends Like These, Who Needs Enemies?

Castilian Spanish has many cognates which look like English words and mean much the same. For example, during the *transición* from Franco's *dictadura* to the current *democracia*, complete with *elecciones*, Spain drew up a *constitución* which offers all its citizens the *garantía* of certain basic *libertades*. Easy, isn't it?

To a certain point. Many words can catch you out, though. Despite looking like an equivalent English word they mean something completely different and are what linguists call 'false friends'. Used incorrectly they can cause misunderstanding or embarrassment. Some common ones are:

Actual/actualmente: Adjective and adverb referring to things which are **current, at the present time**. The English sense of 'actual' is *real* or *verdadero*.

Aplicar/aplicación: You do not *aplicar* for a job, you *solicitar* it or send in a *solicitud*. *Aplicar* does mean apply if you are talking about a theory or a cream for mosquito bites.

Asistir: This verb means **to attend**, a meeting or a football match. *Atender* is the verb for **to serve, take care of** or **attend to** customers or problems. **To assist/help** is *ayudar*.

Carpeta: Not something from Persia or Axminster but a **file** or **folder** in which you carry documents. Also applies to computers. A **carpet** is an *alfombra*.

Constiparse/Constipado: Also written *costiparse* and *costipado*, the verb means **to catch a cold**, the noun is **a cold**. If you are **constipated**, you are *estreñido*.

Contestar: Means **to answer** (a question, the telephone). If you wish **to contest** an allegation or a decision you *protestar*.

language used by the autonomous authorities. It extends up into the south-west corner of France too (Roussillon, around Perpignan) and in total is spoken by more than 6 million people, more than Danish or Finnish, both official EU languages, Catalan-speakers forming the largest linguistic community in Europe without their own state. It is another Latin-based language, but in some ways is closer to French than Castilian (its closest relative of all is actually Provençal, which still survives to a much weaker extent in France). However, if you can read any Castilian or French you can make a reasonable attempt at reading a newspaper in Catalan; similarly, if your understanding of Castilian is good then you may be able to catch parts of a conversation or the TV news.

The degree to which Catalan has reasserted itself, and the extent to which it is expected of foreigners in particular, varies from region to region. In Catalonia itself (especially in smaller towns and the countryside) and Menorca it has pretty much regained the position of first language of everyday life, but the other islands and most of Valencia are more bilingual (still with variations, Castellón, for example, being much more Catalan-speaking than Alicante). If your chosen destination is a village in the Empordà or a house in the Catalan Pyrenees, learning some Catalan will be just as important as learning Castilian is elsewhere; if you aim to live and work in Barcelona, you need to be able to

Decepción: Is not deception but **disappointment**. **To deceive** someone is *engañar*; advertising may be *engañosa*.

Desgracia: Is a **misfortune**, something **disgraceful** is *una vergüenza*.

Disgusto: Means **displeasure** or an **upset**. Something **disgusting** is *asqueroso*.

Embarazada/Embarazo: Means **pregnant/pregnancy**. **Embarrassment** or **feeling embarrassed** is expressed by *vergüenza* or feeling *avergonzado*.

En absoluto: Actually means **absolutely not!**

Ilusión: Usually means **hope** or a **feeling of expectation**.

Introducir: Can mean **to introduce** in the sense of **to begin** as in new laws, but also means **to put something** (like a diskette) **in** a slot. **To introduce** people, use the verb *presentar*.

Molestar: No sexual connotations here, this means **to bother** or **to annoy**.

Preservativo: A **condom**; preservatives, in foodstuffs, are *conservantes*.

Pretender: This verb means **to try/aim for/aspire to**. **To pretend**, say *fingir* or *simular*.

Realizar: Means **to carry out/make something real** (a plan or project). **To realize** something (mentally) is *darse cuenta de*....

Recordar: Means **to remember** or **to remind**. To record on a cassette or paper, use *grabar* or *anotar* respectively.

Sano: Means **healthy physically**; somebody who is **sane** is *cuerdo*.

Sensible: Is **sensitive**. Somebody **sensible** is *sensato* or *razonable*.

Sopa: **Soup**, not **soap**, which is *jabón*.

Suceso: An **event, a happening**. **Success** is *éxito*. The **exit** is *la salida*.

understand and to a lesser extent use both Castilian and Catalan, otherwise you will find pathways closed to you. Many road and public information signs are in Catalan, as are official forms, so the practical need to be able to understand the written language is obvious. The Catalan regional government provides a range of low-cost or sometimes free courses to help non-Catalan-speaking residents learn the language.

Galician – *Galego*

This language to the untrained ear sounds (and looks, come to that) like a hybrid of Castilian and Portuguese, but is definitely a language in its own right, another Latin language and actually the older parent of modern Portuguese. *Galego* is spoken by the vast majority of people in the Galician autonomous region in the Atlantic northwest, as a second language by many but as first choice in rural areas. Again, many signs are in the local language, and place names have in recent years been converted back to Galician from their Castilian translations. Galicians speak Castilian with a musical lilt, owing to the influence of their own language, and at times it can be difficult to tell which of the two they are speaking. If you have a reasonable understanding of Castilian, though,

Galego should not be too difficult to grasp in conversation. Galicians are traditionally unassertive nationalists but, again, if you live in any small community in Galicia you will have much closer contact with people if you can handle the local language.

Basque – *Euskera*

Basque, or *Euskera*, is spoken by over half a million people in the three provinces of the Basque Autonomous Region (Vizcaya, Guipúzcoa and Alava) and in neighbouring Navarra, and by some 80,000 residents of the French Basque country across the border. No contact with any other language will prepare you for Basque, the misty origins of which are the subject of endless debate, although it was certainly spoken before the introduction of Indo-European languages into France and Spain. Its basic vocabulary and grammatical structure bear no relationship to any other living language. The autonomous government provides courses in the language, but learning it is a tough proposition for anyone who is not a talented or dedicated linguist!

Educating and Bringing Up Children

If you are moving to Spain not just as a free agent or a couple but as a family with young children, another set of questions comes into play. Spain, however, is a very attractive place to bring up children, to the extent that this is cited by many British families as a prime reason for moving there. The old stereotype about Spaniards loving children may have its quirks (as in the peculiarly low modern Spanish birth rate) but, overall, it's one of those that holds up the best. Spain today, of course, has traffic and other modern pressures, but most children growing up in Spain, certainly outside the main cities, are allowed more space and more room to run around in public spaces than many parents in Britain now feel able to allow. The education system has improved greatly, and overall is on a par with those of any northern European country. And small children provide a guaranteed passport into local life. Visit a local shop a couple of times with your child and he or she will be recognised, and the shopkeeper will look out for them. Children everywhere have less reserve in making friends than their parents. And with a child you will necessarily have to make use of schools and other local amenities, and meet up with other parents doing the same.

If you're moving to Spain as a family, along with deciding where to live, finding the appropriate property and finding work or setting up a business, the question of where you send your children to school will be another priority issue. The choices available in most Spanish towns or cities of any size range from free, state-run schools (*escuelas públicas* or *colegios públicos*) through to private ones (*escuelas privadas* or *colegios privados*), with grant-assisted private schools (*colegios concertados*) filling the gap in between. The question of public (state) versus private is one of many dilemmas you will have to ponder.

In Spain, schooling is optional from age three to five, and compulsory for all children from age six to 16. Throughout the country there are many *guarderías* or nurseries for very young children, some of them publicly run. Education is a serious business in Spain, and high on most parents' scale of values. Around two-thirds of all children attend state-run schools, mainly co-educational, with the rest going to a mixture of religious or secular private day schools (many of which are grant-assisted), among which are the international private schools, a popular but expensive option for many foreign families based in Spain. A very small percentage of children in Spain attend boarding schools of different persuasions. The relatively high number of children in private schools reflects a long-held middle-class view that state-run education is inferior, inadequate and offers few guarantees of academic achievement and career success. There was a time when this was perhaps the case, but a great deal has been spent on the public system in Spain in the last few years, and it would be unfair to say that Spanish state schools are now inadequate, even if their study programme and facilities offered for extra-curricular activities cannot match those offered by the most expensive privately run outfits.

For more on all aspects of education, *see* **Settling In**, 'Education', pp.251–4.

State Schools

State schools, *escuelas públicas*, are 'public' in the real sense of the word, not to be confused with élitist British 'public schools'. The state school system is the overall responsibility of central government and the Education Ministry in Madrid but, in line with the decentralisation process that has come with Spain's system of autonomous regions, responsibility for the running of education, budget allocation and a good part of course content now lies with the education authorities in each region; how much independence they have and how much of a supervisory role is retained by the Ministry is a matter of regular argument, especially in Catalonia. In Catalonia practically all teaching is in Catalan, Castilian is taught as a second language and the curriculum often emphasises Catalan history and culture. In Galicia and the Basque country, part of the curriculum is taught in the local languages.

Throughout Spain, state education is free and available to all, except for books and certain other materials, school lunches and extra-curricular activities, which taken together can add up to quite a sum. It spans from pre-school education (*pre-escolar*) to the pre-university baccalaureate (*bachillerato*) stage. Standards have risen over the last decade or so and are now arguably as good as anywhere else in Europe, although many parents who are able to compare the Spanish system with others sometimes find it rather rigid, and over-rooted in traditional, rote-learning methods, with little scope for the child's personal development. This depends largely on the quality of the staff or individual teachers in any given school. As everywhere, sociological factors also intervene in standards: some schools are thought of as 'rough' because they are in socially and economically deprived areas, and in the big cities there are some schools with alarmingly high drop-out rates, poor examination performance and many of the ills that plague inner-city education in the UK, such as bullying, gangs and demoralised teaching staff. Unprecedented levels of immigration in recent years have also brought problems, in the sense that the system and many teachers too, are unprepared and insufficiently funded for dealing with large numbers of children from different linguistic and cultural backgrounds. In choosing where you live you should take these considerations into account.

Under the PP governments, between 1996 and 2004, there was a tendency to reduce funding for public schools and channel it into grant-assisted and private schools. Plans in the controversial Education Act introduced by former minister Pilar del Castillo to introduce tougher exams at all levels, and streaming by ability from an early age, met with resistance from many quarters. The new government is preparing its own ambitious law to revamp and modernise state education. Like all reforms, some of the content will be positive, some not. The problem, as many teachers point out, is that with so many laws in quick succession, they do not know exactly what criteria to adhere to, and those who suffer in the end are the children.

Private Schools

There are over 5,000 private schools of many different types in Spain, but the international English-language schools are the ones chiefly of interest to the foreign resident. These schools provide either a British or American education and are found mainly in the big cities and, as you might expect, in areas with large expat populations, namely the *costas* and the islands. In general they provide a broad, rounded education with emphasis given not only to academic achievement but also to the arts, sports and ethics. Their results can be excellent: students usually come out of these schools completely bilingual in English and Spanish, and often with a third or even fourth language. An extremely high percentage of international school graduates go on to study in Spanish, British or North American universities. Facilities are often superb, too.

Health Services

Spain's public heath system is not the best in Europe, but it's by no means the worst either. It is another public service that has improved greatly in the last two decades, and gives coverage to the vast majority of Spaniards (over 90 per cent) and legal residents, including their families, who contribute to the social security system. Doctors and other health professionals are highly trained and hospitals generally have up-to-date equipment. Waiting lists have been reduced and patients are able to choose their own doctors or specialists. The system is complemented by the private sector, which often deals with 'overspill'.

The Spanish themselves are generally a healthy people, with life expectancy being around 80 for women and 74 for men. The Mediterranean diet and the climate contribute to this, as well as a more relaxed lifestyle overall.

For more on the Spanish health system, *see* **Settling In**, pp.254–7.

Visitors

All visitors from EU and EEA (European Economic Area) countries are entitled to medical and basic dental attention, medicines and hospitalisation during their first 90 days in Spain, provided they have an EHIC (European Health Insurance Card, the replacement for the old E111 form), available from post offices in the UK. Anyone planning to stay for over 90 days but still not resident in Spain should purchase health insurance, for which many options are available; check carefully what is covered and what is not. Failure to do this could mean enormous medical bills. Visitors from non-EU or EEA countries are not, except where bilateral agreements exist, entitled to free medical attention and healthcare, so private insurance is strongly recommended.

Residents

Residents, both EU and non-EU, who work in Spain and contribute to the social security system are entitled to state medical care and, according to contributions made, to daily sickness allowance. Contributions made in the UK and other EU countries may also be taken into account when calculating entitlement to benefits in Spain. Pensioners from EU countries who take up residence are also entitled to healthcare, except for those who retired below the normal pensionable age. Non-EU citizens who do not work and therefore do not contribute to the social security system, mainly pensioners and those living off their own means, are not entitled to Spanish state healthcare and should therefore seek private coverage. Everybody who takes up residence and is entitled to healthcare should register with a local GP (*médico de cabecera*) at the nearest health centre (*ambulatorio*).

Retirement and Pensions

Retiring to Spain is an idea in many people's minds nowadays, especially among those who already own a second home there and think of what it might be like to stay in the sun all year round. In many areas – especially the northern Costa Blanca and the central Costa del Sol – there are sizeable British or German 'retirement communities', a sign of just how easy it has become. Anyone eligible for a state pension in any other EU country is now free to receive it in Spain, and will often find that the lower cost of living stretches it a little further. Recipients of company pensions can do the same, and the money is generally paid wherever the scheme's rules allow – perhaps directly into a Spanish account, or into a UK one and then transferred to the Spanish account. Non-EU pensioners can do the same, and find it easier than people of working age to become legally resident, needing only to show proof of sufficient income. Retired EU citizens are also entitled to the full use of the Spanish healthcare system on the same basis as a Spanish person. Those who have worked in Spain may be entitled to a Spanish pension on retiring, and contributions made in another EU country prior to taking up residence are usually taken into account.

However, retiring to Spain is one more topic that requires careful thought. Above all, you need to make a realistic assessment – often best done with professional advice – of how far your pension and any savings will stretch, and try to make some allowances for possible future currency fluctuations. You may need to look at health services and other amenities more closely than a younger person would. You also need to consider, depressing though it may be, whether the distance from your family, friends and roots, which might be no problem (or even a plus) when you're fit and mobile in your 60s, will seem a whole lot more problematic to you when you're 15–20 years older, and that much more frail. And this also needs to be taken into account in your choice of home: a remote farmhouse or beach villa might look very attractive when you're in your prime, but when you're that much older the sometimes-crowded feel of the *urbanizaciones* closer to towns and with neighbours around might have compensations.

For more on retirement, *see* **Settling In**, 'Retirement', pp.217–19.

Permits, Visas and Other Bureaucracy

When you become a foreign resident in Spain, even if you are from an EU country, there are various bits of paperwork you need to pick up and procedures to go through to formalise your stay. Officially, you should do this once you stay for more than 90 days. It is of course possible, especially if you're not working, to lie low and not bother, but this could be just storing up problems for the future, especially if you ever have any trouble with your home.

Residency procedures have become steadily less time-consuming for EU citizens in the last few years; for agencies that can help you with them if required, *see* 'Dealing with Bureaucracy – Using a *Gestor*', pp.216–17. According to which area you may wish to work in, you might also need to get your qualifications recognised (*convalidado*); this remains a very tedious procedure.

The following is a summary of the main papers you need to get to be an established resident.

The NIE

The NIE, *número de identificación de extranjeros*, equivalent to the NIF or *número de identificación fiscal* borne by all adult Spaniards, is your tax identification number as a foreign resident. It is an essential document for all types of financial and other transactions, and therefore necessary for any kind of work beyond the black economy. It is important to know that, whether you need a residency card or not (*see* below), you must still have a NIE. To obtain one you must go to the foreigners' section of your local Spanish police station. There, fill in a form, and present two passport-size photographs and your passport. The formality is simple and the card is issued automatically.

The Residency Card (*Tarjeta Comunitaria*) for EU Citizens

There is currently considerable confusion about the need for EU citizens to possess a residency card. A Royal Decree, which became effective as of 1 March 2003, removed the obligation for many EU citizens to obtain a residency card. The decree is published on the Interior Ministry's website; go to the following link: **www.mir.es/sites/mir/extranje/regimen_comunitario/residencia.html**.

If you cannot be bothered reading the ministry-speak Spanish, here is an abbreviated version in English:

Madrid, February 14th 2003

The Council of Ministers has approved a Royal Decree which exempts EU Citizens resident in Spain, as well as nationals of Norway, Iceland, Liechtenstein and Switzerland, from the obligation of being in possession of a residency card.

The beneficiaries are, basically, EU citizens who are employed workers or self-employed, students, retired persons or pensioners who have contributed to the Spanish social security scheme and family members of all of these groups. The measure is only not applicable to 'inactive' EU citizens, tourists and family members of EU citizens who are themselves citizens of third countries.

Elimination of Obstacles

The carrier of the aforementioned documents may, therefore, come to our country without the need for any administrative proceedings. A valid passport or the equivalent of a Spanish National Identity Document will suffice for any dealings or transactions such as the purchase of property, the issuing of a driving licence or a simple bank transaction.

Furthermore, possession of a valid passport, or the equivalent of a Spanish National Identity Document, is sufficient for the EU resident to be included on the electoral roll and participate in municipal elections and those for the European Parliament.

So, if you take up a job, become self-employed, start up a business or go to Spain to study, you do not need a resident's card. Nor do you need one if you have worked or have been working in Spain and qualify for a Spanish state pension, in which case you probably have a card anyway but do not need to renew it on expiry. If you are living on a UK state or other pension, or have a private income from outside Spain (thereby qualifying as 'inactive'), you must apply for and obtain a card, as should any family member who is a citizen of a non-EU country.

If only it were that simple in reality! It is possible to apply for a residency card voluntarily and, on balance, there are some very good reasons to do so. First, whatever the Royal Decree says, you may come up against stubborn functionaries at many branches of the state administration who simply will not let you carry out certain red-tape procedures without one, even if you print off the decree and wave it in front of them! Some banks, too, may be reticent about loaning money or giving mortgages to non-card-holders. Also, and possibly most important, as in Spain you must carry some valid form of ID at all times, and Britons do not, as yet, have an ID card, this implies carrying your passport around with you. Having your passport stolen, and arranging for a replacement, is a traumatic and expensive experience. The 'voluntary' resident's card is similar in appearance to a Spanish DNI (National Identity Document) and is the same size as a credit card so fits neatly into any wallet. It also bears your NIE number, photograph, fingerprint and signature so is valid in all situations.

Whether you need one or not, the process these days is very simple and your application would only ever be refused if you were perceived to be a threat to Spanish national security or a public health risk. All you need to do is go to a foreigners' police station with your passport, photocopies of the relevant pages of the same, three passport-type photographs, identical, in colour and with a white background, and application form, duly completed, in block capitals and black ink. To find your nearest foreigners' police station, or *comisarías de extranjeros*, go to the following link: **www.mir.es/sites/mir/extranje/directorio_ oficinasextranjeros.html**.

Retired people or unemployed applicants must be able to prove they have adequate sickness insurance and sufficient financial resources (covering family members also), and entitlement to retirement benefits payable in the place of residence. If the national retirement scheme under which you are insured covers medical expenses, you have the right to the same cover as a retired person in the country where you are living. To qualify for these benefits, you should notify your change of residence to your pension authorities before you leave and ask for form E121 from the health authorities in the country from which you are moving (*see* 'Social Security and Entitlements under EU Law', pp.255–7). The form should be handed to the relevant authorities in the country to which you move.

Non-EU Citizens

Non-EU citizens need not only a residency card but also a work permit. Getting this is much more complicated, and depends on several conditions. A prerequisite is a *visado de residencia*, a special visa which must be obtained from a Spanish consulate in the applicant's home country before travelling to Spain. There are several types of visa:

- **Visa for those who want to retire in Spain.**

- **Visa for those who want to start a business. Applicants have to show that they have approximately $120,000 (€127,000 or nearly £82,000) to invest and that the business will provide work for Spanish nationals.**

- **Visa for those who have been offered a job. Applicants must be able to produce a work contract, proof that the post has been advertised by the Spanish employment office and that no suitable Spanish (or EU) candidate has been found to take it up.**

- **Visa for executives and business employees. This is usually dealt with by the company.**

- **Visa for students. Conditions are practically the same as for EU citizens.**

- **Visa for teachers.**

Applications for the residency and work permit, a separate process from visa application, are made once in Spain, assuming the visa has been granted. Applicants must also be able to show that they have not served a prison sentence and have no criminal record. This is proved by means of a police certificate that must be officially translated. Also, on applying for the permits, applicants must be able to show a clean bill of health and proof of registration with their country's consulate in Spain. Those wanting to become self-employed workers then have to deal with still more complicated paperwork. In general, it is easier to do this 'from the inside' – that is, once established as a legal, working resident by means of a job.

Many non-EU citizens have also been able to benefit from successive amnesties granted by the authorities over the last several years. These amnesties have been designed to 'regularise' the situation of the many non-EU citizens who have been in Spain for some time without a visa, residency or work permit and are aimed principally at the large numbers of North and sub-Saharan Africans, Latin Americans and Eastern Europeans who have arrived in recent years. Each year a certain number are allowed to get their papers in order, and North Americans, Australians and New Zealanders have also been able to 'get legal'. Tougher immigration laws currently being prepared may make this option unfeasible in the future.

Other factors intervene in the granting or not of the visa and/or the permits. The country of origin is one – some countries have bilateral agreements with Spain. Blood ties are another: descendants of Spaniards may be given preferential treatment. The sector of the economy the applicant plans to work in is another, as the labour authorities consider, above all, the level of unemployment. One non-orthodox way of cutting through all this, used by many US, Australian and New Zealand residents in Spain, is by looking back through their ancestry, and acquiring a British, Irish or sometimes Italian passport, the magic pass to EU citizenship and, with it, far less trouble with papers.

Residency and work permits for non-EU workers also vary greatly; they are initially for one year only, but on renewal are usually granted for five years.

Documents to be presented vary depending on the permit applied for and are too numerous to be dealt with here. The most common type of application is that made by a contracted worker, who has to present a valid passport; six photos; a job offer or contract; and proof that the employer legally carries out the business stated, is solvent and is up to date with tax and social security obligations.

Profiles of the Regions

03

Spain has a greater geographical diversity of landscapes than anywhere else in western Europe – from deep-green fjords in Galicia that are as rain-soaked as anywhere in Ireland, through Alpine mountains to real deserts in Murcia and Almería, and the sub-tropical Canary Islands. It is more mountainous than any other European country except Switzerland, and Madrid, at 2,134ft (650m), is the continent's highest capital. Most British people and northern Europeans looking to buy a home in Spain are most interested in places with winter sunshine and within reasonable distance of a beach – and this preference is reflected in the organisation of this chapter – but even staying within a morning's drive of the country's *costas* there is still a wealth of landscapes.

As well as enough changes of scenery to fill a continent, Spain also offers great human diversity. As well as Castilian Spanish, Catalan, Basque and Galician are vigorously maintained in different parts of the country. One big difference between Spain and the other 'pluri-national' conglomerates nearby – the British Isles and France – is that, whereas in those the centres of political and economic power have nearly always been in the same places – London and Paris – in the Iberian Peninsula no such natural hub has ever emerged. Madrid, for example, was plucked out of obscurity to become capital of Spain by King Philip II in the 1560s, but until quite recently was economically less important than Barcelona or Bilbao. While the Pyrenees kept Iberia as a whole apart from Northern Europe, Spain's many other mountains helped keep different regions in partial isolation. Even when they shared the same language, different regions of Spain developed individual characteristics, and most Spaniards remain highly conscious of where they come from, and attached to regional traditions. On top of this cultural background, another essential element in the diversity of modern Spain is that modernity and industrialisation affected different regions at different times, so that there has often been a gulf in living standards – and the whole pace of life – between, say, Barcelona and rural Andalucía or Extremadura.

All these variations add to the spark, charm and fascination of Spain. At times they also have been sources of conflict. The new Spain established since 1975 has for once sought to recognise rather than straitjacket its diversity, and is organised into 17 autonomous regions. For property-buyers, this can have specific practical consequences in that some details such as tax can differ from one region to another.

The Spanish Background

Spain has been touched by a very special mix of influences. Its first people with a name were the Iberians (*Iberos*), who arrived, probably from North Africa, some time around 2000 BC, and they were followed by Celts, who came across the Pyrenees in around 1000 BC and blended with the Iberians to create a new, hybrid culture known as the Celtiberians (*Celtibéricos*). Parts of Spain were also settled and conquered by Phoenicians, Greeks, Carthaginians and especially the Romans. The most distinctive era of all in Iberian history began in AD 711, when an Arab army came across from Morocco and inaugurated six centuries of Muslim pre-eminence, during which *Al-Andalús* was the wealthiest and most sophisticated society in Europe. Medieval Spain was a fascinatingly diverse place, with huge Jewish communities, Christians who lived under Muslim rule, and Muslims ruled by Christians. Even the Christian kingdoms that struggled to take back land from the Muslim rulers were not united. While one major centre of power grew up in the Cantabrian Mountains as the Kingdom of León, later to become Castile, another, the counties in the Pyrenees that developed into Catalonia, had a very different, non-Iberian origin as the southern frontier of the empire of Charlemagne, which is why Catalan's closest linguistic relative is Provençal.

A Global Power

Rulers of Spain with greater than usual powers have often seen it as their role to suppress and control this diversity, most notably on two occasions. The first began in 1469, when Ferdinand of Aragon married Isabella of Castile, bringing together for the first time ever the main Christian kingdoms. Queen Isabella 'the Catholic', intensely devout, detested the religious hotch-potch of medieval Spain and saw it as her duty to do away with it. In 1492 her armies finally took Granada, last remnant of Al-Andalús. She expelled all Jews from Castile and Aragon, and obliged Muslims to convert to Catholicism or leave; also, since so many forced converts could not be fully trusted, she won from the Pope the right to set up one of the most notorious of all Spanish institutions, the Inquisition, to enforce religious orthodoxy. In the same 'Year of Glory', Columbus discovered America. This was the beginning of Spain's 'Golden Century', during which it quite suddenly became the first global power, the centre of the first empire on which the sun truly never set. In line with the 'imperial mission' set by its monarchs, it also took on huge responsibilities as 'God's (Catholic) policeman'. Spain was ever ready to fight continual wars – against all the native peoples in the Americas; against Protestants in Holland, Germany and England; against Muslim Turks in the Mediterranean. As a result, it also became the first global power to burn out. In the 17th century, as the empire slid deeper into crisis, tensions revived between Castile, hub of the monarchy, and the crown's non-Castilian kingdoms. Although Spain is often described as united since 1469, it has actually only existed as one state since 1715, when the new Bourbon King Philip V issued his decree of Nova Planta at the end of the 12-year War of the Spanish Succession, during which he had subdued the rebellious former Aragonese territories (Catalonia, Valencia and Aragón) by force. Only then were their remaining special rights abolished, and the whole country brought under one, centralised administration.

The Road to Modernity

If Spain has often struggled with its own diversity, between Napoleon's invasion in 1808 and 1975 it also grappled constantly with modernity. The two were intertwined, because when the Industrial Revolution came to Spain in the 1830s it was confined almost exclusively to Catalonia and the Basque Country, and so added to cultural differences. For Basques and Catalans, nationalism was seen as inseparable from modernity, in opposition to the backwardness of a Castilian Spain that seemed impervious to change. Spain as a whole was also known for its incompatible extremes, with a jigsaw puzzle of political tendencies.

This did not put a stopper on other developments: the early 20th century, above all, was an age of great cultural energy, with the 'Silver Age' of Spanish literature and culture producing a string of great writers, musicians and artists such as Picasso, Manuel de Falla, Antonio Machado and Federico García Lorca. The era's political conflicts, though, culminated in the explosion of political and social agitation of the 1930s and Spain's great modern tragedy of the Civil War of 1936–9.

The Franco Years

The Civil War led to the second comprehensive attempt to impose a clamp of uniformity on Spain, by the victorious regime of General Francisco Franco. The Franco era divides into two phases. Vindictive in victory, for its first 20 years it was a thoroughgoing fascist regime. A dour Catholicism, looking back to the Habsburg Golden Age, became almost obligatory. Minority nationalities were singled out for special attention, and for publishing, public use or sometimes just speaking, Catalan and Basque were banned. Rigid censorship was imposed, and all independent unions and social or political activity outside of Franco's National Movement prohibited. The country was desperately poor – much poorer in many areas than in the 1930s – and many older Spaniards have more traumatic memories of these 'hunger years' than they do of the Civil War itself. Things began to change in 1959, when a Stabilisation Plan for the economy was drawn up by technocrats of the Catholic lay organisation Opus Dei, which provided the 'brains' of the regime. This opened Spain up to international trade and investment; it also coincided with the Europe-wide boom of the 1960s, which provided another vital element – tourists. Money flooded into the country, filtering into industry and many other sectors as well as tourism, and Spain had one of the highest growth rates in the world. The regime still expected to keep absolute political control; an expanding society, however, was more and more difficult to keep in check. In the 1960s the Basque organisation, ETA, began its armed campaign for independence, and everywhere else union and opposition movements emerged. Even so, the regime hung on until the dictator died, on 20 November 1975.

The New Spain

Spanish stereotypes often celebrate tradition and the past. In fact, Spain has changed more rapidly than any other country in Europe in the past 40 years. The economic boom of the 1960s has been followed by further wide-reaching booms after Spain gained EU membership in the 1980s, and in the late 1990s. From an overwhelmingly rural country in the 1950s it has become urban, with a huge movement to the cities. All these booms have spread industries of different sizes – once confined to pockets like Catalonia, the Basque lands and Madrid – around the country. Economic imbalances between regions are still a Spanish characteristic, but they are much less extreme than before 1939. Another transformation since 1975 has been in the position of women, who were previously confined to the home under a regime that allowed neither divorce nor birth control. Spanish women now work in every area of the economy, and the birth rate, once one of Europe's highest, is among the lowest in the world.

Spain's political 'transition' has been one of its most remarkable changes. Franco had ordained that, on his death, the monarchy should be restored under King Juan Carlos, grandson of Spain's last king dethroned in 1931, but nobody knew what he intended to do. He appointed a former Francoist official, Adolfo Suárez, as prime minister, and charged him with bringing democracy to Spain. Opposition parties were legalised, and the first open elections since 1936 were held in June 1977, and adroitly won by Suárez himself. It became clear that any democratic system in Spain would have to acknowledge some of the demands of the 'historic nationalities', especially the Basques and Catalans. To some astonishment, Suárez offered autonomous governments and devolved powers not only to these strongly nationalistic areas but to Spain's 15 other regions as well (critics argue, probably rightly, that this was in part a ploy to dilute the privileges of the top two). Instead of stamping on regional differences, the Suárez system seeks to manage them. This produced a degree of chaos in its early years, and can still be highly confusing, particularly since there was no uniform pattern as to what powers a region could have (gradually, they have divided into two main blocks: the 'historic nationalities' and large regions like Andalucía or the Canaries that enjoy ample powers such as control over education, health and their own police forces and some tax-raising powers, and smaller regions that function more like arms of local government; but there are still differences in power between all of them). Spain's *Estado de las Autonomías*, or 'Autonomy State' as it is called, has not resolved all national and regional differences, for the Basque pro-independence terrorist campaign remains one of Spain's constant problems. The Partido Popular (PP) governments, in office from 1996 until 2004, tried to reassert the primacy of central government, rooted in a Spanish-nationalist frustration that the powers of the regions have gone too far. However, in most of the country, regional administrations have provided a means by which these issues can be dealt with and for most Spaniards they are now a part of the scenery, an established fact. Since the Socialists, under the leadership of José Luis Rodríguez Zapatero, returned to power in spring 2004, the 'statutes of autonomy' instituted in the late 1970s and early '80s, and the regions' relationships with central government, are once again being reviewed and discussed, with the aim of furthering autonomy. As these pages are being written, the 'Parlament de Catalunya' is about to approve a new statute. Within the terms of the new '*estatut*', Catalonia will be defined as a 'nation' within a 'nation of nations' (i.e. Spain) and a new system of financing and tax-raising, the real issue at stake, will be introduced, reducing what many Catalans see as a historic imbalance and giving the region more control over its own purse strings.

In other areas of politics, the permanence of democracy was confirmed with the election of a socialist government under Felipe González, in November 1982. The new government gave more emphasis to modernisation – including EU membership – than to radical social reforms, and presided over a spectacular boom. Over their 14 years in power the González governments disappointed many of their supporters – above all over unemployment – and in their final years were mired in corruption scandals. However, they had their major achievements, notably in two areas – transport, where they inherited a ramshackle rail network and left behind one of the most efficient systems in Europe (British citizens can only look on in awe); and health, where services, if still patchy, also vastly improved. The conservative Partido Popular government, led by José María Aznar, did recognise these pluses of the González years (especially in transport) by doing little to change them, while pursuing a liberalising, privatising agenda in other areas of the economy. While quite successful in terms of the economy for much of their stay in power, what brought the PP's tenure to an end was the perception that they had mishandled several major crises, especially the *Prestige* oil tanker disaster, the air crash in Turkey in which 62 Spanish military personnel returning from a humanitarian mission in Afghanistan were killed (the rickety Yak 42 plane was rented on the cheap and there was terrible confusion over the identification of the remains) and the March 2004 bombings in Madrid. Aznar's arrogant style, reinforced by an absolute majority in the parliament, and tendency to look for confrontation where dialogue might have been better, were finally enough to coax the undecided and the apathetic out of their homes on 14 March 2004 and vote the Socialists back in, though they rely on support from Catalan nationalists and the United Left party in the house. The current government has ambitious plans in the field of infrastructures including vastly extending the motorway and high-speed rail networks and revamping airports, and extending civil liberties to previously discriminated-against groups such as gays and lesbians, who may now marry and adopt children.

Modern Spain is a pragmatic country. After the see-sawings of the previous century, between years when all kinds of experiments seemed possible and others of silent repression, many Spaniards take little interest in their political

Bombs, Spin and Ballot Boxes

During the morning rush hour on 11 March 2004, three days before the general elections, a dozen bombs, activated by mobile telephone, exploded on four Madrid commuter trains, killing a total of 191 people. This was the worst terrorist outrage in western European history and one that was to bring about an unforeseen U-turn in Spanish politics.

As news of the bombings unfolded, Interior minister Ángel Acebes declared to the press that only the 'meanest of spirit' could doubt that the attacks were the work of ETA, the Basque separatist group that had been responsible for many terrorist attacks over the past 30 years and which, the government claimed, was 'on the ropes'. There was a contradiction in this declaration. ETA as an armed group almost certainly did not have the operative capacity to pull off such a spectacular stunt. Several other factors, when put together, pointed the blame at al-Qaeda.

ETA, despite a bloody history, has rarely carried out indiscriminate bombings, usually gives a telephone warning before the explosions and claims responsibility afterwards. This time the group vigorously denied any involvement and even went so far as to repudiate the attacks, which, however hollow and cynical that may have seemed, was certainly a new departure. The discovery later that morning of a stolen van containing detonators and cassettes with verses from the Koran added weight to the al-Qaeda theory but, despite this, the government insisted on pointing the finger at ETA and President Aznar even telephoned leading newspaper editors in an attempt to persuade them to pursue this line of argument in the special editions of their papers. Foreign minister Ana Palacio also sent telegrams to all Spanish ambassadors abroad exhorting them to 'give the impression' that the attacks were the work of ETA. During the massive demonstration (of two and a half million people) led by government and opposition leaders, Prince Felipe, the Portuguese prime minister, EU president Romano Prodi and other heavyweights, there were many anti-ETA placards and slogans.

The next evening, however, when the news came out, despite government attempts to suppress it, that some Moroccan and Indian citizens with suspected al-Qaeda links had been arrested in connection with the bombings, all hell was let loose. Massive, spontaneous demonstrations took place outside PP headquarters in Madrid and Barcelona to protest about the lack of transparency in the government's handling of the situation and the perceived manipulation of the situation to suit their own electoral interests. The following day, with a large turnout, the PSOE beat the PP, who had led in the polls throughout the campaign.

past. Spain has little sense of nostalgia, and instead something of the exuberance, and occasional assertiveness, of a country that has often felt frustrated. It very much enjoys its pleasures, to a degree that always surprises those with clichés of black-clad Catholic puritans in mind (for years after Franco, it was not thought a good idea to ban anything). It is less set in its ways than some nearby countries like France or Italy. At the same time, since so much change has had to be absorbed so fast, many Spaniards still retain a strong attachment to the traditions of wherever they came from, and – like foreign visitors – to images of an older Spain of villages, quirky little shops and more personal rather than industrialised ways of living. IT experts and leftist radicals can be enthusiastic followers of traditional fiestas, which have boomed in the last few years. This interplay of tradition and total modernity is one of the constants of life in Spain today. *See* also **Settling In**, 'Politics', pp.286–9.

Which Spain?

When you're picking out a part of Spain in which to look for a place to buy, it's worth starting with some basic questions to help you make the right choice.

• **How close do you want to be to a beach?**
If it has to be a sunny beach, then you can only look along the Mediterranean *costas*, the Costa de la Luz and in the two groups of islands, the Balearics and the Canaries. However, there are many attractive places only an hour or so inland, especially in the mountains behind the Costa del Sol.

• **How much sun do you really want?**
For reliable sunshine for at least 10 months a year, you should only look at the Costa del Sol, Almería and Murcia, Ibiza and the Canaries. Anywhere north of Valencia, the true Mediterranean sun is only likely to come out from about Easter to October, and winters can be cool and wet. On the Costa Blanca around Alicante winters are reliably sunny at the southern end, but more changeable towards the north.

• **How much do you want to be near other expats and English-speakers, and English-speaking facilities?**
Many places around the Spanish coasts contain big clusters of foreign home-owners, whether permanent or seasonal residents, with all sorts of English- or other-language speaking services, from shops to lawyers, at their disposal. Many divide by nationality – some developments are orientated to English-speakers, some to Germans, and so on – while a few are more mixed. The largest concentration of British expats and everything to cater for them is on the Costa del Sol (which also has Gibraltar close by). Next in line are the Costa Blanca, Mallorca and the Canaries, but you can find smaller clusters at many points around the southern coasts and islands. If, on the other hand, you don't want to be surrounded by an expat ambience, think about avoiding these same places.

• **Do you want to play golf?**
There are now over 30 golf courses along the Costa del Sol, the western strip of which is marketed as the 'Costa del Golf'; after that, the next biggest cluster

is in the southern Costa Blanca, south of Alicante, and the adjacent La Manga area of Murcia. A growing phenomenon is the dedicated golf resort, with usually two or three courses, all sorts of other sports facilities and villas and apartments, built as one integrated development. Home prices tend to be high, but buyers naturally get privileged access to all facilities. Most luxurious of all are the opulent complexes at Sotogrande and San Roque north of Gibraltar; others are near Torrevieja in Alicante, and at La Manga (*see* 'The Costa Blanca', pp.48–50 and 'Almería and Murcia', pp.47–8). There are also courses and golf resorts at many points along the Costa de la Luz, the Costa Blanca, in Mallorca and in the Canaries. Golf courses are much thinner on the ground from the northern Costa Blanca upwards, and more expensive.

• **How much do you want to go out, be close to culture, and be part of Spanish life in general?**

If you want a lively social life, with a choice of music, clubs, films and so forth, and to be in touch with young Spaniards, then head for one of the main cities, Madrid, Barcelona or Valencia. In the coastal towns near Barcelona you can combine city and beach life, but these towns are becoming oversubscribed, and relatively expensive. If you want to live more quietly by the coast but surrounded by Spaniards rather than expats, try the rest of Catalonia and Valencia, the Costa de la Luz, or the (much cooler) north coast.

• **How much do you want to get away from it all?**

Among the most popular places in which to find rural retreats in Spain are the mountains inland from the Costa del Sol, such as the Serranía de Ronda and the Alpujarras of Granada, which have the bonus that you can get down to the beach in an hour or so, but their popularity has led to rising prices (*see* 'The Costa del Sol', pp.42–5). Elsewhere, you can still find surprisingly quiet villages only a short distance inland from major tourist centres all around the Mediterranean coast, but do check whether developments may encroach on them in the near future. You can also find idyllically peaceful small towns and villages throughout Spain's mountains and inland regions, but to live there you need to be ready to tackle local life head-on.

Urban Spain

Over the last 20 years, both of Spain's main cities have acquired large English-speaking – mostly British – communities running to well over 10,000 each. Both, naturally, tend to attract a younger crowd than those who come to Spain looking for beach homes. Madrid is a vibrant, hugely enjoyable city with a 24-hour social life that's often preferred by those for whom Barcelona has become too cool for its own good, and, as Spain's capital, is the base for a large international business community. Barcelona's status as one of the trendiest, and most beautiful, cities in Europe attracts hundreds of new arrivals every year looking to stay a while and sample the scene.

Next in line are Valencia, also a very lively Mediterranean city, and maybe Seville, which is better for those looking less for cosmopolitan hipness than for a traditional Andaluz ambience and energy.

In general, it has become easier to take advantage of EU citizenship and move out of traditional foreigners''niches' (such as teaching English) into other lines of work, or to open your own business, in Barcelona than anywhere else, although Madrid is now opening up a little more, too. Public services are generally more foreigner-friendly in Barcelona, but do be aware that to get really involved in the life of the city – as in the whole of Catalonia – you need at least to be able to respond to both Castilian Spanish and Catalan. Another thing to bear in mind is that a spell in Barcelona or Madrid is so popular these days that you will not be alone, and finding work will often involve a strong element of luck and being in the right place at the right time. Yet another consequence of the near-glut of young foreigners in Spanish cities these days is that pay, especially for English teachers in Barcelona, can be low.

Spanish cities are traditionally made up of apartments (*pisos* or *apartamentos*), not individual houses; most Spanish flats, though, give you more rooms and more floor space than most small British houses (*see* pp.107–8). In recent years, too, house-and-garden developments have been mushrooming around the main cities, above all on the west side of Madrid; in Barcelona, where there's less open space, they're mostly found in towns outside the city. Ever more popular with middle-class Spanish couples – local papers have pages of ads for them every weekend – they also tend to be preferred by foreign businesspeople transferred to Spain, whose relocation may be handled by their company. They're generally more expensive than city flats, but you usually get huge amounts of space.

The down-side of urban living in Spain is the cost, which is higher than in the great majority of places on the coast, and much higher than in anywhere inland. Property prices in all Spain's cities have been rising since the 1980s. In Madrid and Barcelona, where prices have just about doubled in the last five years, you will not find many flats to buy for under €250,000, and a modern two- or three-bedroom flat with good facilities is more likely to cost a lot more. If you are thinking of renting while you house-hunt, you will be pleased to know that rents have risen slightly less steeply, and there are still good deals to be found (including some pretty shabby old flats), but a pleasant two/three-bed city flat is likely to cost from around €1,000 a month – more encouraging if you are thinking of buying to let.

Inland Spain

The vast majority of foreigners interested in moving to or buying in Spain look to the cities or the coasts but there are, of course, huge areas in between. Regions such as the two Castiles (now organised into Castilla-León and Castilla-

La Mancha), Aragón or Extremadura have plenty of historic culture, spectacular landscapes and character. In among them are corners of rural Spain that seem barely to have entered the 20th century, let alone the 21st – mountain villages in extraordinary locations, that come to life perhaps just once a year for a fiesta of inexplicable antiquity. Elsewhere, much of the countryside is the kind of Spanish landscape that has been likened to a bull's hide (the *piel de toro*): a tough, rugged country, stretched over burnt-brown hills (although it bursts lavishly into life in spring). Land and climate tend to extremes, above all in the north – while much of the Castilian plateau, for example, may look like Morocco in midsummer, it's a fact not often appreciated by foreigners that Burgos has winter temperatures similar to those of Warsaw.

Owing to the scale of the movement into the cities since the 1950s, in small towns and villages all around the inland regions it's easy to find long-closed-up or semi-abandoned – but often huge – farms and houses available for sale very cheaply. The more remote the location, the cheaper they're likely to be, unless it's a celebrated beauty spot. However, they will also nearly always require a great deal of work to bring even basic services up to the standard you'll prob-ably want. These kinds of places can be ultra-attractive to people who are repelled rather than drawn by the tourist clusters of the coast, and want to take on a new life. Since there are few foreigners around, locals will be surprised to see you arrive, and may be welcoming (or alternatively suspicious and reserved, at least at first); local officials, similarly, will be unused to handling foreign busi-ness, and things are liable to move far more slowly than in the geared-up world of Barcelona or the coast. Finding the house you want is likely to be a matter of going to an area and looking and asking around, since few international agen-cies handle these regions. Taking on a house like this is for those who are truly ready to get to grips with Spanish country life, and do everything for them-selves, without any handy English-speaking lawyers nearby.

Spain Region by Region

Andalucía and its *Costas*

Andalucía (or Andalusia) is home to all the classic images of Spain: flamenco, guitars, sherry, avidly followed bullfights, elaborate religious festivals, and whitewashed houses with metal-grille windows and clad in bougainvillaea. It is the hottest part of Spain, and indeed the highest temperatures ever recorded in Europe have all been notched up here (mostly in Almería). The centuries of Moorish rule that gave the region its name left behind countless other traces, in architecture, the layout of towns and villages, place names and food. Moorish architecture still dominates the spectacular great cities of inland Andalucía, Seville, Córdoba and Granada.

Although Spanish-speaking (albeit with a strong local accent), Andalucía, as Spain's largest region and one with the most distinctive character, has since 1975 demanded the same rights as nationalities like Basques and Catalans, and the regional government enjoys wide powers. Inside Spain as well as outside of it, its people suggest any number of stereotypes: to the rest of the country, southerners are impractical and slow-moving, but also witty, silver-tongued, sarcastic, sassy, warm, extrovert and above all ever-passionate when involved in something about which they really care. In the last two centuries Andalucía has often been a 'problem area' of Spain, a reservoir of rural unemployment, and as you go inland there are still large areas where work is always in short supply. Nowadays, though, the coasts of Andalucía contain many of Europe's most popular holiday resorts, with the tourist-industry jobs these bring.

The Costa de la Luz

The Costa de la Luz – the 'Coast of Light' – is the name given to the western-most coastline of Andalucía, between Punta Tarifa, at the southern tip of mainland Europe, and the border with Portugal. Since it faces the Atlantic, not the Mediterranean, the seas are cooler and rougher than those around the point, but in compensation the beaches are often broader and cleaner, with huge stretches of open sand. They're also less busy, as this area long remained less developed than the better-known *costas* further east. In the last few years it has been increasingly popular with Spanish holidaymakers, for hotels and second homes, and is becoming better known to foreigners, although most developments are relatively low-density. Overall, properties here are cheaper than on the Costa del Sol, but a bit more expensive than on the Costa Blanca.

The Costa de la Luz divides into two halves. In the western part, in the province of Huelva, the landscape inland is fairly flat and unexciting, but the beaches are some of Spain's finest. At **Isla Canela**, just south of the town of Ayamonte at the mouth of the Guadiana river, which forms the border with the Portuguese Algarve, a medium-sized development combining villas, apartments and a golf course has been created. East from there stretch miles of beaches, with only a few scattered villages, hotels, moderate-sized developments and beach houses. **Huelva** itself is a busy fishing port with few attractions for outside visitors (remarkable for Andalucía) but **Palos**, on the opposite side of the Río Tinto, was the departure point for Columbus' first voyage, on the back of which the city now tries to attract a few more tourists. East of Huelva there's a certain amount of industrial sprawl, but this gives way to almost 50km (30 miles) of golden beach. There are only two real centres: **Mazagón**, where beach-villa building remains low-key, and **Matalascañas**, where there are already hotel, golf and villa developments of heavyweight Costa del Sol proportions, springing up quite suddenly from the empty shoreline.

What splits the Costa de la Luz into two are the *marismas*, or **marshes**, at the mouth of Andalucía's great river, the Guadalquivir, which begin east of

Matalascañas. Most of the marshes are within the **Doñana wildlife reserve**, the home of wild cattle, deer, eagles and lynxes, the last wild big cats in Europe. Naturally, though, no building is allowed in the reserve. One other utterly distinctive feature of this area is the tiny **sanctuary of the Virgin of El Rocío** (the dew), by the western edge of the national park. This comes alive once a year for one of the most extravagantly folkloric of Andaluz fiestas, the pilgrimage of the Virgin of Rocío at Pentecost (Whitsun), when processions converge on it from Seville, Huelva and Sanlúcar, on horseback or in horse- or ox-drawn carts.

In many parts of Spain there are areas that, for an often hard-to-pin-down set of reasons, are held up to represent something like the 'essence' of their wider regions. One such, in Andalucía, is the core of the province of Cádiz, south of the Guadalquivir and behind the eastern Costa de la Luz. **Jerez de la Frontera** and **Puerto de Santa María** are homes to the region's most internationally popular product, sherry (and most Spanish brandies), and Jerez's riding school is the great showcase for Andaluz horsemanship skills. This is also one of the heartlands of flamenco, and towns like **Sanlúcar de Barrameda**, **Chipiona** and **Puerto de Santa María** have produced any number of singers and performers. The tag 'de la Frontera', attached to many place names, refers to the 250 years when this area was 'the frontier' between Christian Spain and Muslim Granada, and Moorish influences can be detected at every turn. **Cádiz** itself is a fascinating and lively city, the oldest in all Spain, with busy beaches and the most elaborate carnival on the mainland each January or February.

Thousands descend on towns like Sanlúcar, Chipiona or Jerez each year to sample their atmosphere (and their great seafood restaurants). The beaches nearby, though, are relatively small and the US naval base at Rota, to the south on the Bay of Cádiz, makes an unattractive neighbour. In the hills of the **Sierra de Cádiz**, inland to the east and south, however, are the first of the *pueblos blancos* or '**white villages**' – perched on hilltops, and with medieval fortifications, they are celebrated as some of the most beautiful of all the region's traditional villages. **Arcos de la Frontera** is the largest, and the Sierra's main centre. With spectacular mountain scenery of ridges and gorges, this area blends into the already popular **Serranía de Ronda** to the east behind the Costa del Sol (*see* below), and village houses here are becoming highly sought-after by wealthy, fashionable buyers seeking Andalucían country life with much of its tranquillity and historic character intact. So far, the Cádiz side is still a little cheaper than the Ronda area, and it's possible to find a surprisingly wide range of prices.

Back on the coast, more expansive beaches resume south of Chiclana. Medium-scale villa and apartment developments are now springing up along this coast, slightly paradoxically since much of its popularity, especially among Spaniards, has been due to its having a more laid-back, small-scale and trendy feel than the international tourism-on-a-plate zones on other *costas*. From **Barbate** south to Tarifa are some of Europe's best surf beaches, which attract a young, hippyish beach-hanging crowd, while the old Moorish town of **Tarifa** itself, famed for its ocean winds, has become the continent's windsurfing capital. So far, most non-Spanish developments in this area have been directed at German buyers, but other nationalities are gaining a presence. **Zahara de los Atunes**, between Barbate and Tarifa, is the fastest-growing centre, with a whole new *urbanización* (development) called **Nueva Zahara**. In the hills around the town there are some very opulent villas, popular with people looking for a less intensive atmosphere than that of the main *costas*.

The Costa del Sol

The Costa del Sol east from Gibraltar is far the most popular of all Spain's Mediterranean *costas*. The name 'Sun Coast' was not hard for it to come by because, with an average of 320 days of sunshine each year, this really is the sunniest place in mainland Spain. Drawing in millions of visitors every year, it has attractions for every taste and every wallet, from palace-villas and gleaming resorts for Arab sheikhs and fashion glitterati to cosy family holiday centres and archetypally hectic mass-density resorts, like Torremolinos, that offer a young crowd all the essentials of sun, sand, sex, cheap booze and plenty of opportunities for larging it. While some areas are crowded practically year-round, the Costa is big enough to have room for other resorts that are far more discreet. It also has Europe's largest concentration of winter-sunshine golf courses and specialised golf resorts.

The Costa del Sol is also much the most popular area for British property-buyers, with over 60 per cent of all purchasers. Every facility is on hand: there are hundreds of *urbanizaciones* of different sizes spread along this coast, and it has the largest concentration of foreigner-orientated services of all kinds, from bars and supermarkets to specialist property agencies and English-speaking lawyers and doctors. It's extremely easy to get to, via Málaga airport. There is a large and fairly self-contained permanent British and foreign community, many of them running or working in businesses directed at each other and the seasonal tourists. In an ancient town like **Mijas**, for example, 40 per cent of residents are foreigners, and there is a dedicated Foreign Residents Department at the local council to organise activities and keep people informed of what goes on. However, as a result of the massive transformation that has swept over this once-remote part of Andalucía, any traces of its historic character are often fairly synthetic; some developers now bill the area as 'the California of Europe', and stress sports facilities, sun and luxuries ahead of any old Andaluz identity.

Major reasons for buying along this coast would be the range of attractions and activities it offers, and its sheer convenience. Cost alone is no longer likely to be one, since local prices, after falling in the early 1990s, have risen significantly in the last few years. Because of the huge scale of building that has gone on here since the 1960s it's still possible, just, to find often quite well-used apartments in high-density resorts like Fuengirola for around €100,000 but, for something more attractive and/or a bit more spacious, such as a modest two-bedroom villa or village townhouse, you're unlikely to find much for less than €150,000–175,000, and more likely to have to spend close on €180,000–200,000. As the towns along the coast itself have become ever more developed, the preferred areas for more affluent buyers have become the hills and valleys heading inland, with the buying-up of old village houses or the building of often-luxurious new developments, even in out-of-the-way villages. Prices here are as high, or higher, although there are some great bargains to be found. Still more fashionable are the villages of the higher mountains behind the Costa, such as the **Serranía de Ronda**, with deliciously cool air and less intensive tourism, but still only an hour from the beach. On the coast or in the sierra, prices for large properties run into the limitless category.

Costs and building-density aside, there are other reasons why a beach location is not all-important here. One strange feature of the Costa del Sol is that its beaches are not hugely attractive, most of them being narrow and made up of grey sand. Another is that the region's main highway, the A7, follows the coast for most of the way between **Nerja** and **Algeciras** so that, on many beaches, there is at least some constant traffic noise.

Like many *costa*-labels, that of Costa del Sol is a little vague. When coined in the 1960s it tended to be used for the whole Mediterranean coast of Andalucía, from Almería to Algeciras. However, more recently, Costa Tropical has been thought up for the coast of Granada, and Almería has gone its own way, leaving Costa del Sol applying to the 200km (125 miles) between Nerja and Tarifa.

Málaga and Further West

For most of the *costa*'s foreign residents and visitors, Málaga is simply an adjunct to the airport, but it's actually a lively city with plenty of Andaluz character and street- and bar-life. It has its own town beaches, and a lot has been done recently to renovate the once run-down old town centre. Its transport links, by air, rail, road and ferry (to Morocco and the Balearics), make it especially convenient if you need to come in and out of the area frequently, and it's also a lot cheaper than anywhere on the coast outside it, with good-sized flats available for €120,000 or less. However, few of the British-orientated *costa* agencies handle properties in the city so, if you want to buy here, you'll need to work with local Spanish agents.

The mass-throughput, package-holiday Costa del Sol begins about 20km (12 miles) west of Málaga, and runs through the three towns of **Torremolinos**, **Benalmádena** and **Fuengirola**, which have the added convenience of being accessible by train from Málaga (the line ends at Fuengirola). Torremolinos surely needs no introduction, and lives up to its legend, with all the brash nightlife you could want and row on row of high-rise hotels, apartment blocks and timeshares behind a seafront of cafés selling full English breakfast or bratwurst and mustard, surrounded by villa developments that stretch away for miles along the beaches and into the dusty (unless permanently sprinklered) countryside. Benalmádena and Fuengirola are similar but a bit quieter, a bit more 'classy', and Benalmádena is about to go upmarket with a new gated *urbanización* development, complete with the inevitable golf course, country club and sports complex with one-bedroom apartments starting at a little over €150,000. These are places you either love or hate. If you love them, the sheer volume of apartments means that there are still places available at low prices, approaching €100,000, but expect to pay half as much again for something spacious and well appointed, and, even here, villa prices have risen fast.

Between Benalmádena and Fuengirola the A387 road runs inland into the Sierra de Mijas, the first of a succession of ranges of hills behind the *costa*. Here there are several old towns – **Mijas** itself, **Alhaurín el Grande** and **Coín** are the largest – that have become destinations of choice for property-buyers seeking to combine the convenience of the central *costa* with a less intense atmosphere than that of the beach resorts. All are now ringed by generally quite tasteful and spacious, and often pricey, apartment and villa developments, and places like Mijas have huge foreign communities. Anyone who does not want such an expat-orientated atmosphere needs to look further and further inland, and even in the most apparently remote villages there are now properties available.

West of the mass-market Costa del Sol, after a gap of about 30km (18 miles) that's filling up with medium-priced villa developments and golf courses, comes the élite Costa del Sol, with **Marbella** and its purpose-built pleasure port of **Puerto Banús**. This is where the *costa*'s 'Europe's California' tag fits best, in the Beverly Hills architecture of the giant villas, gated estates and apartment complexes, and the gleaming yachts lined up by the Puerto Banús quays. Ever-popular with the kind of celeb faces who fill Spanish and Italian gossip magazines, Marbella is quite a sprawling town, the service centre for a big section of the *costa*, that has extended into whole new areas like the 'new town' of **Nueva Andalucía**. Hence, as well as multi-million-pound villas there are medium-priced apartments available, but don't expect much for under €200,000 and think maybe €30,000–50,000 more for something a little special. Further west again, **San Pedro de Alcántara** and **Estepona** are less glitzy but also growing resorts that are very popular with British buyers. They are more peaceful than Marbella, and far more so than Torremolinos, particularly since the A7 motorway took away their through traffic.

From San Pedro the A376 road winds uphill and inland for 50km (31 miles) to **Ronda**, one of the most spectacular hill towns in Spain, perched above a gorge (it is a stop on the railway line between Algeciras and Seville and Córdoba, which can be handy). It is the capital of the **Serranía de Ronda**, a knot of dramatic valleys with superbly beautiful *pueblos blancos* or white hill-villages like those in the Sierra de Cádiz to the west (*see* 'The Costa de la Luz', pp.40–42). If Marbella is the fashion hub of the beach-*costa*, the Serranía villages, first discovered by foreign bohemians and artists back in the 1950s, have become a target for the fashionable set looking for mountain-village tranquillity near the Costa del Sol. The downside of this is that in **Gaucín**, for example, prettiest and trendiest of all the villages, a house can now easily cost €1 million and counting. However, it is in the nature of this kind of area – which is very extensive – that you can also find properties for far less, although they will almost certainly require a fair amount of work.

Just inland from Marbella there is an area now known as '**golf valley**', but the real 'Costa del Golf' is along the westernmost stretch of the Costa del Sol towards Gibraltar. The largest and finest dedicated golf resorts are at **Sotogrande**, 22km (14 miles) from Estepona, with three full-size courses that include Valderrama, location for the 1997 Ryder Cup, and San Roque, just north of Gibraltar, where Severiano Ballesteros is the occasional pro. Both offer a whole range of other activities as well, such as beach clubs, tennis courts, riding and, at Sotogrande, a world-class polo club and a marina, and are surrounded by luxurious villas built as part of the estate. Prices are to suit.

La Línea and **Algeciras** are two undistinguished industrial towns, mainly visited by travellers taking the ferry to Morocco. **Gibraltar**, that strange piece of British territory across the bay from Algeciras that brings the Costa del Sol to an end, is a regular excursion destination for many British *costa* residents, and not only for its pubs and British chain-store branches with all sorts of products from home. Its airport can be useful, and many people use the high-interest, tax-free accounts offered by Gibraltar banks.

East of Málaga

The relatively short stretch of the Costa del Sol running east from Málaga to Nerja is much less well known than the western part, and so is usually less crowded and often more attractive. Towns along the coast, such as **Cala del Moral** or **Torre del Mar**, are similar in style to the package resorts further west, only smaller. The area's real attractions begin if you turn inland at Torre del Mar to the old Moorish town of **Vélez-Málaga**, at the mouth of a valley famous for its wines. This is the gateway to the **Axarquía**, an area of whitewashed hill villages and isolated *fincas* as pretty as those of the Serranía de Ronda but, so far, much less sought-after. The scenery is stunning, offering the classic Andaluz combination of views that take in dazzling blue sea, lush green valleys and snow-topped peaks in one turn of the head. Some villages nearer the coast, such as **Frigiliana** and **Torrox**, where upwards of €130,000 gets you an attractive two-bedroom apartment, already contain their share of villa estates but, further up in the hills, pretty villages like **Cómpeta** or **Canillas de Aceituno** have still had relatively little new building – most new houses are individual villas, not whole developments – while prices are still quite moderate. **Nerja** itself is a relaxed resort with beaches in small coves, a celebrated cliff-top promenade and a giant cave, the Cueva de Nerja, that's used as a spectacular live music venue.

The Costa Tropical and the Alpujarras

The coast of Granada province is another area with a different atmosphere from the main Costa del Sol, and much less crowded, so the name Costa Tropical has been created to differentiate it more clearly. Its relative quietness is partly due to its special geography, with mountains that come down very close to the shore or fall directly into the sea, leaving between them delicious, intimate coves, while limiting the space available for any high-density development. **Almuñécar** is the only resort of any size, and elsewhere there are mostly small villages or isolated beaches. Villas are spreading up the hillsides behind them – in superb locations, with magnificent Mediterranean views – but most of the new building follows the styles of local village architecture, and consists of individual houses or small clusters rather than estate developments. Prices here seem to be catching up with those to the west, but a spacious three-bedroom apartment a stone's throw from the beach can still be found for around €150,000. The shoreline opens up a bit at **Salobreña**, a lovely, whitewashed old village around a Moorish castle that is one of this coast's most popular – but still not heavily developed – places, with many properties available in town or in the hills around it. The 'Tropical' in the *costa's* name comes from the small, sheltered plain between Salobreña and the town of **Motril** that, for centuries, has been used for growing sugar cane and tropical fruit. East of Motril there are more open beaches, and these are becoming more developed.

Towering up above the Costa Tropical is the Sierra Nevada, the highest mountain range in mainland Spain, and one of the area's special attractions is the possibility it offers, for months each year, of skiing in the morning and swimming in a perfectly warm sea in the afternoon. In between the two are the **Alpujarras**, foothills of the main sierra, with fabulously beautiful mountain scenery and a famously healthy climate. **Órgiva** is the only town, and most villages are tiny. The writer Gerald Brenan lived here for many years and, since the 1960s, many more foreigners have come here in search of back-to-the-good-life rural tranquillity, taking over and restoring the area's often-abandoned old slate farmhouses. Many have a vaguely alternative state of mind, and foreigners in the Alpujarras now do all kind of things for a living, from plumbing to craftwork (there's also a Tibetan Buddhist monastery). One resident is former Genesis band-member, Chris Stewart, the runaway success of whose 'Peter-Mayle-comes-to-Spain'-style book, *Driving Over Lemons*, has attracted a whole new wave of attention to the Alpujarras, which could end up disturbing their laidback-ness a bit. It has also tended to push up prices but, even so, probably due to the time it takes to get into the valleys, it's still possible to find many farms and village houses here for under €75,000. A renovated townhouse in Órgiva itself could cost as little as €110,000, or somewhat less than €100,000 in nearby Lanjarón.

Almería and Murcia

Although Almería province is part of Andalucía, in landscape and from the point of view of visitors it has more in common with Murcia just to the east, one of Spain's few regions made up of a single province. Together they make up the driest and hottest area in all Spain, and Almería contains the one true desert in Europe, an extraordinary expanse of bare grey rock, wadis and caves – not for nothing were the spaghetti westerns of the 1960s filmed here. This is a landscape that some people find hugely compelling, but for others it's just too sparse to be attractive.

Since every part of Mediterranean Spain must have its *costa*, each province here has its own. The current main growth area on the **Costa de Almería** is in beach towns west of Almería city, such as **Aguadulce**, **Almerimar** and **Roquetas**, where there are villa estates, marinas and golf courses. However, they're places with little charm, especially since the land behind them is devoted not to tourism but to the other boom that has made once-ragged Almería a growth area of modern Spain – growing winter vegetables. The grey desert soil is very fertile when watered, and the flat plain to the west is covered with endless plastic-roofed greenhouses that produce year-round crops of tomatoes and iceberg lettuces to be trucked off to Europe's supermarkets. Scenic they are not. Almería itself is an unimpressive city, with surprisingly few traces of the days when it was the main port of Al-Andalus.

A far more exciting part of the Costa de Almería lies south and east of the city, around the giant cape of **Cabo de Gata**, a vast, almost lunar landscape of sand flats, scrub, dunes and bare desert cliffs rising sheer out of the sea. Its isolated beaches are popular for camping and scuba-diving but, despite this being a national park, there are also small resorts such as **San José** and **Agua Amarga**, with a few villa and apartment developments. Prices are accessible. The most renowned tourist centre in Almería is north of the national park at **Mojácar** which, with its fierce summer temperatures, has become a favourite with sun-chasers from all over Europe. Old Mojácar is a remarkable, a completely Moorish-looking whitewashed village perched on a cliff a little inland; below it, villas extend away along the volcanic sand beach. Despite its fashionable status, property prices here can also be quite moderate, though they have risen quite a lot lately.

Murcia, meanwhile, has decided to call itself the **Costa Cálida** or 'Hot Coast', which, given that the other *costas* are hardly chilly, is a sign of how hot it can get here. Most of the south-facing coast of the province is, so far, relatively empty. The main centre is **Mazarrón** and its resort of **Puerto de Mazarrón**, with fine beaches, a marina and villa developments that are mainly sold to Spanish families, and in which you can find quite large houses for between €180,000 and €200,000. Murcia's most unusual geographical feature, though, is the **Mar Menor**, a giant saltwater lagoon east of Cartagena that is separated from the

Mediterranean by a long, thin, beach-lined strip of land, **La Manga** ('the Sleeve') del Mar Menor. Midway along the 'sleeve' is the Club La Manga, a huge sports resort with three full-sized golf courses and every kind of other world-class sporting facility that has become famous by providing winter training facilities for football teams from around Europe. Integrated into the complex are upscale villas and apartments, available for sale or rent. This area has seen a huge amount of recent building, with *urbanizaciones* multiplying either side of the club and in the villages at the north end of La Manga, like **Torre de la Horadada**, blending into the golf resorts of the southern Costa Blanca (*see* opposite). Prices for villas can be very reasonable, but these are places that sell on sun, beaches and sports opportunities, not any local colour.

Valencia and Alicante

The 'Valencian Community' – made up of the provinces of Valencia, Alicante (Alacant, in Catalan) and Castellón (Castelló) – is one of Spain's bilingual regions, with two official languages, Spanish and Valencian (a dialect of Catalan). Road signs, for example, show two ways of spelling nearly all place names. Anyone wishing to get close to local life (not easy to do, if you're living in a Costa Blanca *urbanización*) would be advised to get some understanding of the local language but, in general, Valencians are less culturally assertive than, say, Catalans, and it's usually quite easy to get by in Spanish. Valencia is home to one of the things nearly all foreigners recognise as Spanish – paella – but otherwise the local culture is more elusive than that of Andalucía.

Until recently, anyone buying an individual or rural property in any of Valencia's three provinces had to be careful not to fall foul of the Ley Reguladora de la Actividad Urbanistica de la Comunidad Valencia or LRAU. This planning law allowed developers to compulsorily purchase chunks of rural land from larger plots, rezone them and develop them, in many cases rendering the remainder of the property worthless. This is set to change, however, *see* box, p.50.

The Costa Blanca

Ever since the 1960s, Alicante's Costa Blanca has been among the most popular areas in Spain for British visitors, for holidays and buying homes. Consequently there are large British and foreign colonies here, supported by all kinds of services and with all sorts of facilities on hand, especially for golf. It remains second in popularity only to the Costa del Sol as a target area for British property-buyers in Spain. The climate is only a little less sunny than on the Costa del Sol, but also milder, and has been officially declared by a World Health Organisation report to be among the healthiest in the world. With the recent rise in prices on the Costa del Sol, many parts of the Costa Blanca are now significantly cheaper by comparison.

Traditionally there have been two parts to the Costa Blanca, although it's recently gained a third. The northern Costa Blanca is the prettiest part, with often-lovely rocky coves, backed by rugged green mountains, around the triangular peninsula that ends at Cap de la Nau, easternmost point of mainland Spain. Its main towns – **Dènia**, **Jávea/Xàbia**, **Calpe/Calp** and **Altea** – are very well known and surrounded by villa developments, but at the core of each of them there is still a historic old town of considerable charm. They have some of Spain's longest-established British colonies – especially Jávea and Altea – with many retired people in permanent residence and many more who stay over each winter. The **Jalón Valley**, just inland from Jávea, is a popular area for new villa-building – with two high-standard golf courses – but this is also a partial conservation area, so the villa developments are being kept to a relatively discreet, medium-density scale.

Only 10km (6 miles) south of Altea is **Benidorm**, which dominates the central Costa Blanca. Like Torremolinos, Europe's largest single resort has a reputation that goes before it, and doesn't disappoint. It is always being claimed that the town wants to become less bargain-package-orientated, but there doesn't seem to be much point, and it continues to build yet more high-rise hotels and apartments. Hence there are always moderately priced apartments and villas available around the town but, for something spacious and in an *urbanización* with swimming pool, you are probably looking at over €135,000. As with other mega-resorts, it's a place you either love or loathe. Entertainment is never lacking, and a recent big new family attraction is the theme park just outside the town, Terra Mítica, which, it seems, is headed for bankruptcy so it's anybody's guess how long it will be there. **Vilajoyosa**, 10km (6 miles) south, is to Benidorm what Fuengirola is to Torremolinos, a bit smaller, a bit quieter and a bit more family-orientated. Beyond it there are more smaller beach resorts down to Alicante itself which, like Málaga, is seen by most foreign *costa*-visitors as just an airport, but which has its own beaches and a vibrant old centre buzzing with Spanish bar- and street-life.

The southern Costa Blanca, below Alicante on the map, barely figured as a destination before the 1990s but is now one of the fastest-growing holiday areas in Spain, above all for villa developments. The landscape is much drier than further north, more similar to the Costa Cálida of Murcia (*see* p.47), into which this area blends indistinguishably. Along the coast there are open, sandy beaches and palm trees instead of rocky coves. As at La Manga, winter golf is a major attraction, especially around the so-called 'golden triangle' of courses (Las Ramblas, Campoamor and Villamartín) south of **Torrevieja**, which all have upscale house developments attached. *Urbanizaciones*, restaurants and other facilities are multiplying along this coast and, because of the scale of recent building, this is one of the cheapest areas in which to buy in Spain, with plenty available starting at about €90,000. Torrevieja is the largest town and, although heavily touristed, still has a big food and produce market. Overall, though, since virtually everything here is so new, this is not an area anyone goes to in search of local atmosphere.

The Costa del Azahar

This is the label given to the coast of Valencia and Castellón provinces, although it's not widely known. It means 'Orange Blossom Coast', which is quite apt, since vast groves of Valencia oranges line the flat plain for miles at a time. The biggest interruption to them is Spain's third-largest city, **Valencia**, which has urban attractions of its own as well as a sizeable modern industrial belt. The city aside, this region is agriculturally rich in other things as well as oranges and lemons. South of Valencia city is the **Albufera**, a huge area of freshwater wetlands celebrated for its bird life and special atmosphere, and which is also the traditional source of the rice used in paella and the other rice dishes that are the great specialities of local cuisine. Valencia also produces high-quality wines.

Along the shore there are fine, straight sandy beaches rather than small coves. There are also plenty of villas and apartments, but they are mostly bought or

Valencia Scraps Urbanisation Law

Under a law introduced by the Valencian autonomous government in 1994 (the Ley Reguladora de la Actividad Urbanistica de la Comunidad Valencia or LRAU), developers have until recently been able to move on to property not owned by them. The urbanisation law allowed local developers to submit a plan and acquire rural land, frequently part of somebody's *'finca'*, or estate, at a fraction of the market value. To make matters worse, many British owners were forced to contribute to the developers' construction costs, which meant many faced financial ruin.

The legislation, known as the 'land grab law', was designed to cut through complex planning procedures and to pay for improvements in the infrastructure such as roads and airports but really gave property developers and speculators *carte blanche* to acquire land below the market price from owners who do not want to sell. If they refused, the local town hall could sequester their property. If they sold part of their land, they were left with properties that were practically worthless or drastically reduced in value. The result has been overdevelopment up and down the coast and the undermining of property investment security.

A long campaign led by expat and local home-owners, and taken up by Euro-MP Michael Cashman (formerly an *EastEnders* actor), has led the Valencian government, under pressure from the European Parliament, to scrap the act and begin drafting a replacement law. It is too early to say exactly what the new legislation will entail, and when, or if, victims of the old law will receive compensation. But residents in the region have been able to breathe a huge sigh of relief and feel they have won an important victory.

rented by Spanish families from Valencia, Madrid or other cities inland rather than foreigners. Germans are the only other nationality that seems to have discovered this coast in any numbers.

Gandia, at the southern tip of the Costa del Azahar, is a historic old town like those of the Costa Blanca; set back from the sea, it now has a big beach resort attached to it where you may find a three-bedroom apartment for a little under €150,000. **Cullera**, 20km (12 miles) north, is another popular Spanish family resort, and there are smaller holiday developments beside the Albufera. The most attractive stretch of this whole coast is at the very northern end, above **Castellón**, in the towns of **Vinarós**, **Benicarló** and especially **Peníscola**, where hotels and beach houses spread along the beach either side of a wonderful medieval old town set on a spit of rock jutting into the sea. Here, for upwards of €115,000 or €120,000 you may find a two-bedroom apartment with sea views. Busy with Spanish families every August, they're low-key the rest of the time, and have superb seafood restaurants. The only big resort nearby is **Benicássim**, near Castellón, which has gone all-out for a new audience by hosting beach raves each summer. Inland from this coast is the **Maestrat**, a region of fiercely rugged, dry hills scattered with ancient villages that, like its main centre, the extraordinary walled town of **Morella**, are the kind of places that seem like exhibits from a museum of medieval life. In among them, the resourceful house-hunter can find any number of abandoned or under-used farms and village houses, in need of restoration.

Catalonia

Catalonia was the first region around Spain's Mediterranean coast to open up to foreign tourism back in the 1950s and yet, curiously, is the least 'Spanish' of any of them. It has a strong sense of its own history and culture, to be found in language, food, folklore and the heritage of artists like Gaudí or Miró, and a greater sense of identity than many independent member states of the United Nations. It has always been one of the most economically active parts of Spain and, although it no longer accounts for nearly 70 per cent of Spanish industry, as it did before 1936, its continued importance and overall vibrancy is reflected in Barcelona's rise and rise to become one of Europe's most fashionable cities.

Since 1975 Catalonia has also been among the most assertive of all the Spanish regions in developing its own autonomous government. Catalan is now the primary language in education and most areas of public administration. When dealing with local councils, for example, while Spanish translations of documents will usually be available, things will take longer if you insist on doing everything in Spanish. Anywhere in the Catalan countryside, especially, you will get much further much faster in any kind of contact with local people if you make some effort with their language. The regional government provides a variety of facilities for learning Catalan (*see* p.281).

Most of the Catalan countryside is rugged and rocky, but also much greener than further south, and its old stone villages provide plenty of centuries-old charm. More than in any other part of Spain, except maybe Andalucía, foreign residents in Catalonia now spread into most parts of the country, into villages, small towns and *masies* (*see* below) rather than just sticking to the coast. However, most property-buyers remain closer to the coast, many hoping to combine the benefits of beach living with easy access to Barcelona. There are plenty of villas and apartments along the Catalan coast, but their main buyers are local city-dwellers from Barcelona, with whom you have to compete. Catalonia is also more densely populated than other regions, so land prices are higher overall. The combined result is that house prices here – while not on the scale of the most luxurious parts of the Costa del Sol – are generally higher than in the more tourist-orientated areas further south. Another difference is in the weather: Catalonia is greener because it is more northerly, and from November to March grey, damp days are as likely as winter sunshine.

Inland Catalonia

One of the most characteristic features of the Catalan countryside is its *masia* farmhouses – giant chalet-like structures, often 500 or more years old, with immense stone walls and sloping tiled roofs – that you can see scattered across hills and up mountain valleys. Traditionally, as in a Swiss chalet, livestock was kept on the ground floor while the family lived above, all in the one building. In recent years *masies*, which generally come with some land, have become highly sought-after by Catalans and a growing number of foreigners as country homes – for which purpose they usually need comprehensive renovation, with all-new plumbing, wiring and often whole walls within the rustic old structure. Fully renovated *masies* with modern comforts installed, and often a pool in the grounds, easily change hands for €1,000,000 and upwards, though you may find one in need of restoration for quite a lot less than that. However, such is the demand that *masies* reasonably close to main transport links that come up for sale are snapped up quickly, and finding others often requires a fair amount of exploration, and some luck. An area where more old farmhouses may be available at low prices is the High Pyrenees, with its superb scenery. However, they will almost certainly require a lot of work, while an alpine climate and remoteness magnifies the practical difficulties.

The Coast South of Barcelona and the Costa Daurada

The Catalan coast south and west of Barcelona is now most widely known as the Costa Daurada (or, in Castilian, Dorada) which means 'Golden Coast' although, strictly speaking, this applies only to a part of it. About 40km (25 miles) and – on a good day – 45 minutes from the city is **Sitges**, Barcelona's favourite weekend beach, with an old fishing town at its centre that first attracted an artists' colony in the 1890s. Sitges has managed the trick of becoming a popular family resort while always remaining vaguely trendy, and in particular hosts a thriving gay scene. Recently, with frequent rail connections and a fast motorway link on the A16, it has become increasingly popular as a place to live for people working in Barcelona, especially foreigners. However, this has had the natural effect of pushing up prices, which can reach the €260,000 mark for even medium-sized apartments. **Vilanova i la Geltrú**, 5km (3 miles) west, is a larger, more workaday town with a fishing port. It also has a long beach, but has never had Sitges' fashionable cachet, and so is cheaper.

West of Vilanova is a long string of small and usually tranquil beach towns, such as **Calafell** and **Comarruga**, with villas mostly owned by Barcelona and Tarragona families, and where there are always properties available for moderate (but rarely low) prices. **Torredembarra** has some of the best beaches, and so is one of the busiest; medieval **Altafulla**, 15km (9 miles) from Tarragona, is one of the prettiest. Tarragona is an attractive small city, with fine Roman relics and medieval architecture and some of the features of Barcelona, including a long Rambla promenade, but little of its bustle. Ten kilometres to its west is **Salou**, the one big hub of the Costa Daurada, with all the usual features of big Spanish package resorts – high-rise hotels and apartments, loads of tourist restaurants – but not quite as brash and overpowering as Benidorm or Torremolinos. Just outside it is the Mediterranean's largest theme park and resort complex, at Universal Mediterrània (formerly Port Aventura). Like the other major resorts, though, Salou has lower house prices, a steady supply of properties to buy or rent and plenty of agencies to help you find them. With the rising prices elsewhere in Catalonia it now also serves as a convenient home – or as a first base on arrival, from which to explore the area – for quite a few resident foreigners, including people working in Barcelona, 1hr 20mins away by train. South of Salou is another line of small beach towns spread along 50km (30 miles) of flat, not very attractive coastline, but all accessible by train. They are brought to an end by the vast wetlands of the **Ebro Delta**, wonderful for bird-watching and cycling but, in human terms, very unpopulated.

The Coast North of Barcelona and the Costa Brava

The small towns along the coast north of Barcelona – **Masnou**, **Premià** and even as far as **Canet**, 42km (26 miles) from town – are, still more than Sitges to the south, fast becoming part of a secondary 'commuter belt' to the city, as well as a weekend beach. The coastal strip is very narrow because a steep mountain ridge rises right up behind it, and most of the towns have a lower, beach half and an upper section at the top of the hill, the greater tranquillity of which is much-prized. The package-holiday destinations of the Costa Brava begin as the coastal plain widens at **Calella de la Costa**, which, with the peculiar segregation of some resorts, has been pretty much a German colony since the 1970s. Further north, **Blanes**, big and bouncing **Lloret de Mar**, **Tossa de Mar** and **Platja d'Aro** are more international, and have a long-established popularity with British holi-daymakers. All have the usual range of apartments and villa *urbanizaciones* around them, but properties here are now scarcer and relatively more expensive than on the Costa Blanca or many parts of the Costa del Sol.

Strictly speaking, this is not the Costa Brava at all, as the name ('Rugged Coast') really only applies to the 50km (30 miles) or so of rocky coast just to the north, between Palamós and Begur and centred on the old town of **Palafrugell**. Instead of broad, sandy beaches there are intimate, often spectacularly beau-tiful, rocky coves, backed by green-wooded cliffs and accessible only by winding narrow lanes. There are very few large-scale developments, in part because the geography discourages it, but also because this is one of the preferred areas for the second homes of wealthy Catalans, who have helped to keep things the way they are. There are plenty of large villas up on the hillsides, but prices can be very high, with villas fetching well over half a million euros and even over €600,000.

North of the River Ter, where the coastline broadens out again, are **L'Estartit** and **L'Escala**, two towns that are both working fishing ports and pleasantly un-hectic small resorts, and where there are often villas and townhouses available for a more accessible cost. The largish resort of the northern Catalan coast is **Roses**, which is still smaller than Salou, let alone Benidorm. Like other resorts, though, it contains a wide range of villas and apartments and, on its south side, there is a large villa development at **Empuriabrava**. Roses stands at the landward end of the extraordinary rock outcrop of Cap de Creus, at the far end of which is the famously beautiful village of **Cadaqués**, long-time home of Salvador Dalí, where houses tend to change hands only for very large amounts of money. The fishing villages on the north side of the cape up to the French border, such as **Port de la Selva** or **Llançà**, are more low-key but have a great deal of charm, and many houses there are bought up by Catalans as summer retreats.

Stretching inland behind this whole coast is the **Empordà**, a beautiful region of old stone villages and very fertile green hills. Some of the prettiest villages – such as Pals, near Begur, which is virtually a Gothic monument – are just inland from the Costa Brava proper, and their houses are in great demand as leisure homes. There is a big market in both converted *masies* and new villas, but prices are correspondingly high. The northern or Alt Empordà, around **Figueres**, is larger and flatter, and more likely to yield up a wider range of prices. Fully converted *masies* may still cost €1,000,000 and more but, with some explo-ration, it's also possible to find farms and village houses in need of work for much less.

The Balearic Islands

Synonymous with modern tourism – from Mallorca beach resorts to Ibiza clubbing – the Balearic Islands have been the favourite Med holiday destination for the whole of northern Europe for over 40 years. Curiously, though, among

British people buying property in Spain they lag in popularity behind the Costa Blanca and Costa del Sol. By far the largest number of foreign home-buyers, in Mallorca especially, are Germans, but there are also ample Scandinavian and Dutch colonies. Even so, there are still plenty of British property-owners around the islands, with English-speaking services at their disposal.

The statistics of Balearic tourism are staggering – more hotel beds than entire countries, whole towns that are 90 per cent foreign-owned – but, strange as it can seem, the islands have a life of their own as well. Each of the islands has its own character and climate and, away from the big resorts and foreign-owned enclaves, there are characterful towns and – always surprising – large untouristed stretches of countryside and even shoreline. The Balearics – which form one autonomous region – is also another bilingual, Catalan-speaking area. Locals are less linguistically demanding than Catalans, and more concessions are naturally made to foreigners overall, but the more you use local services, and above all schools, the more useful you will find it to be able to handle Catalan.

In the last few years the Balearics' authorities and publicity agents have often expressed a desire to do away with the islands' quick-and-cheap package holiday image and appeal to a more upscale public. There has also been a feeling among locals that the complete dominance of tourism over local life had become overwhelming, and that the time had come for the local adminis-tration to make its own choices, rather than simply meeting every demand made by the travel trade. One aspect of this has been a series of measures aimed at halting the endless cycle of uncontrolled new building, and limiting development mainly to those (already ample) areas built up since the 1960s. Waste management and recycling has also become a growth industry in itself. This is greatly appreciated by foreign home-owners already established on the islands, since it means that the still-untouched and beautiful coves around them will remain that way. However, it has had the effect of pushing up prices. Even so, it remains a characteristic of the Balearics that, after the huge amount of building that has gone on here ever since the 1960s, there is a wide range of properties and prices available, from plain 1970s apartments for around €100,000 to lavish converted farmhouses for many millions, passing through just about every other price-band in between along the way.

Mallorca

Over 90km (56 miles) wide, Mallorca is too big to be totally consumed by tourism although, at times, it has often looked as if someone was making a serious effort to see if it could be. Its capital of **Palma**, home to over half the 600,000-plus population, is a real city with a life of its own, while in the middle of the island there is an impressively rugged interior scattered with engaging small towns and villages. It has a mild Mediterranean climate, with occasional chilly winters. Such is the number of people that come to the island, though, and spread in from the coasts, that there is scarcely a village on Mallorca that does not have at least some foreign residents or second-home-owners.

There are two sides to Mallorca, especially with regard to property-seeking. The ultra-developed package Mallorca is concentrated primarily around the **Bay of Palma** on either side of the city, and tends to divide up quite neatly with British-dominated resorts like Magaluf and Palma Nova on the west side, and German-favoured S'Arenal and other resorts to the east. Until recently, building and rebuilding has continued here with few let-ups since the 1960s, and so there are small apartments available but not for much less than €125,000. A far more refined Mallorca is found along the northwest coast, in and around old towns like **Sóller**, **Valdemossa** and especially **Deià**, where the poet Robert Graves lived for many years and Michael Douglas has a house. Here, as on the central Costa Brava, a combination of geography – spectacular mountainsides falling into small coves – and the preferences of people already established there have prevented large-scale development. The towns and villages are full of character, and all along the coast there are intimate bays and small wooded valleys with superb views: villas easily cost from €1,000,000 up to several millions. In between these extremes you can find just about every other grade of property, spread through all the beach villages around the island. Townhouses in places like **Pollensa** seem to offer the best mid-range value, costing between €285,000 and €375,000. Some have just one or two *urbanizaciones* and scattered villas, others have several; the southeast corner, around **Felanitx**, is the German buyers' favourite area but you can find very spacious townhouses there for under €400,000. There is now also a big market in converted farms, village houses, old mills and similar in the island's interior. A converted five-bedroom windmill was selling for €530,000 recently and a restored farmhouse might fetch upwards of €325,000. There is, again, a complete range of prices, depending especially on whether a house has been fully renovated or still needs a lot of work, but you will be very lucky to find anything for under €200,000.

Menorca

The northernmost and greenest of the islands, Menorca has a noticeably cooler winter climate and from around October to April is prey to powerful north winds, strong enough to cause the trees to grow bent horizontally on that side of the island. Though small, it has a strong character, and two attractive old towns at either end, **Maó (Mahón)** and **Ciutadella**. Tourist development arrived here slightly later than on the other two islands, and around the coasts there are still many beautiful coves and beaches that are untouched, accessible only by dirt track. As regards homes, as on the other islands there are purpose-built beach villa and apartment developments, mostly on the north coast (**Son Parc**) or the south (**Son Bou**, **Cala Galdana**, and others), which have the most properties available at lower-to-moderate prices (mostly from about €130,000);

elsewhere, there are converted farmhouses and village houses, which are usually more expensive, starting at around €250,000 for something small and stretching way past the million mark. In general, though, prices on Menorca tend to be higher than on Mallorca, but lower than on Ibiza.

Ibiza (Eivissa) and Formentera

A long way further south than the other islands, Ibiza (Eivissa in Catalan) is a burnt-brown desert island for much of the year, but explodes with flowers for a few brief weeks in February and March. Its unstoppable popularity as number-one Mediterranean party venue continues to bring in the plane-loads each year, despite occasional challenges from other sun-spots. Nevertheless, it needs to be pointed out that the real 24-hour club scene on Ibiza has remained surprisingly localised, concentrated mostly in Ibiza Town itself, Sant Antoni (San Antonio) over on the west side of the island and along the road between them, and to a lesser extent in Santa Eulàlia. Elsewhere there are still plenty of rocky coves that are empty or contain just a few villas, which the regional government's new planning laws are intended to preserve from further development.

As elsewhere in the Balearics, after 30 years of building there is a very wide range of property available but, even more than on the other islands, the recent building restrictions have tended to raise prices. Flats in 1970s high-rises in San Antonio can still be found cheaply. Most apartments cost at least €165,000 and more; houses around the coast or inland rarely cost less than €750,000 and often a great deal more and you will be very hard pushed to find houses inland (in need of work) for under €300,000.

Formentera, smallest and least known of the Balearics, is an even smaller island, reachable only by ferry from Ibiza Town. Its relative remoteness and aridity have been enough to deter major development, and it is much loved by serious sun-lovers who prize its tranquillity and often-empty beaches over the lack of nightlife and the small scale of island social life. There are a few relatively small apartment developments, and a few more villas and converted farmhouses. Oddly enough, perhaps because Formentera has never been included in any 'boom', prices are a little lower than on Ibiza.

The North Atlantic Coast

Spain's north coast has long been a popular holiday area for Spaniards who prefer cooler temperatures and fresh breezes in midsummer to sun-baked Mediterranean beaches. For this same reason, it has been passed over by most British visitors. The landscape is one of green, wooded hills, and the many wonderful beaches face ocean seas, often with crashing surf. Winter weather is pretty similar to that of much of northern Europe: cold, grey and wet.

The Basque Country

The Basque provinces have superb scenery, and two very attractive cities in 19th-century **San Sebastián (Donostia**, in Basque) and industrial **Bilbao (Bilbo)**, now 'upgraded' in international terms since the creation of the Guggenheim Museum. The Basques' special culture expresses itself in all kinds of ways, one of the most attractive of which is some of the very best cooking in Spain, especially fish and seafood. The most traditional kind of farmhouse in the Basque valleys is the *caserío*, a giant stone chalet similar to the Catalan *masies*; as in Catalonia, there is a certain trade in old houses to restore, but on a far smaller scale and at lower prices. Beyond the weather, a prime difference is the ongoing conflict around the support by a sizeable section of the population for complete Basque independence, reaching its violent peak in the actions of the ETA terrorist organisation. As in Northern Ireland for most of the last 30 years, this conflict can remain out of sight – especially to outsiders – in most of the country most of the time, but then suddenly flare up in your face. Anyone living in a Basque village would almost certainly be expected eventually at least to give an opinion, and to some extent take sides. Also, you would be required to come to terms – above all if you have children – with the Basque language (Euskera), which is less widely spoken (particularly in the cities) than Catalan or Galician in their home regions but is heavily promoted by the regional government. Learning Basque is more difficult than attaining fluency in any of the Latin-based languages.

Cantabria and Asturias

The two Spanish-speaking regions west of the Basque Country along the coast have equally – or more – spectacular scenery, without the political problems. Along the coast, particularly in **Cantabria** either side of **Santander**, there are some lovely beach villages that come alive each summer, and inland there are some of Spain's most spectacular mountains in the **Picos de Europa**. Central Asturias around the cities of **Gijón** and **Oviedo** is (or was) one of Spain's centres of old-fashioned industry (coal mines and shipyards), but otherwise both regions still have plenty of rural character, and historic villages with distinctive architecture are dotted all around the mountain valleys. In food, **Asturias** is known for rich winter dishes (to keep out the cold) and strong cheeses; cider, as throughout the north coast, is the traditional drink. The summer climate is often delightful and in the last few years the Picos de Europa have become popular for walking and exploring the countryside. Many houses are available for summer lets, and a growing number are available to buy. Prices are a lot lower than by the Mediterranean: fully restored farm and village houses can cost around €200,000 or even less, unrestored properties under €45,000 and sometimes very little at all. Finding them involves exploring; there are plenty of local agents, but they are geared to Spanish buyers.

Galicia

Spain's northwest corner, Galicia is one of its most intriguing regions. Galicians are Celts, and the country has many similarities to Ireland or Brittany – the greenness everywhere, grey-stone villages, folk traditions, the ever-changing and often soggy weather – although its language, *Galego*, is a Latin language that is closely related to Portuguese, not Castilian Spanish. In rural Galicia, especially, it is overwhelmingly the first language of daily life.

A celebrated feature of the Galician coastline is its *rías*, fjord-like inlets surrounded by fine sand beaches, green hills and pretty fishing towns. The largest *rías* contain the region's busiest towns, such as **El Ferrol, A Coruña (La Coruña**, in Spanish) and **Vigo**; inland is one of Spain's most fascinating historic cities, **Santiago de Compostela**. The *rías* are also a prime source of the superb fish and seafoodthat form a mainstay of the local economy and of local cooking. This industry was severely hit by the worst ecological disaster in Spain's history, the sinking of the *Prestige* in November 2002. The tanker, totally unseaworthy, vomited thousands of tons of thick, unrefined oil into the sea and many beaches were affected, with traces of the oil turning up on French Atlantic coast beaches months later. The region is slowly recovering in economic terms but the extent of the long-term damage to the sea bed has yet to be calculated.

Galicia has traditionally been a land of emigration, and many properties in the area are bought by returning migrants who, having made their money in the UK, Germany or elsewhere, buy houses in their home towns or around the *rías*. As in Asturias, prices for village houses and old farms are low-to-moderate, going up just slightly for places with a sea view. A five-bedroom, two-bathroom family home a short walk from the beach can cost as little as €250,000.

The Canary Islands

The seven islands of the Canaries have one overriding attraction for most of their northern European visitors and long-stayers: the subtropical climate, labelled by some the 'eternal spring', which they enjoy thanks to a location closer to Africa than to the Iberian Peninsula. Winter sunshine is guaranteed while conversely, thanks to ocean winds, even midsummer temperatures do not usually reach the heights of the hottest mainland spots, except on Lanzarote. Second after the weather comes the extraordinary mix of landscapes and ecology of these volcanic islands, from the deserts of Lanzarote to the cactus jungles of Tenerife, and including superb beaches. The downside of the Canaries' peculiar geography and lack of rainfall is a shortage of fresh water, especially on Fuerteventura and Lanzarote, which becomes more or less of a problem at different times of year. Colonised from Castile and Andalucía in the 15th century, the islands developed a quirky, slow-moving culture of their own during their long centuries of virtual isolation.

Nearly all the islands have at least some large-scale, well-developed resorts, and there are substantial colonies of foreigners (mainly British and German) with houses on the islands. There is also a full variety of English-speaking services, especially on Gran Canaria, Lanzarote and Tenerife. However, while the all-year sunshine represents an essential draw for some people, for others the islands' isolation and more difficult access (a 3½-hour flight from the UK) is significantly off-putting so, with less demand, property prices are overall a little lower than on the mainland. As on the Costa del Sol and in the Balearics, properties available can be divided between villas and apartments in purpose-built holiday developments, town flats and single houses, whether recently built villas or converted farms and village houses. Prices vary surprisingly little between the main islands: in general, there is a range on offer in apartment and villa *urbanizaciones* from between €90,000 and €130,000, and largish town-houses can be found for upwards of €160,000 while smallish villas can cost as little as €200,000. Paying €50,000 more, you get a reasonable, medium-sized family villa. Among renovated rural houses there are many properties for under €300,000 and some gorgeous country houses for a little under €400,000.

To compensate for the economic effects of their remoteness, the Canaries have always enjoyed special tax privileges within Spain, and these have been maintained in the EU. The Canaries are not considered part of the EU for customs purposes and so many items, cars and large electrical goods among them, are almost tax-free and thus unusually cheap. However, should you ever take them into the EU proper (whether mainland Spain or the UK), you will usually find that you are officially required to pay extra duty on them.

Gran Canaria

In the middle of the archipelago, Gran Canaria contains Las Palmas, the Canaries' capital and largest city, and receives the largest number of visitors each year. Rather like Mallorca, although in a less marked way, it has two sides to it. Gran Canaria's big package resorts are all on the **south coast**, around **Playa del Inglés** and the spectacular sand dunes at **Maspalomas**. On either side, as well as miles of golden-sand beaches, there are now villa developments and timeshare complexes extending around the coast. Some high-density complexes have apartments available at remarkably low prices; among the most sought-after, though, are the more attractive, generally rather more expensive developments west of Maspalomas, towards the pretty marina resorts at **Puerto Rico** and **Puerto de Mogán**. This area also now has three golf courses. The part of the island preferred by those seeking more upscale villas with plenty of land, on the other hand, is over in the much greener **northwest** corner, with a landscape of rugged mountains, lush valleys and banana and fruit farms, and sheer cliffs more often than beaches along the coast. Prices are much lower than for luxury villas in the Balearics.

Fuerteventura

This is the second-largest of the Canaries, but one of the least populated. Much of it is semi-desert, but along the east coast there is mile on mile of fabulous, empty sandy beaches. There are still only a few resorts, widely spread out: **Corralejo** at the northern end, **El Castillo** and **Caleta de Fustes** near the island's capital, **Puerto del Rosario**, on the west coast and **Morro del Jable** at the southern end. Each has a few villa and hotel developments, and elsewhere there are converted houses available in Puerto del Rosario and the dusty villages of the interior. While it has now acquired a golf course, those who most appreciate Fuerteventura are windsurfers and other watersports enthusiasts, fishermen, naturists and others who love to have huge tranquil beaches to themselves.

Lanzarote

Hottest of the islands, Lanzarote has long been popular with anyone in Europe looking for temperatures close to 30°C in January. Almost completely treeless, the bizarre desert landscape, full of strange shapes and colours, makes most of the island a kind of geological park. This is a setting that some people love, but others find it too arid and unbending to stay in for any length of time. **Arrecife**, the island's capital, is a straightforward little town while, inland, the former capital of **Teguise** is a prettier village. Lanzarote is surprisingly undeveloped: a very large proportion of its visitors head for just two resorts, at **Puerto del Carmen**, south of Arrecife, and **Playa Blanca** near the southernmost point, around which there are the usual villas and timeshare developments. Elsewhere, although the pace of building has stepped up, developments tend to be smaller-scale and more isolated, with plenty of empty beach between them.

Tenerife

The largest of the Canaries, Tenerife also offers the greatest variety in villages, towns, landscapes and things to do. Its capital of **Santa Cruz de Tenerife** is by far the most attractive of the island towns, and puts on the biggest carnival in all Spain each January or February, a blast of the Canaries-meets-Rio. Tenerife is also the most popular of the Canary Islands among British people buying homes, as opposed to just holidaying. Its main drawback is that most of its beaches are of grey volcanic sand (except at Santa Cruz, where a whole new beach was created by importing golden sand from the Sahara).

The sheer range of landscapes on Tenerife is astonishing, from beaches through banana fields, cactus plains and woodlands, up to the snow-capped peak at the centre of the island, the giant volcano of **Mount Teide** which, at 3,718m (12,198ft), is the highest mountain in the whole of Spain. Like Gran Canaria, the island has two main sides. The biggest, greyish beach resorts are on the southwest coast, clustered around the very Brit-orientated mega-resort of

Playa de las Américas. A little further north along the west coast, around Adeje, there is an area of more spacious, higher-priced developments that is increasingly popular with buyers wishing to avoid the hyper-intensive constructions further down. The most-prized location for upscale villas on Tenerife, though, is in another part of the island altogether, on the north coast near the older resorts of **Puerto de la Cruz** and **Orotava**. With rich vegetation, charming villages and fine views (but few beaches), this area is particularly popular with retired people. Tenerife has also been fast developing as a golf destination, with six courses around the island.

The Smaller Islands: La Palma, La Gomera, El Hierro

The three small islands at the very west of the Canaries have no direct connections with the outside world, and can only be reached by ferry or local flights from Tenerife. The greenest of all the islands, they have very few beaches, and any tourist development here is still very small-scale; most locals still live from agriculture or fishing. Most of the few outsiders who know and love these islands do so precisely because of their air of quiet isolation.

La Palma, the largest, is best known for its towering mountains that shoot up out of the sea and which, because of the rare climatic conditions here, house one of the world's most important astronomical observatories. The island's capital, **Santa Cruz de la Palma**, is a 16th-century Spanish colonial town with great charm. Around it, especially to the south at **La Breña**, some modest *urbanizaciones* have appeared, and elsewhere there are scattered villas; prices are not as low as on the big islands, but are still moderate.

La Gomera, famous for the idiosyncratic customs of its people, odd ocean weather and its spectacular scenery of steeply terraced hillsides, tends to be visited only as part of a day trip from Tenerife. It is starting to become popular with adventurous foreign buyers looking for something more alternative, and a lot more out-of-the-way, than the main islands, but so far has only one small resort, at **Playa Santiago** on the south coast.

Tiny, rocky **El Hierro** feels still more remote, despite having fine beaches along its south coast.

Selecting a Property

04

Unless you really want to make your life into a Quixotic quest, no sensible person will scour the whole of Spain looking for a property. For one thing, it is just too big – more than three times the size of Britain. It is also, as outlined earlier, a very varied country. Those who don't narrow down the scope of their search early on tend to go round in ever-decreasing circles and fail to buy. Settling on a particular region and type of property to look at depends on a logical selection process that, if done sensibly, can help you make your choice or, perhaps as likely, eliminate others, without too much difficulty.

Once you have decided to look for a place in Spain, an important first step is to do your research and, above all, to get certain things clear in your own mind before embarking on a viewing trip. With the current boom in Spanish

Important: Fix a Budget

As soon as you decide to buy your home in Spain, fix a budget for the whole operation. Ask yourself what the maximum is that you are able and willing to spend to end up with a house that's ready to live in, then proceed accordingly. When matching up your total budget with any properties that you see, include in your figures not just the cost of purchase, but also estimates of any essential repairs or improvements, and the taxes and fees that will have to be paid.

If you are buying a new property, or one that does not need major repairs, these calculations are fairly straightforward. If you are buying a house in need of repair or wholesale restoration, on the other hand, working out a budget will be a lot more difficult. People always underestimate the cost of repairs, and no job ever finishes exactly on budget – or on time. This is as true in Spain as it is in the UK. Buyers create a rod for their own backs with unrealistic costings. Also, the extent of repairs needed in old properties can go far beyond what is obvious. If you are buying a property that needs major work, do not commit yourself until you have had a survey and builders' estimates for the work found to be necessary. If you are told that there is no time for this, and that you will lose the property if you can't sign today/this week/before Easter – walk away.

If you are buying your new property as a second or retirement home, then the amount of money you have available is likely to be fairly clear to you from the outset. If, though, you are moving to Spain to work, and still more if you are setting up your own business, it's a particularly good idea, if possible, to rent a place to live in at first while you settle in. Then, once you have had a little time to see how things are working out, you will have a clearer idea of how much you can afford to spend on somewhere more permanent, and can set your budget to suit.

Unless you are in the happy position that money is no object, stick to your budget and do not exceed it by any significant amount without serious consideration. It is too easy, after a good lunch and in the company of a silver-tongued estate agent, to throw financial plans to the wind. 'Only another £30,000' is a statement you may later come to regret.

property sales, in which houses can change hands fast, you are much less likely to be disappointed if you are well prepared and so can make decisions quickly. It is also strongly recommended that you find an independent lawyer, experienced in Spanish property law and with whom you feel comfortable, at the very beginning of the process, before seeing any properties, to establish a relationship and go over some preliminary questions (for more on the role of legal advice throughout, *see* **Making the Purchase**).

Among the essential things to consider at the outset are:

- How much you want/are able to spend.

- Accessibility – both how easy it is to get to from Britain, and how easy it is to get to the nearest towns and the services that they provide.

- What you want the property for – for a holiday getaway, to start a new life, with a view to retirement and eventual permanent residence, or as an investment (in which last case rental potential may be as important as or more important than your own preferences).

- How much room you need, for yourself and any visitors or tenants.

- How much work you are prepared to put into the property yourselves – or pay to have done.

- What you want to do at your Spanish home once you're there – whether it's get to the beach or golf course as quickly as possible, work, or enjoy the nightlife or countryside.

Getting to Spain

Accessibility is on a par with climate as a factor when choosing an area in which to house-hunt – issues include how you will travel there, how easily your family and friends can come to visit, and how you will get about while staying at the house (of course, if you're deliberately looking to get away from it all, then you may well approach this issue from the opposite direction, and go for 'the more remote the better'). Spain is very easy to get to, with a wide range of flights from many airports around Britain and Ireland. However, some regions (the north coast especially) have fewer flight connections than others, and ticket prices are not equally low to all parts of the country.

Once you have a home in a particular region, and can probably expect to make several trips there each year, the relative cost and time it takes from the nearest airport to your Spanish base loom larger than if you're only planning a one-off holiday. If you intend to let out the property, these considerations will be more important still (*see* **Letting your Property**, pp.291–306). Travel industry research has suggested that if visitors have a journey of more than an hour by road at either end of their flight, 25 per cent will not bother to travel. If it's more than

1 hour 30 minutes, 50 per cent will be put off. This may not concern you, but it is worth bearing in mind as far as family and friends are concerned, and is even more relevant if you hope to attract tenants for holiday lets. If your property is especially distinctive – a huge, superbly converted farmhouse in its own grounds, in a spectacular location, perhaps – then people will not grumble at making the extra effort to get there; if it's more conventional, on the other hand, the deterrent factor of distance will be much more significant.

Whether budget airline flights, regular special-offer tickets with main carriers or cheap flight-only charters are available to a convenient airport is something to take into account. Many people find that once they own a home in Spain, even if they use it mainly for longer holidays, they also tend to go back and forth fairly regularly for shorter breaks at other times, and your family and their friends may want to visit on their own, too. So it is worth considering how easy it is to get to your new house for a weekend trip, and whether a striking but remote location may become irritatingly inconvenient after a while. It's also very likely that you will want to drive to your chosen location at least a few times – especially when first moving in – so proximity to main road and ferry routes will also be something to consider.

By Air

The arrival of no-frills budget airlines has transformed the ease of travel to Spain's cities in particular, but bear in mind that they are not always as cheap as their advertising can suggest (note, too, that with all of them, to get significant extra savings you must book online rather than by phone). Ticket prices on all the budget airlines vary for each flight according to demand and ticket availability and, on the most popular routes (such as to Barcelona) at peak times (July or August, and any weekend), can be as high as or higher than those of the main traditional carriers. The concessions that the no-frills operators have forced on the main carriers – **British Airways** and **Iberia**, between the UK and Spain – can be as beneficial to travellers as the services they offer themselves: both of the 'big two' have been obliged to compete, and Iberia in particular often has limited-period special offers on tickets that are comparable with budget airline prices. The Spanish company has also cut costs by introducing 'Tu Menú', a paid-for catering service on-board which passengers can take or leave as they wish. BA's special price offers to Spain are less frequent than Iberia's, but are always worth checking against no-frills rates. In winter (Nov–Mar), especially, when the budget airlines cut back on many routes, main-carrier special offers will often be your best bet. The rule to follow is always check around all the airlines operating on any specific route, and to airports nearby.

In addition, while new-model, no-frills airlines like **easyJet** have monopolised press attention in the last few years, there are other airlines operating to Spain that are not to be ignored, since they can be very handy for getting to some parts of the country missed by the others, especially in the Balearics and the Canaries. **Monarch Airlines**, well known as a charter carrier, also has regular scheduled routes (known as Monarch Scheduled) to about a dozen destinations including Menorca and Tenerife and others that were previously only served by Spanish domestic flights or charters, such as Granada, Almería or Murcia. Unlike the newer no-frills airlines, it still issues conventional tickets and provides a full, meals-on-board service, but prices are very competitive and, if you book at short notice, tickets can be collected at the airport just before departure. There are still discounts for booking online, and prices are comparable with those of the ticketless no-frills airlines. Monarch also operates many charters, which though cannot be booked direct (*see* below).

The independent Spanish airline **Air Europa** also has regular services from Gatwick to Madrid and Palma de Mallorca and frequently offers good prices on connections to its many domestic routes within Spain (*see* pp.83–4), especially to the Balearics and the Canaries. And there are a still a great many charter flights between most UK airports and many airports in Spain, especially during the Easter–October main holiday season. In principle, of course, most seats on them are booked as part of package holidays, but flight-only tickets are also available on most routes, often at prices that undercut those of the scheduled no-frills carriers. The best way to book them is through ticket operators like Avro (*see* overleaf).

Another heavy hitter in recent times has been **Ryanair**, which flies to a dozen regional airports, some of them places that many have probably never heard of, such as Reus, close to Tarragona.

With all the airlines, on all routes, you will save the most money if you travel in off-peak seasons (low season: January–Easter, October–early December; mid-season, May–June and September) and, with budget carriers, if you travel at the beginning of the week (Monday–Wednesday), never at weekends. Budget carriers also give you lower prices if you book well in advance. If you're flexible, on the other hand, and can travel at short notice, you can also sometimes pick up surprisingly cheap last-minute offers even in summer.

Flight-only Charter Tickets

Good places to find leads to other booking services are the back pages of newspapers' travel supplements, especially in Sunday papers.

• **Avro, t** 0870 458 2841, **www.avro.com**. The largest UK operator offering flight-only tickets on charters to Spain has flights from many UK airports to a big range of Spanish destinations (Alicante, Almería, Girona, Ibiza, Málaga, Menorca, Murcia, Palma de Mallorca and all four main islands in the Canaries – Gran Canaria, Tenerife, Lanzarote and Fuerteventura). Prices are very competitive, and Avro flights are much used by owners of Spanish properties.

- **Dialaflight, t** 0870 333 4488, **www.dialaflight.com**. Reliable ticket-bookers that provide tickets on a very wide range of European flights and charters as well as UK-based airlines.
- **Flightline, t** 0800 541 541, **www.flightline.co.uk**. Offers a wide mix of ticket options.

Airports and Airlines Around Spain

Each of Spain's most popular holiday regions has its own main airport and a few smaller ones, although Madrid still offers the biggest choice of long-haul routes and domestic connections. The airlines listed in the tables following are only some of the main scheduled services to Spain: check all the airlines in the list below, and look on **www.cheapflights.com** for price comparisons, and remember that many, many more airports are also reachable by charter flight. Remember, too, that airline routes and networks change quite frequently, so always check for current routes and any announcements on future plans on websites and in the travel press.

Airlines

- **Aer Lingus, t** 0818 365000, UK **t** 0845 984 4444, **www.aerlingus.com**.
- **Air Berlin, t** 08707 388 880, **www.airberlin.com**.
- **Air Europa, t** 08702 401 501, Spain **t** 902 401 501, **www.air-europa.com**.
- **bmibaby, t** 0870 264 2229, **www.bmibaby.com**. The no-frills offshoot of British Midland.
- **British Airways (BA), t** 0870 850 9 850, **www.ba.com**.
- **British European (flybe)**, UK **t** 0871 700 0535 (10p/min), Ireland **t** 1890 925 532, **www.flybe.com**.
- **British Midland (BMI), t** 08706 070 555, **www.flybmi.com**.
- **easyJet, t** 0905 821 0905 (65p/min), **www.easyjet.com**.
- **EUJet, t** 0870 414 1414, **www.eujet.com**.
- **flyglobespan.com, t** 08705 561 522, **www.flyglobespan.com**.
- **GB Airways, t** 0870 850 9 850, **www.gbairways.com**. Operates as a franchise of British Airways.
- **Iberia, t** 0870 609 0500, **www.iberia.com**.
- **Jet2, t** 0871 226 1737, **www.jet2.com**.
- **Monarch, t** 08705 40 50 40, **www.flymonarch.com**.
- **Ryanair, t** 0906 270 5656, **www.ryanair.com**.
- **Thomsonfly, t** 0870 1900 737, **www.thomsonfly.com**.

Madrid

Madrid's Barajas airport is the hub of all air services within Spain, and of the Iberia route network in particular. From it you can get connections with Iberia, Air Europa or other airlines to every one of Spain's regional airports, the Balearics and the Canaries.

Madrid

From	Carrier
Birmingham	British Airways, Iberia
Bristol	easyJet
Dublin	Aer Lingus
Edinburgh	British Airways, Iberia
Glasgow	British Airways
Liverpool	easyJet
London Gatwick	Air Europa, British Airways, Iberia, easyJet
London Heathrow	British Airways, British Midland, bmibaby, Iberia
London Luton	easyJet
Manchester	British Airways, Monarch

Andalucía

Málaga, right in the middle of the Costa del Sol, is the main airport for tourist traffic in Andalucía, with main carrier and budget flights. Its services are supplemented by the small airport at Jerez de la Frontera, near Cádiz, which is more convenient than Málaga for the Costa de la Luz and some parts of the western Costa del Sol, and has been discovered by budget airlines. The regional capital of Seville also has its own airport. There are also two airports near this region that are not actually on Spanish territory, but still worth remembering: Faro in the Portuguese Algarve, which has budget flights and can be useful for getting to the Costa de la Luz and Cádiz, and Gibraltar, at the very western end of the Costa del Sol (although crossing from Gibraltar into Spain can involve delays).

Faro (Portugal)

From	Carrier
Belfast	easyJet
Birmingham	Monarch
Bristol	easyJet
Cardiff	bmibaby
Dublin	Ryanair
Nottingham East Midlands	bmibaby, easyJet
London Gatwick	Monarch, easyJet, GB Airways
London Stansted	easyJet
London Luton	Monarch, easyJet
Manchester	Monarch
Newcastle	easyJet

Gibraltar

From	Carrier
London Gatwick	GB Airways
London Heathrow	GB Airways
London Luton	Monarch
Manchester	Monarch

Granada

From	Carrier
Liverpool	Ryanair
London Stansted	Monarch, Ryanair

Jerez de la Frontera

From	Carrier
London Stansted	Air Berlin, Ryanair

Málaga

From	Carrier
Aberdeen	Monarch
Belfast	easyJet
Birmingham	bmibaby, Monarch
Blackpool	Monarch
Bristol	easyJet
Cardiff	bmibaby
Dublin	Aer Lingus, Ryanair
Durham Tees Valley	bmibaby
Nottingham East Midlands	bmibaby, easyJet
Liverpool	easyJet
London Gatwick	easyJet, GB Airways, Monarch
London Heathrow	GB Airways, Iberia
London Stansted	Air Berlin, easyJet
London Luton	easyJet
Manchester	bmibaby, Monarch
Newcastle	easyJet
Newquay	Monarch
Shannon	Ryanair

Seville

From	Carrier
London Gatwick	GB Airways
London Heathrow	Iberia
London Stansted	Air Berlin, Ryanair

Getting From the Airports

The following areas can usually be reached in very approximately an hour's journey by road from Andalucía's main airports (from the point of leaving the airport, not necessarily from landing). Another consideration is that, at smaller airports, baggage collection and customs formalities can be quicker than at very busy airports like Málaga.

- **From Gibraltar (so long as you're not held up at the border)**: the western Costa del Sol (San Roque, Sotogrande, roughly up to Estepona and San Pedro de Alcántara); the southern part of the Costa de la Luz (Tarifa, Zahara de los Atunes, Barbate); the southern Sierra de Cádiz (Vejer de la Frontera).

- **From Jerez**: the southern Costa de la Luz and the Sierra de Cádiz, and much of the Serranía de Ronda can be as easy to reach as from Málaga. However, because the roads to the west of Jerez turn inland to go around the Doñana wildlife reserve, the closest airports for the western Costa de la Luz are actually Seville and Faro.

- **From Málaga**: everywhere along the Costa del Sol to the east as far as Almuñécar at the start of the Costa Tropical, and, to the west (where travelling is speeded up by the A7/E15 motorway), through Marbella and Fuengirola roughly as far as Estepona. Inland, within an hour you can get to anywhere in the Sierra de Mijas, but getting into the Serranía de Ronda will usually take longer (about 1½ hours) due to the winding mountain roads. Most of the Costa Tropical in Granada and all of the Alpujarras in Granada are also about 1½ (at least) from any airport, although it can be quicker to get to this part of the coast in the opposite direction from Almería.

Almería and Murcia

The rapid growth of tourist and golf developments around the La Manga area of Murcia has been reflected in the opening of this small region's own – but also rapidly growing – airport, officially called Murcia even though it is actually closer to the coast and the main resort areas (at San Javier) than it is to Murcia city. Almería airport, just across the Andalucían border to the west is used by many well-priced charter flights but now receives scheduled flights from Manchester operated by Monarch.

Almería

From	Carrier
London Gatwick	easyJet
London Stansted	Air Berlin, easyJet
Manchester	Monarch

Murcia

From	Carrier
Birmingham	bmibaby, Monarch
Bristol	easyJet
Dublin	Ryanair
Nottingham East Midlands	bmibaby, Ryanair
Glasgow	Ryanair
Liverpool	easyJet
London Gatwick	easyJet
London Stansted	Air Berlin, Ryanair
London Luton	Ryanair
Manchester	bmibaby

Getting From the Airports

Murcia (San Javier) airport is very close to La Manga, the Costa Cálida and the southern Costa Blanca in Alicante province, around Torrevieja. All are within half an hour of the airport, and traffic is light, so Murcia is preferred to Alicante airport by many home-owners in the southern Costa Blanca. Mojácar is about 1hr 45mins drive to the south. From Almería airport the Cabo de la Gata, Mojácar and the Costa Tropical are all within about an hour's drive.

Valencia and Alicante

Alicante is the region's busiest tourist airport and the main entry point for the Costa Blanca, although Murcia airport can now give faster and easier access to the southern Costa Blanca (*see* above). The regional capital Valencia also has its own airport, with many internal and some international flights.

Alicante

From	Carrier
Belfast	easyJet
Birmingham	bmibaby
Bristol	easyJet
Cardiff	bmibaby
Dublin	Aer Lingus
Durham Tees Valley	bmibaby
Nottingham East Midlands	bmibaby, easyJet
London Gatwick	British Airways, easyJet, GB Airways, Iberia, Monarch
London Heathrow	bmibaby
London Stansted	Air Berlin, easyJet
London Luton	easyJet, Monarch
Liverpool	easyJet
Manchester	bmibaby, Monarch
Newcastle	easyJet

Valencia

From	Carrier
Bristol	easyJet
London Gatwick	easyJet
London Heathrow	GB Airways, Iberia
London Stansted	Air Berlin, easyJet, Ryanair

Getting From the Airports

Travelling is speeded up along most of the Costa Blanca by the A7/E15 motorway, which runs inland behind much of the coast. Within an hour of arrival at Alicante you can expect to reach the northern Costa Blanca through Benidorm up to Calpe/Calp and Punta Moraira (Jávea/Xàbia and Denia can take over an hour, according to traffic); to the south, you can get to the whole of the southern Costa Blanca through Torrevieja, and down to La Manga. From Valencia, you should be able to reach the northern Costa Blanca, and most of the Costa del Azahar as far north as Castellón, also within an hour. However, heavy traffic around Valencia itself can slow things up.

Catalonia

Barcelona airport is almost as busy a hub as Madrid for European and Spanish internal flights, although it receives fewer intercontinental, long-haul flights. There are plenty of flights from the UK, but tickets to Barcelona are in huge demand, above all for summer weekends, so it's usually more than worth looking around to find the best price. The only other airports in the region are at Girona, the main airport for Costa Brava charter flights but which now also has no-frills scheduled services from a great many UK and Ireland departure points, all operated by Ryanair, and Reus, near Tarragona and Salou just inland from the Costa Daurada, also a major charter and scheduled Ryanair destination.

Barcelona

From	Carrier
Birmingham	British Airways, Iberia
Bristol	easyJet
Dublin	Aer Lingus, Iberia
Nottingham East Midlands	bmibaby
Glasgow	British Airways
Liverpool	easyJet
London Gatwick	British Airways, easyJet, Iberia
London Heathrow	British Airways, Iberia
London Stansted	Air Berlin, easyJet
London Luton	easyJet
Manchester	Iberia, Monarch
Newcastle	easyJet

Girona

From	Carrier
Blackpool	Ryanair
Bournemouth	Ryanair
Dublin	Ryanair
Nottingham East Midlands	Ryanair
Glasgow (Prestwick)	Ryanair
Liverpool	Ryanair
London Stansted	Ryanair
London Luton	Ryanair
Shannon	Ryanair

Reus

From	Carrier
Dublin	Ryanair
Liverpool	Ryanair
London Stansted	Ryanair
London Luton	Ryanair

Getting From the Airports

Barcelona airport is just south of the city and is well connected to public trans-port and the motorways, though getting away can still take time due to heavy, and slow, traffic. Within an hour's travelling time of arrival, going north, you should (with luck) be able to get along the coast as far as Blanes at the beginning of the Costa Brava. Travelling south is easier, since the airport is on the south side of Barcelona and so you do not have to negotiate the city ring road: within an hour you can expect to get as far as El Vendrell and Comarruga on the Costa Daurada. Reus is within an hour or less of anywhere on the Costa Daurada.

The Balearics

All three main islands have their own airports, and for a few months every summer Palma joins Heathrow, Paris Charles-de-Gaulle and a select few others as one of the busiest airports in the entire world. Listed here, as before, are only the island's scheduled connections from the UK, but all three also receive a huge number of charter flights.

Ibiza

From	Carrier
Nottingham East Midlands	bmibaby
London Stansted	Air Berlin, easyJet

Menorca

From	Carrier
Birmingham	Monarch
London Luton	Monarch
Manchester	Monarch

Palma de Mallorca

From	Carrier
Birmingham	Monarch
Bournemouth	Air Berlin
Bristol	easyJet
Cardiff	bmibaby
Durham Tees Valley	bmibaby
Nottingham East Midlands	bmibaby
Liverpool	easyJet
London Gatwick	Air Europa, easyJet, GB Airways, Iberia
London Heathrow	bmibaby, British Midland
London Stansted	Air Berlin, easyJet
London Luton	easyJet
Manchester	bmibaby, Air Berlin, Monarch

Getting From the Airports

Everywhere on the three main islands is within an hour's journey by car or bus of their respective airports. The smallest of the Balearics, Formentera, can only be reached by ferry from Ibiza Town.

The North Atlantic Coast

This area has the fewest direct flight connections with the UK but the budget airlines are beginning to take an interest, as are visitors looking for something other than hot, overcrowded Mediterranean resorts. It is currently possible to fly to Bilbao, Santander, Asturias (Oviedo) and Santiago de Compostela, in Galicia, and there are domestic flights to these airports and La Coruña and Vigo from Madrid, Barcelona and other departure points.

Asturias (Oviedo)

From	Carrier
London Stansted	easyJet

Bilbao

From	Carrier
London Gatwick	Iberia
London Heathrow	British Airways
London Stansted	easyJet

Santander

From	Carrier
London Stansted	Ryanair

Santiago de Compostela

From	Carrier
London Gatwick	British Airways
London Heathrow	Iberia
London Stansted	Air Berlin, Ryanair

Getting From the Airports

Traffic is often heavy around Bilbao but, on a good day, within an hour of leaving the airport you can expect to reach San Sebastián, Pamplona or get just into Cantabria; reaching Santander, Asturias and into the Picos de Europa mountains will take more like 1½–2 hours, or more. From Santiago de Compostela you can reach all of central and southern Galicia in about an hour's travelling, but roads are often winding, and slow.

The Canaries

None of the no-frills airlines has yet extended its routes to the Canaries, so ticket-only charters (especially with Avro, *see* p.67), more than elsewhere, are your best bet for getting the best prices, though Monarch now does scheduled flights to Gran Canaria, Lanzarote and Tenerife. All four main islands (Gran Canaria, Tenerife, Lanzarote and Fuerteventura) have airports that handle international flights and direct connections to mainland Spain, and Tenerife has two (Tenerife-Norte and Tenerife-Sur). Scheduled connections with the UK are dwarfed in number by charter flights.

Gran Canaria (Las Palmas)

From	Carrier
London Gatwick	GB Airways
London Luton	Monarch

Lanzarote

From	Carrier
London Luton	Monarch

Tenerife

From	Carrier
London Gatwick	GB Airways, Iberia
London Luton	Monarch
Manchester	Monarch

Getting From the Airports

Everywhere on the main islands (Gran Canaria, Tenerife, Lanzarote, Fuerteventura) is within an hour's drive of each island's airports. Within the Canaries there is a comprehensive network of inter-island flights, operated by Binter Canarias (*see* p.83), which also includes the three small western islands, and a range of local ferries (*see* pp.92–3). Tenerife is the best hub for inter-island connections, by air or sea.

By Road and Sea

Understandably, because of the distances and time involved, driving to Spain is much less popular than flying as a way of getting there. However, many second-home owners like to have the convenience of their own car while they are there (for more on buying or renting a vehicle in Spain, *see* pp.84–9 and 232–4). Also, once you have a home in Spain it's very likely that, at some point, you'll want to take over there more things at one time than it's ever really practicable to take along as airline baggage.

It's possible to get from any of the Channel ports across France to the Spanish border in about 17 hours, and then through Spain to the Costa del Sol in another 18, if you so wish. However, for non-masochists and any car-load without at least two drivers to share the work of driving, it's much better to make more of a trip of it, allow three or four days and take in some of the glories of France along the way. Also, to get down through France and Spain at a really fast pace you have to travel on motorways (*autoroutes* in France, *autopistas* in Spain) which, in both countries, carry substantial tolls: to go by *autoroute* all the way from Calais to the Spanish border, for example, would cost at least £50 in tolls. If you take a bit more time, stay on minor roads and stop for a couple of nights in hotels, you may find that the extra costs are not much more than you would have spent on tolls had you driven straight through, and you can arrive feeling a lot fresher.

By the time it reaches the Spanish border, most traffic gets funnelled into just two roads, one at the Atlantic end of the Pyrenees via Bayonne and Irún and the other, the more popular route, on the Mediterranean side along the motorway that runs south from Narbonne and Perpignan to cross the frontier at La Jonquera (now called European route E15; in France it's better known as the A9, and in Spain as the A7). The routes in between, through the Pyrenees, are very scenic but take a good deal longer – except perhaps in mid-summer, when the La Jonquera route in particular can get hugely busy. The beautiful Puerto de Somport road across the border, reached via Bordeaux and Pau in France and which then takes you down to the Spanish Mediterranean coast via Jaca, Huesca and Zaragoza, is liked by many summer drivers with time to take things a little easier. In mid-winter, the mid-Pyrenees routes become very slow (and are even closed at times) due to snow.

To get down to the border from Britain, on the other hand, there are a great many possible routes through France, and which one you choose will depend on what kind of journey you want to have. The western cross-Channel routes (Newhaven–Dieppe, Portsmouth–Le Havre, Portsmouth–Caen, Portsmouth or Poole–Cherbourg, Portsmouth, Poole or Weymouth–St-Malo) are used by many home-owners who drive regularly to Spain because they allow you to avoid Paris and, with it, the most traffic-congested part of France. Anyone wishing to make a trip of it can have an enjoyable drive from any of these ports down through Normandy and the Loire valley, maybe joining the *autoroutes* at Tours, Poitiers or Limoges to speed things up. The advantage of the Dover–Calais routes (tunnel or ferries), however, is that, although the distance to Spain may be greater, they put you directly on to the main French motorway system (via the Paris ring roads), allowing a fast getaway. Another alternative is to cut out France completely, with one of the ferries that run to northern Spain (*see* p.81).

Crossing the Channel to France

Overall, after a long period in which the cost of crossing the Channel had been falling, fares have risen in the last five or six years, so the relative advantages of taking a car rather than flying need to be worked out carefully. Assuming that you are going to stay at your Spanish home for more than five days, with most companies you will need a standard rather than an economy return. In the summer season this will probably cost around £350 for a car and four people – on any of the routes, as prices vary by demand rather than by distance travelled. Fares on the **Eurotunnel** shuttle may appear higher than those of ferries in the first instance, but note that these are per vehicle, whatever the number of passengers, whereas on ferries you pay a fare per car plus something extra per person. If there are several of you in a people-carrier, say, the tunnel will tend to win out on price. Fares vary at all times, though, so even in summer it's worth checking around for cheaper deals; as with flights, there are agencies and

The Mysteries of Cross-Channel Fares

Technology is supposed to make life easier, but it's not clear how this works in relation to fares across the Channel. Fares on all the ferry routes and the Channel Tunnel vary enormously by season, which day of the week and what time of day you travel, so finding the best price available at any time demands a bit of research. All the companies now suggest that you book online, and most no longer list fares in any published brochure. However, their fare structures are so complicated that the websites generally fail to present them clearly, and when you tap in a given date-time combination, as you are required to do, there's no way of telling whether you could travel for less just a day or so earlier or later. Hence, this is one area where it's much more effective – and saves time – just to phone up and persist long enough to get through to a human, to whom you can ask the magic question: 'What is the cheapest fare available that week, and when would I have to travel to get it?' In general, night and early morning crossings are the cheapest, midday ones the most expensive. One website that does list current fares in a fairly straightforward way is Eurotunnel's (**www.eurotunnel.com**), for which it deserves gratitude.

websites offering discount Channel crossings, of which two of the larger ones are **www.channel-travel.com** and **www.cross-channel-ferry-tickets.co.uk**. Also check out **www.ferrybooker.com**.

Each company also offers a complicated and ever-changing range of special offers, discounts for booking well in advance and loyalty schemes for frequent travellers. These range from fairly simple points systems, like supermarket reward cards, where with each trip you earn points towards discounts on future journeys, to much more generous discount packages aimed especially at owners of homes abroad. Some companies, such as Condor Ferries, offer their own discount schemes for regular travellers; P&O has a home-owners' discount and Hoverspeed a frequent users' club.

Whenever you take your car to France or Spain you do, of course, need comprehensive insurance for you and your vehicle, and preferably breakdown cover, for the whole trip. Under current European law, UK motor insurance policies now include basic third-party insurance cover valid in all EU countries, and extensions to this basic level, including fully comprehensive insurance and breakdown assistance, are available from most companies for only a limited extra premium. The breakdown and travel insurance packages offered by motoring organisations like the AA and RAC tend to be more expensive, but generally include a wider range of extras.

In planning your journey down to Spain, websites that are well worth consulting (both available in English) are **www.autoroutes.fr**, which has maps of the French autoroute system, and, most important, the current toll rates, and **www.bison-fute.equipement.gouv.fr**, the website of the French National Traffic Centre, which has all sorts of useful information on roadworks, potential blockages, likely extra-traffic days – such as local holidays – and so on, throughout France. The similar official website for Spain is not quite as wide-ranging, but still has current Spanish motorway toll rates, and can be found at **www.dgt.es**, but only in Spanish.

Eurotunnel and Ferry Operators

- **Brittany Ferries, t** 08703 665 333, Rep. of Ireland **t** (021) 427 7801, **www.brittanyferries.com**.
- **Condor Ferries, t** 0870 243 5140, **www.condorferries.co.uk**.
- **Eurotunnel, t** 08705 35 35 35, **www.eurotunnel.com**.
- **Hoverspeed, t** 0870 240 8070, **www.hoverspeed.com**.
- **Irish Ferries**, UK **t** 08705 17 17 17, Rep. of Ire. **t** 0818 300 400, N. Ire. **t** 00 353 818 300 400, **www.irishferries.com**. £10 surcharge for phone bookings.
- **Norfolkline, t** 08708 70 10 20, **www.norfolkline.com**.
- **P&O Ferries, t** 08705 20 20 20, **www.poferries.com**.
- **Sea France, t** 08705 711 711, **www.seafrance.com**.
- **Speedferries, t** 08702 200 570, **www.speedferries.com**. £10 surcharge if you book over the phone.
- [a] **Transmanche, t** 0800 917 1201, **www.transmancheferries.com**.

Car Ferry and Tunnel Services to France

Going from east to west.

Dover and Folkestone–Calais

- **Eurotunnel**: There are three departures an hour through the tunnel at most times; journey time is around 35 minutes, and you need to check in at least 25 minutes before departure; note, though, that with the tunnel – unlike, other than in exceptional circumstances, on the ferries – it is quite common at busy times to find yourself 'booted' on to a later departure than the one for which you booked.
- **Hoverspeed**: Hoverspeed's 'Super Seacat' giant catamarans are faster than the standard ferries, often making the crossing in under an hour, but are more likely to be affected by bad weather. Usually 13 crossings daily.
- **P&O Ferries**: Largest ferry operator on the Dover–Calais route, with 36 sailings a day in each direction in mid-summer and around 20 a day even in January. Journey time around 1hr 15mins.
- **Sea France**: Fewer sailings than P&O, but the French-owned company has recently greatly improved its fleet, and offers very competitive prices.

Dover–Boulogne

- **Speedferries**: One of the cheapest ferries across the channel.

Dover–Dunkerque

- **Norfolkline**.

Newhaven–Dieppe

- **Hoverspeed**: Usually April–October only: three crossings daily by 'Super Seacat' (around 2½–3 hours, and so quite expensive) and two or three by conventional ferries (3½ hours).
- **Transmanche Ferries**: French company offering two sailings daily all year round; a straightforward service, so prices can be a bargain.

Portsmouth–Caen

- **Brittany Ferries**.

Portsmouth–Cherbourg

- **Condor Ferries**: One crossing daily, July–September only. Journey time about 5 hours.
- **Brittany Ferries**.

Portsmouth–St Malo

- **Brittany Ferries**: Usually one sailing daily, with restricted service October–March. Journey time about 8½ hours.

Poole–Cherbourg

- **Brittany Ferries**: Three sailings a day in summer, and a much more limited service October–March. Journey time about 4½hours.

Poole and Weymouth–St Malo

- **Condor Ferries**: Channel Islands-based company with fast Seacats offering two sailings daily on each route. Good prices, but they all stop in Guernsey on the way, which complicates the journey. Journey time about 6 hours.

Plymouth–Roscoff

- **Brittany Ferries**: Two to three sailings daily in high season, and a more restricted service at other times. Journey time about 6 hours. Note that, for anyone going to Spain, travelling via Roscoff involves quite a long drive to get out of Brittany before heading south.

Cork–Roscoff

- **Brittany Ferries**: One sailing a week in each direction; journey time about 15 hours.

Rosslare–Cherbourg/Roscoff

- **Irish Ferries**: One to two sailings a week on each route for most of the year, but extra services in July–September; journey time about 19 hours to

Cherbourg, 17 hours to Roscoff. Again, Cherbourg is a much more convenient arrival point if you are driving south to Spain.

Ferry Services Direct to Spain

There are two direct ferry services between Britain and northern Spain, which give you a more relaxing first stage to your journey in place of the drive through France. Of course, if your destination in Spain is on the southern Mediterranean coast you will still have from about 10–18 hours of driving ahead of you when you arrive.

• **P&O Ferries** (*see* p.79): Two sailings each week between Portsmouth and Bilbao. Journey time is about 35 hours out and 29 hours back.

• **Brittany Ferries** (*see* p.79): Two sailings weekly, from Plymouth to Santander (out Monday, Wednesday; return Tuesday, Thursday). Journey time is a little less, at around 24 hours.

Since this is a proper ocean crossing, both companies' ships are larger and more comfortable than Channel ferries, with plenty of amenities and entertainments on board, so that the trips have something of the leisurely feel of a cruise rather than just a car ferry service (although some travellers may notice rough weather more, too). Fares – although they also vary a lot according to when exactly you want to go, like those for the cross-Channel routes – are accordingly quite high, for example around £550–750 per standard (over five-day) return for a car and four people in summer. Even so, these routes are very popular with owners of property in Spain, and need to be booked well in advance for the summer season.

By Rail

It is, of course, still possible to get to most parts of Spain travelling all the way from Britain by train but, perhaps sadly, nowadays this will nearly always work out more expensive than getting there by plane. A return from London to Alicante, for example, by Eurostar and then high-comfort, high-speed sleeper trains from Paris and in Spain will probably cost around £300 in summer, although it is possible to get cheaper fares by travelling on standard trains, and there are sometimes good special-offer fares available. It also naturally takes much longer (around 24 hours or more) but, as compensation, you see much more on the way. The French TGV ultra-comfortable, high-speed trains provide very fast connections between Paris and the Spanish border, and combine with similarly superior-grade services, known as Talgos or Trenhoteles (sleepers) run by Spanish railways; note, though, that all these luxury services have higher fares than standard trains.

As a first stage you need to get to Paris, most easily done on **Eurostar** (**t** 08705 186 186, **www.eurostar.com**). For western Spain or the Costa del Sol, take a train from the Gare d'Austerlitz down towards the Basque border at Irún, and continue on through Spain via a change in Madrid. If you're going to anywhere on the Mediterranean coast down to the Costa Blanca, catch a train from the Gare de Lyon in Paris towards the eastern end of the border and Barcelona.

Constructed in the 19th century – and cursed by transport planners ever since – nearly all of Spain's railways were built to a broader gauge than that of the rest of the European rail network. Hence, with a few exceptions such as the luxury services, which have special wheels to adapt to the change in the track, trains cannot cross the border, and you have to transfer on to a Spanish one at the border crossing (Hendaye–Irún on the west side, Cerbère–Port Bou at the Mediterranean end). This does not usually involve much delay. Eventually, Spain's own high-speed network, still in its infancy, will reach the French border, but this is not imminent.

Through **Rail Europe**, **t** 08708 371 371, **www.raileurope.co.uk**, the reservation and information service run by French railways in Britain, you can book train tickets on any of the main European rail networks. French railways' own website (**www.sncf.com**) and the Spanish railways' (RENFE) site (**www.renfe.es**) are both available in English.

Getting Around Spain

As well as proximity to transport links from abroad, you also need to think about how easily you can get to your home in Spain from the nearest airport or motorway, and how you will get around once you are there. You will want to be able to get to attractions like beaches or the nearest large town without hours of travelling, and you'll probably want quick and easy access to local shops and restaurants. You'll need to consider access to necessary amenities like doctors and hospitals, and, if you have children, how they will get to school. Your friends, family, children and their friends will almost certainly want to visit, too, so look at how they would get to your house by public transport from other airports or other parts of Spain, and how easily you can get to pick them up.

You may expect to use a car for most journeys, but there will often be times when you or your guests want to get around by other means – or your car may be off the road – so you'll need to know how close the nearest public transport is. Spain has a good and wide-ranging rail system and, in areas that have heavy summer traffic, local rail lines provide a useful, stress-free means of getting in from the coast to regional centres like Málaga, Alicante and Barcelona. More immediately useful to you if you're living in a village behind the coast or out in the country will be local buses, which run between most villages and the nearest towns.

A great many owners of second homes in Spain, and who travel there by air, either hire a car for every trip or own their own Spanish car, which they leave at their house or (better) in the airport car park, waiting for their next visit (for more on owning a car in Spain, *see* **Settling In**, 'Buying, Selling or Importing Cars', pp.232–4). It's worth doing a careful price comparison here: surprisingly often the cost of insuring, taxing and maintaining your local car, plus airport parking and depreciation, can amount to nearly as much as – or more than – renting a new car each time. Renting also means that you can choose the type and size of car you need for each trip. Check the availability of car hire locally – cheap, local companies as much as, or maybe ahead of, the big names. A related question is how your visitors and any teenage-and-upwards children will travel around on their own when they're in the area, and whether they will want or be able to hire a car for themselves. Some car hire companies have a minimum age limit of 25. Hence, again, your children and guests may need to use buses, unless you're willing to provide a permanent taxi service.

By Air

Spain has an extensive domestic airline network. The busiest routes are between Madrid and Barcelona, and those connecting the two groups of islands and the mainland. For years, domestic routes were a monopoly of Iberia and its subsidiaries, and fares were kept artificially high, but more recently there has been much wider competition from independent airlines, especially Air Europa. It's possible to find very good fare offers so it's always worth checking. Current offers can be found on the airlines' websites. In addition, anyone resident in the Balearics or the Canaries can get significant discounts on Iberia and Air Europa flights between the islands and the mainland; you only need to show your residency card, bearing proof of your address, when booking your flight.

The main airlines operating domestic routes are:

• **Air Europa**, Spain **t** 902 401 501, **www.air-europa.com**. Flights between Madrid and Barcelona and all Spain's main cities, the three main Balearic islands and the Canaries. It usually has the best fare offers, and Air Europa tickets can be bought at any branch of Halcón Viajes, Spain's largest chain travel agency.

• **Binter Canarias**, Gran Canaria **t** 928 579 601, Tenerife **t** 922 635 644, **www.bintercanarias.es**. Internal flights in the Canaries, with frequent services between all the islands, centred on Gran Canaria and Tenerife.

• **Iberia**, Spain **t** 902 400 500, **www.iberia.com**. The most comprehensive flight network within Spain, with routes to every part of the country including the islands, mostly centred on Madrid (many journeys involve changing there) but also focused on regional hubs like Barcelona, Valencia and Seville. Many flights to and from the Balearics are by **Air Nostrum**, Spain **t** 902 400 500, **www.airnostrum.es**, a wholly owned subsidiary.

• **Spanair,** Spain **t** 902 131 415, **www.spanair.com**. A slightly smaller operation than Air Europa that also has flights to most parts of Spain and the islands, centred on Madrid. Again, very competitive fare offers.

By Car

Huge sums have been spent on road-building and improvements in Spain since the 1980s, and nearly all major roads have been widened, resurfaced, diverted into bypasses around main towns and, especially in the case of hill roads, given good crash barriers and other safety features. Most minor roads have also seen some improvements, and such things as road markings and signing have been upgraded. The backbone of the highway system is the *Carreteras Nacionales*, or **main trunk roads**, roughly corresponding to British A-roads and until 2003 identified by an N and a Roman numeral. Since then they have been redenominated and now begin with an A followed by an Arabic number. Thus the six main roads that radiate outwards from Madrid to different far-flung parts of the country which appear on pre-2003 maps as NI (Madrid to Burgos), NII (Madrid to Barcelona) through to NVI (Madrid to A Coruña) are now identified as A1 through to A6. The A stands for *'autovía'*, which means a dual carriageway with a central reservation. They are of near-motorway standard, the equivalent of the A(M) roads in the UK, and have the same speed limit, 120kph, as motorways, themselves called *'autopistas'*. *Autopistas* are also usually indicated by an A. You may, in fact, go from being on a stretch of *autovía* to one of *autopista*, and then back again, without even being aware of the fact. The difference is that on *autovías* you may encounter a roundabout, impossible on an *autopista*, and that signposting on *autovías* is in green whereas on *autopistas* it is blue, as in the rest of Europe.

Circumventing all larger cities and provincial capitals are the **ring roads**, *'carreteras de circunvalación'*, whose denominations can also be a little confusing. They are usually of *autovía* standard but take their lettering from their province – as did car number plates until quite recently. Thus Madrid's manic ring roads are the M-30, M-40 and the still unfinished M-50.

Elsewhere, many N roads retain their original numbering, either because the administration has not yet got around to relabelling them or they have not yet been upgraded. This is the case of the N340, well known to many holiday visitors, which follows the Mediterranean coast all the way from the French border round to Cádiz. The quality of N roads can vary considerably but they have come a long way from being simple two-lane blacktops.

Spain's central roads and traffic agency, the **Dirección General de Tráfico**, provides a range of (sometimes not entirely up to date) information on routes and road regulations, but in Spanish only, on its website (**www.dgt.es**).

Spain's **motorways**, or *autopistas*, are, as pointed out already, also indicated with an A and a number. They form an extensive but not entirely connected network. They invariably follow more or less the same route as an older trunk road, stretches of motorway often taking over in the busiest sections of the road. *Autopistas* keep the same number for the whole route, though, so that, for example, all the motorway sections that parallel the N340 – including Spain's longest single motorway covering all the 700km (435 miles) from the French border down to Alicante and an entirely separate section around Marbella – are equally considered to make up the A7. Major routes now have European route numbers, too, so the A7/N340 can also be signed as the E15, which can sometimes be a little confusing. Some *autopistas* are state run and toll-free; others are operated by private companies and charge tolls, known as *'peaje'*. These are indicated by the initials 'AP' (*Autopista de Peaje*). To make life more confusing still, around Madrid there are radial toll motorways, indicated with an 'R'. Different *autopistas*, and separate sections of the same one, are administered by various private companies, and the tolls can be quite high (around €45 from the French border to Alicante). Current rates can be found on the DGT website; alternatively go to that of the toll companies' association (**www.aseta.es**), which has information in English and links to the operating companies' websites. The AA's website also has up to date toll information; see **www.theaa.com/allaboutcars/overseas/ european_tolls_results.jsp**.

Since *autopistas* always follow alongside existing trunk routes, those who do not want to pay tolls can easily take a slightly slower, but parallel, route. As a consequence, some N-roads often get very congested with toll 'refuseniks'. This is why so many *autovías* have been upgraded to near-motorway status. The extent of the major road network varies by region, being most complete around Madrid, in Valencia and in Catalonia (one additional reason for the Catalan coast's ongoing popularity with more affluent British house buyers, since it's much the easiest part of Mediterranean Spain to drive to, using the A7/E15). Driving tends to be slowest along the north coast, where many roads are still narrow and winding. Even quite remote provincial towns have been reached by *autovías* in the last few years, though, and it's now quite easy to drive reasonably swiftly between all Spain's main towns.

Off the main highways, and sometimes providing a more scenic alternative, there are **provincial and regional roads**, roughly equivalent to British B-roads. They can be identified by a confusing mixture of prefixes, according to which provincial or regional administration is in charge of them. Spanish local administrations, as well as the state, have spent a great deal of energy on road improvements lately, and most country roads are now in quite good condition, although you can still find some that have an interesting assortment of ruts and potholes. Smaller **rural roads**, or *carreteras comarcales*, can still be bumpy dirt tracks in a few increasingly scarce cases, but if their surface is in a good state, driving along them can be a pleasure – a nearly traffic-free cruise through stunning scenery. **Mountain roads** usually have some hair-raising bends with, on the most minor roads, little or no fencing on the outside edge. In villages and

Stiffer Penalties...

During 2003 there were 3,446 fatal accidents on Spanish roads with a total of 4,032 deaths – that is, one every approximately two hours. A further 2,061 people were seriously injured. A series of new measures, aimed at reducing these appalling statistics, was introduced on 1 January 2004. Generally speaking, sanctions for most infringements have been stiffened with more severe penalties for repeat offenders. In brief, the new measures are as follows:

- **On-the-spot withdrawal of driving licences**. Drivers who, in the view of traffic police officers, are not in a condition to drive may have their licence taken away temporarily.

- **New drivers**. All 'new drivers' – those who have obtained their licence within the last 24 months – who are found guilty of three 'grave infractions' (such as speeding, overtaking where not permitted, jumping red traffic lights, etc.) or two 'very grave infractions' (such as refusing to do a breathalyser test or driving at over 50 per cent of the speed limit) will have their licence withdrawn for a year.

- **Driving without a licence**. Anybody caught driving without a valid licence will be barred from obtaining one for 12 months and have their vehicle impounded for a month or two months if they repeat the offence.

- **Withdrawal of motorcycle riders' licences**. Motorcyclists who commit two 'grave' or one 'very grave' infractions during a period of two years will lose their licence though may apply for a licence to drive a car.

- **Loss of licence**. Any driver found guilty of three 'very grave' infractions will lose their licence indefinitely and may only obtain a new one on following, and passing, a 'recycling' course. If they pass the course, the ban is reduced to 12 months.

- **Drinking and driving** is now taken seriously; drivers who show an alcohol level of over 0.05 per cent face heavy fines, loss of licence or even prison for recurring offenders.

... and a New Traffic Code

More or less at the same time, the government introduced a new traffic code whose main points are as follows:

- **Drivers**. The use of mobile telephones or any other means of communication, except for 'hands-free' models, while driving is no longer permitted.

on country roads, as you might expect, you need to watch out for children, old people, dogs, flocks of sheep, very slow-moving tractors and trucks, and helmetless kids on mopeds, none of whom may expect you to be there.

Driving in towns is generally best avoided. In the biggest cities, like Madrid and Barcelona, traffic is pretty nightmarish at most times of the day, so that

- **Any devices which may distract the driver are prohibited**. This includes computer screens with Internet access, televisions, video or DVD players. GPS and other navigational aids are permitted.

- Previous regulations ordered **the engine and the lights to be turned off** when filling up at the petrol station. Now, **radios and mobile telephones must be turned off** also.

- **Seatbelts are obligatory**, both in front and rear seats.

- **Children aged between 3 and 12 or less than 150cm in height** must travel with a seatbelt adjusted to their size and weight and may not sit in the front.

- **Children under 3 years of age** must travel in a child seat.

- When stopping on the hard shoulder **drivers must wear a reflecting waistcoat or jacket** on alighting from the car.

- **Cyclists, motorcyclists and moped and scooter riders** are now subject to the same alcohol limits as other drivers – 0.05mg. Cyclists must also now wear officially approved head protection and reflecting jackets when travelling on main roads outside built-up areas

- **Motorists must also carry at all times:**
  - **Two warning triangles** – officially approved by the Ministerio del Interior, bearing a round symbol E9 and the code 27R03.
  - **A spare tyre** and the tools necessary to fit it.
  - **A spare set of bulbs** and the tools necessary to replace any broken ones.
  - **A spare pair of glasses** if you use spectacles to drive.
  - **Insurance documentation**.

As of 1 October 2004, recent reforms made to the Penal Code regarding driving under the influence of alcohol also came into effect. These include prison sentences of between three months and a year and/or community service for a period of between 31 and 90 days for driving 'under the influence of toxic drugs, narcotics, psychotropic substances or alcoholic beverages'. In addition, those caught can expect to lose their licence for a period of more than a year and up to four years. Speeding while under the influence may also mean longer prison sentences and a ban of up to six years, according to the gravity of the offence.

driving is often one of the slowest ways of getting around, as well as raising stress levels. In smaller towns traffic density is not so bad, but the historic centres of most Spanish towns are a higgledy-piggledy confusion of narrow streets and alleys, not suited to cars, and often with labyrinthine if not incomprehensible one-way systems. When visiting a city, large or small, you are best advised to park somewhere on the outskirts, possibly near a bus or metro stop, and proceed by public transport or on foot. Many larger cities have park-and-ride schemes, with large car parks by accessible metro stations or bus termini.

Driving Safely

Outside of towns and busier spots along the *costas*, though, traffic is often very light, much more so than in Britain. This, however, gives encouragement to some noticeable bad habits of Spanish drivers, in the first place a marked speeding tendency. Spain has a poor reputation for road safety, and the accident rate is high. The latest response of the authorities, introduced at the beginning of 2004, has been a much stricter, if still perhaps not drastic, set of traffic laws (*see* box, previous pages) together, perhaps more importantly, with a declaration of intent to be far more rigorous in enforcing them. Police checks on drivers are more frequent, and the legal limit for a driver's blood-alcohol level, 0.05, is now lower than that in Britain.

The frequently abused official **speed limits** are 120kph (75mph) on *autopistas* and *autovías*, 100 or 90kph (62 or 56mph) on most N and country roads, and 50kph (30mph), or sometimes less, in towns. Note that these limits are reduced for vehicles towing caravans or trailers.

To reduce the risk of accidents and unfortunate experiences overall, the following are some basic points to keep in mind while driving in Spain:

- **Local drivers are often impatient, and road discipline is erratic, so drive extra cautiously, especially on narrow roads. Further spice is added in tourist areas by the large numbers of foreign drivers about, who may not be clear about where they are going or the rules of the local road (and so add to locals' impatience). Stick tightly to the correct side of the road, and keep a look out for cars cutting corners on bends or trying to overtake recklessly on tight bends and the crests of hills, either from behind you or coming towards you.**

- **At traffic lights, most drivers will expect to follow through until the light has changed to red. Do not brake quickly as it changes to amber, as the driver behind will not be anticipating this and may run into the back of you.**

- **When an oncoming driver in Spain flashes their lights at you, this means that they are *not* giving way or letting you in – the opposite of British practice. If a driver flashes lights at you on an open road this is usually a helpful tip that there is a police check ahead.**

- **When you park your car, including at motorway service areas, do not leave anything on view inside it. Thefts from cars are very common (*see also* 'Car Crime', p.268).**

Petrol in Spain is currently a little cheaper than in Britain but, like everywhere, prices have taken a hike in recent times. The same EU-recognised fuel grades are on sale: unleaded is *sin plomo* (or *sense plom* in Catalan), regular, lead-replacement petrol is *super*, and diesel is *gas-oil*.

For more on owning a car in Spain, driving licences and other information, *see* **Settling In**, pp.242–4.

Car Rental

The Spanish for car hire is *alquiler de coches* (or *autoalquiler, alquiler de autos* or *alquiler de vehículos*) and is listed under this or *Automóviles de Alquiler* in the local *Yellow Pages*. In Catalan-speaking regions you will also see *Autolloguer* or *Lloguer de Autos*, which mean the same thing. There are franchises of the major car-hire chains (Hertz, Avis, Europcar, National-Atesa and others) throughout the country, especially in tourist areas. In addition, it's well worth seeking out small, locally based agencies, of which there are usually a few in each area, as these are likely to be both cheaper overall and more ready to offer flexible weekly or longer-term rates, and yet are still generally reliable. Every system has its own pricing structure and range of special offers and long-term deals, but rates overall are highly competitive so, with a bit of checking around, it's usually possible to get a small car, for example, for around €200 a week or less. Lower-rate deals are also available pretty much everywhere in winter, off-season months. If you expect to be hiring a car every time you visit your Spanish home it's well worth finding a hire agency you like and suggesting to them that they give you a price that takes this into account.

To hire a car in Spain you need to be at least 21 years old and to have had a driving licence for at least a year. Some companies have a minimum age of 25, or impose this or another age limit for higher grades of car, people-carriers or four-wheel-drives, and some also have an upper age limit of 65, 70 or 75. When hiring, check that the price given to you includes insurance, tax (IVA, or VAT, at 16 per cent) and unlimited mileage (*kilometraje ilimitado*). Most rental agencies now give unlimited mileage as standard, and any deals that do not will probably waste your money. All rental contracts must by law include basic third-party insurance (*seguro obligatorio*), but check whether your agency will add in comprehensive cover, including collision damage waiver (CDW or *cobertura de daños*), theft cover (*cobertura contra robos*) and personal accident insurance (*daños personales*). If this is not included, it's worth paying the extra required to have it, for peace of mind. To hire a car you will also, effectively, need a credit card. In theory it's possible to leave a large cash deposit instead, but this is so inconvenient that it hardly ever happens.

By Bus

Buses make up Spain's most unsung but most comprehensive transport system. You can get to just about any part of the country by long-distance coach (*autocar*), and there's an enormous web of local and regional bus services (*autobuses*). Buses are modern and comfortable; they're also cheaper than trains, if slower.

Services are operated by a great many different private companies, most of them based in a particular region, although one large company that has long-distance routes throughout the country is **Alsa-Enatcar (www.alsa.es)**. Provincial capitals and sometimes other, medium-sized towns act as hubs for local bus routes to every part of their surrounding areas, and virtually every village has a bus at least once a day, and often more frequently, with extra services on the local town's market days. Each island also has its own bus service.

Most mainland towns have a central bus station (*estación de autobuses*) that is used by most companies in the area, but in some cities there may be more than one, and some companies operate from their own, separate depots. Local tourist offices will be able to give details of departure points and how bus routes work in any particular area. In small towns and villages, buses nearly always have a stop on the main *plaza*, or as near to it as possible, and timetables will usually be posted up there too. To avoid the strain of having to drive everywhere, it's very worthwhile getting to know your local bus service.

By Rail

Virtually all of Spain's trains are operated by the **RENFE**, the state-owned national railway corporation. As with other areas of transport infrastructure in Spain, a huge amount of money and attention has been invested in RENFE since the 1970s, and overall, while it still has its quirks, the network has improved almost beyond recognition. Virtually all the rolling stock has been replaced, and trains are modern and comfortable. At the same time, they have remained very amenably priced when compared to fares in the UK: a second-class adult ticket on a fast express from Barcelona to Alicante (515km/320 miles), for example, costs from €45.50, and slower, stopping trains are cheaper still. Punctuality can still be a little erratic sometimes on regional and local services (though still far better than that of equivalent trains in the UK), but the network's safety record is one of the best in Europe. Full information on all RENFE services is available on the website (**www.renfe.es**, in Spanish and English) and through a centralised phone line that has English-speaking operators (in Spain t 902 24 02 02; t 00 34 93 490 11 22 if calling from abroad). **Tickets** for all long-distance and many regional trains can also be booked online or by phone.

There are several different grades of trains, which can be confusing. Fares vary according to the speed and comfort of the train. The jewel in the RENFE crown is the super-fast, ultra-comfortable *AVE* high-speed train, a sleek piece of advanced engineering built for the 1992 Expo in Seville, and which runs between Madrid and the Andalucían capital in just 2½ hours, with reimbursement of your ticket price in full for any delay. There is also now an AVE line from

Profiles
of the Regions

Andalucía and its *Costas*: Costa de la Luz, Costa del Sol and Costa Tropical

<< *see page 39*

With its coastlines of sun and light, this is the Spain of flamenco and bullfighting, of sherry and seafood, and of whitewashed villages cloaked in bougainvillaea. With 320 days of sunshine each year on the Costa del Sol, it's also a magnet to millions, from billionaires and movie stars to teens on the loose, young families and retirees. Within the space of a few miles the *costas* can be brash or classy, peaceful or package-holiday-land. You'll find everything from high-density developments and country-club resorts to fishing villages. Inland, you could not be further away from the Torremolinos lifestyle, with mountain hamlets and farmhouses frozen in time – except in terms of price, of course.

1 Costa de la Luz beach
2 Costa de la Luz beach
3 Cádiz
4 Jerez de la Frontera

1 Bendalid, Ronda
2 Gaucin
3 Casares
4 Almond trees, Sierra Nevada
5 Granada
6 Villa, Frigiliana

4

5

6

1 Frigiliana
2 Fuengirola
3 Frigiliana
4 Near Nerja
5 Costa Tropical

Almería and Murcia

<< *see page 47*

Home to Europe's only desert, these regions are hot, hot, hot, and yet the arid soil, when watered, is verdant not only as Spain's winter vegetable garden but also as home to world-class golf and sporting developments such as Club La Manga, where Europe's top football teams train in winter. The southern coast on which it sits is quiet but developing fast, with marinas and villas still attracting a mostly Spanish clientele. Property prices are quite reasonable considering the fine beaches, excellent leisure facilities and good weather, so sun worshippers and sports fans might choose to seek their dream home here.

1 Villa, Mojácar
2 Almería

Valencia and Alicante: the Costa Blanca

<< see page 48

The Costa Blanca has lured Britons here since the 1960s – golf, a year-round mild climate and an established British community make it especially popular with older buyers. Again a *costa* of contrasts, its quiet and ruggedly pretty northern part and its sandy-beached, upmarket southern stretch are divided by both infamous Benidorm and often-overlooked Alicante with its vibrantly Spanish old centre. Valencia's 'orange blossom coast' is not just about its vast groves of citrus – along here are the freshwater wetlands that produce the best paella rice. At its northern end, smart Spanish families snap up summer houses around medieval Peñíscola while, up in the hills, there's a wealth of farm and village houses waiting to be restored.

1 Benidorm, Old Town
2 Vilajoyosa
3 Benidorm beach

1 Altea
2 Calpe
3 Altea
4 Costa Blanca

Catalonia: the Costa Daurada and Costa Brava
≪ see page 51

Catalonia has its own regional government, language, culture and history. A rugged, green countryside harbours centuries-old stone villages and traditional, chalet-style farmhouses. Most property-buyers stick close to the coast but the climate can be variable in winter. Nonetheless, both the southerly Costa Daurada and the northern Costa Brava offer charming fishing ports and custom-built developments, busy package-holiday centres and smaller resorts, so there's something for everyone within easy reach of Barcelona.

1 Sitges
2 Coast
3 Morning fishing

1 Catalonian bridge
2 Coast
3 Calella de Palafrugell
4 La Pera
5 Fishing boats

The Balearic Islands

≪ *see page 54*

Despite its being synonymous with modern tourism, there are still vast untouched areas of countryside and shoreline in the Balearics. Mallorca can offer you the most ultra-packaged experience around Palma, with cheap and cheerful holiday property to match, while the northwest coast is the chosen home of writers and movie stars, with villa prices accordingly high. Menorca is the greenest island, though cool and windy in winter, with lovely coves and far less tourism – but higher property prices – than Mallorca. Ibiza is mostly arid and brown, but offers unspoilt coastline protected from overdevelopment.

1 Pollenca
2 Farmhouse, inland Mallorca
3 Old Town, Ibiza
4 Deya, Mallorca

5 North coast, Mallorca
6 Cluc Alcavi
7 Fields, Mallorca
8 Fornacutx

The North Atlantic Coast

‹‹ *see page 57*

Spaniards escape here in summer for wonderful, empty beaches and ocean breezes – which are a far cry from the Mediterranean *costas*. The forests and Picos de Europa mountains are also popular for walking, and holiday homes are being snapped up while prices are still low. In winter, visitors leave the northern European climate to the locals. Local character is evident everywhere – in folk traditions, in rural architecture, in language and culture. Most distinctive of all is that of the Basque Country, centred on newly revived Bilbao. The downside of such a strong identity is the passion aroused by it, and that is the Basque region's darker heritage.

1 Coast, Basque Lands
2 Puente la Reina
3 La Rioja

The Canary Islands

<< *see page 59*

These seven subtropical islands are closer to Africa than to the Iberian peninsula. The islands' landscapes range from the deserts of Lanzarote to the cactus jungles of Tenerife, and superb beaches may be of black volcanic sand. Gran Canaria and Tenerife are the most visited islands, with spectacularly varied landscapes and wide beaches. Lanzarote's landscape is matched by its temperatures. Fuerteventura's huge, tranquil beaches are watersport heaven, while the other islands are lovely but remote.

1 *Mount Tie de, Tenerife*
2 *Maspacimas Dunes, Gran Canaria*
3 *Lanzarote del Carmen*
4 *Southern Tenerife*

Madrid to Lleida (Lerida in Castilian), passing through Zaragoza, which will eventually reach Barcelona and then the French border, connecting up with France's TGV network. Another line is under construction to Valencia. Travel times by train between London, Paris, Barcelona and Madrid will then be greatly reduced. Next after the AVE are the *Grandes Líneas*, or long-distance trains, which also have subdivisions within them: the best trains for long journeys between the major cities are *Talgos*, fast expresses that are now almost as quick (around 220kph/137mph) and as comfortable as the AVE. Included among them are several special services that have a name and identity of their own, such as the *Alaris* trains between Madrid and Valencia, or the *Arco* between Barcelona and Valencia. Slower and cheaper long-distance trains are known by the English tag Intercity, and there are also sleeper trains known as *Trenhoteles* or (slightly more basic) *Trenes Estrella*. The next main category is that of *Regionales* which, unlike those described so far, stop at every (or nearly every) station on their route. Lastly, several of Spain's conurbations, among them Madrid, Barcelona, Bilbao, Cádiz, Málaga, Murcia and Valencia, have *Cercanías* or local rail networks of varying sizes, with lines running out into the suburbs and smaller towns around them.

Until recently, **fares** were complicated because they were generally quoted as a basic price with supplements for the more expensive services, but now the system has been simplified. Discounts are available on certain days midweek (identified on the timetable as Días Azules, 'Blue Days') and for regular travellers there are various multi-journey or period-pass tickets, which also save you money. At larger stations there are separate ticket windows for long-distance and regional services (identified by Largo Recorrido, or in Catalan Llarg Recorregut) and Cercanías (in Catalan Rodalies).

Many of the remaining idiosyncrasies of Spanish railways are due to the structure of the track as it was first laid out by private companies in the 19th century, and which has been much harder to upgrade than the rolling stock. One, as mentioned, is the gauge, which is broader than that used in other European countries. Owing to uncooperative mountain terrain, lines often follow strangely out-of-the-way routes, and some regional lines are still single track. And, while there are lines to all major cities, some parts of the country are much less well served by railways than others: along the north coast and in Galicia, for example, there are more lines running inland towards Madrid than between different parts of the same region. Among the areas with the most comprehensive and useful rail network is Catalonia, where there are, in particular, two Cercanías lines along the coast north and south of Barcelona that provide a very handy, efficient alternative to congested highways for getting from the city to the beach towns and vice versa. The southern line continues down the coast all the way through Valencia to Alicante and Murcia, making it easy to get up and down the Costas Daurada, del Azahar and Blanca. From Alicante, there is also a branch line to Torrevieja. Further south, it used to be a rule that as soon as any train entered Andalucía you could always expect it to slow down, for no obvious reason. This is no longer the case, but this is still a region where the rail system has many oddities. Chief among them is that, due to their having been built long ago by separate companies, the region's two main lines – one connecting Córdoba, Seville, Algeciras and Huelva and the other Málaga, Granada and Almería – meet only at the strange little town of Bobadilla, and many longer journeys involve extended waits to change trains there. On the other hand, the Málaga Cercanías line, along the busiest part of the Costa del Sol through Torremolinos to Fuengirola, provides a good alternative to the N340 highway.

As well as the RENFE network there are some **independent lines** in Spain, run by private companies or regional governments. The most important are the Catalan government's FGC, which has lines from Barcelona out into the suburbs and country towns, and the FEVE, along the Basque coast from San Sebastián to Bilbao and on to Santander. Mallorca has three narrow-gauge lines of its own, from Palma out to Sóller, Sa Pobla and Artà.

By Sea

There are plenty of options for travelling between the mainland and the Balearics by sea. Car and passenger ferries run to the Balearics from Barcelona (Palma de Mallorca, usually two to three sailings daily; Menorca, from three sailings a week; Ibiza, one daily except Sunday), Valencia (Mallorca, one to two daily, Menorca, from one a week, Ibiza, from three a week) and Denia (two to three daily, to San Antonio, Ibiza, only). Schedules change frequently through the year and there are always extra sailings from mid-June to September. There are three grades of ferries on most routes, from conventional ship-ferries (simply called 'Ferry'), which are also the cheapest, through 'Super-Ferries' to catamaran style 'Fast Ferries' (or *Alta Velocidad*). Journey times vary from 3½ hours on a Fast Ferry to 7 hours on the basic, overnight ferry on the Barcelona–Mallorca route, or from 6½ to 7½ hours from Valencia–Mallorca; Denia–Ibiza, which is Fast Ferry-only, takes 4 hours.

Three main companies operate these services: **Transmediterranea** (**t** 902 454 645 in Spain, **www.trasmediterranea.es**); the rapidly growing **Balearia** (**t** 902 160 180 in Spain, **www.balearia.com**); and **Iscomar Ferries** (**t** 902 119 128 in Spain, **t** 00 34 971 437 500 from abroad **www.iscomarferrys.com**). All three offer information in English on their websites and online booking facilities. The booking procedure is as long and complex; you have to follow several steps, choosing ferry type, sailing, date, number of passengers, car length etc. before you get to find out how much it will cost and whether there are any places available. It can be most frustrating to complete all the steps to then find that there are no places available on the date you wish to travel. Balearia (going via the site map) and Iscomar (click on 'Schedules and Fares') do give you an at-a-glance guide to fares, which is helpful.

Unless you really want to take your own car to the islands, you will almost certainly find it cheaper to fly. Transmediterranea's cheapest fare, for one person travelling in a seat, one-way, is currently around €76 on a Fast Ferry, from Barcelona or Valencia, or €55 on a basic ferry, and cabins naturally cost extra; a car costs around €149 by Fast Ferry, about €137 by ferry, plus fares for each person travelling. There are also all-in 'packet' (*paquete*) fares for a car and four people, of around €388 one-way on a Fast Ferry. All these routes often need to be booked up months ahead for summer, especially for the beginning and end of August. Balearia and Iscomar both offer fares that are competitive with Transmediterranea's; Balearia will take you from Barcelona to Ibiza for €48.60 and Iscomar charges €29 one-way for a foot passenger from Barcelona to Palma de Mallorca. They also have some interesting offers, but you have to get in quickly, and of course the dates must coincide with when you want to travel. Transmediterranea appear not to offer discounts for Balearic Island residents while the other two do.

Transmediterranea is also the only company operating car ferries to the Canaries, from Cádiz. There is roughly one sailing a week on each route to Las Palmas, Lanzarote and Tenerife; sailing times are long, around 36–38 hours. Ticket prices are also high and, again, uncompetitive with air fares unless you want to have your vehicle with you, although anyone officially resident in the Canaries is entitled to discounts of from 25 to 33 per cent on all ferry tickets. The minimum fare per passenger is at least €300 for non-residents, or around €135 for residents, and a 'packet' ticket for a car and four people costs about €770 for non-residents, €570 for residents. The many ferry routes between all the islands within the Canaries are operated by Transmediterranea, **Naviera Armas (t** 902 456 500 in Spain, **www.naviera-armas.com**) and **Líneas Fred Olsen (t** 902 100 017 in Spain; **www.fredolsen.es**). Fares are much more competitive, for passengers and vehicles.

Climate

Stereotypically, Spain can be considered to divide into two main regions as far as weather is concerned. One of them, much the smaller, is north of the Cantabrian mountains along the Atlantic coast, stretching westwards from the Pyrenees through the Basque Country, Asturias and the whole of Galicia, and can be roughly labelled 'wet Spain'. The Atlantic Ocean gives this area a distinctly maritime, northern climate, with only moderate variations in temperature between warm, pleasant summers and mild, or sometimes pretty cold, winters. Rainfall is quite heavy and frequent through the year, too, if a little less so in summer. Another aspect of the ocean weather is its unpredictability, so rain and cloudy skies can occur here at any time, and the weather can also be quite stormy, above all in winter and spring.

The remaining two-thirds of the country is 'dry Spain', although this in itself can be divided into two. Virtually all of Spain's central regions are several hundred metres higher in altitude than the coastal areas to their east and south, and form an arid plateau with a typically continental climate of very hot, dry summers and sometimes fiercely cold winters. An old saying describes the mountain climate of Madrid as 'six months of winter (*invierno*), followed by six months of hell (*infierno*)', which is a piece of poetic exaggeration, but local weather is characterised by extremes. Even in winter there is not much rainfall, which can be as low as 350mm (14in) per year in some areas, although snow is quite common in northern Castile. In Madrid in July you can go around in minimum clothing 24 hours of the day (and maybe still feel too hot), but anyone who thinks they won't have to put on several extra layers by November is in for a big shock.

The more low-lying eastern and southern coasts, most of Andalucía and the Balearics, on the other hand, have a classic Mediterranean climate pattern of hot summers, cooled a little by sea breezes, and mild, balmy winters. Although this is all part of 'dry Spain', its dryness is not uniform, and Catalonia and Menorca, for example, are far greener and less dry than Andalucía, which includes areas like Almería that receive scarcely any rain at all. Towards the north, in particular, in between the beautifully clear days with dazzlingly blue skies, there are spells of heavy humidity leading to thunderstorms. Throughout these regions, rain, if and when it arrives, very often does so in the concentrated form of brief, torrential storms, which happen mainly in spring and at the end of summer in late September and October, when the hot weather often markedly 'breaks' to give way to milder temperatures.

As well as hot sun and occasional rain, some other, less well-known features of the Spanish coast are its winds: strong sea winds are found throughout the Mediterranean, and blow especially strongly on Menorca, the northern Catalan coast and the Costa Brava, the Costa Blanca and the Costa del Sol, particularly in spring and autumn. Although often celebrated in local folklore, blasting winds that can set in for days on end are something of a guilty secret as far as tourist and property promoters are concerned, and if you're especially averse to high winds you should ask about whether an area is prone to them, especially if you visit in July when the weather is calm.

Finally, another characteristic of Mediterranean Spain stems from the variety of the landscape: no matter how hot it may be by the coast, as soon as you go into the hills inland, temperatures will be cooler and fresher, so that hill villages are especially prized as places to live. Remarkable contrasts are most marked in Andalucía, with its mix of semi-deserts, lush oases and alpine mountains. One of the region's classic experiences is to look up on a baking day in Granada and see snow on the peaks of the Sierra Nevada, away to the south.

The Canary Islands, naturally, form an entirely separate climatic area. Although they lie off the Sahara, their almost permanently sunny climate is moderated

Scorched Earth

It seems marvellous, doesn't it? A laid-back life, mostly spent outdoors in the glorious sunshine; home is a villa built into a golfing complex, or a short drive from the nearest links. A gentle round in the morning, or maybe a leisurely game of tennis, followed by a pre-lunch dip in the private pool, then rinse off the chlorine in your power-shower, or perhaps soothe in the Jacuzzi those aching joints brought on by many years of cold, damp British winters. Heavenly, isn't it?

This lifestyle, that so many buy into, is an industry that moves many, many millions of euros every year. It is the subject of numerous TV programmes and sells a great many books, such as this one. It keeps the construction industry very busy and provides local councils with previously unimaginable sources of revenue. It is fed by, and at the same time feeds, the low-cost air travel business. It stimulates service industries and provides employment for locals.

But it is also under threat and may eventually become a victim of its own success. Because this lifestyle needs lots of water, and water is precisely something that the areas most people choose to up-sticks and move to does not have.

Spain is at the time of writing experiencing its worst drought since reliable records started being kept. Many reservoirs in central and southern Spain are at less than 50 per cent of their capacity, and some are even below 20 per cent. Aquifers in coastal regions are so low as to become invaded and polluted by seawater. Whether this is all the result of worldwide weather trends, global warming, toxic emissions and deforestation, or just part of a cycle, is open to debate. But the results are there for all to see. Water for domestic use is being rationed in many parts of Mediterranean and inland Spain. Parks are left un-watered. Fruit and vegetable growers in Spain's market-garden regions such as Murcia are facing ruin, losses in the sector are already calculated in billions. And forests were ablaze all over the country throughout the summer of 2005: 30,000 hectares went up in the province of Guadalajara; 11 volunteer fire-fighters died. Much of Spain's scarce water is squandered, by inefficient irrigation techniques, poor infrastructures that allow much of it to filter out or evaporate before it ever reaches the tap.

Oh, and golf courses. The number of golf courses in Spain has doubled in the last five years, to 276. A further 150 are planned. Keeping one course green and lush uses the same amount of water as that needed by a town of 12,000 people. Maybe within a few years, golfers will have to get used to putting on the 'brown' and ponds will no longer be an obstacle. It's worth thinking about.

greatly by the Atlantic all around them. Lanzarote and Fuerteventura, the furthest east, are near-desert-like and have so little rainfall that water has to be found by other means, but the further west you go, the more the islands become greener, slightly wetter and a little cooler.

For a chart allowing you to compare temperatures and rainfall in Spain, *see* pp.332–3. Bear in mind, though, that figures like these only tell part of the story. Wind, the amount of shelter or the lack of it, altitude, daily variation and many other factors can affect how you actually experience the weather in any location.

Selecting a Property

Once you've chosen a region of Spain that appeals to you, and worked out how to get there, you naturally need to move on to specifics and make a preliminary selection of the type of property you're going to look for. This is not always as straightforward and rational a process as you might think. The application of common sense and systematic thought can help inform your decision but, mercifully, the human spirit often ignores such considerations. If you or any of your family falls in love with an abandoned farmhouse in the middle of the countryside while reason tells you that you ought to be looking for an apartment near an airport, you will probably buy the farmhouse. And with luck you'll enjoy it all the more. It is too easy to forget, as you get immersed in the detailed planning for the purchase, that this whole exercise is supposed to be fun, for pleasure, since nobody really needs a villa by the Mediterranean. If you want to throw reason to the wind and buy the house of your dreams there is nothing wrong with doing so – provided you understand that this is what you are doing.

This does not mean, however, that it isn't worth spending some time working out what those dreams might be (in a roughly practical way) and so thinking about the type of property that would suit you best before you travel to Spain to look at buildings. Buying an inappropriate property can prove very expensive and, worse still, can put you off the whole idea of a home abroad. Here, again, it is useful to be in contact with an independent legal adviser from an early stage, to clear up any initial queries. In particular, of course, you need to get a basic idea of whether your preliminary choices are in line with your budget – with a little flexibility to allow for any pleasantly cheap surprises that may turn up.

As well as helping you focus your ideas, thinking about these issues will allow you to give estate agents a clear brief about what you are looking for. This will help them help you and avoid your time being wasted by their showing you totally inappropriate properties. Always discuss your requirements with the local agents who are helping you find a property, rather than dictate those requirements to them. They may well say that what you are asking for is not obtainable in their area – but that something very similar is. And do not be afraid to change your mind. It is quite common for people to start off looking at rural properties for restoration and end up deciding that, for them, a new property is a better bet – or the other way round. If you do change your mind don't forget to tell the estate agents. Better still, discuss your developing views with them regularly, and get confirmation that what you want is achievable.

Location, Location, Location

You may have settled on which region of Spain most attracts you for its weather, landscape, culture, general atmosphere, food or whatever, and on whether you want to live in a town, on the coast or in a village, but deciding on a particular town, village, development or hillside in which you will want to spend a lot of your time, or even live permanently, involves a whole series of much more individual, more intimate choices. Before you commit yourself to anything you should also try to get a much better idea of what a place really feels like, as a place to live, than you would get just from passing through. The way to do so that is most fun – and undoubtedly the best – is to travel exten-sively, and get to know an area (or areas) both in summer and in winter. The need to see them in both seasons cannot be overemphasised. Some summer resorts close down almost completely in the winter months, and the climate that was so agreeable in June can be drab in January. Somewhere else that was a tranquil 20-minute drive from town in May might be accessible only with a two-hour nose-to-tail driving ordeal in August.

Few people will have the time or staying power to drive around every corner of any particular region in search of their ideal location, but this isn't really necessary anyway. If you find a locality that you like, and would like a home there, it scarcely matters that there are 10 other villages further up the road. Most people tend to select an area to buy in from those they already know plus, perhaps, another couple that they have read about and decide to visit before making their final decision. A fair substitute for, or preliminary to, an initial visit is a bit of reading, beginning with general guides to Spain. Follow that up with some more specific reading about the areas that interest you, TV programmes, information from the Internet and other sources, and you can gain more of a feel of what a place will be like.

Sooner or later, though, there is no substitute for getting over there and exploring. A two-week self-drive holiday, staying in inexpensive small hotels, can cover a lot of ground. Most people know within a few minutes of arriving in a town whether it is somewhere they could see themselves living or not. Take a large-scale map or road atlas. Use it as a tool. Write your comments about places you visit on the page, otherwise you will never remember which was which. Take plenty of pictures or videos, and/or buy postcards to remind you of the scenery. Pick up a copy of the local paper for each area: even if you do not speak Spanish it will give you some idea of what goes on in the area, and will invariably have ads from most of the local estate agents. Visit the local tourist office, and pick up as much information and brochures as you can carry about the area, and of what goes on throughout the year. Look in estate agents' windows, and make a note – again on the map – of the sorts of prices you might have to pay for the type of property that interests you. However, *do not go inside*. The purpose of this first visit is to decide as freely as possible on your feelings about the town or area, not specific properties, so make it an absolute rule that you will not look at any. If you do you will be caught in the classic trap of focusing on bricks and mortar rather than the area around them. As the old estate agent's saying goes, location is the most important factor when buying any property, ahead of the details of individual houses and, when you are moving to a new country, location includes the whole community and area around it. You can find attractive houses anywhere, but which combination of house and location will be right for you is a different matter.

Provided the initial look at prices hasn't ruled out this area for you, if you like the town mark it with a big ✔ and move on to the next place. If it is not for you, mark the map with a ✘ and, likewise, move on. Shortlist your two or three most likely places, and visit them again, in summer and winter. Spend a little time there. Make contact with estate agents, and start looking at as many properties as you can handle.

If you are intending to move to Spain permanently, to work or to retire – unless you have known a place for many years already, maybe as a holiday home – it is advisable first to find a place to rent in your chosen town, settle in for a while and decide whether the life really is for you, rather than go straight into house buying. For more on renting, see 'Renting Before, or Instead of, Buying', pp.142–4.

Setting Your Priorities

Within each area, there are then more individual features to be considered, as well as the obvious ones that might make you fall in love with a place, such as a fabulous view or a spectacular setting. You will need to think differently about location according to whether you just want a place in which to spend your leisure time, or if you ever intend to live permanently, work or retire there, and if you have children. A different set of considerations comes into play if you expect to let your property while you're not there, which can potentially limit your choices (for more on all aspects of letting, see **Letting Your Property**). If you are going to be travelling to work, meeting clients and/or getting kids to school you should think about whether you can do so reasonably easily throughout the year, not just in June, and after the initial novelty of your new situation has worn off a little. If, on the other hand, you deliberately take on somewhere that is more remote and rural, you should accept that you will have to be much more self-sufficient than if you were within easy reach of town shops and services. If you are not going back to the land, and do not have work organised, you will need to be somewhere where you have a reasonable hope of finding it. Most kids, too, will almost certainly want some kind of social life. You need to be especially realistic about location if you are thinking of retiring to your Spanish home. A spectacular mountain track that provides the only access to your restored farmhouse may seem an added attraction when you're still in full vigour, but you may not feel so good about driving up and down it every time you need to visit the shops 20 years on. Access to public transport and medical services will become more important as you get older, too, and you may well find that the closeness of other expats, from whom you might have shied away in earlier years, becomes much more comforting, and helpful.

Within these general considerations, these are some specific points to look at:

• **Town or country.** As already outlined, this is a basic choice to make, but even those who decide to go for a country or beach home should think about just how far away from the madding crowd they want to be. Most people find it handy to stay within about an hour's drive of a reasonable-sized town, for those occasions when you need a bit more than the village shop can provide.

• **How much outside space you want, and how close you will be to your neighbours.** This, again, is an obvious consideration anywhere in the world, but is made particularly prominent in Spain because so many of the properties on sale to foreigners are in *urbanización* developments, of greater or lesser density. When looking at any development properties you need to find out what the future of the *urbanización* is going to be, and whether it is likely ever to contain many more properties than it does when you see it.

• **How close you are to local shops, bars and restaurants.** How good the nearest shops and other essentials are, and what range they offer, and whether you can stroll down to them on a Sunday morning, or will have to take the car every time. How far it is, also, to the nearest larger-scale shopping centre and/or supermarket, and whether you can get there if you are ever without a car.

• **The nearest public transport.** How frequent and useful it is, and also ease of access from the property to major transport links.

• **Proximity to a beach.** Of course. Also, you might think about whether the nearest beach is one that you'll be happy to go back to time and again.

• **Schools.** If you have school-age children you will need to know that the local schools are reasonably accessible, and check out what they are like. If you want to have your children educated in English at one of the international private schools in Spain (and do not want to send them away to board) your choice will be much more restricted (*see* pp.20–22 and 251–4).

• **Health and social services.** In most towns and villages there will be a health centre and doctor's surgery run by the Spanish health service. Find out how easy it is to get to, take a look at it and, since these centres do not usually have emergency services, check how far it is to the nearest hospital with an emergency department (*urgencias*). Try to find out, too, whether there are any English-speaking doctors, dentists or private clinics in the locality. Other foreign residents and expat magazines are good sources of this kind of information. This will, naturally, be more or less prominent in your mind according to your state of health, and whether you have small children. For more on health services, *see* pp.22–3 and 254–7.

• **Golf and other sports.** If, as many people do nowadays, you intend to make golf a major part of your life in Spain, you will want to be somewhere where you have a choice of courses within a reasonable distance. The western Costa del Sol, La Manga in Murcia and the southern Costa Blanca are Spain's biggest golf regions, but there are courses and developments growing up in the Canaries, Mallorca and many other areas too. For maximum convenience there is the fast-expanding phenomenon of the dedicated golf resort, where courses and housing are built together as parts of one development. If you or you family are interested in other sports – windsurfing, scuba-diving and other watersports, sailing, riding, skiing – look into how easy it is to get to these facilities as well.

• **Arts and entertainment.** Unless you're completely uninterested in this kind of thing, find out where the nearest cinema is, whether there are any cinemas within 100km (60 miles) that show films in English, undubbed (identified as VO, or *versión original*, in newspapers) and whether you can hear any live music in the locality. Take a look too at what kinds of arts events are available in the surrounding towns.

• **Youth culture.** If you have older children or teenagers, their demands for entertainment and a social life are likely to be higher than yours are.

• **Compatriots, and how much you want to see them.** This is another of the basic choices to be made by anyone buying property in Spain. All around the Spanish Mediterranean coast, but most of all on the Costa del Sol and Costa Blanca, there are big communities of foreign residents, quite a lot of them in self-contained developments that are 100 per cent British, or 100 per cent German, which allow their inhabitants to isolate themselves from every aspect of Spanish life except cheap drink and cigarettes. They are supported by a complete range of English-speaking businesses. Whether or not you want to be in one of these clusters while you live in Spain is a matter entirely of personal preference, but this can become a fairly marked choice. Should you go to live in a development like this and yet still want to come into contact with Spanish life, you may find it difficult, as locals are accustomed to regarding these estates as alien places that they have little or nothing to do with. In some of these expat *urbanizaciones*, a high proportion of residents are retired people, which naturally sets the atmosphere. Be aware, also, that some all-foreign developments where a high proportion of the houses are used as second homes are virtually deserted in winter, and even the shops and services may close down or run on a limited schedule.

Elsewhere along the coast, on the other hand, and in towns and villages just inland, there are places with smaller foreign communities that are more mixed – even on *urbanizaciones* – less concentrated and less self-contained, and therefore offer the option of talking about familiar things when you want to, but without having to chew over the English football results every time you go into a bar. And if you want to make your own way, avoid all hints of 'expat-dom' and get as much into Spanish life as possible, then you should head in another direction and find somewhere without any recognisable foreign community at all. If you do so, though, you should take on board the need to learn the local language (whichever one it is) to at least a decent standard and take some trouble to break the ice with your neighbours in order to get along.

• **Neighbours.** Beyond the nationality of the community as a whole, you will want to get some impression of what the specific people who will be living next door, or above you, will be like – whether they are noisy or tranquil, friendly or offhand, cooperative or suspicious, and so on. This is particularly important if you buy an apartment, in which case you and your neighbours will have to deal with various things in common. Spanish people are used to knowing their neighbours, and friendly neighbours help each other out in all sorts of ways, so a good neighbour is a great plus – especially if you are ever going to leave your property vacant for any stretch of time, and need someone to leave the key with. Conversely, if your neighbours are remote or uncommunicative, you will be missing out. In some *costa urbanizaciones* , as mentioned, you may have no neighbours at all for long periods, or the next villa may be let out to a continually changing stream of holiday tenants, which can be irritating.

• **Summer crowds.** Tourist towns along the coast and in the islands are very often quite placid for much of the time, but bear in mind that each year from July to September, and at some other times such as Easter, the bigger resorts especially will become hugely crowded, and shops, roads, beaches and restaurants will all be packed, 24 hours a day. Services may get overloaded, leading to power cuts and water shortages. If you don't want to handle this summer deluge, look away from the beach and a bit further inland, especially if you want a place to live in and not just a seaside second home.

• **Noise.** A related question. Spain is often spectacularly noisy. Aside from the tourist crowds, check whether any buildings near your prospective buy are used for industrial purposes, whether any roads nearby get periodically busy, or whether the anonymous building at the end of the street that's closed all day becomes a club venue at night (quite common in Spain). Get your lawyer to check whether any land nearby has been zoned for business use. And visit the site after dark to check on the noise.

• **Parking.** If you are buying or renting in a city or town, and have a car, always check that some kind of off-street parking is available. Street parking is severely restricted and car break-ins and minor accidents are common. Most modern Spanish apartment blocks have a car park underneath them, but there may be an extra charge to use it. Commercial and council-run car parks in cities are expensive, and there may be waiting lists to get into them. In small communities parking is much less of a problem, but check that it is safe to leave a car in the street.

• **Crime.** Get an idea of the local crime rate, and whether there is a noticeable incidence of break-ins, car thefts or muggings aimed at foreigners and foreign-owned properties. While nowhere near plague proportions, this is a significant problem in some high-density tourist areas, one result of which is increased insurance premiums in those places. Isolated but opulent houses that are often left vacant can be a particular target for burglaries. In villages, on the other hand, the likelihood of any sort of theft is far less.

• **Planning problems.** Over the past four decades of Spanish tourist expansion, holiday developments and villas have quite often been built with little attention to the local planning laws, to which the various authorities have responded recently with a range of new regulations and penalties, leading to back-and-forth litigation in the middle of which innocent, and often uncompre-hending, foreign buyers have been caught. If you are looking at anywhere on an established development, especially, you should be aware of whether any such problems have occurred in the area. This is another reason why it is very important to have good legal advice from the start (*see* 'Lawyers and How to Use Them', pp.131–2). Planning laws in the Valencian region (Castellón, Valencia and Alicante provinces) have until recently posed problems for anyone considering buying there and, though scrapped, what will replace them remains to be seen – *see* box, p.50, and p.110.

• **The local council.** It's a good idea to get some impression, maybe by talking to other residents, of how well or otherwise the local municipal council (*ayuntamiento*, or in Catalan *ajuntament*) is run, and take a look at the services it provides, such as a well-kept public swimming pool. If you expect to be doing much building work, especially, a helpful council will make your life easier. Many towns on the *costas* with big foreign communities have a special foreign residents' department to keep them informed of things that affect them.

• **Rural services.** If you are looking at isolated rural properties, they may not be connected up to mains water or electricity. If you don't want to have to deal with your own generators, tanks and so on, find out how far away the nearest mains supply is, and what it will cost to be connected.

• **Water shortages.** Lack of water is a serious problem in many parts of Spain, despite vast engineering projects to bring water from north to south, which were anyway scrapped by the PSOE government on taking power, and the building of desalination plants at various points around the coast. The continual building of tourist developments and water-guzzling golf courses has only exacerbated the situation (*see* box, p.95). The problem is most acute in Andalucía, Murcia and the southern Costa Blanca and, naturally, is most noticeable in times of peak summer demand, when there can be shortages leading to occasional restrictions or even cuts in supply. Before buying anywhere in 'dry Spain', always get an idea of the state and reliability of the local water supply, preferably from other local residents. Water in these areas is also more expensive; aside from the water companies' charges, in some developments the water supply is controlled centrally by the developer, who may charge you well over the odds for guaranteeing water at all times. If you are in an area with water problems, it's a great asset to have some alternatives to the mains supply, such as a storage tank or well (*see* pp.112–13). For more on water in general, *see* **Settling In**, p.241.

• **Fire and flood.** Sudden but very damaging brush fires are another problem in some areas, especially in the very driest months of summer. And another aspect of the lack of water is that houses in dry areas that are on steep hillsides, or next to gullies, may be affected by flash floods during the torrential storms that tend to come in late summer or early autumn. Properties in locations with a record of either problem will be harder to insure.

• **Dirt tracks.** Something else mainly relevant to rural properties: if you move into an idyllic old farmhouse on a hillside, the only access to it will very possibly be by dirt track. Check that this will be passable at all times, including after heavy rain, and whose responsibility it will be to repair it (and pay for it).

Spanish Homes: Property Types

Half-abandoned castles and converted sheds aside (although these are out there), most of the properties you will find on offer in Spain divide up roughly between villas, apartments and townhouses (in towns and villages), and *fincas*, farmhouses and other rural properties. You also, naturally, have a choice between new or nearly new and old properties. Another very important distinction arises in Spain, though, because of the sheer amount of tourism-orientated building since the 1960s: that between properties specifically built as holiday, leisure or retirement homes for outside buyers, and those which were not. This split is becoming a little fuzzy at the edges – there are so many beach villas on some parts of the coast that locals sometimes find them cheaper and more convenient than old-style town houses – but overall it still marks a noticeable choice. A majority of the places built to be second homes and/or for foreign sales are in *urbanizaciones*, or purpose-built developments.

Urbanizaciones

Travel just about anywhere along the Mediterranean coast of Spain and its islands and you will see any number of villa *urbanizaciones*, lining beaches or running into the countryside and up hills around the resort towns. They cover the whole market, from low-budget bargains to ultra-luxurious: some are high-density estates of 100 or so identical whitewashed-walled and red-tile-roofed villas with just tiny terraces between them, while others are discreet clusters of a few very grand villas amid vast gardens spread over whole hillsides. In between these extremes you can find every other grade of spaciousness as well. By no means are they all intended for foreigners. Spaniards are actually more enthusiastic second-home-buyers than British people: traditionally, people with money in Spain lived in a big flat in town but kept another home outside it, where they spent the whole summer or escaped to at weekends. In the past, the most favoured spots for second homes were cooler places up in the hills but, in modern Spain, beach houses have become far more popular. As more people have had the wherewithal to acquire a weekend retreat, demand has naturally soared and, depending on the area, the growing affluence of urban Spain has probably contributed as much as foreign tourism to the mushrooming of *urbanizaciones* in the last 40 years. Also, since *urbanización* is really just Spanish for 'housing estate', they do not have to be by the coast. Over the last two decades or so, in a break with centuries of tradition, the full social consequences of which have not yet been checked out, a fast-growing number of Spanish families have forsaken their city flats and moved to houses with gardens in neat and shiny *urbanizaciones* around the major cities (especially Madrid), in all-new, rather un-Spanish-looking suburbs.

A great many of the *urbanizaciones* on or near the coast, though, are pitched predominantly at foreign buyers. This may not be stated upfront, but when the development company is foreign-owned and all the promotional material is primarily in English or German, the developers' aims are clear. Developments like this are found above all in the major expatriate clusters of the Costa del Sol, Costa Blanca, Mallorca and the Canaries, but there are plenty elsewhere. Beach-frontage for *urbanizaciones* is now very much at a premium in the best-known areas, which is why building has gained so much pace in previously overlooked areas like the Costa de la Luz and, especially, the southern Costa Blanca around Torrevieja and La Manga in Murcia – currently the biggest area for new villa development-building in Spain, still with surprisingly low prices, and very popular with British buyers. Elsewhere, there are also many *urbanizaciones* a little inland from the coast where in return for forgoing your beach frontage you will usually get a good deal more space, in the villa itself and in land around it, for the same amount of money.

Urbanización properties are heavily promoted by developers and through all the property agencies specialising in foreign sales based along the *costas*, and if you look through property magazines or go to any of the international property exhibitions in the UK this is predominantly the kind of properties you will find on offer there too. Developers and agencies generally offer a complete sales service that covers all the formalities, allowing you to buy virtually 'off the peg', so this is by far the easiest way to buy property in Spain – but even so, and with no reflection on the other party, you should always have your own independent lawyer working on your behalf as well, and have them check any contracts before you sign. Many developments have a range of properties, to cater for different buyers – from studio apartments and two-bedroom apartments to two-bedroom villas, four-bedroom villas and more. Many also include a variety of shared facilities – swimming pools (the most common), the beach itself, gardens, tennis courts, a bar and restaurant, maybe a fitness centre and a golf course, reaching up to a fantastic range of facilities at the most lavish of them all, Club La Manga in Murcia and the Sotogrande golf resort on the Costa del Sol. In most – especially those with a lot of facilities – there will also be a caretaker, administrator or management office to which you can turn, even if you have bought your property outright, if you have a problem.

Urbanización developers frequently offer properties on a range of terms – outright sale, leaseback, sometimes timeshares (*see* 'Types of Ownership', pp.119–20). The most popular option is outright sale, with which, whatever your relationship with the developer, under Spanish law you will become a member of the *comunidad de propietarios* or 'community of owners' for the whole *urbanización* (*see* pp.115–17 and 171–2). If you only use your villa or apartment as a second home, the developers' agents or management company, where there is one, will also probably be willing to take charge of letting it the rest of the year on your behalf, for a sizeable commission.

The attractions or otherwise of *urbanizaciones* are a matter of taste in how you prefer to spend your time in Spain. Whatever your preferences, if you're considering buying in an *urbanización* it's always a good idea to try and get some sense of how the *comunidad* works and the general atmosphere to decide whether it's for you, which is best done by talking to people already there. Some developments are attached to older Spanish villages, which you can wander into to find cafés, local shops, markets and so on, while others are entirely out on their own between golf course and beach, so that residents looking for local atmosphere have to get in the car. Some form rather claustrophobic little communities in which everyone is expected to meet up at the same bar every night, others are more open-ended; some are entirely of one nationality, others are more mixed; while in some most residents are elderly and retired people. Some *urbanizaciones* have scarcely any permanent residents, and become virtual ghost towns in winter. You should also consider whether any communal facilities such as swimming pools, that appear ample and peaceful in April, may be completely overrun when every single property on the development is occupied in August. With cheaper and older *costa* properties, especially, be aware also that many of them are planned specifically as holiday homes with, for example, only basic kitchens, minimal storage space and no provision for heating. If you ever want to live there more permanently they have limitations that become very apparent once you have been installed for a few weeks.

The advantages of buying in an *urbanización* are, first of all, sheer convenience, both in the process of house purchasing and later in offloading many of the responsibilities of looking after your property, maintenance and so on. Then there are all the community facilities; ready-made social contacts; greater security, both when you are there and when your home is empty; lower taxes; and the possibility of owning a home in locations – such as next to a beach near Marbella – where fully detached properties are hugely expensive. Disadvantages can be high community charges, inflexible and restrictive community rules and problems with other members of the *comunidad*, difficult neighbours, lack of space and privacy, and lack of control over the future of the development, especially if you do have any disagreements with other residents (for all *comunidad*-related issues, again, *see* pp.115–17 and 171–2).

Buying 'Off-plan'

Prospective buyers looking around agents in Spain or property exhibitions in the UK are often given the opportunity to buy properties 'off-plan' – meaning homes or whole *urbanizaciones* that have not been built yet – on the basis only of a show home or just the development plans and perhaps a model. Payments are made in instalments, with final payment after the finished building is 'delivered', but a substantial initial deposit will be required. This is obviously not an ideal way to buy, and publications like this one often advise buyers against it, but, in a sellers' market and with properties in especially desirable locations, this may not always be an entirely practical caution. If you do consider buying off-plan, you must get as much information from the developer and agents about the property as possible. And, most importantly, you should get a 'termination guarantee' from the developer that both your home and every aspect of the development (landscaping, roads, water, and so on) will be properly finished, backed up by a full insurance policy. This is another area where the support of your own lawyer is essential. In addition, even if your own home is completed when you buy it, be sure to ask if there are any plans in the pipeline for changes to the development. In a worst-case scenario, you can find that your property is only part of 'Phase I' of an *urbanización*, and that 'Phase II', when it arrives, will block off your view of the beach.

Villas

As well as development properties there are a great many fully detached, purpose-built holiday villas dotted around the *costas*, especially in rather more upmarket areas like the Marbella section of the Costa del Sol, the northern Costa Blanca and northern Mallorca. You will nearly always pay more for a detached villa than for a house of equivalent size and comfort on an *urbanización*. A big advantage, of course, is that you do not have a *comunidad* to deal with. Special caution is required at the moment, though, when looking at any such non-development properties on the Costa Blanca and in other parts of the Valencian region as while the 'land grab' law there has been suspended, no one knows quite what will replace it (*see* box, p.50, and p.110).

Apartments

With flats in Spain, perhaps more than with any other kind of property, it's worth distinguishing between places built as holiday homes and the rest. A huge (sometimes scarcely believable) number of holiday flats has been built around the *costa*s since the 1960s, in developments and in resort towns. The biggest resorts, such as Benidorm, Torremolinos or Playa de las Américas on Tenerife, have row on row of holiday apartment blocks beside their beaches and, because supply so often now outstrips demand, these are now near invariably the cheapest places to buy properties anywhere on the Spanish coast. Even in generally expensive areas – Ibiza, the Costa Brava – there are always some cheap flats around. Some of these holiday flats are quite comfortable, and their designers have struggled to give nearly all of them some view of the beach. Anyone looking to buy at the bottom of the market, though, should be aware of what they are getting. Many of these apartments are designed to be used by undemanding tenants for around two weeks at a time, maximum, and still more than villas offer very limited comforts for anyone living in them any longer. Older apartment blocks may also have been built to poor standards, or – if, say, they were built in the 1970s – have reached the time when they need substantial maintenance work. The cheapest holiday flats, too, are often so cheap because they're right in the middle of resort towns, the streets that get most congested each summer and where clubs and their crowds are likely to be rowdy all night. If what you want is somewhere as cheap as possible near a beach and party-town, that's fine, but if this isn't your scene it's best to think again.

Elsewhere in the resort towns, in quieter areas away from the centre or a little back from the beach, there are plenty of more comfortable, spacious and high-standard apartments. They naturally require a higher outlay than the bargain holiday-flats, but are still generally cheaper than *urbanización* villas along the coast.

Urban Spaniards are traditionally flat-dwellers, and apartments (*pisos*), rather than individual houses also make up far the greater part – or all of it, in city centres – of housing in all Spanish cities. Spanish city flats range from tiny, quaint spaces with sloping walls and low ceilings in 17th-century blocks in the historic centres of the main towns to spectacular modern duplexes with two whole floors and acres of room. Old British preconceptions that a flat is auto-matically second-best to house-with-garden need adjusting in Spain: most Spanish flats built since the 19th century give you more floor space than most British semi-detached or small detached houses, even if you may not have your own outside space. A drawback can be that natural light only enters at either end of the flat, leaving the middle rooms dark, but this is less common in modern buildings. Some upmarket modern apartment blocks have similar communal facilities to *costa* developments, such as swimming pools and tennis courts. In the grand old 19th-century apartment blocks of Barcelona and Madrid the most-valued flats were initially the huge opulent ones on the lower floors, which often have wonderful architectural details, while the upper floors at the top of the stairs were much plainer and cheaper. More recently, with the addition of lifts, the top floors, which get more light, have become much more desirable, and among those most sought-after nowadays are rooftop flats or *áticos*, which often have delightful roof terraces.

In all Spanish cities and towns, old flats – dating any time from the 16th century to about 1930 – are available for sale quite frequently and, if they have any distinguishing architectural features, especially, are highly prized. Quite often they are surprisingly cheap, but this usually means that they need a good deal of work, both to maintain their historic structures and to give them modern services. Young foreigners, though, have acquired something of a reputation for taking on crumbling piles that many Spanish buyers can't be bothered with. If you do look at any old flats, you need not only to look at the condition of the apartment itself but also to find out as much as possible about the state of the whole block, its plumbing, wiring and so forth.

Whenever you buy any apartment in Spain, whether a holiday flat or in a city block, you become a member of a *comunidad de propietarios* for the whole block, on the same terms as buyers of villas in development (*see* pp.115–17).

Town and Village Houses

In the same way that Spanish city-dwellers have traditionally lived close to each other in flats, so too the people of small towns and villages have tended to cluster together, and nearly all traditional houses in small communities – especially in the south – are next to each other in terraced-style or attached to each other in various other ways, rather than detached. This means they have only a little outside space, which is nearly always at the back – rarely ever at the front – and generally takes the form of a paved patio, although houses in Andalucía and the Balearics often have some flat roof space up above as well, ideal for drying clothes and lazy sunbathing. In this type of house you will automatically have a fair amount of contact with your neighbours, especially if your patios adjoin each other, which can be a very helpful, and enjoyable, introduction to local ways. Behind their generally plain exteriors, village houses in southern Spain often have a surprisingly large number of cool, shady rooms, frequently with timber-beam roofs, although old houses may well also require a fair amount of checking and new work with regard to wiring and plumbing. In hill villages, the arrangement of rooms snaking up hillsides within the same house is often extraordinarily ingenious and varied, and, invisible from the street, gives these houses great concealed character. Some of the most attractive traditional village houses in Spain, far away from the Mediterranean, are those of Cantabria and Old Castile, with veranda-like balconies along both ground and upper floors.

In addition, most towns and villages behind the *costa*s and in the islands contain a great many recently built houses, which local agents advertise equally as 'townhouses'. They may be detached villas, or small terraced developments, or villa complexes like those in *urbanizaciones*.

Fincas – Rural Properties

The Spanish word *finca* means a plot of land or an estate, irrespective of what is built on it. Hence properties advertised as *fincas* by local agents can run from tumbledown converted farmhouses to lavish modern villas with every convenience. They have in common that they are on their own land in the countryside, outside or in between towns and villages. *Fincas* generally come with a substantial amount of land, which may include olive groves and fruit orchards as well as a certain amount of land.

In Andalucía the most attractive type of traditional farmhouse – often called a *cortijo* – consists of a house and several outbuildings around a shady courtyard, and these often make for the most striking, characterful conversions. In the same areas there will also be much smaller whitewashed cottages, former smallholders' or labourers' cottages, but which also usually come with some land. Anywhere near the coast there are now few such properties that have not been at least looked at by foreign buyers and property agents, and if you want to find any farm courtyards that are still in their pure, rustic state, and thus much cheaper, you will probably have to look further inland – although it's still possible to turn up some remarkable bargains even around fashionable hill villages, so long as you're ready to take on all the renovation work that will almost certainly be required. In these same areas behind the *costa*s there is also a very large resale market in modern villas newly built or converted – often out of all recognition – from old properties over the last 30 years, which commonly have pools, gardens, wonderful locations and other attractions.

Every region of Spain also has its own traditional rural architecture. In much of central Spain, older farms often follow the same 'house, outhouses and court-yard' pattern as in Andalucía. In the hilly and mountainous regions of the north, the most characteristic traditional country buildings are isolated, often spectacularly large chalet-style farmhouses in which livestock was kept on the ground floor while the family lived above, like the *caseríos* of the Basque Country or the *masies* of Catalonia. In Catalonia especially, these magnificent buildings are now in great demand for conversions, and consequently some – but by no means all – carry high prices (*see* 'Guide Prices', pp.121–6).

If you buy any rural property, be it a villa or a farm, there are additional legal issues to consider, regarding any communal rights or by-laws that may affect the *finca*, which your lawyer should look into. And special conditions may apply to all non-development properties – which can include modern villas as well as rural *fincas* or building land – in the three provinces of the **Valencian region** (Castellón, Valencia and Alicante), due to a local planning law called the **LRAU** (Ley Reguladora de la Actividad Urbanística). This law, considered something of a developer's charter, has contributed greatly to the recent rapid acceleration in *urbanización*-building on the Costa Blanca, but its consequences for private owners of properties so far considered 'non-urbanised' are that a developer can have an *urbanización* approved that includes part of their land and can then have it compulsorily purchased, at a very low price. Many people have received nasty shocks (and lost a great deal of money) this way, and the opposition this law has aroused (among local farmers as well as foreigners and leisure-home owners) has led to it being referred to Spain's Supreme Court and the European Court. The latest news is that the law has been suspended but it is unclear quite what will replace it, and whether those affected by it will ever receive compensation is also unclear. There is therefore currently less risk than before in buying any non-development property anywhere in the tourist areas of the Valencian region but do stay abreast of any new legislation and check its implications with your lawyer.

The law never applied to development properties (which are already considered 'urbanised') but your lawyer should make especially clear to you the current situation, both regionally and locally. Some town councils see their main role as promoting large-scale tourist activity and make a habit of approving developments irrespective of environmental considerations or the effects on private *finca*-owners.

Features to Look For

Whichever kind of property you're hoping to buy, there are some basics to be kept in mind.

Air-conditioning

British people often downplay the importance of air-conditioning, regarding it as an unnecessary luxury, but if August night-time temperatures begin to hover around 25–30°C and you cannot sleep you won't deny its value. Traditional southern Spanish houses are cleverly built to keep out the heat as much as possible, which is why they're often so peculiarly dark, and it's worth making a note of whether a property is well enough aired, usually through a breezy location, to give it 'natural air-con'. More modern properties, though, have sadly moved away from these practical styles and in many, especially apartments, you'll find that at least some form of air-conditioning is a necessary feature – you may not need it often, but when you do you really need it. It is particularly important for people buying a home for retirement, or with elderly relatives who will visit. As we get older, everyone gradually loses their ability to adjust to extremes of temperature, and a temperature that is just unpleasantly hot for someone of 55 can be seriously disturbing for an 80-year-old. If an air-con system has not already been installed, portable coolers can be bought for around €450 and upwards that also do the job quite well, provided the room or flat can be reasonably closed off against the hot air outside.

Basic Utilities – Gas and Electricity

With both, you need to know about the form and reliability of supply, and the costs, and if there are ever any problems or cuts. This is especially important with rural properties, which may rely on their own generator and periodic deliveries of bottled gas. If you wish, you should also look at how the supply can be improved. For more on all aspects of these utilities, *see* **Settling In**, pp.238–41.

Heating

The other side of the coin of Spanish flats and houses, built with tiled floors and concrete-block walls to stay as cool as possible in summer, is that they also magnify the effect of any cold temperatures in winter. In Spanish flats it's a common experience in January to feel colder at home than you do in the street. This might seem a minor consideration when you're there in July but, even on the Costa del Sol, cold snaps can turn up later in the year, and if you have a house anywhere north of about Alicante you will definitely need some kind of heating for a few weeks at a time, even if it's only to fend off a drop of a few degrees from the 28°C you've got used to. Many villas and, especially, apartments built for holiday use have no fixed provision for any kind of heating, and the only way you can heat them is with portable electric and gas heaters – adequate in a small space, but very expensive in large rooms.

Parking

As mentioned earlier, secure off-street parking is a major asset in towns with cramped, narrow streets. Check whether a parking space is included with the property, or whether (as is quite often the case with apartment blocks and *urbanizaciones*) it has to be paid for separately.

Septic Tanks

An important consideration if you are looking at rural *fincas*, or any villas that are a little isolated from town and village drainage systems. Most such rural properties in Spain depend on their own septic tanks for their drainage. This is no great problem, but requires a little maintenance, and before you buy a house with one the tank should be checked by your surveyor, who should confirm that it is in good condition and adequate for your needs – taking into account whether you intend to make changes, install new bathrooms and so on.

Space

Many people underestimate the space they will need in their home abroad, especially if they expect to use it mainly for holidays – no one ever quite accurately calculates how often they will want to get over there themselves, or how many visitors may turn up. The combination of your own accommodation needs, the needs of visitors and the requirement for storage space – once you have your own place, you won't want to carry everything back and forth on the plane every time – means that, if the budget permits, it is worth thinking of buying one more bedroom than you first contemplated.

Swimming Pools

A pool is something most people would like to have next to their Spanish home, but they can also be very expensive. If you're looking at a property that already has a pool, find out how much maintenance it needs, and the cost per year. Check too that there are no ongoing problems, such as with the water supply. Even if you only use the house for holidays and let it infrequently you will still need someone at least to check the pool from time to time, or you will only face bigger bills when you come back. If you hope to have a pool built on a property, check whether the land is suitable, and double-check that there is an adequate water supply. It's also a good idea to make some preliminary enquiries, either directly or through a lawyer, with local pool-building companies on potential costs, whether there are any problems with pool-building in that particular area, whether there are any difficulties with the local council (which would have to give planning permission).

Water Supply

As well as finding out about the general water situation in your area, as mentioned, you need to be fully informed about the water supply system in the specific property in which you are interested, and its costs, which can vary a great deal.

This is especially the case with isolated or rural properties. *Fincas* and villas that are some distance from any village water system will usually only have a storage tank (*depósito*), which is filled in regular deliveries from a tanker, at extra cost. It's very useful to have a tank that collects rainwater and, even in properties that are connected to the main supply, a *depósito* is a major asset, whether filled by rain or from the mains (most modern systems keep the tanks filled automatically, and refill them after water cuts), since it provides invaluable back-up whenever there are water shortages. *Depósito* tanks can be installed on the roof (often the case in apartment blocks) or underground.

For more on water supply, *see* **Settling In**, 'Utilities', p.241.

Wells

Because of all the problems with water supply, the presence of a well is another great plus in rural properties. Even if you don't use it for drinking water it will be an excellent and cheap way of watering a garden or filling a swimming pool. Some wells, though, dry up in summer, while others have become too saline, and so are useless. If you are interested in a property with a well and you think it is going to be important to you, check it over, and make sure that your rights to it and its water are protected in your contract of purchase. If you hope to use your well for drinking water you should get it checked by the town health department or by your local water company, who will issue a certificate that its water is fit for human consumption (*agua potable*).

New or Old?

There is no right answer as to whether it is 'better' to buy newly built or old properties in Spain. Instead, like location, style and just about every other aspect of house-buying, this is, as everywhere, a matter of personal preference. Traditionally Spanish people, except for the very wealthy, have tended to scorn older, restored property in favour of new-build. For a long time this left the market open for foreigners to buy up older, rustic homes for a pittance, love them, restore them and live happily ever after. Things, though, have changed. In many areas the Spanish have developed their own interest in older 'character' property while, at the same time, the once-seemingly inexhaustible supply of houses and cottages abandoned as a result of rural depopulation and drought has, in areas like the provinces of Málaga and Alicante, almost run out. Prices have been rising, above all behind the Costa del Sol, and in most places old rural residences, even in need of work, can no longer be found for a song.

New Property

Advantages

- The technical specification and design will be better than in an older property. This is particularly so in areas such as insulation and energy-efficiency.
- It will have been inspected and built to known standards.
- Most people prefer new kitchens, which get more sophisticated each year.
- It will probably have a reasonable heating system.
- Electrical and plumbing installations will be to a superior standard.
- Few people will have used the bathrooms.
- Provision will probably have been made for car parking.
- You may share the cost of expensive common resources such as pools or tennis courts with other people.

- The building will require a lot less maintenance than an older property, certainly for the first few years.

- It should be cheaper to run.

- You can design your own property or, at least, often fine-tune the design to your special requirements.

- The fabric will be guaranteed.

- If you buy 'off plan' you may see some pre-completion growth in value.

Disadvantages

- The building will be new and brash, not mellow.

- It can be hard to envisage what you are going to get from a plan and specification.

- You will have to sort out all the small snags inevitable in any new building.You may spend all your holidays chasing the builder or doing this – difficult if you don't speak Spanish very well.

- You will have to sort out an immature garden.

- You may have to decorate.

- Although technical design may have improved, the aesthetic appeal may be less than that of an older property and the detailed workmanship less rewarding than that of a time when labour was cheap.

- As a rental property most (British) people prefer either a property with close access to golf or entertainment or a villa with a pool.

Older Property

Advantages

- The property has 'character'. Its design may be classically beautiful and the detailed workmanship will probably be superior to today's product.

- The garden will be mature.

- It may occupy a better site than a newer property – on the basis that the best were often built on first.

- It may be a more attractive rental proposition than a new property, especially in rural areas.

- You will feel that you are living in a truly Spanish property.

- What you see is what you get. You turn on the taps, there is water. You can see the room sizes and how the sun lies on the terraces. You can see the views and the distances to adjacent properties.

- It may be cheaper than a comparable new property.

- It will probably have more land than a comparable new property.

Disadvantages

- Older properties can need a lot of maintenance and loving care.
- It will be more expensive to heat and run.
- You may need to spend significant sums on, say, the kitchen and bathrooms to bring the property up to modern standards.
- You may have to sort out an overgrown garden.
- You may have to decorate.

Types of Ownership

There is no such thing as leasehold, ground rent and so on in Spain, except to a certain extent for some commercial properties. Instead, there is only outright (freehold) ownership and renting. There are, however, certain variations or refinements to outright ownership, the most important of which to know about are the *comunidad de propietarios* and the various limited-period ownership schemes such as timeshares.

The *Comunidad de Propietarios*

In Spain, whenever a property shares certain common areas or parts with other adjacent properties – as in the case of an apartment in a block, a villa in an *urbanización* or sometimes even an old terraced house in a village – these common parts are 'co-owned', under a system similar to the American idea of the condominium or the British idea of commonhold. As the buyer of a villa or flat you get outright, freehold ownership of your own property and also shared freehold ownership of – and responsibility for – all the common areas around you, together with your neighbours, in what is known as a *comunidad de propietarios* or 'community of owners'. These common areas include, in an apartment block, the lifts, lobby, stairs and the roof, and in larger developments can run from just a few estate roads and gardens through swimming pools and communal satellite TV systems right up to a marina or golf courses. Whenever you buy a property that shares facilities – which means the great majority on offer, except fully detached villas and *fincas* – you automatically become a member of the relevant *comunidad*. Virtually all holiday home developments form *comunidades de propiedades* in law, and indeed you should never buy in any development that does not have a properly constituted *comunidad*. This is, therefore, by far the most common form of ownership for foreign buyers.

Each *comunidad* has to be registered in the local property registry for each town, and should have a set of statutes (*estatutos*) defining exactly what its common parts are, and which parts are the responsibility of individual homeowners. By law it should also hold at least one general meeting (*asamblea general*) of all the residents each year, and elect one of its members as its president (*presidente*), perhaps assisted by a committee. In small *comunidades*, such as an eight-flat apartment block, the post of *presidente* may be rotated among all the residents, while big developments will usually have a more complicated structure and often employ a professional administrator (*administrador*) or whole office to carry on routine estate management. In mainly foreign-owned *urbanizaciones* this role is often taken on by the development company or an *administrador* is first appointed by the developers on behalf of the *comunidad*, a situation with which many foreign owners are quite happy.

The central purpose of this structure is to ensure that the common parts are maintained, to set the community charges or fees (*gastos de comunidad*) required, and to oversee the spending. Where the properties are not all exactly the same size, the amount you pay within the overall community charge (your personal *cuota*) varies according to the size of your property, the exact percentage being set down in the deeds when you first buy; voting rights in the *comunidad* are weighted according to the same calculation, so that if you have a bigger property you have more clout.

The community *gastos*, set at each year's AGM, can vary a great deal and, when looking at property in any *comunidad*, it is essential to find out their current level; on top of that, you should also ask to see the seller's charge receipts for the previous five or six years, to check whether there have been any big increases, and also the minutes of the last AGM, to see what matters were raised. These documents will normally be kept in Spanish, so ask your lawyer to go through them if necessary (all official community records must be in Spanish, or Catalan in some areas, but translations with equal official status can be requested, and meetings can be held in other languages if every resident accepts it). High community charges can be good value, if a development is well maintained and you get a lot for your money; they cover maintenance of many kinds, such as cleaning, lighting and, in apartment blocks, a buildings insurance policy for the whole block. They can pay the wages of full-time staff, such as a concierge (*portero*) in a block of flats, or gardeners. In modest apartment blocks there is often only a limited regular community charge, with the option of calling a special meeting to arrange a one-off payment whenever any extra expenditure is required, such as repairs to a roof.

For more on the legal details of the *comunidad de propiedad*, *see* pp.171–2. The *comunidad*, though, is much more than just a legal construct: it is also a human institution, one of the inescapable features of modern Spanish life, and swapping tales of goings-on in *comunidad* meetings is as common among Spaniards as passing on stories of soaring house prices and wily estate agents is among Britons. By becoming part of a *comunidad* you quickly get to know your neighbours in a very practical way, whether they are Spanish or foreign. All the quirks of neighbourhood existence turn up in *comunidades*: the people who just love being on committees; those who question the spending of every last euro-cent;

the ones who are just plain uncooperative. As well as administering joint expenses, each *comunidad* also has to agree a written set of rules (*reglamento*) for the community, which in some cases – especially in developments – can be quite comprehensive and restrictive: some *urbanizaciones* have severe rules against noise, making parties out of the question, or rules against pets, or restricting children playing in the street, or even on when you can hang out washing. Some *urbanizaciones* have an ongoing history of feuds and bad relationships, so that meetings are repeatedly taken up with tedious arguments, while in others there are splits between different nationalities. When problems arise it is often, predictably, because of money, when some residents wish to take on an extra expense and others do not. By law, when at least 25 per cent of the members disagree with a majority decision they can go to court to have their interests acknowledged but, since you will all have to live together afterwards, this is obviously a solution of last resort.

When owners are non-resident – as in the case of second-home-owners – they can cede their voting rights in the *comunidad* by proxy, perhaps to the *presidente* or the administrator. This can be another bone of contention in developments where there is a large block of non-resident owners and the permanent residents feel they should have more influence over decisions. Community fees also need to be paid whether you are in residence or not, so a direct debit should be set up to take care of this. In the past there have been serious problems of accumulated debt in *comunidade*s due to avoidance of charges by residents, but the law has recently been tightened to make it much easier for the *presidente* to make an official complaint, go to court and, *in extremis*, have the property seized and sold by auction to clear the debt.

Listing potential problems in this way inevitably highlights the downside of *comunidades*. Many run entirely smoothly, and do not obstruct their residents' lives in any way. They can also be a very friendly and practical way of managing a property, and give you more control than if you were just leasing from a property company.

Timeshares and Other Period-ownership Schemes

Apart from outright ownership, the main alternatives available in Spain are the various schemes that give you access to a property for a set time each year, for an (apparently) much lower cost than normal purchase.

Timeshares

Timeshares remain a very popular way of getting access to holiday property in Spain, especially in the major resort areas. With them you buy the right to occupy a property for a set period each year – often just two weeks – rather than the property itself, for a much lower cost than if you were to buy the property outright, spread over a few years to further soften the blow. As well as the price, another attraction is that most of the responsibilities of home ownership, maintenance and so on are offloaded on to the management company. Timeshares are most frequently available in big developments and apartment and resort complexes. Their popularity remains high, rather perversely, in spite of the fact that the timeshare business is utterly notorious for scams, rip-offs and other disasters. Most of the horror stories about property-buying in Spain are to do with timeshares, and there are far, far more unhappy timeshare-owners than there are freehold buyers who have major problems with their *comunidad de propietarios*.

Because of timeshares' bad reputation, other names are often now used for these schemes, such as 'vacation ownership', 'holiday ownership' or the Spanish *multipropiedad*, but the basic timeshare concept is the same. Many of the problems associated with timeshares stem from the way many of them have been sold. For years one of the features of big Spanish resorts has been the number of touts and *'proppers'* (from propaganda, actually the Spanish word for publicity), nearly always young foreigners, who go round buttonholing every tourist they can find. Kids are given invitations and discount coupons to clubs and bars; couples and anyone older are mostly given initial pitches for time-shares (sometimes disguised behind non-existent prize draws or surveys). Should you take the bait, you will be whisked off, probably the same day, to a 'presentation', usually in an out-of-town restaurant that you can't escape from easily, where in return for a mediocre meal and a drink you will be held semi-captive for an afternoon and given a ferociously intensive sales pitch for the timeshare, with various carrots such as a free extra week included in your first year, until (they hope) you give way and sign up for one. The sales team will almost certainly ask for a hefty deposit, preferably (for them) on your credit card. The scams that have been perpetrated around sales like this are too many and varied to list here, but the Timeshare Consumers' Association website (*see* **www.timeshare.org.uk**) gives a very handy guide to the most common of them. *See also* **www.crimeshare.com**.

The problems of timesharing have also been due to its rather vague status in law, especially in Spain, somewhere between ownership and renting. Because of the number of bad experiences that have occurred, new, semi-standardised laws were introduced in all EU countries in 1998 to regulate the business. Their most important features are that timeshare companies must guarantee that the property is as advertised, that all timeshare buyers have a ten-day cooling-off period after signing up during which they can back out of the deal without forfeiting any money, and that buyers cannot be asked to pay over any deposit larger than the first payment for the timeshare. In Spain, buyers can also demand that their timeshare purchase be registered with a notary and lodged in the local property registry, although there is still no automatic obligation for the vendor to do this as there would be with a freehold sale. Even so, it is in the nature of the trade that some dubious timeshare companies have found ways to get around these laws.

Another point to be held against timeshares is that, in spite of the low up-front cost, they are actually pretty poor value. It's easy to work out why: a two-week annual timeshare slot for several years can easily cost around €15,000, in an apartment which would have a market value of around €100,000. If the developers sell just 15 such slots, their profit is already well over 100 per cent, and the margin is often much higher. On top of this there are also management fees (another scam-ridden area), the equivalent of community charges in a development, but without the control over them that you would have as a freehold owner. In addition, timeshares have very little resale value, and owners who tire of them rarely get back the price they paid for them. If you can get the finance together, it is a far better deal overall to go for an outright buy rather than timeshare.

Nevertheless, thanks to low cost and convenience, timeshares are still a very significant part of the property market, and many people – it should also be said – surmount all the obstacles and are perfectly happy with them. Some of the best timeshare-related schemes are the ones that are a little more expensive, such as those of the big American resort corporations **Resort Condominium** International (**t** 0870 6090 141 in the UK, **www.rci.com**), **Interval International** (**t** 0870 7444 222 in the UK, **www.intervalworld.com**) and **Marriott** (**www.marriott.co.uk**), which give you the option of using your time slot in the company's other resorts around the world rather than always in the same place. A simpler, cheaper but reliable British-based scheme is the **Holiday Property Bond** which, rather than being a strict timeshare, gives you access to a wide variety of properties around the UK and Europe (HPB Management, **t** (01638) 660 066, **www.hpb.co.uk**). If you are interested in Spanish timeshares, a first rule to follow is never to go to any off-the-street presentations but, if you're ever trapped in one, never sign up for anything that day. If the company is serious they should be perfectly happy to let you go and think about it and then call into their office in a day or two. It's also a very good idea to get in touch first with the **Timeshare Consumers' Association** (**t** 01909 591 100, **www.time share.org.uk**), who produce several leaflets and whose website gives an excellent, comprehensive guide to the pitfalls and positives of timeshare-buying. And another important suggestion is to treat timeshares in the same way as you would any other property purchase and get the advice of your own lawyer before taking it on, even though this goes against the bargain-priced, off-the-peg convenience of timesharing that many people find appealing.

Leaseback

Leaseback is a system, found mainly in large mixed developments, golf resorts and so on, through which you buy an apartment or villa at a substantial discount (often around 30–40 per cent), in return for which you agree to occupy it for only a few weeks each year and to 'lease it back' to the developer the rest of the time to be let to holiday tenants. The developer also retains responsibility for maintenance and managing the property. This arrangement lasts for a fixed period (usually around 10 years), after which you gain full, unrestricted ownership like any other buyer in the *comunidad*. You are, however, registered as the freehold owner in the local property registry throughout the life of the agreement, and the full price, not the discount price, is recorded in the registry.

If you are sure that all you want at first is a holiday home, but may want to make more frequent use of it later, and you like the look of a development, then leaseback can be a very efficient way of getting more for your money, and is much better value than timesharing, above all because you have fully established freehold rights to the property. Most leaseback schemes, too, are also much more generous in the amount of time you can use the property – often around six weeks each year – than most timeshares. Note, though, that leaseback is most often available in fairly upmarket *urbanizaciones* rather than the bargain developments that tend to offer timeshares. Also, something that you and your lawyer should look out for when joining a leaseback scheme is that there are not any hidden 'redemption charges' or other fees for getting full possession of your property when the agreement expires.

Co-ownership

Co-ownership refers to any arrangement whereby ownership of a whole property, not just the common parts as in a *comunidad*, is shared between several people, who divide up the amount of time they can each use it each year proportionately. The names of all the individuals involved feature in the property register as the joint owners of the property. Schemes along these lines are offered by quite a few *urbanización* developers, such as the four-owner schemes in which you buy the right to use a property for a quarter of the year, while the developer stays in charge of ongoing management. Be aware, though, that one reason property companies are keen on these schemes is because the price of all four 'shares' will nearly always amount to more than they would have got for the villa if they had sold to a single buyer.

Other co-ownership arrangements are set up entirely privately, by groups of people who, by banding together, can afford to take on a much larger and maybe more spectacular place than they could ever pay for on their own. Arrangements like this often begin when one person sees, for example, a magnificent old Catalan farmhouse, and then gets together as many like-minded friends and relatives as possible to be able to buy and restore it. This can be done before you buy the property or afterwards.

The legal aspects of these arrangements can be a bit complicated but a decent lawyer should be able to sort them out. The financial stakes, and so the share of ownership, need not be equal but could follow, for example, a 30–20–20–10–10–10 per cent split, although the more complicated the breakdown, the more difficult it will be to manage. How well such arrangements work in practice and how 'formal' they need to be depends to a large extent on the personalities and dynamics in each group; it helps if the property is large enough so that several of the 'co-owners' can be there at the same time without getting in each other's way. In developers' co-ownership schemes things can get complicated over the allocation of time slots, since nearly everyone wants part of their quarter-year to be in summer while no one may want to go there in October, and a certain amount of juggling is required. If any co-owners want to sell out of the agreement, the others normally have right of first refusal.

According to how business-minded you are, one efficient way of handling a private co-owned property is to set yourselves up as a Spanish company, which then officially manages the property. Any shareholder who wishes to sell up can then be bought out or sell on their shares in the company to a third party fairly easily, thus lessening the danger that the whole property might need to be split or sold off.

Guide Prices

The ultimate question with any property purchase is, of course, how much – how much you want to spend, how much you can possibly spend, and how much you will have to spend to get something near what you want. As outlined in **Profiles of the Regions**, there are considerable regional differences in Spanish property prices: of the coastal areas, the most expensive are the central Costa del Sol, the central Costa Brava, northern Mallorca and Ibiza; among pockets of relative cheapness are the eastern Costa del Sol and Costa Tropical, the southern Costa Blanca and Murcia, most of Valencia and most of the Canaries. A special feature of the Spanish coast is that in every resort of any size there will be a sizeable number of 1970s–'80s holiday apartments available for under €75,000, making up the cheapest block of properties on the market, but these are not always very attractive places. Everywhere you go around the coast, purpose-built apartments and development villas will almost invariably be cheaper than comparable detached properties, but often more expensive than conventional flats built for the local market. As in any part of the world, you will pay a good deal more for a special location, and above all for beach frontage and/or sea view; buying inland, around the *costa*s, means paying less.

However, one peculiarity of the property market around the Spanish coasts and countryside is that, owing to the sheer amount of property available, it is oddly unpredictable, and you can still find inexplicably large price variations even in the same highly prized area. If you like an area it's always worth a little investigation. Price levels are particularly erratic for properties that are in need of restoration or at least some work to bring them up to scratch, so that you can often turn up very pleasant surprises.

On top of the prices listed here and quoted to you by agents, you will also have to pay the transaction charges needed to complete the purchase (notaries' fees, taxes and so on), which in Spain are quite high, amounting to around ten per cent of the purchase price. For a breakdown of these, *see* **Making the Purchase**, pp.182–3.

Remember, also, that in addition to local inconsistencies, in any volatile property market, as currently exists in Spain and the UK, average price levels can shift very quickly. Hence those listed here are very approximate, and should only be taken as guidelines. They were all found during Internet research for this book, and are, if they have not yet been sold, real properties on sale.

Under €30,000

• Tiny house situated in the centre of Lanjarón, needs a complete makeover; two bedrooms, one bathroom, one toilet, 45 square metres of living space.

Under €80,000

• Five-bedroom village house in need of some work, one bathroom and two toilets; Lanjarón (Granada province, Alpujarra mountains).

• Small country house in peaceful setting with possibility to extend; large plot of land to one side included in price; two bedrooms, one bathroom, living area 85 square metres, plot 7,000 square metres; Irixoa, province of A Coruña (Galicia).

€80,000–100,000

• First-floor apartment with lift, two bedrooms, one bathroom, American kitchen, lounge/diner, south-facing balcony; living area 55 square metres in Torrevieja (Alicante).

• Two-bedroom top floor apartment (three floors) with lounge, American style kitchen and bathroom. Large balcony with spiral staircase leading to roof terrace. 46 square metres of living space, in Arona, Tenerife.

• Two-bedroom apartment with balcony and communal swimming pool in Torrevieja (Alicante).

€100,000–120,000

• Three-bedroom, one bathroom traditional village house in Cabo de Gata (Almería); in need of some work but structurally sound.

• Three-bedroom upstairs apartment with one bathroom, fully furnished, large solarium, phone, communal pool, close to all amenities; Málaga city.

• Townhouse, 120 square metres in the heart of Órgiva town (Granada province, in the Alpujarra mountains), close to all amenities; three bedrooms, one bathroom.

• Two-bedroom bungalow apartment with lounge and one bathroom in Peñíscola, province of Castellón. Terraces with views of castle and sea.

€120,000–140,000

• Brand new, two-bedroom apartment with two bathrooms; totally furnished kitchen equipped with linen goods; video entryphone; pre-installation for air-conditioning; sauna for two people. Chimney, garden. Living area, 58 square metres. Mojácar (Almería).

• Restored traditional stone house with two further properties to be restored. The restored house has three bedrooms, one bathroom and 150 square metres of living space, all with good quality finishing. The remaining plot 8,100 square metres) has a lot of potential. Pontedeume (A Coruña).

• Two-bedroom, one bathroom apartment, 800 metres from the beach, shops, cafés, bars and other amenities within minutes walking distance. Alcúdia (Mallorca).

• Two-bedroom apartment with large terrace plus communal pool and garden area. Sea and mountain views. Living area, 70 square metres. Peñíscola (Castellón).

€140,000–150,000

• Two-bedroom apartment, 85 square metres of living space. Close to golf course, partly furnished, fitted kitchen, parking space included. Communal pool and garden. Jávea/Xàbia (Alicante).

• Apartment with three bedrooms plus two bathrooms and extra toilet, in third line from beach front. Good condition, living area 75 square metres. Playa de Gandia (Valencia).

• Apartment, 100 square metres, with three bedrooms, large lounge, bathroom and fitted kitchen. 100 metre walk from Velilla Beach, Almuñécar (Granada).

• Townhouse with seven bedrooms and two bathrooms, renovated. Órgiva (Granada, Alpujarra mountains).

€150,000–165,000

• Two-bedroom apartment with one bathroom in Cortijo Torreblanca, a private closed residential complex with gardens and pool; Fuengirola (Málaga).

€180,000–200,000

• Traditional townhouse, with 120 square metres of living space, two bedrooms and two bathrooms, located in the village of Benitachell, close to Jávea/Xàbia (Alicante).

• Duplex apartment with garden and sea views, parking space included. Ground floor terrace with garden, rear terrace, two bedrooms, one bathroom. Master bedroom leads on to terrace. Total living area, 60 square metres. Peníscola (Castellón).

• Three-bedroom, two bathroom apartment overlooking the 18th hole of a golf course, two minutes walk to the beach. Resale property, partly furnished, ready to live in. Mojácar (Almería).

• Brand new two-bedroom apartment with living room, large terrace, sea and mountain views, fitted kitchen. Living area, 60 square metres. Torreblanca (Fuengirola).

€200,000–240,000

• Large corner village house, no decorating necessary. Ground floor has entrance hall leading to lounge/dining room with fireplace and kitchen. Six bedrooms, two bathrooms. Gandia (Valencia).

• End of terrace bungalow on golf resort. Close to amenities and sports facilities. Two bedrooms, one bathroom, one extra toilet. Living area 60 square metres. Jávea/Xàbia (Alicante).

• Family duplex, four bedrooms, two bathrooms, two extra toilets. Utility room, lounge with fireplace, fitted kitchen. Living area 170 square metres. Puerto de Mazarrón (Murcia)

• Beachside house, furnished, with fitted kitchen three bedrooms and two bathrooms. Off-road parking, communal pools, pleasant views. Built in alarm system. Jávea/Xàbia (Alicante).

€240,000–275,000

• Country house, 100 square metres, three bedrooms, one bathroom, one toilet, barbeque area garden on 1,960 square metre plot. Shares a well with others. Solar power installed, swimming pool. Es Castell (Menorca).

• Renovated apartment, living area 78 square metres, three bedrooms (two doubles), one bathroom. Sitges (Barcelona).

• Two-bedroom duplex apartment with sea view, two minutes' walk to beach. Upper level has entrance hall, master bedroom with balcony. Living area on lower level. Palmanova (Mallorca).

• Townhouse with three bedrooms, one bathroom, private rear terrace, living room with fireplace, air conditioning in all bedrooms. Living area 100 square metres. Quiet area. Mojácar (Almería).

€275,000–300,000

• Renovated town house in Pollensa (Mallorca). Ground floor with small living room, kitchen/dining area, and patio, work room and toilet. Two bedrooms with en-suite bathrooms on first floor; main bedroom opens on to a balcony.

• Duplex apartment in exclusive area, two bedrooms, two bathrooms, views over sea to Africa. Living area, 90 square metres. Marbella (Málaga).

€300,000–325,000

• Townhouse, four bedrooms, two bathrooms, ample living area, patio and roof terrace with views over town, port and sea. Renovated, living area 230 square metres. Andratx (Mallorca).

• Apartment, 80 square metres, totally refurbished, three bedrooms (two doubles), one bathroom. Sitges (Barcelona).

• Country house, with 235 square metres of living space on a plot of over 1,000 square metres with fruit orchard and views. Five bedrooms, one bathroom, barbecue area and splash pool outside. Twenty minutes' drive to Palma. Sineu (Mallorca).

€350,000–400,000

• Large country house with sea views. Three bedrooms in the house plus flat with two bedrooms, three bathrooms in total, living area 175 square metres on a plot of 2,000 square metres. El Perelló (Tarragona).

• Town house with commercial local on ground floor. Three bedrooms, two bathrooms, one extra toilet. Living area 350 square metres, on a plot of 160 square metres. Mazarrón (Murcia).

• Restored townhouse, two floors, four bedrooms, two bathrooms, terrace, basement and garage for two cars. Living area 210 square metres. Mahón (Menorca).

• Waterside property with a freehold 9 x 4 meter mooring. Six bedrooms, three bathrooms, three extra toilets. Living area 180 square metres. Empuriabrava (Girona).

• Rustic villa with six bedrooms, four bathrooms, mostly furnished. Living area 297 square metres, plot 465 square metres. Arona (Tenerife).

€400,000–500,000

• Large four-bedroom villa with pool and spectacular views above the coast near Mijas, Costa del Sol.

• Three-bedroom villa with pool, near Pals, central Costa Brava.

€500,000–600,000

• *Masia* on 3.5 hectares of land with private pine forest, swimming pool, pond and cave. Six bedrooms, two bathrooms, two extra toilets. L'Ametlla de Mar (Tarragona).

• Converted windmill on 10,000 square metre plot of land with approximately 380 square metres of living space, more available if further renovation work done (mill tower and stable still to be converted). Five bedrooms and two bathrooms in main house. Close to Felanitx (Mallorca).

• Modern country villa with three double bedrooms, plus master bedroom with en-suite bathroom plus three bathrooms. On a 3,000 square metre plot. Santa Cristina d'Aro (Girona).

€750,000–1,000,000

• Private hill villa overlooking the bay of Cala Llonga. Four bedrooms and bathrooms, numerous terraces, large pool. Santa Eulalia (Ibiza).

• Large house (250 square metres) on 18,000 square metre plot. Three bedrooms, two bathrooms, one shower room, swimming pool. Close to harbour in Mahón. Es Castell (Menorca).

• Large and amply modernised townhouse with distinctive features, Gaucín, Serranía de Ronda.

• Large converted *cortijo* farmhouse with original features and courtyard, outside Alhaurín, Sierra de Mijas, Costa del Sol.

• Very large, architect-designed hilltop villa with large pool, near Costa del Sol.

€1,000,000 and upwards

• Three-bedroom (each with en-suite bathroom) beachfront villa with huge living/dining area, fitted kitchen, laundry room, spacious terraces, swimming pool and separate guest accommodation. Close to Pollensa (Mallorca).

• *Masia*, 400 square metres of living space plus separate 85 square metre guesthouse. Four bedrooms, three bathrooms pluas extra toilet. Sant Feliu de Guíxols (Girona).

• Multi-room villas with pool, gardens and many other features around Marbella.

• Very large, secluded villa in extensive garden with many extras, near Mijas.

• Seven-bedroom converted *masia* with pool, outside Girona, Catalonia.

• Multi-room villas in own grounds near Deia, northern Mallorca.

• *Finca*/country house. Main house: three double bedrooms, kitchen, fireplace with mantelpiece, living room, TV room, three bathrooms, rooftop terrace. Separate guest area with two bedrooms and bathrooms. Total living area, 690 square metres on a 15,000 metre plot. Sant Antoni de Portmany (Ibiza).

Research and Information Sources

When you first begin thinking about a future home in Spain, whittling down choices and defining your preferences, there are a great many sources of information available to you in the UK and Ireland. So big is the Spanish holiday-home-buying business these days that all the agencies and companies dealing in Spanish properties are almost impossible to list or pin down. The main information sources accessible 'at a distance' divide into three – press, exhibitions and the Internet. With them it will always be far easier to find out about purpose-built developments and holiday homes – above all on the Costa del Sol and the Costa Blanca, overwhelmingly the main focus of most UK-based companies dealing in Spanish property – than about more individual, out-of-the-way locations but, with some searching, useful pointers towards these kinds of places can be found. If you are interested in properties outside the 'holiday development belt', you should get used to looking for information from local Spanish agents, many of which will have their own websites.

Press Sources

The travel supplements of daily and especially the Sunday broadsheet papers such as the *Sunday Times* can be a good place to start, since they carry articles on buying abroad and property ads with increasing frequency. The biggest range of informative articles and useful advertising, though, will be found in the specialist magazines, of which the most important available in the UK and Ireland are:

- *Homes Overseas* (**t** (020) 7939 9888, **www.homesoverseas.co.uk**). The leading publication in the field; a lively, attractively produced monthly that covers the whole world, but always has many Spain-related features and advertising in each issue. Widely available, and a useful reference point.

- *International Homes* (**t** (01245) 358877, **www.international-homes.com**). Smart, glossy magazine, often featuring spectacular properties.

- *Living Spain* (**t** (01234) 710992, **www.livingspain.co.uk**). New magazine published bimonthly, sister publication to Living France.

- *Spain* (**t** (0131) 226 7766, **www.spainmagazine.info**). Informative, glossy monthly with articles on all aspects of living in Spain and, in every issue, property features, advice and advertising. Good for leads on non-development properties.

- *Spanish Homes Magazine*, formerly known as *Spanish Property News* (**t** (020) 8469 4381, **www.spanishhomesmagazine.com**). A useful, quite simply produced magazine that covers every end of the market and carries a wide range of advertising.

- **World of Property** (t (01323) 726040, **www.outboundpublishing.com**). Another of the long-established magazines in the field, dealing with the whole world but always with features, tips and ads on Spain. Published every two months.

Once you get to Spain, a great many more English-language publications are available. Many are sponsored by property companies, and the large property agents also often produce their own brochures in a magazine-style glossy format, but they can all give useful leads. The expat- and property-sales-orientated press in English, like the British-orientated Spanish property trade in general, is disproportionately centred on the Costa del Sol. Other areas have their own publications, but they tend to be fewer and less glossy.

English-language magazines can be found in the main tourist areas on news-stands and in the many English-language bookshops, or, if they are free sheets, in many estate agents' offices, tourist offices, bars and other businesses. In any of the main resorts and expat centres they are quite easy to find, but elsewhere distribution is patchy, so it's best to pick them up whenever you see them.

The main English-language publications with more or less 'Spain-wide' distribution are:

- **The Broadsheet**. Free monthly magazine in English, based in Madrid but also distributed on the Costa del Sol, Costa Blanca and some other areas. Useful range of ads, from estate agencies and removal companies to classifieds.

- **Lookout**. Long-running Costa del Sol-based free magazine for the expat community, with features on many areas of living in Spain, and a lot of advertising.

- **Villas**. Glossy magazine on luxury living in Spain. Good for finding that special place, if you can afford it.

The most prominent local magazines and papers to look for are these, but there are several more mostly glossy publications available, especially on the Costa del Sol. All of them carry a big range of property advertising, and features.

- **123Property News** (**www.123propertynews.com**). Very useful advertising-led free sheet featuring a wide range of properties all around the Costa del Sol, and an enterprising range of articles. Also has an informative website, with loads of local links.

- **Absolute Marbella**. As the name suggests, a self-consciously glossy, upscale magazine advertising some of the Costa del Sol's most opulent properties.

- **Costa Blanca Weekly Post**. Straightforward weekly paper in English, with classifieds.

- **Costa del Sol News**. The same for the Costa del Sol, and also weekly.

- *Majorca Daily Bulletin*. The Balearics' main English-language paper.
- *Real(i)ty News*. All-property magazine based in Marbella.
- *Tenerife News*. Another English-language local paper, with small ads.

Property Exhibitions

Property exhibitions have grown in popularity as rapidly as has foreign-property buying in general. The most important are those run in association with the main international property magazines, *Homes Overseas* and *World of Property*, but there are many more hosted by other companies all around the UK and Ireland throughout the year. Exhibitions enable prospective buyers to make contact with, and get a first look at the wares of, a wide range of people and companies working in the field – specialist lawyers, financial advisers and, of course, a great many estate agents and developers – all under one roof and in the course of a few hours. Note, though, that the agents and developers who exhibit at property shows on Spain in the UK deal overwhelmingly with the mainstream market, with development properties and similar purpose-built homes in the main tourist areas. A few of the regular exhibitors do handle individual properties but, in general, anyone looking for more unusual and off-the-beaten-track properties will not find many of them here, although you may pick up some leads.

The main exhibition organisers are listed here; others advertise in national papers and the property magazines. A smallish admission fee is usually charged.

- **Evening Standard Homebuyer Show (t** (020) 8877 3636, **www.homebuyer. co.uk**). Large-scale, high-profile shows held in the London area, mainly dedicated to local property matters but with a fast-growing international section.

- **Homes Overseas (t** (020) 7939 9852, **www.blendoncommunications.co.uk**). The largest international property exhibition organisers, running some 10–15 exhibitions each year in venues around Britain and Ireland.

- **International Property Show (t** (01962) 736712, **www.internationalproperty show.com**). Hosts several shows each year in London, Manchester, Bristol and other centres.

- **Spain on Show (t** (0500) 780878, **www.spainonshow.com**). Spain-only exhibitions in venues around Britain, with around three shows each month for most of the year.

- **World Class Homes (t** (0800) 731 4713, **www.worldclasshomes.co.uk**). An international agency that presents its own exhibitions – rather than letting space to others – in smallish venues throughout Britain, all year round.

- **World of Property** (t 01323 745130, **www.outboundpublishing.com**). The publishers of the magazine present at least three large exhibitions each year, normally two in southern England and one in the north.

The Internet

The amount of Spanish property information now available online is, of course, huge. As well as all the magazines and organisations listed above, virtually every property agency and developer now has its own website. Listed here are some sites that can be particularly useful (for Andalucía, also try the 123 *Property News* site, *see* p.128), and which you may not come across easily without being directed towards them, but any search combining 'property' with 'Costa del Sol', 'Mallorca' or any other area will turn up many more. It's always best to look under a specific area, to make the search a bit easier to handle. Once you've been through English-language sites for your preferred location(s), be sure to look under the Spanish ones, where you may well find the best bargains (*inmobiliaria* is the best word to look under for property). Remember, though, that, as with most things except books and air tickets, it is never a good idea to buy or commit yourself to anything over the Internet. It should be used for information-gathering and making initial contacts only. The sites that follow are only an infinitesimally small percentage of those that are out there!

- **www.buyaspanishhome.com**. English-language site run in association with a nationwide Spanish estate agency, Fincas Corral, offering a very wide range of properties in Spain's main cities and all around the coasts, and also a page for private ads.

- **www.countrylife.co.uk/international**. The international page of *Country Life*'s website is one of the top places to find leads to luxury properties in Spain, and agencies that deal in them.

- **www.segundamano.es**. The magazine *Segunda Mano* is a bit like a modern Spanish version of *Exchange & Mart*, with local editions in most parts of the country. As well as ads selling most things it has a large property section, for sales and rentals, much of which is also on its excellent website. Click on *inmobiliaria* for property, choose a region, and then *ventas* for sales. There are ads from both agencies and private sellers, and you can find real bargains. In Spanish only.

- **www.spanish-property-in-spain.com**. Despite the name, this site mainly deals with the Costa del Sol, but it carries a wide range of properties.

- **www.vivendum.com**. The website of the *Guía Inmobiliaria*, an information service for Spanish estate agents, with address details or – in most cases – links to the websites of a huge number of local agencies in every part of the country. Some have English translations. A great help if you're looking to live outside the 'tourist belt'.

- **www.thinkspain.com**. A useful site which allows you to search for properties and whittle your search down by region, province, town, type, size and maximum/minimum price. Good Spain-centred news and articles too.

- **www.spanishpropertyco.com**. A site designed for and by expats. They do sell property themselves but have a lot of useful information for the general public.

Lawyers and How to Use Them

As has already been touched on several times in this book, one of the basics of buying a property in Spain is that you should always have the advice of your own independent lawyer with proper experience in Spanish law throughout the purchasing process, rather than just bringing one in towards the end to formalise the sale after you have found and decided on the property all by yourselves, as you might if you were buying in the UK. One reason for this is that there will be so many unfamiliar areas of law, tax and so on related to the purchase that you will be much clearer about what you are doing if you can consult regularly with your lawyer as you go along. Beyond this, there are certain specific features of some common types of Spanish properties that make it very important to have the input of your lawyer while you are still choosing your new home, rather than after you have spent hours trying to make your mind up about it.

Some local estate agents may tell you that you do not need to use a lawyer, because the services of the local *notario* (notary public) will be sufficient, as they would be for most Spanish buyers. This, though, is a false economy for foreign purchasers, for there will be many issues on which you need guidance that it is no part of the notary's duty to provide. Also, a Spanish notary will usually know nothing about UK law and so will be unable to give you any help with such vital issues as making the best arrangements to avoid being caught between different Spanish and UK tax systems. Again, your own lawyer experienced in the field is essential. For more on the role of the notary, *see* 'The Notary Public', pp.167–8.

One reason for working with a lawyer throughout is related above all to development properties, and especially older ones. During the great Spanish tourist boom from the 1960s to the 1980s, and in some cases even recently, *urbanización* developers quite commonly played fast and loose with the already inadequate planning laws, building villa complexes without any legal permits, getting planning permission for 20 villas and then building 100, building villas on land zoned for conservation and so on. Over the last 25 years, municipal councils around the country have struggled to make sense of this situation, not infrequently with sweeping penalties, fines, dispossessions and similar measures, going as far as demolition with minimal or no compensation in some cases. Some of the most dramatic Spanish property 'horror stories' have occurred when innocent and uncomprehending foreign buyers have been caught in the middle, in tangles of litigation that drag on for years. In some cases, councils have adopted a policy of reversing the uncontrolled over-building of early years and decreed that whole developments should be returned to open woodland, in the process effectively penalising the foreign buyer more than the developer who built the villas or apartments illegally in the first place. This is far less likely with any development initiated after 1985, but your lawyer should at least check whether a development has any history of legal disputes or problems with the local authorities, and give a summary of its current planning status, and should be able to advise you on the general atti-tude of any particular local council on these issues. In addition, the internal rules of any *comunidad de propietarios* can be a complicated document, and you should show a copy of it to your lawyer and get his or her advice while you are deciding on whether you want the property.

A second area in which a lawyer's input is especially important is in relation to rural properties of all kinds with land attached. Rural properties in Spain are often subject to a wide range of local and customary laws and rights – from foot-path rights and grazing rights for local farmers and their sheep to more problematic matters such as hunting rights (very important in the Spanish coun-tryside) and prohibitions on new building or any change of use – of which, as a foreigner, you'll probably be totally unaware. Rural properties quite frequently also have disputed boundaries. Your lawyer should check these matters over carefully and inform you of just what accumulated strings any *finca* may come with. In particular, most buyers of rural properties would like at least the possi-bility of building a swimming pool. As a first step, your lawyer should make sure there are no local or legal blockages to you doing so, and that the local council does not have a history of refusing planning permission for pools.

All these considerations make a good, ongoing relationship with your lawyer so important. For more on working with your lawyer, and all the questions they should clarify for you in the course of your purchase, *see* **Making the Purchase**.

Estate Agents and How to Use Them

Most, by far, of British and Irish people who buy property in Spain do so through estate agents – called *agentes de fincas* or *agentes de propiedad inmo-biliaria* in Spain, although the most common signs to look for on agency offices are just *Fincas* or *Inmobiliaria* followed by the company name (*finca* can refer to any property as well as more specifically to rural land). With Spanish property sales being such a huge business nowadays, they come in all guises but, very roughly, they can be divided into three main types, although all of them blend into each other: large-scale development and property sales companies that specialise in holiday-home and foreign sales; Spanish-based estate agencies (which themselves run the gamut from national chains to one-office local operations); and a range of smaller-scale foreign-run agencies and operations, based in Spain or abroad, that deal in property in different ways. Each of them offers different levels of service.

The role of an estate agent in Spain is similar to that in the UK – their basic job is to find buyers for properties entrusted to them by a seller. Beyond that there are, though, significant differences. Most agents in Spain offer a more comprehensive service than just finding a property. The big holiday-property companies in particular pride themselves on giving an at-your-convenience service that can take care of every aspect of a purchase for foreign buyers, with their own staff available to look after all the ancillary questions such as arranging a mortgage, tax or residency status (for a proportionate cost). Even local agencies without such lavish resources will be willing to offer advice on the various associated legal and bureaucratic matters as well as the purchase itself and, while they may not have their own staff to deal with them, they will have a network of connections that they can either contact directly on your behalf, or point you in the direction of and let you deal with them yourself, with the aid of the agent's personal recommendation of course. Nearly all will be able to recommend a local lawyer, if you haven't got one already, but it is always better to find one for yourself first, and one who is used to dealing with both Spanish and British law.

The big international companies are the ones that advertise most frequently in the property press, and which you are most likely to find at exhibitions – among the largest are **Viva Estates (www.vivaestates.com)**, based on the Costa del Sol, **Interealty (www.interealtynet.com)**, with offices all around the coast and the Canaries, and **Superior Real Estate (www.4avilla.com)**. Most of them will also be ready to assist you with your travelling plans to Spain to view properties, on 'inspection tours', sometimes throwing in such things as free car hire and/or accommodation. Many offer to take care of managing and letting your property whenever you are not in residence, and may provide a complete after-sales service that can include supplying furniture and fixtures, electrical appliances, gardening, car purchase and hire and even information on schooling and other such matters. According to what you want – whether, for example, you are interested first and foremost in development properties and villas in the main tourist areas – this can be a very pain-free way of buying; the drawback can be that, once you have signed up with an agency, you are pressured to choose only from their stock of properties, so it's best to avoid those companies that deal only with a set, limited number of developments. A few big agencies – most notably Viva – deal with many individual properties as well as developments, and so give you more options.

At the other end of the scale, local Spanish agents may seem to you to be less 'proactive' and organised than they would be in Britain, especially in nontouristy rural areas. They are much less likely to have printed particulars or photographs available that you can take away and mull over; on the other hand, they will probably be more thorough and punctilious than you are used to in showing you round a set of properties, and maybe introducing you to the sellers. Finding a good local *agente de fincas* is invaluable, above all if you are looking for out-of-the-way properties: they can be a mine of useful information, knowledge of the area and practical help. The great majority will be genuinely enthusiastic about their region, and about your joining their community. Local agents, as much as the big companies, will also usually be willing to help in managing and letting your property if you only use it as a second home. The best way of all to proceed, in any area, is to find an agent – or maybe a few – in your preferred region and with whom you feel comfortable, build up a relationship and try to work closely with them, explaining what you're hoping to find and listening to their ideas as to how you might adjust your plans as you go along. Personal relationships help things along in most parts of the world, and especially in rural Spain.

However, whichever agent you use and wherever they are based, do remember that they are being paid by the seller to sell the property, not by you to look after your interests. However helpful and professional they may be, in the last resort they have to get contracts signed to receive their commission; they have their own interests to look after, which broadly coincide with those of the sellers but might not coincide with yours. Hence, the rule is to take advantage of what they have to offer, form a rapport with them, buy a property through them, but get everything checked by your legal adviser, just as you would in the UK.

In the Spanish property market, it is not always the seller who pays the estate agent's commission. This is the most common practice, especially in tourist areas, but there are local variations in different towns and regions. In some places, paying the commission actually falls to the buyer, while in others they might be expected to contribute half. Be clear when you are looking at property whether the price mentioned includes or excludes these fees; this is particularly important, as fees are usually between 5 and 15 per cent of the price. Cheaper properties generally carry a higher percentage commission than more expensive ones, and properties in main tourist areas tend to carry more commission than those in less sought-after areas. In some cases, in order to protect his commission, an agent may ask you to sign a document before he takes you to see a property. This does not necessarily mean that you will have to pay anything, but is a statement that it is he who has introduced you to the property, so avoiding later arguments about who should be paid the commission due.

One last general tip: if you are going around properties on your own, and meeting up with agents en route, take a mobile phone. Rural *fincas* and modern developments can all be exasperatingly hard to find if you're unfamiliar with the territory and don't have very complete directions.

Spanish Agents and Professional Qualifications

A notable difference between estate agents in the UK and in Spain is that, in Britain, a person can be a plumber today and, without any qualifications or experience of any kind, set up an estate agency tomorrow. It has not traditionally been so in Spain. There, in order to practise as an estate agent, until very recently you were officially obliged to be professionally qualified and hold a licence to practise. While in part this reflected Spanish officialdom's traditional liking for certificates and red tape it has also been, as anyone can appreciate, a very useful consumer protection measure.

There are two recognised professional bodies for estate agents in Spain, membership of which should ensure a professional service. One is the nationwide **Gestores Intermediarios en Promociones de Edificaciones** or **GIPE**, which is the only organisation with direct links to the Confédération Européenne de l'Immobilier (CEI), through whose website (**www.web-cei.com/gipe**) you can find a listing of GIPE members in Spain. The other association is the older and much larger **Agentes de la Propiedad Inmobiliaria** or **API**, of which there is a different *colegio oficial* for each province. Until 2000, only estate agents associated with one or other of these two bodies could be licensed to practise, and they in turn only gave membership to agents with professional qualifications. However, these regulations were often abused in practice – in resort areas, especially, there were always plenty of 'cowboy operations' about – and new laws that were passed at that time to liberalise the property market also removed the obligation to be a member of a professional association and so, by extension, to have relevant qualifications to trade in property.

This has, of course, opened up the profession to a much wider range of people, as in the UK, and inevitably some are far less reliable than others, if not best avoided entirely. It is still very important, therefore, to choose a Spanish agent who is a registered member of either API or GIPE (most of the large-scale property companies also have fully qualified Spanish agents on their staff). These initials and the registration number are usually clearly identified in all promotional material for such agents, who should also have their licence on display in their offices and give details of their licence and the liability insurance and bond they have in all correspondence and contracts (if you are dealing with an agency by phone, fax or e-mail, they should not take offence if you ask for proof of registration). In addition, you should enquire as to who actually holds the API or GIPE licence in the agency – it may be just the proprietor, in which case you should insist that he deal with your business and not an unqualified junior. Hence, it's also important to call ahead and make an appointment, rather than just drop in to the office, to make sure that you meet a qualified member of the staff, and to establish a professional relationship. Another useful plus is if the agent has access to a multi-listings network, thus allowing you to see a wider choice of properties and reducing the need to deal with many different agents.

Most local and rural agencies cover an area about 40km (25 miles) in diameter, and there are a great many throughout the country. Apart from just walking around for a while in a town near where you want to house-hunt, other ways of finding them are through local papers, the local *Yellow Pages* (under *Agentes Inmobiliarias*) or through the GIPE or the provincial API, which will also be in the phone book (possibly under *Colegio Oficial* rather than *Agentes*). *Yellow Pages* for some popular places in Spain, such as Málaga and Alicante, can quite often be found in public libraries in the UK. Many provincial APIs, but not, so far, any central body, also have their own websites. Other great sources of online information, that cover the less-obvious parts of Spain as well as tourist spots, are the 'noticeboard' websites for Spanish local agencies listed earlier.

UK-based Estate Agents, and Foreign Agents Operating in Spain

As well as Spanish agents and the big property companies there is a growing number of smaller-scale operations based in the UK that sell Spanish property, foreigners who work in the property field in Spain, and people who go back and forth between the two. Many advertise regularly in the international property magazines, and most of the popular regions are covered. Although, under English law, they are entitled to call themselves estate agents, it is worth remembering that in the great majority of cases these 'foreigners selling to foreigners' in Spain are not licensed Spanish estate agents. Some have fully established offices and a solid infrastructure behind them, while at the other end of the scale there are quite a few people running property businesses from their own villas with just a phone, website and a set of personal contacts.

Small-scale foreign property agents often work in association with one or more Spanish agents, generally covering a wider area than a single Spanish agent would. They advertise or market the properties through exhibitions, magazines and so on, and then act as the intermediary between potential buyers and the Spanish agent (who may not speak English). Because they deal with British and foreign buyers all the time, they should be able to anticipate some of the common problems that arise, and smooth the progress of the sale. In most cases they should share the commission of the Spanish agent – who is usually very pleased that he can expand his potential buyer base. Thus the services of the foreign intermediary should cost you, as the buyer, nothing extra.

People like this can be very useful, particularly if you have little experience of dealing with Spain and don't speak Spanish. Even though they may not be entirely 'legitimate' property agents in Spanish terms, some of them are excellent, skilled people who offer a service at least as good as that of many fully licensed local agents. Unfortunately, though, this is not the end of the story, as there are also some who operate a range of sharp practices that in some cases amount to scams, exploiting the tendency of foreign buyers to feel safer with someone from home rather than dealing with Spanish agents direct. Some charge substantial extra commissions for their services, a fact which is often not disclosed to the buyer. There is nothing wrong with paying some commission to someone who is doing a useful job, but you should be told that you are expected to do so, so that you can then decide whether the convenience of dealing with someone in the UK is worth the extra cost. When dealing with agents in this way, always ask for confirmation that the price you will be paying is exactly the same as you would have paid in Spain, or, if there is an extra charge, how much it is.

Some UK-based agents advertise their prices as a global fee that includes the price of the property, tax, notary's fees and all commissions. This can simplify things very helpfully for British buyers unused to big foreign transactions, but can also, when manipulated, be a way of masking large chunks of hidden commission. Say, for example, that Señor Martínez has agreed to sell his apartment for €50,000; commission has been agreed at 5 per cent (€2,500), while notaries' fees and taxes may amount to another 8 per cent (€4,000). An all-inclusive price to the buyer of €60,000 therefore adds a hidden extra charge of €3,500. If you are offered property on this basis, always ask for a breakdown of what the price includes.

Many of these UK-based sellers are highly experienced and very reputable. Before deciding which to use ask about their level of experience. It is more difficult to assess whether they are reputable. A good starting point is to see whether they are members of the **Federation of Overseas Property Developers, Agents and Consultants** (**FOPDAC**; **t** (020) 8744 2362). This is a non-profit organisation that agents and developers can join if they are experienced in the field, and are prepared to be scrutinised and abide by its code of conduct. The website lists member companies working in specific countries.

Looking for Yourself – Private Sales

It is far more common in Spain for property to be sold privately, 'person to person', than it is in the UK, especially in big cities and in the countryside. Depending on the area, private sales can amount to between 10 and 20 per cent of all property transactions. Provided you have the help and advice of your lawyer behind you, there is no reason to shy away from them. Cutting out agents and property companies will, of course, save a significant amount of money and, if you have found the property you want, don't want to look any further and have hit on an amenable vendor, will also probably allow your deal to go ahead quite a bit faster.

There is a variety of ways to find out about properties available for private sale. First of all, wherever you go in Spain, in the entrance halls of city apartment blocks or at the end of farm tracks, you will see a wide assortment of DIY for-sale signs (with the words *se vende* or *en venta*), nearly always with a contact phone number. To take advantage of property offered in this way you obviously have to be in the area, and will probably need to speak at least some Spanish. Even if you can't carry on much of a conversation in Spanish, though, it's still worth a trial phone call; if the person who answers does not speak English, there may be a local English-speaker – perhaps in your hotel – who can make contact on your behalf. With rural properties you can often just walk up and knock on the door but, if a phone number is given, it's best to call first, and the chances of finding any English-speakers are wholly unpredictable. As a last resort you can phone your lawyer, who should be able to find out the necessary details for you and, if you wish, make arrangements to view. He will charge for this but the saving on estate agents' fees will still work out to your advantage.

Local newspapers (which in Madrid and Barcelona include the local editions of national papers like *El País*) also carry lots of property ads in their classified sections, especially, in most cities, on Sundays. Most will have been placed by agencies, but there will be plenty from private sellers too. Another very good place to find private sales ads placed by Spanish owners is the free advertising magazine *Segundamano*, which has editions in many parts of the country, and a good website (*see* 'The Internet', pp.130–31). Again, you will have to phone to make contact with the vendors. Local English-language papers also carry plenty of property ads, but beware of anyone advertising in this way who suggests a friendly Brit-to-Brit sale cutting out some of the Spanish formalities – there have been reports of property sharks working a variety of scams on other foreigners by this means, especially on the Costa del Sol. It is surprisingly common for people in the big expat clusters to think that they can agree property sales 'between themselves', ignoring most or all of the Spanish legal obligations, failing to register proper title and so on, without storing up big problems for themselves in the future. Even leaving aside the types who make a living out of exploiting this sort of naïve chumminess, this is absolutely to be avoided. Get a lawyer and do things by the book.

Buying at Auction

Property in Spain can be bought at auction, just as in the UK. Some auctions are voluntary, while others are run by court order following compulsory repossession. Low prices can make them very attractive – a few years ago, during Spain's last major recession, it was possible to find incredible bargains at auctions, with prices equivalent to only 30 per cent of normal market value. Today auctions no longer offer such spectacular discounts, but the prospect of getting large properties at prices well below the local norm still draws many buyers. Prices are so low primarily because, in judicial auctions in particular, the process is intended first and foremost to recover debts of various kinds, and once these and the costs have been covered there is little reason for auctioneers to press for a higher price.

Buying property at an auction is not simple for non-locals, and if you are interested in trying it out it is vitally important that you have taken all the normal preparatory steps – including seeing a lawyer – before you embark on the process. Auctions are usually advertised six to eight weeks in advance: auctions ordered by the court will be officially announced in local papers and notices posted in the area, while non-judicial auctions will just be advertised in the press. Brief details of properties to be sold are published, but these are often very uninformative. To make any preliminary decisions you will need to inspect the property and decide whether it is of interest, a time-consuming and potentially costly process. An alternative to looking yourself is to get someone to do it for you: this is not as satisfactory, but a local estate agent will, for a fee, go to look at the property and give you a description of it, and can perhaps post or e-mail you some photographs. Buying blind at auctions, on the other hand, is for confirmed gamblers.

Another important preliminary, before the date of the auction, is to check out the legal situation of the property and, since many properties sold at auction are not in the best condition, to get estimates of the likely cost of repairs or improvements, to make sure that the price you are going to bid plus these costs is not so high as to make the whole project non-viable. Finally, you should appoint a lawyer to act for you at the auction itself – only very brave or foolish foreigners take on these events without a lawyer to represent them or at least help them on the day. Your lawyer will explain precisely what needs to be done at each stage, while you will have to tell him the maximum price you want to offer and give him the bidding deposit – a refundable deposit levied by the auctioneer to allow you to enter a bid. Your will also have to give the auctioneer various personal details, and a deposit amounting (usually) to 10 per cent of the price you are offering, less the bidding deposit. This deposit must be paid over at the time your bid is accepted. You do not need to attend the auction in person, as your lawyer can do so for you, for which he will require power of attorney and the required funds.

Although auction prices are low, you should be aware that you will face additional costs over and above those you would have to pay in a normal house purchase, including the extra fees you will owe to your lawyer for dealing with the auction. These costs are likely to raise the overall transaction costs of the sale from the 10–11 per cent of the purchase price normal in Spain to around 13–15 per cent.

Building from Scratch or Renovation

Between villas, developments, apartments and converted *fincas* there is a huge variety of property available to buy around Spain but, if you don't find exactly what you want, you could have a house built for you from scratch, exactly to your own requirements. Many estate agencies, in resort areas and elsewhere, offer plots of vacant land (*parcelas*) as well as existing homes. Having your own home built in Spain, though – as everywhere – is not something to be taken on lightly, especially by anyone not resident in the country. You cannot expect simply to buy some land, go through some formalities, approve a design, contract a builder and then go away, ring up every few weeks and then come back next summer to find everything finished as you wanted it. Instead, there will be lots of bureaucratic niggles to get over and surprise problems to sort out. To get your ideal home in the sun just as you hoped for, you need to be able to be personally involved throughout and to visit regularly or, failing that, to appoint a reliable, local professional architect or engineer (who will expect to be quite well paid) to supervise things on your behalf. Building your own home will work best if you plan things carefully, and take your time, without building up over-optimistic ideas of when things will be done. You should also approach the project with much more than the usual slack in your budget, since unforeseen costs will often arise.

As with any purchase in Spain, you should discuss your plans with your lawyer before you set out. When commissioning a house to be built, still more than with other kinds of property-buying, you need contact with local networks to be sure of getting good service, and a good lawyer should be able to recommend and maybe introduce you to other reliable professionals – architects, surveyors – whose services you may need later. The next step is to find a suitable piece of land, the price of which can vary greatly, from about €30 to €50 per square metre. Before you get to buying it, though, a number of vital enquiries have to be made. Most importantly, your lawyer has to clarify the planning status of the land, and ensure that there are no regulations attached to it that could obstruct your plans entirely. All local councils in Spain now have a *plan general de urbanización* or town plan, available for consultation at the town hall, indicating the zoning of different types of building, conservation areas and so on. In areas that have already been built up or classified as *fincas urbanas*, or building land, it is fairly clear from the outset that permission to build will be given, but in rural areas the situation may be much more complex. Rural properties can also be subject to customary and local laws and special rights, such as grazing, hunting and water rights, all of which need to be checked over. Assuming you will probably want to build a swimming pool at some point, your lawyer should enquire specifically if there are any planning obstructions to that. Aside from these legal matters, you will also need to get an architect or surveyor to check over the physical features of the plot, such as its water supply – again, hugely important if you hope to build a pool – and get good estimates of how much it will cost to connect it to sewers, water, electricity and other services.

If all your lawyer's enquiries proceed smoothly, after some time he will be able to give you an assurance that there is no obstruction in principle to your being issued with a *permiso de edificar*, or building permit, the equivalent of planning permission, for that piece of land. This is your green light to begin buying the plot, the procedure for which is the same as for any other property purchase (*see* **Making the Purchase**). Actually to be issued with the *permiso* and begin building, though, you need to submit a detailed set of plans, together with a detailed specification for the building, its plumbing, wiring and so on, called a *memoria*. There are two main ways to obtain these: one is to go to one of the larger local builders – most of whom will have a stock of set 'patterns' for villas and other types of home, that can be combined and altered to your require-ments – who can arrange for the plans to be drawn up; the other, more interesting way is to have the plans drawn up by an architect, local or from anywhere in the EU, in line with your own specific ideas and requirements. At the same time you can also go about contracting a builder, although if you have contracted a design from one you will already have committed yourself. Your architect, or possibly your lawyer, should be able to suggest to you which of the local builders is most reliable, and if you are on good terms with any property companies or development administrators nearby, they are also a good source of recommendations for builders with whom they work.

Always get at least three different quotes for the work, and bear in mind that these are estimates only, and that some variation from them is inevitable. When you contract your builder, the official *memoria* should be incorporated into the contract, and be the basis of pricing. Payment terms vary a greatly deal, but you should hold out to ensure that as large a part of the fee as possible is to be paid at termination, not up front. Under Spanish law, a builder guarantees his work for 10 years, and an architect is also responsible for the same period for mistaken instructions to the builder and undetected defects in the land, like subsidence. However, getting any recompense if things get so bad that you take your builder to court can be a very long-drawn-out process.

As potentially attractive as having your own dream house built in Spain is the idea of finding a tumbledown old rustic pile and returning it to life. The number of semi-derelict old farms and cottages in Spain that nobody has yet begun to restore is fast diminishing, but there are still many around the countryside. Again, there are bureaucratic procedures to be dealt with: if your renovation work on an old house will involve any external changes to the structure (which can be broadly interpreted) your lawyer has to obtain for you from the local town hall a *licencia de obra*, or building licence. More important will be to check that the house is restorable in the first place – that is, that the walls and basic structure are not decayed beyond repair. You will also need to get realistic esti-mates of the potential cost of all the repairs needed – which might include new beams and a whole new roof – and of installing water, drainage, electricity (whether through the main supply or from generators) and other services, septic tanks and so on. These things can be extremely expensive, even if you work on a DIY basis. Restoration is, in general, less popular than building new in Spain, in part because it's usually three times more expensive.

Renting Before, or Instead of, Buying

As has already been touched on in many places in this book, it is a very good idea to rent somewhere for an extended period, such as a year, in the part of Spain that most appeals to you, before you commit to buying. You will get to know the place properly in all seasons, and find out whether you want to stay there or not; you will also have plenty of time to look around local properties for sale, without the time pressures of a short reconnaissance trip. This is especially to be recommended if you intend to work or retire there, or otherwise take up permanent residence in Spain, since you avoid committing yourself to one place too early, when there may be more attractive places to discover a few miles down the road. Even if you're only after a second home, renting beforehand can be a good strategy, since it gives you more freedom to think over your choices and avoid feeling that you always have to holiday in a certain spot because you've bought a place there. Depending very much on the area, renting can save you money too, especially if there's any likelihood you'll change your mind: if you buy, on top of the purchase price you will probably have to pay out another 10 per cent in transaction charges, and if you then decide to sell shortly afterwards you will lose another 5 per cent in more fees, plus capital gains tax.

In addition, depending on your circumstances, it may be worth considering renting long term beyond the first year, especially in the cheaper parts of the country and if, for example, you're starting up a business and don't want to have all your capital tied up in property from the outset. There are, however, problems and drawbacks in renting. In the resort areas, while there are always plenty of short-term holiday lets available, longer-term rentals at acceptable prices can be hard to find. A much bigger financial glitch is that, in these same ultra-popular areas – the central Costa del Sol, especially – the current Spanish holiday-property boom has caused prices to rise rapidly and created a strong seller's market. So far, there's no sign of this situation coming to an end. If you are sure you're staying on in Spain and will want to buy eventually, but carry on renting for too long, you'll find that you lose considerably on the property-price escalator and miss out on many properties. In major cities like Barcelona and Madrid, rental prices have also risen significantly, though over a longer period, and there you may find that you can pay less for a mortgage than you would in rent. Plus, of course, any money that you pay in rent is gone, and does not benefit you in the long term. The choice between renting and buying can be a difficult one, and depends on many different factors in each case. Overall, renting generally works best, in purely financial terms, in rural areas, less-touristed areas and smaller cities.

Advertisements offering properties for short- or long-term let can be found in nearly all Spanish estate agents, local papers and magazines and websites like *Segundamano* (*see* 'The Internet', pp.130–31). They will be listed under *alquileres* (rentals), subdivided usually between *pisos* (flats) and *chalets* for individual houses. You also often see *ad hoc* ads, as you do sales, posted up in the doorways of apartment blocks. Holiday lets can also be arranged in advance through many companies in Britain.

There are two basic types of **tenancy agreement** (*contrato de alquiler* or, in Catalan, *contracte de lloguer*) in Spain – *por temporada*, or seasonal, which covers all holiday lets, and *de vivienda* or long term. A *por temporada* contract can have a maximum validity of one year, although most are for much less than that, with no automatic right of extension for the tenant. Most, but not all, properties let this way are furnished, and the contract should include a detailed inventory of contents. Contracts *de vivienda*, on the other hand, are initially valid for one, two or three years, and the tenant has the automatic right for it to be extended to five, during which time the rent can only be raised in line with the official national inflation index. Even after the first five years a tenant can still obtain an extension, but the rent has to be renegotiated. In resort areas, land-lords often struggle hard not to give *de vivienda* contracts, even if you have been in residence for several months, in order to avoid conceding any permanent rights and so losing the option of getting you out for the summer and letting the property at higher rates in the peak holiday season. They may well prefer just to give successive *por temporada* contracts.

Rent in Spain is always paid monthly, and in advance, so you have to pay your first month's rent before you enter the property. Current tenancy law lays down the basic structure of rental contracts but it does not stipulate their every detail, which can vary a great deal. This is another area where you need to check things over with your solicitor and make sure you understand what you are agreeing to before you sign. One feature of all Spanish tenancies is that when you first sign the contract, in addition to the first month's rent, you will be required to hand over a **deposit** (*depósito* or *fianza*), normally equivalent to one month's rent in unfurnished properties and two months' in furnished ones. This is meant to cover the landlord against any damage or breakages that occur during your stay and, unless you have caused serious problems, is returnable when you leave. By law you can now insist that this be held by an official body (there are different ones for each region and sometimes province), rather than passed directly to the landlord, although many landlords will resist this strongly. Deposits are a long-standing bone of contention between landlords and tenants in Spain. There are countless stories of landlords finding spurious reasons for not paying back a deposit, while many tenants, who resent paying what is in effect an extra month's rent for nothing in the first place, simply refuse to pay the last month's rent when they decide to leave, rather than haggle over a refund. Non-return of deposits is far less of a problem, though, with short-term lets, although a landlord may deduct a small amount for breakages. If either landlord or tenant wishes to terminate a rental contract before its full term, they have to do so in writing by notarised letter with good notice, usually of at least two months.

Other points to look out for in rental contracts are any clauses on responsibility for repairs, and any requiring the tenant to pay community charges or local taxes. Such payments are illegal, and should be queried immediately: in law, if community charges or taxes are to be paid by the tenant, they should be included in the rent, not added on as an extra. With regard to the *comunidad de propietarios*, no matter how long you occupy a flat it is your landlord, not you, who is a member of the *comunidad* and gets officially informed of meetings. How much you are kept informed of decisions that might affect you in, say, an apartment block depends to a great extent on how good your relations are with your landlord and with your neighbours who are owner-occupiers.

Rental levels naturally vary widely around Spain, but in tourist areas such as Mallorca or even the Costa del Sol, it's possible to find decent two- to three-bed flats for around €500 a month, or less for short-term lets through the winter, and in cities nearby, such as Málaga or Alicante, larger flats are obtainable for the same prices.

Where to Stay While You House-hunt: Temporary Accommodation

The best way to find a place that really suits you in Spain, as we have said, is first to rent a place nearby and take your time looking. However, not everyone has huge amounts of time at their disposal. Even if you can only allow yourself a month or so to look around in your chosen area, though, renting will still be far the most cost-effective way to base yourself while you house-hunt. And the place to do so, in resort areas, will be the biggest resorts – Salou, Benidorm, Torremolinos and so on. You may have decided that these places are absolutely not for you, but all of them have huge numbers of small holiday apartments that, because there are so many of them, are available in the winter season for short-term lets at very favourable rates. Any local estate and letting agent will have a selection available for instant occupation. Big resorts also tend to be at the hub of local road networks, making visiting other places nearby easier, too. Failing that, other good places to find economical rentals are the main regional cities, like Málaga or Alicante. Small flats will not be as cheap or easy to find as in the resorts, but a plus could be the possibility of getting a proper taste of Spanish everyday life.

If, on the other hand, you stay in hotels you will find that room rates are lower in resort towns in the winter months – especially those to the north that don't really have a winter season – but can actually be higher in cities, because there are more business customers. Virtually every town in Spain has some sort of hotel but, other than guidebooks, there are no good general directories of them. Two big chains with hotels throughout the country and centralised booking services are **NH Hoteles** (**www.nh-hoteles.com**) and **Tryp Hoteles**, part of the giant Melià leisure group (**www.solmelia.com**). Both have well-equipped smallish modern business hotels – bland and unexciting, mid-priced, but reliably comfortable.

What If It Doesn't Work Out?

Anyone setting out to buy a property abroad and start a new life naturally does so with a feeling of optimism and a sense of adventure, otherwise no one would bother. In such a mood it can seem dog-in-the-manger to start thinking 'what if it all goes wrong, we all change our minds, or we find we don't like it here after all,' but it's wise at least to consider these 'what ifs' before taking the plunge. Family circumstances can change, you may have relatives to whom you need to be closer, you may be offered the job of the century, or many other reasons beyond your control might make you want to return home. If you're planning to sell up and go to live and work permanently in Spain and/or retire there, above all, it's only realistic to be aware of what the possibilities and consequences might be of going back on your decision while you consider the big move. You may still decide to gamble all on your new life, but at least you'll know what you're doing. It's much better to think about this first rather than feel trapped a few years down the line.

The fundamental question is, of course, how much real money you will have at your disposal if, having sold your UK home and moved to Spain, you then have to sell up a few years later to move back to the UK or elsewhere. Property prices have been rising in much of Spain for several years, so it is not currently the case, as it would be in many European countries, that your property would have fallen far behind the ever-rising price levels of the UK and Ireland. However, it is very unlikely that the increase in value on your Spanish property will have matched (or even got near) the rate of house-price rises in, for example, the southeast of England; prices may have shot up in the most popular second-home regions of Spain since the late 1990s – especially on the Costa del Sol – but this is not necessarily typical of the Spanish housing market and you cannot rely on your Spanish home's appreciating in value by large amounts. Depending on where you aim to move back to in the UK, therefore, you are likely to find that you have dropped at least a few rungs on the housing ladder, especially if, for example, you spent the surplus from the sale of your old home on renovating your new one, so that you have no spare cash left to 'top up' your purchase when once again you have to buy in the UK. So, if you can avoid it, don't sink everything you have into your new property – at least for a while – but keep a reasonable amount of cash back for unforeseen circumstances.

Another important factor to be aware of here is **capital gains tax** which, on property sales in Spain, is charged at different rates according to how long you have owned the property. If you sell a property within about three years of buying it, you will be taxed on almost 100 per cent of the difference between the price you sell at and the one you paid, so that much of your profit will go in tax. Capital gains tax is charged at 35 per cent for non-residents and around 20 per cent for Spanish residents, depending on their tax band. The exact rate of allowances varies for each year, by a complicated formula, but you need to have owned a property for at least four to five years before the tax demand drops markedly. If you have to move in advance of this, it's financially better to keep the property and let it, rather than sell up immediately. For more on capital gains tax, *see* **Financial Implications**.

Some people keep open an 'escape route' by not selling up at home when they move to Spain and letting their old house instead. Whether you can afford to buy a new home without selling your old one depends, of course, on your financial circumstances. If you haven't got abundant funds behind you, the problems involved in managing a rented property in the UK while living in Spain are often more trouble than they are worth. If you have any doubts about making a permanent move to Spain, this is another reason to rent for a time there, while letting your old home short-term, to be sure of your decision before ever getting into buying property.

Making the Purchase

05

Buying a property in Spain is as safe as buying a property in England. On reading a book such as this – which must explain the potential pitfalls if it is to serve any useful purpose – it can seem a frightening or dangerous experience. If you go about the purchase in the right way it is not dangerous and should not be frightening. The same or similar dangers arise when buying a house in England. If you are in any doubt, look briefly at a textbook on English conveyancing and all of the horrible things that have happened to people in England. You do not worry about those dangers because you are familiar with them and, more importantly, because you are shielded against contact with most of them by your solicitor. The same should be true when buying in Spain. Read this book to understand the background and why some of the problems exist. Ask your lawyer to advise you about any issues that worry you and leave him to avoid the landmines!

Law

This book is intended primarily for people from England and Wales. For this reason we have drawn comparisons with English law. Scottish law is somewhat different. Where the points apply also to Scottish law we have tried, depending on the context, to refer to either UK or British law. The law is intended to be up to date as at 1 April 2005.

Disclaimer

Although we have done our best to cover most topics of interest to the buyer of a property in Spain, a guide of this kind cannot take into account every individual's personal circumstances and the size of the book means that the advice cannot be comprehensive. The book is intended as a starting point that will enable people who are thinking of buying property to understand some of the issues involved and ask the necessary questions of their professional advisers. **IT IS NO SUBSTITUTE FOR PROFESSIONAL ADVICE**. Neither the author nor the publishers can accept any liability for any action taken or not taken as a result of this book.

Planning to Buy a Property in Spain

At the moment we are in a property 'boom'. It is, in most popular areas, a seller's market. Property – and, in particular, attractive, well-located and well-priced property – sells very quickly. Ten years ago it was fairly simple to go to Spain, look around, see a few properties and then come back to England to ponder which to buy. Today someone doing this could well find that the house they wanted to make an offer on had sold to someone else in the few days after they saw it.

As a result of this, people who are serious about buying property in Spain should do some research and make some preparations before they go on a visit to look at property. When they go on a visit they should do so with the intention that, if they see something that they really like, they will make an offer and commit themselves (at least in principle) to the purchase whilst they are still in the area.

What Preparation Should You Make?

Understand the System

The system of buying and selling property in Spain is, not surprisingly, different from the system of buying property in England or Scotland. On balance, neither better nor worse – just different. It has many superficial similarities, which can lull you into a false sense of familiarity and overconfidence. The most important thing to remember is that buying a home in Spain is just as safe as buying a home in Cardiff – as long as you take the right professional advice and precautions when doing so. If you do not take such advice, there are many expensive traps for the unwary.

See a Lawyer

It will save you a lot of time and trouble if you see your lawyer before you find a property. There are a number of preliminary issues that can best be discussed in the relative calm before you find the house of your dreams rather than once you are under pressure to sign some document to commit yourself to the purchase. These issues will include:

- **who should own the property, bearing in mind the Spanish inheritance rules and the Spanish and British tax consequences of ownership.**
- **whether to consider mortgage finance and if so in which country.**
- **what to do about converting the purchase price into euros.**
- **how to structure your purchase to minimise taxes and cost.**
- **if you are going to be living in Spain, sorting out the tax and investment issues that will need to be dealt with before your move if you are to get the best out of both systems.**

Only UK lawyers who specialise in dealing with Spain will be able to help you fully. Your normal English solicitor will know little or nothing of the issues of Spanish law and a Spanish lawyer is likely to know little or nothing about the British tax system or the issues of English or Scottish law that will affect the way the transaction should be arranged.

The lawyer may also be able to recommend estate agents, architects, surveyors, banks, mortgage lenders and other contacts in the area where you are looking.

A physical meeting is still the best way to start an important relationship. It has a number of advantages. It allows you to show and be shown documents and to wander off more easily into related topics. Most importantly, it is usually easier to make certain that you have each understood the other in a face-to-face meeting than it is by letter. But, these days, 'seeing' your lawyer does not need to involve an actual meeting. If it is more convenient to you it could be done by telephone conference call, by videoconference or over the Internet.

Some estate agents will tell you that you do not need to use a lawyer – that the services of the local notary public (*notario*) will suffice. Ignore that advice. It is quite true that the average Spanish person would not use the services of an independent lawyer when buying a house unless there was something complex about the transaction or about their own circumstances. For a foreigner, however, this is generally not good enough. There are many issues on which you will need guidance that it is not part of the notary's duty to provide. Furthermore, your Spanish notary will almost certainly know nothing about British law and so will be unable to give you any help as far as such vital issues as who should own the property in order to make the most of UK and Spanish tax and inheritance rules. As to the function of the notary, *see* 'The Notary Public', pp.167–8.

Decide on Ownership

Who should be the owner of your new home? This is the most important decision you will have to make when buying a property. Because of the combination of the Spanish and British tax systems, getting the ownership wrong can be a very expensive mistake indeed. It can lead to totally unnecessary tax during your lifetime and on your death. Even on a modest property this unnecessary tax can amount to tens of thousands of pounds. This subject is dealt with more fully later.

Get an Offer of Mortgage/Finance

These days, with very low interest rates, more and more people borrow at least part of the money needed to buy their home in Spain. Even if they don't need to do so, for many it makes good business or investment sense.

If you want to borrow money to finance your purchase it is better to get clearance before you start looking at property. Your lawyer should be able to get a preliminary mortgage offer within about 72 hours.

Property Inspection

Whatever property you are thinking of buying, you should think about having it inspected before you commit yourself to the purchase. It costs just as much and causes just as much disruption to repair property in Spain as in the UK, so you don't want any surprises. In fact – foolishly – very few buyers of property in Spain do this.

A new property will be covered by a short guarantee running from the date of handover and covering minor (but not trivial) defects in a new property. The property will also benefit from a guarantee in respect of major structural defects that will last for 10 years. As a subsequent purchaser you assume the benefit of these guarantees. After 10 years you are on your own. For property more than 10 years old (and, arguably, for younger property too) you should consider a survey.

If you decide on a survey there are a number of options available to you. For a start, there are several things that you can do yourself. These will help you to decide when to instruct a surveyor to carry out a proper survey and to give directions about any specific points of interest (*see* **Appendix 1**). You can also ask a professional to carry out a survey on your behalf, as discussed below. Most surveys can be carried out in seven to ten days.

Who Can Provide a Survey?

Estate Agent

It may be possible to arrange for another local estate agent to give the property a quick 'once-over' to comment on the price asked and any obvious problem areas. This is far short of a survey, and is more of a valuation. It is likely to cost about £200.

Mortgage Lender

This is also no substitute for a proper survey. Many lenders don't ask for one and where they do it is normally fairly peremptory, limited to a check on whether a property is imminently about to fall over and whether it is worth the money the bank is lending you.

Spanish Builder

If you are going to do a virtual demolition and rebuild then it might make more sense to get a builder to do a report on the property. A reputable and experienced qualified builder will also be able to comment on whether or not the price is reasonable for the property in its existing state. Make sure you ask for a written quotation for any building work proposed. As in any country it is as well to get several quotes, though this can be tricky. There is a lot of work for builders at the moment.

Spanish Surveyor

Your lawyer can put you in touch with the right people. In most rural areas there will be limited choice but if you prefer you can select 'blind' from a list of local members supplied by the surveyors' professional body. The cost of a survey is typically £500–1,500.

You will find that the report is different from the sort of report you would get from an English surveyor. Many people find it a little 'thin', with too much focus on issues that are not their primary concern. It will, hardly surprisingly, usually be in Spanish. You will need to have it translated unless you speak very good Spanish and have access to a technical dictionary. Translation costs amount to about £60–100 per thousand words, depending on where you are located and the complexity of the document; incidentally, always use an English native speaker to translate documents from Spanish into English. An alternative to translation of the full report would be to ask your lawyer to summarise the report in a letter to you and to have translated any areas of particular concern.

A few Spanish surveyors, mainly in the popular areas, have geared themselves to the non-Spanish market and will produce a report rather more like a British survey. They will probably also prepare it in bilingual form or at least supply a translation of the original Spanish document.

UK-qualified Surveyor Based in Spain

A number of UK surveyors – usually those with a love of Spain – have seen a gap in the market and have set themselves up in Spain to provide UK-style structural surveys. As in this country, they usually offer the brief 'Homebuyers' Report' or the fuller 'Full Structural Survey'. This is not as simple as it would first appear. To do the job well they must learn about Spanish building techniques and regulations, which are different from those in Britain. Without this knowledge the report will be of limited value. Prices are generally slightly more expensive than for a Spanish report, but it will be in English and so avoid the need for translation costs. Your UK lawyer should be able to recommend a surveyor able to do a survey in your area. Alternatively, look for advertisers in the main Spanish property magazines.

Check that the surveyor has indemnity insurance covering the provision of reports in Spain. Check also on the person's qualifications and experience in providing reports on Spanish property and get an estimate. The estimate will only be an estimate because they will not know for sure the scope of the task until they visit the property and because travelling time means that visits just to give estimates are not usually feasible.

UK-based Surveyor

Some UK surveyors provide reports from a base in the UK. These can be very good but travelling time often makes them impractical – especially in remote areas – and expensive. Make the same checks as for a UK surveyor based in Spain.

Contracts 'Subject to Survey'

This is unusual in Spain. Legally there is nothing to stop a Spanish preliminary contract containing a get-out clause (*condicion resolutoria*) stating that the sale is conditional on a satisfactory survey being obtained. It is unlikely to meet with the approval of the seller or his agent unless the transaction is unusual. In an ordinary case the seller is likely to tell you to do your survey and then sign a contract.

General Points about Surveys

Whichever report you opt for, its quality will depend in part on your input. Agree clearly and in writing the things you expect to be covered in the report. If you don't speak Spanish (and the surveyor doesn't speak good English) you may have to ask someone to write on your behalf. Your UK lawyer would probably be the best bet. Some of the matters you may wish to think about are set out below. Some of these will involve additional cost. Ask what will be covered as part of the standard fee and get an estimate for the extras.

Here is a list of things you may ask your surveyor to check:

- **Electrical condition and continuity check.**
- **Septic tank check.**
- **Drains check, including assessment of drain to point where they join mains sewers or septic tank.**
- **Adequacy of foundations.**
- **Rot check.**
- **Check on cement quality in property constructed out of cement.**
- **Check of underfloor areas, where access cannot easily be obtained.**
- **Check on heating and air-conditioning.**
- **Check on pool and all pool-related equipment and heating.**
- **Wood-boring insect check.**
- **Evidence of asbestos.**

Raising Finance to Buy a Property

In these days of low interest rates, many more people are taking out a mortgage in order to buy property in abroad.

If the property is viewed simply as an investment, a mortgage allows you to increase your benefit from the capital growth of the property by 'leveraging' the investment. If you buy a house for £200,000 and it increases in value by

£50,000 that is a 25 per cent return on your investment. If you had only put in £50,000 of your own money and borrowed the other £150,000 then the increase in value represents a return of 100 per cent on your investment. If the rate of increase in the value of the property is more than the mortgage rate, you have won. In recent years property in most popular areas has gone up in value by much more than the mortgage rate. The key questions are whether or not that will continue and, if so, for how long.

If you decide to take out a mortgage you can, in most cases, either mortgage (or extend the mortgage on) your existing UK property or you can take out a mortgage on your new Spanish property. There are advantages and disadvantages both ways.

Many people buying property in Spain will look closely at fixed-rate mortgages so they know their commitment over, say, the next five, 10 or 15 years. Again there are advantages and disadvantages.

Mortgaging Your UK Property

At the moment there is fierce competition to lend money and there are some excellent deals to be done, whether you choose to borrow at a variable rate, at a fixed rate or with one of the hybrid schemes now on offer. Read the Sunday papers or the specialist mortgage press to see what is available, or consult a mortgage broker. Perhaps most useful are mortgage brokers who can discuss the possibilities in both the UK and Spain. It is outside the scope of this book to go into detail about the procedures for obtaining a UK mortgage. A number of people have found that re-mortgaging their property in the UK has reduced the cost of their existing borrowing so significantly that their new mortgage – including a loan to buy a modest Spanish property – has cost little more, in monthly payments, than their old loan.

Advantages

• **The loan will probably be very cheap to set up.** You will probably already have a mortgage. If you stay with the same lender there will be no legal fees or land registry fees for the additional loan. There may not even be an arrangement fee. If you go to a new lender, many special deals mean that the lender will pay all fees involved.

• **The loan repayments will be in sterling.** If the funds to repay the mortgage are coming from your sterling earnings, then the amount you have to pay will not be affected by fluctuations in exchange rates between the pound and the euro. If sterling falls in value, then your debt as a percentage of the value of the property decreases. Your property will be worth more in sterling terms but your mortgage will remain the same.

- You will be familiar with dealing with British mortgages, and all correspondence and documentation will be in English.
- You can take out an endowment or PEP mortgage or pension mortgage or interest-only mortgage, none of which is available in Spain. Normally only repayment mortgages are available in Spain.
- You will probably need no extra life insurance cover. This can add considerably to the cost of the mortgage, especially if you are getting older.

Disadvantages

- You will pay UK interest rates which, at the time of writing (September 2005), are higher than Spanish rates. British rates are about 4.5 per cent variable. Spanish rates vary from about 3 per cent variable. Make sure you compare the overall cost of the two mortgages. Crude rates (which, in any case, may not be comparable as they are calculated differently in the two countries) do not tell the whole tale. What is the total monthly cost of each mortgage, including life insurance and all extras? What is the total amount required to repay the loan, including all fees and charges?
- If sterling increases in value against the euro, a mortgage in euros would become cheaper to pay off. Your loan of €60,000 (now worth about £41,500 at €1 = £0.69p) would only cost about £33,000 to pay off if the euro rose to about £0.55. This seems unlikely to happen.
- If you are going to let the property it will be difficult or impossible to get Spanish tax relief on the mortgage interest.
- Many people do not like the idea of mortgaging their main home – which they may only just have cleared after 25 years of paying a mortgage.
- Some academics argue that, in economic terms, debts incurred to buy assets should be secured against the asset bought and assets in one country should be funded by borrowings in that country.

All in all, a UK mortgage is generally the better option for people who need to borrow relatively small sums and who will be repaying it out of UK income.

Spanish Mortgages

A Spanish mortgage is one taken out over your Spanish property. This will either be from a Spanish bank or from a UK bank that is registered and does business in Spain. You cannot take a mortgage on your new Spanish property from your local branch of a UK building society or high street bank.

The basic concept of a mortgage is the same in Spain as it is in England, Wales or Scotland. It is a loan secured against land or buildings. Just as in the UK, if you don't keep up the payments the bank will repossess your property.

The Main Differences Between an English and a Spanish Mortgage

- Spanish mortgages are almost always created on a repayment basis. That is to say, the loan and the interest on it are both gradually repaid by equal instalments over the period of the mortgage. Interest-only mortgages have become available over the last few years, although endowment, PEP and pension mortgages are not known in Spain.

- There are often restrictions on the ability to impose penalties for early payment of the loan.

- The formalities involved in making the application, signing the contract subject to a mortgage and completing the transaction are more complex and stricter than in the UK.

- Most Spanish mortgages are usually granted for 15 years, not 25 as in England. In fact the period can be anything from five to (in a few cases) 25 years. Normally the mortgage must have been repaid by your 70th (sometimes 65th) birthday.

- The maximum loan is generally 80 per cent of the value of the property, and 75 or 66 per cent is more common. As a planning guide, you should think of borrowing no more than two-thirds of the price you are paying.

- Fixed-rate loans – with the rate fixed for the whole duration of the loan – are more common than in England. They are very competitively priced.

- The way of calculating the amount the bank will lend you is different from in the UK. As you would expect, there are detailed differences from bank to bank but most banks are not allowed to lend you more than an amount the monthly payments on which amount to 30–33 per cent of your net disposable income. *See* 'How Much Can I Borrow', below.

- There will usually be a minimum loan (say £20,000) and some banks will not lend at all on property less than a certain value. Some will not lend in rural areas.

- The way of dealing with stage payments on new property and property where money is needed for restoration is different from in England. *See* below.

- The paperwork on completion of the mortgage is different. There is often no separate mortgage deed. Instead the existence of the mortgage is mentioned in your purchase deed (*escritura de compraventa*). It is prepared by and signed in front of a notary public (*notario*).

How Much Can I Borrow?

Different banks have slightly different rules and slightly different ways of interpreting the rules.

Generally they will lend you an amount that will give rise to monthly payments of up to about 30–33 per cent of your net available monthly income.

The starting point is your net monthly salary after deduction of tax and National Insurance contributions but before deduction of voluntary payments such as to savings schemes. The following income is also taken into account:

- **Two salaries if there are two applicants.**

- **Any investment income or a pension.**

- **If you are buying a property with a track record of letting income (this may or may not be taken into account).**

- **Leaseback rental income if you are buying a leaseback (*see* pp.119–20).**

- **Your pension and investment income if you are over 65 (but your earnings will not be taken into account).**

If your circumstances are at all unusual, seek advice as approaching a different bank may produce a different result.

e.g.		
	Mr Smith – net salary	£3,000
	Mrs Smith – net salary	£2,000
	Investment income	£1,000
	Total income taken into account	**£6,000**

The maximum loan repayments permitted will be 30 per cent of this sum, less your fixed commitments.

i.e.   Maximum permitted loan repayment £6,000 x 30% = £1,800

Regular monthly commitments would include mortgage payments on your main and other properties, any rent paid, HP commitments and maintenance (family financial provision) payments. Repayments on credit cards don't count. If there are two applicants, both their commitments are taken into account.

e.g.		
	Mr and Mrs Smith – mortgage on main home	£750
	Mr and Mrs Smith – mortgage on flat in France	£400
	Mrs Smith – HP on car	£200
	Total pre-existing outgoings	**£1,350**

Maximum loan repayment permitted = £1,800–£1,350 = £450 per month. This would, at today's rates, equate to a mortgage of about £60,000 over 15 years.

If you are buying a property for investment (rental), the bank may treat this as commercial lending and apply different criteria.

Applications for a Spanish Mortgage

Once again the information needed will vary from bank to bank. It will also depend on whether you are employed or self-employed. Applications can receive preliminary approval (subject to survey, confirmation of good title and confirmation of the information supplied by you) within a few days.

The Mortgage Offer

Allow four weeks altogether from the date of your application to receiving a written mortgage offer, as getting the information to them sometimes takes a while. It can take longer.

Have the mortgage explained in detail by your lawyer. Once you receive it, you will generally have 30 days from receipt of the offer in which to accept the offer, after which time it will lapse.

Payments for New Property

In Spain, when buying a new property one normally makes payments as the development progresses and takes title at the end. This can pose problems for banks, as you do not own anything you can mortgage until you make the final payment and take title. In most cases the mortgage will therefore only be granted to cover the final payment. As this is often 60 or 70 per cent this is seldom a problem. In some cases if the earlier payments are more substantial the banks will offer a credit facility to make the earlier payments. Once the property has been delivered to you (and thus the full loan has been taken) the normal monthly payments will begin.

Property Needing Restoration

Not all banks will finance property that needs restoration. If you have enough money to buy a property but need a mortgage to renovate it, you must apply for the mortgage before buying, as it can otherwise be difficult to find a lender.

The Cost of Taking Out a Mortgage

This will normally involve charges amounting to about 4 or 5 per cent of the sum borrowed. These charges are in addition to the normal expenses incurred when buying a property, which normally amount to about 10–11 per cent of the price of the property.

You will probably be required to take out **life insurance** for the amount of the loan, though you may be allowed to use a suitable existing policy. You may be required to have a medical examination.

You will be required to **insure the property** and produce proof of insurance – but you would probably have done this anyway.

The offer may be subject to **early payment penalties**. These are of particular concern in the case of a fixed-rate mortgage.

The Exchange Rate Risk

If the funds to repay the mortgage are coming from your sterling earnings then the amount you have to pay will be affected by fluctuations in exchange rates between sterling and the euro. Do not underestimate these variations. In the period since the launch of the euro it has varied from €1 = £0.53 to €1 = £0.73. This can make a tremendous difference to your monthly mortgage repayments. A monthly mortgage repayment of €725 (about £500 today) would on some occasions during the last three years have meant paying £384 and on other occasions £529. Equally, if sterling falls in value, then your debt as a percentage of the value of the property increases in sterling terms. Your property will be worth more in sterling terms but your mortgage will also have increased in value. If sterling rises in value against the euro, the situation is reversed.

Mortgaging your Spanish Property: Summary

Advantages

- **You will pay Spanish interest rates which, at the time of writing (September 2005), are lower than UK rates.** British rates are about 4.5 per cent variable. Spanish rates vary from about 3 per cent variable. Make sure you compare the overall cost of the two mortgages. Crude rates (which, in any case, may not be comparable as they are calculated differently in the two countries) do not tell the whole tale. What is the total monthly cost of each mortgage, including life insurance and all extras? What is the total amount required to repay the loan, including all fees and charges?

- **If you are going to let the property you will usually be able to get Spanish tax relief on the mortgage interest.**

- **The loan repayments will usually be in euros.** If the funds to repay the mortgage are coming from rental income paid to you in euros, this will give you something to spend them on!

- **Many people do not like the idea of mortgaging their main home – a debt which they may only just have cleared after 25 years of paying a mortgage.**

- **Some academics argue that, in economic terms, debts incurred to buy assets should be secured against the asset bought and assets in one country should be funded by borrowings in that country.**

Disadvantages

- **The loan will probably be expensive to set up.** Arrangement fees, inspection fees, notaries' fees and land registry fees will come to about 4 per cent of the amount borrowed.

- **You will incur further fees to clear the record of the mortgage of your title once it has been paid off.** This will usually only be a problem if you want to sell the property during the two years following paying off the mortgage.

- **The loan repayments will usually be in euros.** If the funds to repay the mortgage are coming from your sterling earnings then the amount you have to pay will be affected by fluctuations in exchange rates between sterling and the euro. At the time of writing (September 2005) most experts are predicting that the pound will fall further in value against the euro. Equally, if sterling falls in value then your debt as a percentage of the value of the property increases in sterling terms. Your property will be worth more in sterling terms but your mortgage will also have increased in value.

- **You will be unfamiliar with dealing with Spanish mortgages and all correspondence and documentation will be usually be in Spanish.**
- **Normally only repayment mortgages are available – i.e. mortgages where you pay off the capital and interest over the period of the mortgage.**
- **You will probably need extra life insurance cover.** This can add considerably to the cost of the mortgage, especially if you are getting older.

Generally speaking, Spanish euro mortgages will suit people letting their property on a regular basis.

Saving Money on Your Euro Repayments

Your mortgage will usually be paid directly from your Spanish bank account. Unless you have lots of rental or other euro income going into that account you will need to send money from the UK in order to meet the payments.

Every time you send a payment to Spain you will face two costs. The first is the price of the euros. This, of course, depends on the exchange rate used to convert your sterling. The second cost is the charges that will be made by your UK and Spanish banks to transfer the funds – which can be substantial.

There are steps that you can take to control both of these charges.

As far as the **exchange rate** is concerned, you should be receiving the so-called '**commercial rate**', not the tourist rate published in the papers. The good news is that it is a much better rate. The bad news is that rates vary from second to second and so it is difficult to get alternative quotes. By the time you phone the second company, the first has changed! In any case, you will probably want to set up a standing order for payment and not shop around every month.

There are various organisations that can convert your sterling into euros. Your bank is unlikely to give you the best exchange rate. **Specialist currency dealers** will normally better the bank's rate, perhaps significantly. If you decide to deal with a currency dealer you must pick one that is reputable. They will be handling your money and, if they go bust with it in their possession, you could lose it. Ask your lawyer for a recommendation.

As far as the **bank charges** are concerned, differing banks make differing charges. This applies both to your UK bank and to your Spanish bank. Discuss their charges with them. In the case of your UK bank there is usually room for some kind of deal to be done. In the case of the Spanish bank the level of these charges will probably – after their ability to speak English – be the most important reason for choosing one bank over another.

Another possibility for saving money arises if you '**forward buy**' the euros that you are going to need for the year. It is possible to agree with a currency dealer that you will buy all of your euros for the next 12 months at a price that is, essentially, today's price. You normally pay 10 per cent down and the balance on delivery. If the euro rises in value you will gain, perhaps substantially. If the euro falls in value – *la vida es dura*! The main attraction of forward buying is not so much the possibility for gaining on the exchange rate but the certainty that the deal gives you. Only enter into these agreements with a reputable and, if possible, bonded broker.

Bearing in mind the cost of conversion and transmission of currency, it is better to make **fewer rather than more payments**. You will therefore have to work out carefully whether, taking into account loss of interest on the funds transferred but bank charges saved, you are best sending money monthly, quarterly or every six months.

Foreign Currency Mortgages

It is possible to mortgage your home in Spain and to borrow not in euros but in sterling – or US dollars or Swiss francs or Japanese yen.

There may be some attractions in borrowing in sterling if you are repaying out of sterling income. The rates of interest will be sterling rates, not euro rates. This will currently mean paying more. Usually the rates are not as competitive as you could obtain if you were remortgaging your property in the UK, as the market is less cut-throat. You will have all the same administrative and legal costs as you would if you borrowed in euros – i.e. about 4 per cent of the amount borrowed.

This option is mainly of interest to people who either do not have sufficient equity in their UK home or, for whatever reason, do not wish to mortgage the property in which they live.

Who Should Own the Property?

There are many ways of structuring the purchase of a home in Spain. Each has significant advantages and disadvantages. The choice of the right structure will save you possibly many thousands of pounds in tax and expenses during your lifetime and on your death. Because, in Spain, you do not have the total freedom that we have in the UK to deal with your assets as you please on your death, the wrong choice of owner can also result in the wrong people being entitled to inherit from you when you die, for example if you were to die intestate. This is a particular problem for people in second marriages and unmarried couples.

The Options

Sole Ownership

In some cases it could be sensible to put the property in the name of one person only. If your husband runs a high-risk business, or if he is 90 and you are 22, this could make sense. It is seldom a good idea from the point of view of tax or inheritance planning.

Joint Ownership

If two people are buying together they will normally buy in both their names.

Your half is yours and your fellow owner's is theirs. On your death your half will (subject to the requirement of your matrimonial regime – *see* pp.170–71) be disposed of in accordance with Spanish law. A person who owns in this way, even if they own by virtue of inheritance, can usually insist on the sale of the property. So if your stepchildren inherit from your husband they could insist on the sale of your home.

If you decide to buy together then, in certain cases, it can make sense to split the ownership other than 50/50. If, for example, you have three children and your wife has two then to secure each of those children an equal share on your death you might think about buying 60 per cent in your name and 40 per cent in your wife's name.

It is very important to seek clear advice from your lawyer about the form of ownership that will suit you best, both with regard to the consequences in Spain and the consequences in the UK.

Adding Your Children to the Title

If you give your children the money to buy part of the property and so put them on the title now, you may save quite a lot of inheritance tax. On your death you will only own (say) one-fifth of the property rather than one-half. Only that part will be taxable. It may be such a small value as to result in a tax-free inheritance. This only works sensibly if your children are over 18. Of course, there are drawbacks. For example, if the gift is not properly structured it could become subject to gift tax in Spain immediately. If the children fall out with you, they can insist on the sale of the property and receiving their share.

Putting the Property in the Name of Your Children Only

If you put the property only in the name of your children (possibly reserving for yourself a life interest – *see* below) then the property is theirs. On your death there will be little or no inheritance tax and there will be no need for them to incur the legal expenses involved in dealing with an inheritance. This sounds attractive. Remember, however, that you have lost control. It is no longer your property. If your children divorce, their husband/wife will be able to claim a share. If they die before you without children of their own, you will end up inheriting the property back from them and having to pay inheritance tax for the privilege of doing so.

A **life interest** (*usufructo*) is the right to use the property for a lifetime. So, on your death, your rights would be extinguished but your second wife or partner, who still has a life interest, would still be able to use the property. Only on their death would the property pass in full to the people to whom you gave it years earlier. This device can not only protect your right to use the property but also save large amounts of inheritance tax, particularly if you are young, the property is valuable and you survive for many years. As ever there are also drawbacks, not least being the fact that after the gift if you wish to sell you need the agreement of the 'owners', who will be entitled to their share of the proceeds of sale and who would have to agree to buy you a new house.

If you wish to do this you must structure the gift carefully. Otherwise it could be taxable at once in Spain.

Limited Company

For some people owning a property via a limited company can be a very attractive option. You own the shares in a company, not a house in Spain. There are various types of company.

Spanish Commercial Company

Ownership via a company will mean that the income from letting the property is taxed in the way usual for companies – basically, you pay tax only on the profit made – rather than at the flat rate applicable in the case of an individual owner who is not tax resident in Spain. This can reduce your tax bill. Ownership in the form of a company also gives rise to certain expenses – accountancy, filing tax returns, etc. Buying through a Spanish company gives rise to a host of potential problems as well as benefits. The plan needs to be studied closely by your advisers so that you can decide whether or not it makes sense in the short, medium and long term.

UK Company

It is rare for a purchase through a UK company to make sense for a holiday home or single investment property. This is despite the fact that the ability to pay for the property with the company's money without drawing it out of the company and paying UK tax on the dividend is attractive. Once again you need expert advice from someone familiar with the law of both countries.

Offshore (Tax Haven) Company

This has the added disincentive that you will have to pay a special tax of 3 per cent of the value of the property every year. This is to compensate the Spanish for all the inheritance and transfer taxes that they will not receive when the owners of these companies sell them or die. This tax treatment has more or less killed off ownership via such companies, yet they still have a limited role to play. A 93-year-old buying a £10,000,000 property, or someone who wishes to be discreet about the ownership of the property, might think that 3 per cent is a small price to pay for the avoidance of inheritance tax or privacy respectively.

SIPPs (Self-invested Personal Pensions)

SIPPs have been around for a number of years, but in April 2006 the rules change to allow residential property to be put into the name of a SIPP. This can have great advantages if you are thinking about owning property as a long-term investment and do not intend to use the property yourself very often. This can have great tax advantages in the UK (no income tax, no capital gains tax, no inheritance tax and the money that you put into the SIPP is tax-deductible) but there will still be tax payable in Spain (although the rate may be less than it would be if the property was not in the name of a SIPP).

Trusts

As a vehicle for owning a property, trusts are of little direct use. Spanish law does not fully recognise trusts and so the trustees who are to be named on the title as the owners of the property would be treated as 'private individual' owners, having to pay all of the income, wealth and inheritance taxes applicable in their case. In a few cases this could still give some benefit but there are probably better ways of getting the same result. This does not mean that trusts have no place for the owner of property in Spain. A trust could still, for example, own the property via a limited company if this fitted the 'owner's' overall tax and inheritance planning objectives. Again, careful specialist advice is essential.

Which is Right for You?

The choice is of fundamental importance. If you get it wrong you will pay massively more tax than you need to, both during your lifetime and on your death. The tax consequences arise not only in Spain but also in your own country. For each buyer of a home in Spain one of the options set out above will suit perfectly. Another might just about make sense. The rest would be an expensive waste of money.

The trouble is, it is not obvious which is the right choice. You need in every case to take advice. If your case is simple so will be the advice. If it is complex, the time and money spent will be repaid many times over.

The Process of Buying a Property

The Law

As you would expect, this is complicated. A basic textbook on Spanish property law might extend to 500 pages. There are certain basic principles, however, that it is helpful to understand.

1. The main legal provisions relating to property law are found in the civil code. The analysis of rights reflects the essentially agrarian society of late 18th-century Spain and pays limited attention to some of the issues that today would seem more pressing. That has only partly been remedied by the later additions to the code.

2. The civil code declares that foreigners are to be treated in the same way as Spanish people as far as the law is concerned.

3. Spanish law divides property into two classes – moveable property (*bienes muebles*) and immovable property (*bienes inmuebles*). The whole basis of ownership and transfer of ownership depends on which classification property belongs to. The distinction is similar to the English concept of real and personal property but it is not exactly the same. Immovable property includes land and buildings, but not the shares in a company that owns land and buildings.

4. The sale of *inmuebles* located in Spain must always be governed by Spanish law.

5. The form of ownership of land is always absolute ownership. This is similar to what we would call freehold ownership.

6. It is possible to own the buildings – or even parts of a building – on a piece of land separately from the land itself. This is of particular relevance in the case of flats, which are owned 'freehold'.

7. Where two or more people own a piece of land or other property together they will generally own it in undivided shares (*pro indiviso*). That is to say the piece of land is not physically divided between them. Each owner may, in theory, mortgage or sell his share without the consent of the others – though the others might have certain rights of pre-emption, that is the right to buy the property in preference to any outsider.

8. Where a building or piece of land is physically divided between a number of people, a condominium (*comunidad de propietarios*) is created. The land is divided into privately owned parts – such as an individual flat – and communally owned areas. The management of the communally held areas is up to the owners of the privately held area, but can be delegated to someone else.

9. In the case of a sale of land certain people may have a right of pre-emption. One is the co-owner mentioned above. Others are (in each case only in certain circumstances) the municipality or a sitting tenant and certain statutory bodies.

10. Transfer of ownership of *inmuebles* is usually by simple agreement. This need not be in writing, but usually is. That agreement binds both the parties to it but is not effective as far as the rest of the world is concerned, who are entitled to rely on the content of the land register (*registro de la propiedad*). Thus between buyer and seller ownership of land can be transferred, for example, by signing a sale contract (*contrato privado de conpraventa*) even if the seller remains in possession and some of the price remains unpaid. But that ownership would not damage the interests of someone other than the buyer or seller (such as someone owed money by the seller), who is entitled to take action against the person named as owner in the land registry. Ownership can also be acquired by possession, usually for 30 years.

11. Other rights – short of ownership – can exist over land. These include rights of way, tenancies, life interests, mortgages and option contracts. Most require some sort of formality in order that they are valid against third parties but are always binding between the people who made the agreements. The current planning situation of the land and property needs particularly thorough investigation in the Valencian region, which includes the Costa Blanca (*see* p.50 andp.110).

12. There are *two* land registers. Each area maintains a tax register (*registro catastral*). In this, all the land in the district is divided into plots and assessed for tax purposes. The second register is the deed and mortgage register (*registro de la propriedad*). Not all land is registered here. The entries (size, boundaries, etc.) do not necessarily correspond in the two registries.

General Procedure

The general procedure when buying a property in Spain seems, at first glance, similar to the purchase of a property in England: sign a contract; do some checks; sign a deed of title. This is deceptive. The procedure is very different and even the use of the familiar English vocabulary to describe the very different steps in Spain can produce an undesirable sense of familiarity with the procedure. This can lead to assumptions that things that have not been discussed will be the same as they would in England. This would be a wrong and dangerous assumption. To be on the safe side, work on the basis that the system is totally different.

Choosing a Lawyer

The Notary Public (*Notario*)

The notary is a special type of lawyer. He is in part a public official but he is also in business, making his living from the fees he charges for his services. Notaries also exist in England, but they are seldom used in day-to-day transactions.

Under Spanish law only deeds of sale (*escrituras de compraventa*) approved and witnessed by a notary can be registered at the land registry (*registro de la propiedad*). Although it is possible to transfer legal ownership of property such as a house or apartment by a private agreement not witnessed by the notary, and although that agreement will be fully binding on the people who made it, it will not be binding on third parties. Third parties – including people who want to make a claim against the property and banks wanting to lend money on the strength of the property – are entitled to rely on the details of ownership recorded at the land registry. So if you are not registered as the owner of the property you are at risk. Thus, practically speaking, all sales of real estate in Spain must be witnessed by a notary.

The notary also carries out certain checks on properties sold and has some duties as tax enforcer and validator of documents to be presented for registration.

His or her basic fee is fixed by law:

Price more than	Up to	Charge	Cumulative total fee
€0	€6,000	€90	€90
€6,000	€30,000	4.5/1,000	€200
€30,000	€60,000	1.5/1,000	€240
€60,000	€150,000	1/1,000	€330
€150,000	€600,000	0.5/1,000	€600
€600,000	No upper limit	0.3/1,000	

For an average property, however, it will be about 0.4 per cent of the price, though there can sometimes be 'extras'.

The notary is, in theory, appointed by the buyer but, in many cases – particularly with new property – the seller will stipulate the notary to be used. This is a practical time- and cost-saving measure. The notary will already have drafted the documents gathering together all the bits of land bought by the seller (*agrupacion*) and then split off the various individual plots to be sold (*segregacion*). It makes sense for him to deal with all the resultant sales. Otherwise all of the powers of attorney and so on would need to be produced before lots of different notaries, potentially all over the country

The notary is strictly neutral. He is more a referee than someone fighting on your behalf. He is, in the usual case, someone who checks the papers to make sure that they comply with the strict rules as to content and so will be accepted by the land registry for registration.

Many Spanish notaries, particularly in rural areas, do not speak English – or, at least, do not speak it well enough to give advice on complex issues. Very few will know anything about English law and so will be unable to tell you about the tax and other consequences in the UK of your plans to buy a house in Spain. In any case, the buyer will seldom meet the notary before the signing ceremony and so there is little scope for seeking detailed advice. It is, in any case, rare for notaries to offer any comprehensive advice or explanation, least of all in writing, to the buyer. *For the English buyer the notary is no substitute for also using the services of a specialist UK lawyer familiar with Spanish law and international property transactions.* This is the clear advice of every guidebook, the Spanish and British governments and the Federation of Overseas Property Developers, Agents and Consultants (FOPDAC).

Spanish Lawyers (*Abogado*)

Most Spanish people buying a home in Spain will not use the services of a lawyer (as opposed to the notary public) unless there is something unusual or contentious about the transaction.

English Lawyers (Solicitors)

For English people the services of the notary are unlikely to give them all the information or help they need to buy a home in Spain. They will often require advice about inheritance issues, the UK tax implications of their purchase, how to save taxes, surveys, mortgages, currency exchange and so on, which is outside the scope of the service of the notary. They should retain the services of a specialist UK lawyer familiar with dealing with these issues. The buyer's usual solicitor is unlikely to be able to help as there are only a handful of English law firms with the necessary expertise.

The Price

This can be freely agreed between the parties. Depending on the economic climate there may be ample or very little room for negotiating a reduction in the asking price. At the moment (2005) there is more scope to negotiate on the price than there has been over the last few years, although in popularly priced properties in the main cities and tourist areas, which are in short supply, there is still little scope for negotiation.

How Much Should be Declared in the Deed of Sale?

For many years there was a tradition in Spain (and other Latin countries) of under-declaring the price actually paid for a property when signing the deed of sale (*escritura*). This was because the taxes and notaries' fees due were calculated on the basis of the price declared. A lower price means less property transfer taxes for the buyer and less capital gains tax for the seller.

The days of major under-declarations have now largely gone. In rural areas you can still sometimes come under pressure to under-declare to a significant extent, but it is now rare. In many areas the seller will still suggest some more modest form of under-declaration.

Under-declaration is illegal and foolish. There are severe penalties. In the worst case the state can buy the property for the price declared. In the best case there are fines and penalties for late payment. In addition, unless when you sell your buyer also under-declares, you create an entirely artificial capital gain – taxed at 35 per cent.

Nonetheless, you may find that you have little choice but to under-declare. The seller will often refuse to sell unless you do. Fortunately, there is a semi-legitimate 'grey area' for manoeuvre over declared price, rather like doing 40mph where there is a 30 limit; for example, you might agree to buy some furniture for a certain sum, separate from the property itself. It is wrong but you will not get into serious trouble. Seek advice from your lawyer.

Where Must the Money be Paid?

The price, together with the taxes and fees payable, is usually paid by the buyer to the seller in front of the notary. This is the best and safest way. You can, in fact, agree to pay in whatever way and wherever you please. So, for example, in the case of a British seller and a British buyer the payment could be made in sterling by bank transfer. In the case of a seller who is not tax resident in Spain the buyer is obliged to retain 5 per cent of the price and pay it to the taxman (*agencia tributaria*) on account of the seller's potential tax liabilities. *See* below for more details.

Try to avoid arrangements, usually as part of an under-declaration, where part of the money is handed over in cash in brown-paper parcels. Apart from being illegal, it is dangerous at a practical level. Buyers have lost the bundle – or been robbed on the way to the notary's office. Sometimes there is even a suspicion that the seller, who knew where you were going to be and when, could be involved.

General Enquiries and Special Enquiries

Certain enquiries are made routinely in the course of the purchase of a property. These include, in appropriate cases, a check on the planning situation of the property. This *informe urbanistico* will reveal the position of the property itself but it will not, at least directly, tell you about its neighbours, nor will it reveal general plans for the area. Checks on planning status (both current and future) need to be especially thorough for any non-development property in the Valencian region, including the Costa Blanca (*see* p.50 and p.110).

If you want to know whether the authorities are going to put a prison in the village or run a new AVE line through your back garden (both, presumably, bad things), or build a motorway access point or railway station 3km away (both, presumably, good things) you will need to ask. There are various organisations you can approach but, just as in England, there is no single point of contact for such enquiries. If you are concerned about what might happen in the area then you will need to discuss the position with your lawyers at an early stage. There may be a considerable amount of work (and therefore cost) involved in making full enquiries, the results of which can never be guaranteed.

Normal enquiries also include a check that the seller is the registered owner of the property and that it is sold (if this has been agreed) free of mortgages or other charges.

In order to advise you what special enquiries might be appropriate, your lawyer will need to be told your proposals for the property. Do you intend to let it out? If so is it on a commercial basis? Do you intend to use it for business purposes? Do you want to extend or modify the exterior of the property? Do you intend to make interior structural alterations?

Agree in advance the additional enquiries you would like to make and get an estimate of the cost of those enquiries.

Your Civil State (*Estado Civil*) and Other Personal Details

This is something you will have given no thought to. For most of the time it is a matter of no importance in the UK. It is something the Spanish get very worked up about.

When preparing documents in Spain you will be asked to specify your civil state. This comprises a full set of information about you. They will not only ask for your full name and address but also, potentially, for your occupation, nationality, passport number, maiden name and sometimes the names of your parents, your date and place of birth, date and place of marriage and, most importantly, your matrimonial regime (*regimen matrimonial*). A *regimen matrimonial* is something we do not have in the UK. In Spain when you marry you will specify the *regimen matrimonial* that will apply to your relationship. There are two main options for a Spanish person – a regime of common ownership of assets (*comunidad de bienes*) or a regime of separate ownership of assets (*separacion de bienes*). Under the first, all assets acquired after the marriage, even if put into just one party's name, belong to both. Under the second, each spouse in entitled to own assets in his own name, on which the other spouse has no automatic claim. The effect of marriage under English law is generally closer to the second than the first. If possible the notary, when specifying your matrimonial regime, should state that you are married under English law and, in the absence of a marriage contract, do not have a regime but your situation is similar to a regime of *separacion de bienes*.

This is no idle point. The declaration in your *escritura* is a public declaration. It is treated in Spain with great reverence and as being of great importance. It will be hard in later years to go against what you have declared.

If appropriate you will declare that you are single, separated, divorced, widowed, etc. at this point.

The authorities are entitled to ask for proof of all of these points by birth certificates, marriage certificates, and so on. If the documents are required the official translations into Spanish may be needed. Often the notary will take a slightly more relaxed view and ask you for only the key elements of your *estado civil*. It is worth checking in advance as to what is required, as it is embarrassing to turn up to sign the *escritura* only to find the ceremony cannot go ahead because you do not have one of the documents required. In the worst case that could put you in breach of contract and you could lose your deposit!

Tax Identification Number (NIE)

To own a property in Spain you need to obtain an NIE – foreigner's tax identification number. This is obtained from the foreigners' department at your local Spanish police station (*see* p25). You will need to fill in a simple form and produce your passport and two passport photographs. Alternatively, your lawyer can obtain this for you.

The Community of Owners (*Comunidad de Propietarios*)

This is a device familiar in continental Europe but most unusual in England.

The basic idea is that when a number of people own land or buildings in such a way that they have exclusive use of part of the property but shared use of the rest then a *comunidad de propiedtarios* is created. Houses on their own plots with no shared facilities will not be members of a *comunidad*.

In a *comunidad* the buyer of a house or an apartment owns his own house or apartment outright – as the English would say, 'freehold' or more accurately 'commonhold' – and shares the use of the remaining areas as part of a community of owners. It is not only the shared pool that is jointly owned but (in an apartment) the lift shafts, corridors, roof, foundations, entrance areas, parking zones, etc.

The members of the *comunidad* are each responsible for their own home. They collectively agree the works needed on the common areas and a budget for those works. They then become responsible for paying their share of those common expenses, as stipulated in their title.

The community is managed by an elected committee and appoints a president and secretary – both of whom are residents in the community. Day-to-day management is usually delegated to an administrator, who need not be a resident in the community.

The charges of the *comunidad* are divided in the proportions stipulated in deed creating the *comunidad*. You will pay the same *comunidad* fees whether you use the place all year round or only for two weeks' holiday. Of course your other bills (water, electricity, etc.) will vary with usage.

The *comunidad* should provide not only for routine work but, through its fees, set aside money for periodic major repairs. If they do not – or if the amount set aside is inadequate – the general meeting can authorise a supplemental levy to raise the sums needed.

The rules (*reglamento*) set by the *comunidad* are intended to improve the quality of life of residents. They could, for example, deal with concerns about noise (no radios by the pool), prohibit the use of the pool after 10pm, ban the hanging of washing on balconies, and so on. More importantly they could control pets or any commercial activity in the building. These *reglamentos* are important documents. Every buyer of a property in a *comunidad* should insist on having a copy of the rules. If you do not speak Spanish you should have them translated or, at least, summarised in English.

See also **Selecting a Property**, 'Types of Ownership', pp.115–17.

Initial Contracts

In Spain most sales start with a preliminary contract. The type of contract will depend on whether you are buying a finished or an unfinished property. Signing any of these documents has far-reaching legal consequences, which are sometimes different from the consequences of signing a similar document in the UK. Whichever type of contract you are asked to sign, always seek legal advice before doing so.

Generally the preliminary contract is prepared by the estate agent – who is professionally qualified in Spain – or by the developer. Estate agents' contracts are often based on a pre-printed document in a standard format. Some contracts coming from estate agents are legally muddled and not properly thought through. They can blur or mix different types of contractual obligation, often referring to mutually exclusive concepts in the same document – for example, referring to it as a contract of sale and an option contract.

Sometimes the contracts are extremely one-sided, giving their client – the seller – all the rights and taking away all the rights of the buyer.

It is very important that these contracts are not just accepted as final. In many cases they will need to be modified, in some cases extensively.

If You Are Buying a Finished Property

You will be invited to sign one or more of three different documents. Each has different features. Each has different legal consequences. Each is appropriate in certain circumstances and inappropriate in others.

Offer to Buy

This is, technically, not a contract at all. It is a formal written offer from the potential buyer to the potential seller. It will state that you wish to buy the stated property for a stated price and that you will complete the transaction within a stated period. The offer will normally be accompanied by the payment of a deposit to the estate agent or seller. The deposit is not fixed but will usually range from 2 to 5 per cent of the price offered.

This document binds you. It is not a mere enquiry as to whether the seller might be interested in selling. If he says that he accepts the offer, then you (and he) become legally bound to proceed with the transaction.

Generally we do not like written offers. We prefer the idea of making a verbal enquiry as to whether the seller would accept a certain price and, once he says yes, for a binding bilateral contract of sale (*contrato privado de compraventa*) to be signed.

Reservation/Option Contract

This is a written document in which the seller agrees to take a stated property off the market for a fixed period and to sell it at a stated price to a stated person at any time within a stated period.

The seller will usually require that any person taking up his offer pays him a **deposit**. Once he has received this deposit, the seller must reserve the property for you until the end of the period specified in the contract.

This is similar to an English option contract. If you want to go ahead and buy the property you can but you are not obliged to do so. If you do not go ahead, you lose your deposit.

The contract could contain special '**get-out clauses**' (*condiciones resolutorias*) stipulating the circumstances in which the buyer will be entitled to the refund of his deposit if he decides not to go ahead. The drafting of these clauses is of vital importance. See your lawyer.

If you do want to go ahead you can exercise the option at any point up to the end of the agreed period. If the seller refuses to go ahead, the buyer is entitled to claim compensation.

Full Preliminary Contract (*Contrato Privado de Compraventa*)

This is, in most parts of Spain, the most common type of document. It is called a *contrato privado* (private contract) not because it is secret but because it is not recorded in the public register kept by a notary. It is an agreement that commits both parties. The seller must sell a stated property at a stated price to a stated person on the terms set out in the contract. The buyer must buy.

This is the most far-reaching of the three documents covered in this section and so it is particularly important that you are satisfied that it contains all of the terms necessary to protect your position. Take legal advice. Remember that under Spanish law, by signing and completing this contract you become, in some senses, the owner of the property, though you will need to sign a deed of sale (*escritura*) and register your ownership to be safe as far as third parties are concerned.

The contract will contain a variety of 'routine' clauses.

- **The seller and buyer should both be stated fully.**

- **The property should be described fully, both in an everyday sense and by reference to its land registry details.**

- **A date for the signing of the deed of sale (*escritura*) will be fixed or the contract will permit either party to require the signing of the *escritura* at any point by giving notice to the other.**

- **A statement will be made as to when possession will take place – normally on the date of signing the title.**

- **The price is fixed.**

- **A receipt for any deposit is given.**

- **The property should be sold with vacant possession.**

- **The property should be sold free of any charges, debts or burdens and all bills should be paid up to date before signing the *escritura*.**

- **The contract will provide for who is to pay the costs of the purchase.**

- **The contract may confirm the details of any agent involved and who is to pay his commission.**

- **The contract will set out what is to happen if one or both of the parties breaks the contract.**

- **The contract will establish the law to cover the contract and the address of the parties for legal purposes.**

If the buyer or seller drops out of the contract or otherwise breaks it, various arrangements may be made.

A special **deposit** (*arras*) might be payable by the buyer. If he fails to complete he will lose the deposit. If the seller fails to complete, he will have to return double the deposit paid.

Alternatively the contract may provide for a deposit to be paid as a simple part of the price of the property. The contract can provide for all or part of this deposit – and any other sums paid up to the relevant moment – to be lost if the buyer does not proceed.

If the parties fail to comply with their obligations there is the ultimate remedy of seeking a court order. As in any country this is very much a last resort as it is costly, time-consuming and there is no guarantee of the outcome of a court case. If a court order is made in your favour, this order can be registered at the land registry.

If You Are Buying an Unfinished Property

Reservation Contract

Usually in these cases there is a preliminary contract. This is the reservation contract (*see* above). This allows you to reserve a plot when you see it and allows you time to sign one of the other types of contract when you have made the necessary enquiries.

Full Contract

There are three possible types of contract in this case:

• **Contract for immediate sale of the land.**

You sign a contract agreeing to sign the title deed in respect of the land – and anything the seller has so far built on it – now. This involves paying for the land and work so far undertaken in full at this stage. At the same time you enter into a contract to build your house on the land.

As the building continues, it automatically becomes the property of the buyer. The buyer, of course, has the obligation to pay the agreed price, usually by instalments dependent on the progress of the building work.

This has the great advantage of securing the money you pay to the builder. If the builder goes bust, you own the land and everything built on it. It only really works for property built on its own plot rather than, say, apartments. It can be tax- and cost-inefficient.

• **Contract 'on plan'.**

You agree to buy a property once it has been built and agree to make payments in stages as the construction progresses. Sometimes the payments are dependent on the progress of the building works. On other occasions they are due on set dates. The latter are now the more common option, though less attractive to the buyer.

Once the property has been built you will sign the deed of sale and pay the balance of the price. It is only then that you become the owner of the property and register your title. Until then, if the builder goes bust you are simply one of many creditors.

Since 1968 the law has required that the contract must give details of a guarantee to secure completion of the construction in the event, for example, that the seller went bust. In most parts of Spain these guarantees are furnished with no problems. In other places builders simply refuse to give the guarantee. 'I am your guarantee. I am a man of honour. I have been building for over 30 years!' This is part of the commonplace experience in Spain of the law saying one thing but people blatantly doing something entirely different. Why do they do it? They think that they save money (guarantees have to be paid for and the bank will probably not release all the money until the property is finished) and they think the law is a bureaucratic imposition. In Spain there is a saying (*refran*): 'Spain is a constitutional monarchy with 40 million kings'. Most of these areas were poor and backward. The peasant mentality of 'build now, paperwork later' still prevails although many peasants are now multi-millionaires. How do they get away with it? Remember that big companies and honourable men do go bust. Rolls-Royce. Barings Bank. Enron.

• **Contract to buy once the property has been built**
You agree to buy a plot of land and building. You agree to pay once it has been built. Simple! You take title and pay the money at the same time. This is really the same as buying a resale property. This type of contract is little used.

Flipping

If you intend to sell an 'off-plan' property prior to its completion to somebody else with the intention of making a profit (a 'flip'), make sure that the contract that you are signing allows you to do this – some developers do not like the fact that you are making some money and will refuse to allow anybody else other than you to sign the title deed (although many developers use this possibility as a selling point and actively encourage people to do a 'flip').

Other Documentation

Does the property have planning permission/a building licence?

You should be given a full specification for the property, a copy of the community rules and constitution if the property shares common facilities, and a copy of any agreements you have entered into regarding ongoing management or letting of the property. All are important documents. Pay particular attention to the specification. It is not unknown for the show flat to have marble floors and high-quality wooden kitchens but for the specification to show concrete tiles and MDF.

Checklist – Signing a Contract

Property in the Course of Construction	Existing Property
Are you clear about what you are buying?	
Have you taken legal advice about who should be the owner of the property?	
Have you taken legal advice about inheritance issues?	
Are you clear about the property lines (boundaries)?	
Are you clear about access to the property?	
	Are you sure you can modify/add to the property as you want?
	Are you sure you can use the property for what you want?

Is the property connected to water, electricity, gas, etc?

Have you had a survey done?

Have you included 'get-out' clauses for checks not yet made?

Have you made all necessary checks *or* arranged for them to be made?

Is your mortgage finance arranged or a 'get-out' clause inserted in the contract?

Is the seller clearly described?

If the seller is not signing in person, have you seen a power of attorney/mandate to authorize the sale?

Are you fully described?

Is the property fully described with regard to land registry details?

Is the price correct?

Can the price increase and are the extra expenses described fully?

Are the stage payments fully described?	Does contract say when possession will be given?
Are arrangements for stage payments satisfactory?	Receipt for the deposit paid?
Is the date for completion of the work agreed?	In what capacity is the deposit paid?
Does the property have planning permission/licence to build?	Does the property have a habitation licence?

Is the date for signing the *escritura* agreed upon?

Does the contract provide for the sale to be free of charges and debts?

Does the contract provide for vacant possession?

Who is the notary?

Is the estate agent's commission dealt with?

What happens if there is a breach of contract?

Are all the necessary special 'get-out' clauses included?

Steps Between Signing the Contract and Signing the Deed of Sale (*Escritura*)

Power of Attorney (*Poderes*)

Very often it will not be convenient for you to go to Spain to sign the *escritura* in person. Sometimes there may be other things that, in the normal course of events, would require your personal intervention but where it would be inconvenient for you to have to deal with them yourself. Just as often you will not know whether you will be available to sign in person. Completion dates on Spanish property are notoriously fluid and so you could plan to be there but suffer a last-minute delay to the signing that makes it impossible.

The solution to this problem is the power of attorney. This document authorises the person appointed (the *apoderado*) to do whatever the document authorises on behalf of the person granting the power (the *apoderante*).

The most sensible type of power to use will be the Spanish style of power that is appropriate to the situation. The power will be signed in front of a notary either in the UK or in Spain. If it is signed in front of a UK notary it has to be ratified by, of all people, the Foreign and Commonwealth Office for use overseas. This sounds very grand but is actually quick and simple.

The type of Spanish power of attorney that you will need depends on what you want to use it for. Your specialist English lawyer can discuss your requirements with you and prepare the necessary document. Alternatively you can deal directly with the Spanish notary who will ultimately need the power.

In theory an English-style power should be sufficient, but in practice the cost and delay associated with getting it recognised can be unacceptable.

Even if you intend to go to Spain to sign, it is sensible to think about granting a power 'just in case'. It is not something that can be done at the last moment. From the decision to getting the document to Spain will take at least seven and more likely 10 days. If you are able to go, the power will not be used.

Even if you have granted a power of attorney, if you get the opportunity to go to Spain at the time of the signing it is worth doing so. It is quite interesting but, more importantly, you will be able to check the house to make sure that everything is in order before the *escritura* is signed.

Getting the Money to Spain

There are several ways of getting the money to Spain.

Electronic Transfer

The most practical is to have it sent electronically by SWIFT transfer from a UK bank directly to the recipient's bank in Spain. This costs about £10–35 depending on your bank. It is safer to allow two or three days for the money to arrive in a rural bank, despite everyone's protestations that it will be there the same day.

Europe has now (2005) introduced unique account numbers for all bank accounts. These incorporate a code for the identity of the bank and branch involved as well as the account number of the individual customer. These are known as IBAN numbers. They should be quoted, if possible, on all international currency transfers.

You can send the money from your own bank, via your lawyers or via a specialist currency dealer. For the sums you are likely to be sending you should receive an exchange rate much better than the 'tourist rate' you see in the press. There is no such thing as a fixed exchange rate in these transactions. The bank's official inter-bank rate changes by the second and the job of the bank's currency dealers is to make a profit by selling to you at the lowest rate they can get away with! Thus if you do a lot of business with a bank and they know you are on the ball you are likely to be offered a better rate than a one-off customer. For this reason it is often better to send it via your specialist UK lawyers, who will be dealing with large numbers of such transactions. This also has the advantage that their bank, which deals with international payments all the time, is less likely to make a mistake causing delay to the payment than your bank for which such a payment might be a rarity.

You or your lawyers might use a specialist currency dealer to make the transfer of funds instead of a main UK bank. Such dealers often give a better exchange rate than an ordinary bank. Sometimes the difference can be significant, especially compared with your local branch of a high street bank. This author regularly carries out spot checks. His secretary, anonymously, once asked a major high street bank to convert £50,000 into euros and send it to Spain. They offered a rate of 1.6125. A currency dealer offered 1.6311. This is a saving of €930 – or £575.

Although these dealers use major banks actually to transfer the funds, you need to make sure that your dealer is reputable. Your money is paid to them, not to the major bank, so you could be at risk if the dealer is not bonded or otherwise protected.

However you make the payment, ensure that you understand whether it is you or the recipient who is going to pick up the receiving bank's charges. If you need a clear amount in Spain you will have to make allowances for these, either by sending a bit extra or by asking your UK bank to pay all the charges. Make sure you have the details of the recipient bank, its customer's name, the account codes and the recipient's reference precisely right. Any error and the payment is likely to come back to you as undeliverable – and may involve you in bearing the cost of it being converted back into sterling.

The bank in Spain will make a charge – which can be substantial – for receiving your money into your account.

Banker's Drafts

You can arrange for your UK bank to issue you with a banker's draft (bank certified cheque), which you can take to Spain and pay into your bank account. Make sure that the bank knows that the draft is to be used overseas and so issues you with an international draft.

Generally this is not a good way to transfer the money. It can take a considerable time – sometimes weeks – for the funds deposited to be made available for your use. The recipient bank's charges can be surprisingly high. The exchange rate offered against a sterling draft may be uncompetitive as you are a captive customer.

Cash

This is not recommended. You will need to declare the money on departure from the UK and on arrival in Spain. You must by law do this if the sum involved is over €8,000. You are well advised to do so for smaller amounts. Even then, if you declare £200,000 or so they will think you are a terrorist or drug dealer! That suspicion can have far-reaching consequences in terms of listings in police files and even surveillance. To add insult to injury the exchange rate you will be offered for cash (whether you take sterling and convert there or buy the euros here) is usually very uncompetitive and the notary may well refuse to accept the money in his account. We have even heard reports of some people being mugged after coming out of the bank with huge amounts of cash. They have then lost the cash and therefore cannot afford to complete the purchase. Don't do it.

Exchange Control and Other Restrictions on Moving Money

For EU nationals there is no longer any exchange control when taking money to or from Spain. There are some statistical records kept showing the flow of funds and the purposes of the transfers.

When you sell your property in Spain you will be able to bring the money back to the UK if you wish to do so.

Final Checks about the Property

All of the points outstanding must be resolved to your satisfaction, as must any other points of importance to you.

Fixing the Completion Date

The date stated in the contract for signing the *escritura* could, most charitably, be described as flexible or aspirational. Often it will move, if only by a day or so. For this reason it is not sensible to book your travel to Spain until you are almost sure that matters will proceed on a certain day.

Checklist – Steps Before Completion

Property in the Course of Construction	Existing Property
Prepare power of attorney	
Check what documents must be produced on signing the *escritura*	
Confirm all outstanding issues have been complied with	
Confirm all other important enquiries are clear	
Receive draft of proposed *escritura* – one month in advance if possible	
Confirm arrangements (date, time, place) for completion with your lender if you have a mortgage	
Confirm arrangements (date, time, place) for completion with notary	
Send necessary funds to Spain	
Receive rules of community	
Insurance cover arranged?	
Sign off work or list defects	Proof of payment of community fees
	Proof of payment of other bills

The Deed of Sale (*Escritura*)

As has already been said, this must be signed in front of a Spanish notary either by the parties in person or someone holding power of attorney for them.

It will contain a statement that the notary has advised you of your fiscal obligations arising out of the sale. Because it is rare for notaries actually to perform this important part of their duty it is worth setting out some of these sanctions.

- **The right to raise a supplemental demand for tax not paid plus interest plus a penalty.**

- **If the amount declared is less than 80 per cent of the value as assessed by the tax office – or the apparent under-declaration exceeds €12,000 – to treat the balance as a gift from the seller to the buyer. This is a taxable gift.**

- **If there is a clear and intentional understatement, the right to buy the property at the price stated.**

There are other consequences of under-declaration, referred to above.

Formalities

Certain procedures are followed at the signing of the *escritura*.

The parties are identified by their passports or identity cards. This will normally be done, initially, by the notary's clerk and then also by the notary.

The notary's clerk may also go through the content of the *escritura* with the parties. This tends to be very superficial and often the person concerned will have limited English.

The parties will then be ushered into the presence of the notary. In addition to the buyer and seller it would be possible for the group to comprise also the notary's clerk, your lawyer, a translator, a representative of your mortgage lender, the estate agent and any sub-agent appointed by the estate agent. Most of these people are there to receive money! Needless to say, if they all turn up it can get a little loud and confusing!

Translators

If you do not speak Spanish an interpreter should be present when you sign the *escritura*. The attitude of notaries when it comes to assessing when an interpreter is necessary varies enormously. No written translation is provided as a matter of course.

After the *Escritura* has been Signed

The taxes must be paid. Once the taxes are paid, your title and any mortgage should be presented for registration at the land registry. This should be done as quickly as possible. He who registers first gets priority.

After several months the land registry will issue a certificate to the effect that the title has been registered.

The Cost of Buying a Property

There are certain fees and taxes payable by a buyer when acquiring a property in Spain. They are sometimes known as completion expenses or completion or closing costs. They are impossible to predict with total accuracy at the outset of a transaction, because there are a number of variable factors that will not become clear until later. We can, however, give a general guide.

These costs are calculated on the basis of the price that you declared as the price paid for the property in the *escritura*. The size of these expenses, coupled with the Spanish dislike for paying tax, has led to the habit of accidentally under-declaring the price in the *escritura*. These days are now largely over and we can only suggest that the full price of the property is declared. *See* 'How Much Should be Declared in the Deed of Sale', pp.168–9.

Notary's Fees

These are fixed by law, so are not negotiable. They will depend on the type of property being bought and its price.

Typical fees would be:

Price more than	Up to	Charge	Cumulative total fee
€0	€6,000	€90	€90
€6,000	€30,000	4.5/1,000	€200
€30,000	€60,000	1.5/1,000	€240
€60,000	€150,000	1/1,000	€330
€150,000	€600,000	0.5/1,000	€600
€600,000	No upper limit	0.3/1,000	

As a general guide, if you wish to avoid the detailed calculation, allow up to 0.4 per cent.

If you have asked the notary to do any additional work over and above the transfer of title to the property or for any advice there will be additional charges.

Taxes

VAT (*Impuesto sobre el Valor Añadido – IVA*)

This applies only to properties bought from a company. It is 7 per cent of the declared purchase price of the property. This is sometimes, but not always, included in the price of the property quoted to you. Check to see whether it is in your case.

There is no IVA in the Canaries. Instead there is a local tax called IGIC which is charged at 5 per cent.

Property Transfer Tax
(*Impuesto sobre Transmisiones Patrimoniales – ITP*)

This is an additional tax of payable on property that is subject to VAT. In most areas it is 7 per cent.

Stamp Duty
(*Impuesto sobre Actos Juridicos Documentados – AJD*)

This is an additional tax payable on the property that is subject to VAT. It is 1 per cent.

Land Registration Fees

This is normally roughly the same as the notary's fee.

Mortgage Costs (if applicable)

If you are taking out a mortgage there will be additional costs. *See* 'Raising Finance to Buy a Property in Spain', p.158. These typically amount to around 4 or 5 per cent of the amount borrowed.

Estate Agent's Charges (if payable by the buyer)

If an estate agent has sold the property the seller usually pays his fees. This can be varied by agreement. *See* 'Estate Agents', pp.132–9.

These fees will be subject to IVA.

Miscellaneous Other Charges

Architect's fees, surveyor's fees, UK legal fees (typically 1 per cent), first connection to water, electricity, and so on. Most of these will be subject to Spanish IVA at varying rates, but your UK lawyer's fees will be outside the scope of UK VAT.

Property Insurance

Most owners of property in Spain take out a multi-risk household policy. This covers the fabric of the building, its contents and any civil responsibility landing on the owner of the property other than in certain specified circumstances, such as liability incurred in connection with the use of a motor car.

Premiums are comparatively cheap in rural areas, more expensive in Madrid and the Costa del Sol.

There are three important points to bear in mind when choosing a suitable policy.

• **Make sure that the level of cover is adequate.**

Just as in the UK, if you under-insure the building and the worst happens, the company will not pay you out for the full extent of your loss.

The amount for which you should be covered as far as civil liability is concerned should be a minimum of one million euros and preferably higher. Because the risk of a claim under this category is small, the premiums for this part of the insurance are low and so high levels of cover can be provided at low cost.

The amount of cover you should have for the building itself should be the full cost of reconstruction of the building. If you own an apartment then the cost of the building insurance for the whole block of apartments should be included in your service charge. You will then only need contents and public liability insurance.

Once this insurance value has been established, it should be increased each year in line with the official index of inflation of building costs. As far as contents are concerned, you should make a detailed estimate of the value of your furnishings and possessions likely to be in the property at any time. Remember to allow for items such as cameras that you may take with you on holiday. Pay particular attention to the details of this policy and study the small print about what you have to specify when taking out the insurance and any limitations on claims that can be made against it. Notice in particular whether there is a requirement to stipulate items of high value. If you have any items of high value it is worth having them photographed and, possibly, valued.

The insurance company might specify any number of security measures that must be in place in your home. If you don't use them, you may find that you are not covered.

• **If you are using the property as holiday accommodation, you must specify a policy which is a holiday policy.**

If you don't, you are likely to find that one of the conditions of the policy is that cover will lapse if the property is empty for 30 or 60 days. Premiums will be higher for holiday homes because the risk is higher.

• **If you intend to let your property you must notify the insurance company and comply with any requirements of the insurance company with regard to the lettings. Otherwise your cover could be void.**

Your premiums will be higher.

There are some UK-based insurance companies who offer cover in respect of properties in Spain. The main advantages in dealing with a UK company are that the documentation is likely to the English and that, if you have to make a claim, the claim will be processed in English. There are some Spanish companies that also have the facility for dealing with claims in English. This should not be under-estimated as an advantage. Unless your Spanish is fluent, you would otherwise have to employ somebody to deal with the claim on your behalf or to translate what you have said into Spanish – something that is never entirely satisfactory.

If you have to make a claim, note that there are usually time limits for doing so. If the claim involves the theft or break-in you will usually have to report the matter to the police. This should normally be done immediately after discovery of the incident and in any case within 24 hours. The claim should be notified to the insurance company without delay. Check the maximum period allowed in your policy, which could be as little as 48 hours.

As with all important documents in Spain the claim should be notified by recorded delivery post.

See also **Settling In**, 'Insurance', pp.235–6.

Key Points

Property under Construction

When buying a new property the key points to look out for are:

• **Make sure you understand exactly what you are buying. How big is the property? What will it look like? How will it be finished? What appliances are included? What facilities will it enjoy?**

• **Who should own the property so as to minimise tax and inheritance problems?**

• **Make sure the contract has all of the necessary 'get-out clauses' required to protect your position.**

• **Try to obtain a bank guarantee if you are buying 'off-plan'.**

• **Be clear about the timetable for making payments.**

• **Think about whether you should forward-buy currency.**

• When you take delivery of the property, consider carefully whether it is worth incurring the expense of an independent survey to confirm that all is in order with the construction and to help draft any 'snagging list'.

Resale Properties

When buying a resale property, the key points to look out for are:

• Make sure you understand exactly what you are buying. Are the boundaries clear? What furniture or fittings are included?

• Think about whether to have the property surveyed, especially if it is nearly 10 years old and your statutory guarantee will soon be expiring.

• Think about who should own the property so as to minimise tax and inheritance problems.

• Make sure the contract has all of the necessary 'get-out' clauses required to protect your position.

• Think about whether you should forward-buy currency.

• When you take delivery of the property, make sure that everything agreed is present.

Old Properties

When buying an old property - by which is meant a property built more than, say, 50 years ago, there are one or two additional points to look out for:

• Are you having a survey? Not to do so can be an expensive mistake.

• Are you clear about any restoration costs to be incurred? Do you have estimates for those charges?

• Are there any planning problems associated with any alterations or improvements you want to make to the property?

• When you take delivery of the property, make sure that everything agreed is present.

Rural Properties

• Such properties have often acquired a number of rights and obligations over the years. Are you clear about any obligations you might be taking on? There are currently special problems to be looked at with rural properties in the tourist areas of the Valencian region (see pp.50 and 110).

• You are probably buying for peace and quiet and the rural idyll. Are you sure that nothing is happening in the vicinity of your property that will be detrimental?

• If you have any plans to change the property or to use it for other purposes, will this be permitted?

• If you intend to build on the site be very clear about minimum permitted plot sizes – which can vary up to 25,000 sq m – and other planning limitations.

City Properties

• City properties will usually be apartments, *see* below.

• Unless you are used to living in a city – and, in particular, a continental city – don't underestimate the noise that will be generated nearby. If you are in a busy area (and you are likely to be) this will go on until late at night. How good is the sound insulation?

• Are your neighbouring properties occupied by full-time residents, are they weekday only *pieds à terre* or are they holiday homes? Think about security issues.

• If you intend to use a car, where will you park?

Apartments and Houses Sharing Facilities

• Have you thought about a survey of the property? Will it include the common parts?

• Make sure you understand the rules of the community.

• Make sure you understand all the charges that will be raised by the community.

• Make contact with its administrator. Ask about issues affecting the community. Are there any major works approved but not yet carried out? Make sure that the contract is clear about who is responsible for paying for these.

• Make contact with other owners. Are they happy with the community and the way it is run? Remember that no one is ever fully happy!

• Understand how the community is run. Once you are an owner, try to attend the general meetings of the community.

Things to Do After Buying a Property

• Insure the property and its contents. Make a full photographic record of the property. This is useful in the event of an insurance claim and for your scrapbook.

• Make arrangements for your bank to pay your *IBI* (local property tax), water and electricity bills, and so on.

• Make a will in the Spanish form covering your assets in Spain. This will usually mean making small changes in your existing UK will as well.

• Appoint a fiscal representative. This is your point of contact with the Spanish tax office. He will also usually complete and file your annual tax return. Your lawyer may provide this service or should be able to suggest a suitable person.

Financial Implications

Taxation

All tax systems are complicated. The Spanish system is no exception. The Spanish would say that it is nearly as complex as ours! Fortunately, most people will only have limited contact with the more intricate parts of the system. For many owners of holiday homes in Spain, their contact with the system will be fairly minimal.

It is helpful to have some sort of understanding about the way in which the system works and the taxes that you might face. Be warned: getting even a basic understanding will make your head hurt. You also need to be particularly careful about words and concepts that seem familiar to you but which have a fundamentally different meaning in Spain from in the UK. Of course, just to confuse you, the rules change every year.

There are several points in this book where I have said that the contents are only a general introduction to the subject. There is nowhere where this is more true that in this section. Books (and lengthy ones at that) have been written about the subject of Spanish taxation. This general introduction does little more than scratch the surface of an immensely complex subject. It is intended to allow you to have a sensible discussion with your professional advisers and, perhaps, to help you work out the questions that you need to be asking them. It is not intended as a substitute for proper professional advice.

Your situation when you have a foot in two countries – and, in particular, when you are moving permanently from one country to another – involves the consideration of the tax systems in both countries with a view to minimising your tax obligations in both. It is not just a question of paying the lowest amount of tax in, say, Spain; the best choice in Spain could be very damaging to your position in the UK. Similarly, the most tax-efficient way of dealing with your affairs in the UK could be problematic in Spain. The task of the international adviser and his client is to find a path of compromise which allows you to enjoy the major advantages available in both countries without incurring any of the worst drawbacks. In other words, there is an issue of compromise. There is no perfect solution to most tax questions. That is not to say that there are not a great many bad solutions into which you can all too easily stumble.

What should guide you when making a decision as to which course to pursue? Each individual will have a different set of priorities. Some are keen to screw the last ha'penny of advantage out of their situation. Others recognise that they will have to pay some tax but simply wish to moderate their tax bill. For many the main concern is a simple structure which they understand and can continue to manage without further assistance in the years ahead. Just as different clients have different requirements, so different advisers have differing views as to the function of the adviser when dealing with a client's tax affairs. One of your first tasks when speaking to your financial adviser should be to discuss your basic philosophy concerning the payment of tax and management of your affairs, to make sure that you are both operating with the same objective in mind and that you are comfortable with his or her approach to solving your problem.

Are You Resident or Non-resident for Tax Purposes?

The biggest single factor in determining how you will be treated by the tax authorities in any country is whether you are resident in that country for tax purposes. This concept of tax residence causes a great deal of confusion.

Tax residence can have different meanings in different countries. In Spain tax residence is known as *domicilio fiscal*.

Let us first look at what it does not mean. It is nothing to do with whether you have registered as resident in a country or with whether you have obtained a residence permit or residency card (though a person who has a card will usually be tax resident). Nor does it have anything to do with whether you simply have a home (residence) in that country – although a person who is tax resident will normally have a home there. Nor has it much to do with your intentions.

Tax residence is a question of fact. The law lays down certain tests that will be used to decide whether you are tax resident or not. If you fall into the categories stipulated in the tests, then you will be considered tax resident whether you want to be or not and whether it was your intention to be tax resident or not.

It is your responsibility to make your tax declarations each year. The decision as to whether you fall into the category of resident is, in the first instance, made by the tax office. If you disagree with the decision, then you can appeal through the courts.

Because people normally change their tax residence when they move from one country to another, the basis on which decisions are made tends to be regulated by international law and to be pretty, but not totally, consistent from country to country.

The Rules that Determine Residence

You will have to consider two different questions concerning tax residence. The first is whether you will be treated as tax resident in the UK and the second is whether you will be treated as tax resident in Spain.

United Kingdom

It is outside the scope of this book to go into any details about UK taxation but some basic points will have to be dealt with for the explanation of Spanish taxation to make any sense.

In the UK there are two tests that will help determine where you pay tax. These assess your domicile and your residence.

Domicile

Your domicile is the place that is your real home. It is the place where you have your roots. For most people it is the place where they were born. You can change your domicile but it is often not easy to do so. Changes in domicile can have far-reaching tax consequences and can be a useful tax reduction tool.

Residence

Residence falls into two categories. Under UK law there is a test of simple residence – actually living here other than on a purely temporary basis – and of ordinary residence.

Residence falls into two categories. Under English law there is a test of simple residence – actually living here most of the time – and of ordinary residence.

People are generally treated as **resident** in the UK if they spend 183 or more days a year in the UK. Visitors are also treated as resident if they come to the UK regularly and spend significant time here. If they spend, on average over a period of four or more years, more than three months here, they are treated as tax resident.

A person can continue to be **ordinarily resident** in the UK even after they have stopped actually being resident here. A person is ordinarily resident in the UK if their presence is a little more settled. The residence is an important part of his life – it will normally have gone on for some time.

The most important thing to understand is that, once you have been ordinarily resident in this country, the simple fact of going overseas will not automatically bring that residence to an end. If you leave this country in order to take up permanent residence elsewhere then, by concession, the Inland Revenue will treat you as ceasing to be resident on the day following your departure. But they will not treat you as ceasing to be ordinarily resident if, after leaving, you spend an average of 91 or more days a year in this country over any four-year period.

In other words, they don't want you to escape too easily!

Until 1993 you were also classified as ordinarily resident in the UK if you had accommodation available for your use in the UK, even though you might spend 364 days of the year living abroad. This very unfair rule was cancelled, but many people still worry about it. It is not necessary to do so, provided you limit your visits to the UK to less than the 91 days referred to above.

Spain

Tax residence in Spain – *domicilio fiscal* – is tested by a number of rules, the main ones of which are as follows:

- **If you spend more than 183 days in Spain in any tax year, you are tax resident in Spain. This time can be in one block or in bits and pieces through the year. The tax year runs from 1 January to 31 December.**

• If you spend less than 184 days in Spain but do not have a home elsewhere or your principal residence is in Spain, you will be treated as tax resident in Spain.

• If your centre of economic interests is in Spain, you are tax resident in Spain. Your centre of economic interests is where you have your main investments or business or other sources of income and, usually, where you spend much of your money.

• If you work in Spain, except where that work is ancillary to work elsewhere, you will be tax resident in Spain.

• If you have a Spanish resident's card, you will usually be tax resident in Spain.

• If your family is resident in Spain, you will be assumed to be resident in Spain unless you show the contrary. If you satisfy the taxman that you are not resident in Spain, then you will pay tax on your income and assets as a non-resident but your husband/wife will pay taxes on their income and assets as a resident. *See* below for details.

Tax Residence in More than One Country

Remember that you can be tax resident in more than one country under the respective rules of those countries. For example, you might spend 230 days in the year in Spain and 135 days in the UK. In this case you could end up, under the rules of each country, being responsible for paying the same tax in two or more countries. This would be unfair, so many countries have signed reciprocal 'Double Taxation Treaties'. The UK and Spain have such a treaty. It contains 'tie breakers' and other provisions to decide, where there is the possibility of being required to pay tax twice, in which country any particular category of tax should be paid. *See* 'Double Taxation Treaty', pp.206–7.

Decisions You Must Make

The most basic decisions that you will have to make when planning your tax affairs is whether to cease to be resident in the UK, whether to cease to be ordinarily resident in the UK and whether to change your domicile to another country. Each of these has many consequences, many of which are not obvious.

The second consideration is when in the tax year to make these changes. Once again, that decision has many consequences.

For many ordinary people getting these decisions wrong can cost them tens of thousands of pounds in totally unnecessary taxation and a great deal of irritation and inconvenience. It is vital that you seek proper professional advice before making these decisions. You will need advice from specialist lawyers, accountants or financial advisers, all of whom should be able to help you.

Taxes Payable in the UK

The significance of these residence rules is that you will continue to be liable for some British taxes for as long as you are either ordinarily resident or domiciled in the UK. Put far too simply, once you have left the UK to live in Spain:

- You will continue to have to pay tax in the UK on any capital gains you make anywhere in the world for as long as you are ordinarily resident and domiciled in United Kingdom.

- You will continue to be liable for UK inheritance tax on all of your assets located anywhere in the world for as long as you remain domiciled in the UK. This will be subject to double taxation relief. Other, more complex rules also apply in certain circumstances.

- You will always pay UK Income tax (Schedule A) on income arising from land and buildings in the UK – wherever your domicile, residence or ordinary residence.

- You will pay UK income tax (Schedule D) on the following basis:

  - Income from 'self-employed' trade or profession carried out in the UK (Cases I and II) – normally taxed in the UK if income arises in the UK.

  - Income from interest, annuities or other annual payments from the UK (Case III) – normally taxed in the UK if income arises in the UK and you are ordinarily resident in the UK.

  - Income from investments and businesses outside the UK (Cases IV and V) – normally only taxed in the UK if you are UK domiciled and resident or ordinarily resident in the UK.

  - Income from government pensions (fire, police, army, civil servant, etc.) in all cases taxed in the UK.

  - Sundry profits not otherwise taxable arising out of land or building in the UK – always taxed in the UK.

- You will pay income tax on any income earned from salaried employment in the UK (Schedule E) only on any earnings from duties performed in the UK unless you are resident and ordinarily resident in the UK – in which case you will usually pay tax in the UK on your worldwide earnings.

If you are only buying a holiday home and will remain primarily resident in the UK, your tax position in the UK will not change very much. You will have to declare any income you make from your Spanish property as part of your UK tax declaration. The calculation of tax due on that income will be made in accordance with UK rules, which will result in a different taxable sum than is used by the Spanish authorities. The UK taxman will give you full credit for the taxes already paid in Spain.

On the disposal of the property you should disclose the profit made to the UK taxman. He will again give full credit for Spanish tax paid. Similarly on your death the assets in Spain must be disclosed on the UK probate tax declaration but, once again, you will be given full credit for sums paid in Spain.

Capital Gains Tax

If you are either resident or ordinarily resident in the UK, you may be liable to capital gains tax on gains arising when you dispose of assets situated anywhere in the world. Disposing of an asset means selling, exchanging, transferring, giving it away or realising a capital sum from it. Usually you will not pay capital gains tax on:

- **the transfer of an asset to your spouse.**
- **the disposal of private motor vehicles.**
- **the disposal of household goods and personal effects up to a value of £6,000 per item.**
- **the disposal of a private home which has been treated as your main or only residence during the time you have owned it.**

'Overseas assets' are assets located outside the UK under capital gains tax rules. For assets such as land, and most types of immovable property, the asset is situated where it is located.

If you are resident or ordinarily resident in the UK, and dispose of such assets, you will normally be liable to capital gains tax on any gains arising from them. But if you are not domiciled in the UK (i.e. if you have elected to take Spanish domicile), you are taxed on such gains only to the extent that they are brought in or 'remitted' to the UK in a tax year during which you are resident or ordinarily resident in the UK.

There is no capital gains tax charge on gains remitted to the UK before you become resident in the UK.

Inheritance Tax

Domiciled in the UK

Liability to UK inheritance tax depends on your domicile at the time you make the transfer. For inheritance tax purposes, there is the concept of '**deemed domicile**'. Even if you are not domiciled in the UK under general law, you will be treated as domiciled in the UK at the time of a transfer if you were domiciled in the UK within the three years immediately before the transfer or if you were ordinarily resident in the UK for at least 17 of the 20 income tax years of assessment, ending with the year in which you made the transfer.

You or your personal representatives may be liable to UK inheritance tax if you transfer anything of value, such as a lifetime gift or a willed transfer to your personal representatives on your death.

Which Assets are Taxable in the UK?

Generally, if you are domiciled or deemed to be domiciled in the UK, inheritance tax applies to your assets wherever they are situated. If the value of your gift or the assets in your estate is above the threshold then you may be liable to inheritance tax. If you are domiciled abroad, e.g. in Spain, inheritance tax applies only to your UK assets. However, if you are domiciled abroad there is no charge on excluded assets, so the taxman may remove certain other types of UK assets from the tax charge.

The location of the assets is decided according to general law but is subject to any special provisions in a double taxation agreement. The normal rules are:

- **Rights or interests in or over immovable property (such as land and houses) and chattels are situated where the property is located.**

- **Coins and bank notes are situated wherever they happen to be at the time of the transfer.**

- **Registered shares or securities are situated where they are registered.**

- **Bearer securities are situated where the certificate of title is located at the time of the transfer.**

- **Goodwill is located where the business to which it is attached is carried out.**

- **An interest in a partnership is situated in the country whose law governs the partnership agreement.**

- **Debts are situated where the debtor resides.**

- **Bank accounts are situated at the branch where the account is kept.**

Should You Pay Tax in Spain?

Under Spanish law, it is your responsibility to fill in a tax return in each year when you have any taxable income. The rules are applied more strictly every year, and if you are caught not paying the taxes you owe, the penalties are substantial. The irritation can be even more substantial.

The tax office is generally known as **Hacienda**, though its proper name is now **Agencia Estatal de Administración Tributaria**. It is organised by province. The tax office provides a lot of help and advice – including tax forms and guidance notes – over the Internet. It is, not surprisingly, almost all in Spanish.

Local Spanish Taxes

Both residents and non-residents pay these taxes. The taxes payable fall into various categories.

IBI (*Impuesto sobre Bienes Inmuebles*)

The IBI is paid if you own a residential property and use it yourself (or have it available for your use). It is paid by the person who occupied the property on 1 January in any year. It is not usually apportioned if they later move.

The tax is raised and spent by the town hall (*ayuntamiento*) of the area where you live. It is calculated on the basis of the notional rental value (*valor catastral*) of your property. You can appeal against the valuation decision, but the sums involved are usually so small it is not worthwhile.

The amount you will be charged will be the rental value multiplied by the tax rate fixed in your locality.

Refuse Tax (*Basura*)

Rubbish collection charges are, in some areas, raised separately.

Other Local Taxes

Town halls can also raise taxes for other projects and to cover shortfalls.

Payment of Local Property Taxes

A demand for payment is sent each year. The sum claimed must be paid by the specified date (which varies from place to place). Failure to do so incurs a 20 per cent penalty. It is probably simplest to arrange for payment from your bank by direct debit.

The combined total of these taxes is low, perhaps £100 for a small cottage or £400 for a larger house.

Other Taxes Payable in Spain – Non-residents

In general, a person who is non-resident for tax purposes has few contacts with the Spanish tax system and they are fairly painless.

Please bear in mind the complexity of the Spanish tax system. What follows can only be a very brief summary of the position.

Income Tax (*Impuesto sobre la Renta de no Residentes*)

As a non-resident you will generally only pay tax on:

- **Income generated from land and buildings located in Spain. If you own a building in Spain and let it out, the Spanish government collects the first wedge of tax from you.**
- **Income from Spanish securities and capital invested in Spain.**
- **Income from business activities in Spain.**

- **Earned income if you are employed or self-employed in Spain.**
- **A purely notional or theoretical income based on 2 per cent of the valor catastral of any property they own in Spain. This rate drops to 1.1 per cent of the official value (*valor catastral*) if this has been revised since 1994.**

Income tax is calculated on these amounts at, generally, 25 per cent. Note that if you are letting out your property you will usually have to pay tax on every cent earned, without deductions or allowances. For some people it can therefore be more sensible to set the rental up as a business and thus claim the normal business reliefs and allowances.

If you *only* own a home and have to pay the *notional* income tax, your tax returns may be submitted at any point during the year on form 214. A couple jointly owning a property must each make a declaration in respect of their part of the property.

If you have other income – including rental income – you must file the 'full' form 210, technically within 30 days of receipt of the income.

Tax on your income for the year 1 January 2005 to 31 December 2005 is declared and paid in 2006.

Corporation Tax

A company will pay tax on the profits it makes from activities in Spain but not its activities elsewhere. The tests of company residence and these taxes are not considered further here.

Taxes on Wealth (*Patrimonio*)

You will pay Spanish wealth tax on your assets in Spain.

You can deduct from your taxable assets any debts you owe in Spain or secured against the asset.

Tax is applied at the rates shown on the table below.

Wealth Tax Rates – 2005 (Payable 2006)

Assets from (€)	Up to (€)	Rate (%)	Total Tax Payable at Top of Band (€)
Nil	167,129	0.2	334
167,129	334,253	0.3	836
334,253	668,500	0.5	2,507
668,500	1,337,000	0.9	8,523
1,337,000	2,673,999	1.3	25,904
2,673,999	5,347,998	1.7	71,362
5,347,998	10,695,996	2.1	183,670
Over 10,695,996		2.5	

Tax on Real Estate Owned by 'Foreign' Companies in Spain

This tax – 3 per cent of the value of the real estate held – applies to all foreign companies with property in Spain.

The tax is based not on the market value of the property but rather on the lower *catastral* value and is payable unless all of the following apply:

- **The company is fiscally resident in a country that has a double taxation treaty with Spain.**

- **The tax treaty has provisions permitting disclosure of information between the two countries. This includes most countries except tax havens such as Gibraltar, Isle of Man, Channel Islands, and so on.**

- **The true (beneficial) owners of the company are also tax resident in such a 'tax treaty' country.**

- **The company makes an annual declaration of the identity of its shareholders and produces proof of payment of its taxes in its 'home' country.**

There are other exemptions of limited application.

If the real estate is owned by a chain of companies, the test is applied all the way up the chain.

British companies do not have to pay this tax but 'tax haven' companies, including the Channel Islands and Isle of Man companies, do.

If your property is owned in a way that attracts this tax, it is probably worth seeking advice as to how to restructure the ownership to avoid the tax.

Taxes on Capital Gains

You will pay tax on the capital gain you make on the sale of real estate in Spain or on any other capital gain made from property or a business in Spain. This is taxed at 35 per cent of the gain, after various allowances. The calculation of the tax-free allowance is complex.

If the property was bought before 31 December 1986 – and it has not been improved during this period – there is no capital gains tax.

Otherwise the gain is calculated. The real price of the purchase – in effect, the price declared in the title – is adjusted by adding the costs and taxes of acquisition, except interest charges. Provided you have owned the property for at least one full year, this adjusted purchase cost is then further adjusted by multiplying by a coefficient published annually by the tax office, of between 1 and 1.2. The cost of any improvements to the property is then adjusted in the same way and added to the figure calculated. The resulting figure is deducted from the sale price – realistically the price declared in the deed of sale (*escritura*) – and tax is paid on the profit.

If the property was acquired before 31 December 1994, then the taxable gain is further reduced. You will pay tax on the following percentage of the gain:

Full Years' Ownership Completed before 31 December 1996	Percentage Taxable
1	100
2	100
3	88.89
4	77.78
5	66.67
6	55.56
7	44.45
8	33.34
9	22.23
10	11.12
Over 10	0

If the seller is not tax resident in Spain and the property was acquired after 31 December 1986, the payment of the tax on the gain is partly collected by a withholding deposit of 5 per cent, taken at the time of the sale. The buyer must pay 5 per cent of the price to the tax office instead of to the seller. The other 95 per cent is paid as normal to the seller. The buyer supplies the seller with a completed form 211 showing the payment made to the taxman. To recover any balance due, the seller will need to submit a tax return within three months. This will usually require a little tax advice.

If the buyer does not pay this five per cent retention to the tax office, he will be liable for any tax owed by the seller.

Taxes on Death

Inheritance tax is paid in Spain on the value of any assets in Spain as at the date of death.

The tax is an inheritance tax rather than, as in the UK, an estate tax. That is, the tax is calculated by reference to each individual's inheritance rather than on the basis of the estate as a whole. Thus two people each inheriting part of the estate will each pay their own tax. Even if they each inherit the same amount, the amount of tax they pay may be different, depending on their personal circumstances.

All of the assets will have to be declared for the purposes of UK taxation (*see* pp.195–6). Again, double taxation relief will apply, so you will not pay the same tax twice.

The overall value of the part of the estate you inherit is calculated in accordance with guidelines laid down by the tax authorities. Real estate, for example, is valued at market value, *valor catastral* or the tax office's estimated value – whichever is the greatest. Furnishings and personal effects are valued – unless you choose to the contrary – at 3 per cent of the value of the real estate. Other assets such as shares and bank accounts are generally valued as at the date of the death. This is declared by the person who inherits but is subject to challenge by the tax authorities.

Inheritance Tax Rates – 2005

Assets from (€)	Amount of Gift Up to (€)	Rate of Tax (%)	Total Tax Payable at Top of Band (€)
Nil	7,993.46	7.65	611.50
7,993.46	15,980.91	8.50	1,290.43
15,980.91	23,968.36	9.35	2,037.26
23,968.36	31,955.81	10.20	2,851.98
31,955.81	39,943.26	11.05	3,734.59
39,943.26	47,930.22	11.90	4,685.04
47,930.22	55,918.17	12.75	5,703.50
55,918.17	63,905.62	13.60	6,789.80
63,905.62	71,893.07	14.45	7,943.98
71,893.07	79,880.52	15.30	9,166.06
79,880.52	119,757.67	16.15	15,606.22
119,757.67	159,634.83	18.70	23,063.25
159,634.83	239,389.13	21.25	40,011.04
239,389.13	398,777.54	25.50	80,655.09
398,777.54	797,555.10	29.75	199,291.41
Over 797,555.08		34.00	

Any debts (including mortgage or overdraft) are deducted from the asset value as are medical bills and funeral costs.

Some gifts on inheritance are partly tax exempt:

Partially Exempt Gifts on Inheritance – Allowances – 2005

To wife/husband, parents, children, brothers/sisters	€15,957
Extra allowance for children under 21 – for each year over 13 and under 21	€3,990
To uncles, aunts, cousins, nephews and nieces	€7,955

The tax rates on the taxable amount of any gift are as shown in the box above.

But this is not the end of the matter. The rates of tax payable depend on the relationship between the deceased and the person inheriting and their pre-existing wealth in Spain.

The tax rate is multiplied by the following amounts:

Existing Wealth of Person who Inherits	Group 1	Group 2	Group 3
€0–402,678	1.0000	1.5882	2.0000
€402,678–2,007,380	1.0500	1.6676	2.1000
€2,007,380–4,020,770	1.1000	1.7471	2.2000
Over €4,020,770	1.2000	1.9059	2.4000

The groups are as follows:

- **Group 1:** Gifts to your parents or children (including adopted children but not stepchildren) or gifts to your husband/wife.

- **Group 2:** Gifts to other relatives up to the fourth degree – includes cousins, uncles, nephews.

- **Group 3:** Gifts to any other person – including same sex partners or common law wives/husbands.

So, for example, a very large gift to someone to whom you are not related and who is worth over €4,020,770 will attract tax at 81.6 per cent. Ouch!

The tax is calculated in tranches. A gift of €10,000 will therefore be taxed at 7.65 per cent for the first €7,993.46 and 8.5 per cent on the balance.

The tax is paid by the person who inherits, not as in the UK by the estate as a whole. The tax is due at the time of accepting the inheritance by signing the deed of acceptance of inheritance.

In some areas of Spain (notably Pais Vasco, Navarra, Cantabria and Andalucia) the amount of tax paid on gifts between spouses and close relatives is either abolished or signigicantly reduced. It appears that many other areas of Spain will follow this, but as at the time of writing (2005) they have not.

If these figures alarm you there are many legal ways of limiting the amount of tax payable in Spain. Seek advice *before* you buy a home there.

Taxes Payable in Spain – Residents

Taxes on Income (*Impuesto sobre la Renta de las Personas Fisicas; IRPF*)

The Spanish tax system is very complex. What follows can only be a very brief summary of the position. The detail is immensely complicated and is made worse because it is so different from what you are used to. This section is written with reference to the person retiring to Spain. Issues arising out of employment or self-employment are not considered here.

Tax Threshold – Gross Income

If your income is less than €8,000 you need not file a tax return unless you are running a business or are self-employed.

If you are over these limits you are best consulting a tax adviser, at least for the first couple of years. It is not usually expensive to do so.

Types of Income Tax

Income is divided, as in the UK, into various categories. Each category of income is subject to different rules and allowances.

For a married couple, income tax is generally assessed by reference to the income of your household, rather than on your sole income. Unmarried couples are assessed as two households – which is, generally, a disadvantage.

When assessing the income of the household, the income of any dependent children is included.

As a tax resident you will generally pay tax in Spain on your worldwide income.

Remember that Spain is (taken overall, not just in relation to income tax) a high tax society. Whether for this reason or out of an independence of spirit, many people suffer from selective amnesia as far as the tax man is concerned and significantly under-declare their income. Perhaps 30 per cent of Spanish people and 50 per cent of foreign residents do this. This is dangerous and the penalties are severe. There are, however, quite legitimate tax-saving devices that you can use to reduce your liabilities. These issues are best addressed *before* you move to Spain, as there are then many more possibilities open to you.

Deductions from Taxable Income

From your gross income you can deduct:

- **any payments made to the Spanish social security scheme.**
- **your (or your family's) personal allowances.**
- **75 per cent of any *plus valia* tax paid in the year.**

The personal allowances are a scale of allowances for the first two children, which are different if they are under 3 or aged 3–16; then for 'extra' children under 3 or aged 3–16; extra allowances for handicapped children; allowances for you and your spouse if you are below retirement age, and if you are over retirement age.

There are other deductions too. See your adviser.

Tax Rates

The tax payable is calculated using the table overleaf. The tax is calculated in tranches; that is, you calculate the tax payable on each complete slice and then the tax at the highest applicable rate on any excess.

Taxes are paid partly to the national government and partly to the regional government. The table shows the combined total.

Tax Credits

Various tax credits are available. These are deducted from the tax otherwise payable as calculated above.

The rules are complex. They include credits for:

- **mortgage interest and other housing costs in certain cases – usually 15 per cent of applicable amounts.**
- **tax paid abroad (or part of it) on income also taxable in Spain.**

Payment of Tax Due

You must complete your tax form 210 and submit it between 1 May and 30 June each year. Late submission incurs a penalty.

Income Tax Rates – 2005 (payable 2006)

Income from (€)	Up to (€)	National Income Tax Rate (%)	State Tax Rate (%)	Total Rate (%)	Total Tax Payable at Top of Band (€)
Nil	4,080	9.06	5.94	15	612.00
4,080	14,076	15.84	8.16	24	3,011.04
14,076	26,316	18.68	9.32	28	6,438.24
26,316	45,900	24.71	12.29	37	13,684.32
over 45,900		29.16	15.84	45	

The state tax varies in the Basque Country, Navarra and in certain others.

Personal Allowances
Single person   €3,400 (under 65)
Married couple   €6,800

Notional Income Tax

This is a purely notional or theoretical income tax based on 2 per cent of the *valor catastral* of any property you own in Spain. This rate drops to 1.1 per cent of the official value (*valor catastral*) if this has been revised since 1994. This tax no longer applies in the case of your first residence in Spain but will still apply to any other properties owned.

The tax is paid by adding it to your other income and calculating the tax accordingly.

Corporation Tax

These taxes are not considered further here.

Taxes on Wealth (*Patrimonio*)

You will be taxed on your worldwide wealth. That includes any sums hidden in tax havens. Wealth includes:

- **real estate (land and buildings).**
- **cars, boats and other personal property in Spain.**
- **shares in Spanish companies.**
- **debts due to you in Spain.**
- **cash, gold, jewels, and so on.**
- **any shares in a non-Spanish company owning mainly real estate in Spain.**

You can deduct from your taxable assets any debts you owe in Spain or secured against the asset.

The primary purpose of wealth tax, when it was introduced in 1978, was to force people to disclose their assets so that they could be taxed effectively on those assets when they died or sold them. It was not to raise money. Remember that no one ever told the tax man anything! The rates of tax are therefore, for most people, quite low. Tax is applied on your wealth, after any deductions, at the rates shown in the table on p.198. An individual resident in Spain can also have €108,182.18 of otherwise taxable wealth without paying tax. A couple will each have the benefit of the allowance. Most people who are tax resident in Spain in fact – because of the deductions and allowances – pay no wealth tax.

The autonomous regions (the Canaries, Andalucía, and so on) have been given the right to fix wealth tax rates for their area, so the rates could in the future vary from one part of Spain to another.

Your tax return must be filed (if you are British) by 16 July. Tax must accompany the declaration. Assets are valued as at 1 January.

Taxes on Capital Gains

You will pay tax on your worldwide gains. Gains are generally only taxed when the gain is crystallised – e.g. on the sale of the asset.

Gains are taxed as part of your income, subject to a maximum of 15 per cent.

If a resident sells his or her main residence and then uses the money to buy another, then the gain will not be taxed. People over 65 who sell their main residence will pay no capital gains tax whether they reinvest or not.

Taxes on Death

The taxes are similar to the taxes paid by non-residents (*see* pp.200–202) except that, subject to the provisions of double taxation treaties, tax is paid on your worldwide assets as at the date of your death.

Residents in Spain who leave their real estate to their husband/wife or children will find the tax on that asset reduced by 95 per cent for the first €120,000. If it is worth more than that, then tax will be paid as normal on the balance. The person who inherits must keep it for 10 years or pay the tax. There are also reliefs in respect of businesses left to wives or children.

VAT

VAT is a major generator of tax for the Spanish. Detailed consideration of VAT is beyond the scope of this book. *See* **Settling In**, p.274.

Other Taxes

There is a miscellany of other taxes and levies on various aspects of life in Spain. Some are national and others local. Individually they are usually not a great burden. They are beyond the scope of this book.

New Residents

New residents will be liable to tax on their worldwide income and gains from the date they arrive in Spain. Until that day they will only have to pay Spanish tax on their income if it is derived from assets in Spain.

The most important thing to understand about taking up residence in Spain (and abandoning UK tax residence) is that it gives you superb opportunities for tax planning and, in particular, for restructuring your affairs to minimise what can otherwise be penal rates of taxation in Spain. To do this you need good advice at an early stage – preferably several months before you intend to move.

The Double Taxation Treaty

The detailed effect of double taxation treaties depends on the two countries involved. Whilst treaties may be similar in concept, they can differ in detail. Only the effect of the Spain/UK treaty is considered here.

The main points of relevance to residents are:

- **Any income from letting property in the UK will normally be outside the scope of Spanish taxation and, instead, will be taxed in the UK.**

- **Pensions received from the UK – except for government pensions – will be taxed in Spain but not in the UK.**

- **Government pensions will continue to be taxed in the UK but are neither taxed in Spain, nor do they count when assessing the level of your income and calculating the rate of tax payable on your income.**

- **You will normally not be required to pay UK capital gains tax on gains made after you settle in Spain except in relation to real estate located in the UK.**

- **If you are taxed on a gift made outside Spain, then the tax paid will usually be offset against the gift tax due in Spain.**

- **If you pay tax on an inheritance outside Spain, the same will apply.**

Double tax treaties are detailed and need to be read in the light of your personal circumstances.

Tax Planning Generally

Do it and do it as soon as possible. Every day you delay will make it more difficult to get the results you are looking for. There are many possibilities for tax planning for someone moving to Spain. Some points worth considering are:

- **Time your departure from the UK to get the best out of the UK tax system.**

- **Think, in particular, about when to make any capital gain if you are selling your business or other assets in the UK.**

- Arrange your affairs so that there is a gap between leaving the UK (for tax purposes) and becoming resident in Spain. That gap can be used to make all sorts of beneficial changes to the structure of your finances.
- Think about trusts. Although the Spanish system has more restrictions on their effective use than many continental systems, they can be very effective tax planning vehicles.
- Think about giving away some of your assets. You will not have to pay wealth tax on the value given away and the recipients will generally not have to pay either gift or inheritance tax on the gift.

Inheritance

The Spanish Inheritance Rules

The Spanish cannot do just as they please with their property when they die. Inheritance rules apply. These rules for Spaniards are much more restrictive than the rules under English law. Certain groups of people have (almost) automatic rights to inherit a part of your property. Fortunately, if you are not Spanish you can dispose of your property in whatever way your national law allows. For British people this is, basically, as they please.

Making a Will

It is always best to make a Spanish will. If you do not, your English will *should* be treated as valid in Spain and will be used to distribute your estate. This is a false economy, as the cost of implementing the UK will is much higher than the cost of implementing a Spanish will and the disposal of your estate set out in your UK will is often a tax disaster in Spain.

If you are not a resident in Spain, your Spanish will should state that it only applies to immovable property in Spain. The rest of your property – including movable property in Spain – will be disposed of in accordance with English law and the provisions of your UK will. If you are domiciled in Spain (as to the meaning of which *see* p.192) you should make a Spanish will disposing of all of your assets wherever they are located. If you make a Spanish will covering only immovable property in Spain, you should modify your UK will so as to exclude any immovable property located in Spain.

Always use a lawyer to advise as to the contents of your will and to draft it. Lawyers love people who make home-made wills. They make a fortune from dealing with their estates because the wills are often inadequately drafted and produce lots of expensive problems.

What If I Don't Make a Will of any Kind?

A person who dies without a will dies intestate. This gets complicated. Will the UK rules as to what happens in this event apply (because you are British) or will it be the Spanish rules? This gives rise to many happy hours of argument by lawyers and tax officials. All at your (or your heirs') expense.

It is much cheaper to make a will.

Gay Marriage

On 4 July 2005 Spain changed its laws to allow 'gay marriages'. This means that people of the same sex can marry in Spain. Gay spouses are entitled to the same rights as heterosexual spouses. Because this law is very new at the time of writing (September 2005), the exact way that this works is still settling down. In fact, there are currently some legal challenges to the law which claim that gay marriage is unconstitutional. There is debate as to whether two same sex people from different nationalities can marry in Spain, as this has on some occasions been accepted and on other occasions rejected by the authorities.

The position is likely to clarified over the next couple of years, but in the meantime it is highly advisable that you take legal advice on this if you are affected, as the situation seems to be changing constantly.

Investments

The Need to Do Something

Most of us don't like making investment decisions. They make our head hurt. They make us face up to unpleasant things – like taxes and death. We don't really understand what we are doing, what the options are or what is best. We don't know who we should trust to give us advice. We know we ought to do something, but it will wait until next week – or maybe the week after. Until then our present arrangements will have to do. I

f you are moving to live overseas you must review your investments. Your current arrangements are likely to be financially disastrous – and may even be illegal.

What Are You Worth?

Most of us are, in financial terms, worth more than we think. When we come to move abroad and have to think about these things it can come as a shock.

Take a piece of paper and list your actual and potential assets. A suggested checklist can be found in **Appendix 2**. This will give you an idea as to the amount you are worth now and, just as importantly, what you are likely to be worth in the future. Your investment plans should take into account both figures.

Who Should Look After Your Investments?

You may already have an investment adviser. You may be very happy with their quality and the service you have received. They are unlikely to be able to help you once you have gone to live in Spain. They will almost certainly not have the knowledge to do so. They will know about neither the Spanish investment that might be of interest to you nor, probably, many of the 'offshore' products that might be of interest to someone no longer resident in the UK. Even if they have some knowledge of these things, they are likely to be thousands of miles from where you will be living.

Nor is it a simple question of selecting a new local (Spanish) adviser once you have moved. They will usually know little about the UK aspects of your case or about the UK tax and inheritance rules that could still have some importance for you.

Choosing an investment adviser competent to deal with you once you are in Spain is not easy. By all means seek guidance from your existing adviser. Ask for guidance from others who have already made the move. Do some research. Meet the potential candidates. Are you comfortable with them? Do they share your approach to life? Do they have the necessary experience? Is their perform-ance record good? How are they regulated? What security/bonding/guarantees can they offer you? How will they be paid for their work? Fees or commission? If commission, what will that formula mean they are making from you in 'real money' rather than percentages?

Above all be careful. There are lots of very dubious 'financial advisers' oper-ating in the popular tourist areas of Spain. Some are totally incompetent. Some are crooks, seeking simply to separate you from your money as cleanly as possible. Fortunately there are also some excellent and highly professional advisers with good track records. Make sure you choose one.

Where Should You Invest?

For British people the big issue is whether they should keep their sterling investments. Most British people will have investments that are largely ster-ling-based. Even if they are, for example, a Far Eastern fund they will probably be denominated in sterling and they will pay out dividends, etc. in sterling.

You will be spending euros.

As the value of the euro fluctuates against sterling, the value of your investments will go up and down. That of itself isn't too important because the value won't crystallise unless you sell. What does matter is that the revenue you generate from those investments (rent, interest, dividends and so on) will fluctuate in value. Take, for example, an investment that generated you £10,000 a year. Then think of that income in spending power. In the last three years the euro has varied in value from €1 = £0.53 to €1 = £0.73. Sometimes, therefore, your income in euros would have been around €18,900 a year and at others it would have been around €13,700 a year. This is a huge difference in your standard of living in Spain, *based solely on exchange rate fluctuations*. This is unacceptable, particularly as you will inevitably have to accept this problem in so far as your pension is concerned.

In general terms investments paying out in euros are preferable if you live in a euro country.

Trusts

Trusts are an important weapon in the hands of the person going to live in Spain. Trusts offer the potential benefits of:

- **allowing you to put part of your assets in the hands of trustees so that they no longer belong to you for wealth tax or inheritance tax purposes.**
- **allowing you to receive only the income you need (rather than all the income generated by those assets) so keeping the extra income out of sight for income tax purposes.**
- **allowing a very flexible vehicle for investment purposes.**

So how do they work?

After leaving the UK (and before moving to Spain) you reorganise your affairs by giving a large part of your assets to 'trustees'. These are normally a professional trust company located in a low tax regime. The choice of a reliable trustee is critical.

Those trustees hold the asset not for their own benefit but 'in trust' for whatever purposes you established when you made the gift. It could, for example, be to benefit a local hospital or school or it could be to benefit you and your family.

If the trust is set up properly in the light of the requirements of Spanish law, then those assets will no longer be treated as yours for tax purposes. On your death the assets are not yours to leave to your children (or whoever), and so do not (subject to any local anti-avoidance legislation) carry inheritance tax.

Similarly, the income from those assets is not your income. If some of it is given to you it may be taxed as your income, but the income that is not given to you will not be taxed in Spain and, because the trust will be located in a nil/low tax regime, it will not be taxed elsewhere either.

The detail of the arrangements is vitally important. They must be set up precisely to comply with Spanish tax law. If you do not do this, they will not work as intended.

Trustees can manage your investments in (virtually) whatever way you stipulate when you set up the trust. You can give the trustees full discretion to do as they please or you can specify precisely how your money is to be used. There are particular types of trusts and special types of investments that trusts can make that can be especially beneficial in Spain.

Trusts can be beneficial even to Spanish resident people of modest means – say £350,000. It is certainly worth investing a little money to see if they can be of use to you as the tax savings can run to many thousands of pounds. If you are thinking of trusts as an investment vehicle and tax-planning measure you must take advice early – months before you are thinking of moving to Spain. Otherwise it will be too late.

Keeping Track of Your Investments

Whatever you decide to do about investments – put them in a trust, appoint investment managers to manage them in your own name or manage them yourself – you should always keep an up-to-date list of your assets and investments and tell your family where to find it. Make a file. By all means have a computer file but print off a good old-fashioned paper copy. Keep it in an obvious place known to your family. Keep it with your will and the deeds to your house. Also keep in it either the originals of bank account books, share certificates, and so on, or a note of where they are to be found.

As a lawyer it is very frustrating – and expensive for the client – when, after the parents' death, the children come in with a suitcase full of correspondence and old cheque books. It all has to be gone through and all those old banks contacted lest there should be £1,000,000 lurking in a forgotten account. There never is, and it wastes a lot of time and money.

Conclusion

Buying a home in Spain – whether to use as a holiday home, as an investment or to live in permanently – is as safe as buying one in the UK.

The rules may appear complicated. Our rules would if you were a Spanish person coming to this country. That apparent complexity is often no more than lack of familiarity.

There are tens of thousands of British people who have bought homes in Spain. Most have had no real problems. Most have enjoyed years of holidays in Spain. Many have seen their property rise substantially in value. Many are now thinking of retiring to Spain.

For a trouble-free time you simply need to keep your head and to seek advice from experts who can help you make the four basic decisions:

- **Who should own the property?**
- **What am I going to do about inheritance?**
- **What am I going to do about controlling my potential tax liabilities?**
- **If I am going to live in Spain, what am I going to do about my investments?**

If you don't like lawyers, remember that they make far more money out of sorting out the problems you get into by not doing these things than by giving you this basic advice!

Settling In

Once you have exchanged all the papers, made all the financial arrangements and clinched the purchase of your Spanish home, you can finally begin the process of moving in and starting to enjoy it. There will still be a whole lot of other things to sort out – getting connected to utilities, finding out how to use local banks, and a hundred and one other aspects of local life and living in Spain that you'll want to make sense of as you settle in. This chapter is a brief introduction to the most important issues that new homeowners in Spain need to deal with; you'll discover many more at your leisure, as you go along.

Making the Move

Just how many of your possessions you need and/or want to take to your new home in Spain is very much a matter of personal preference. You may prefer to start afresh, buy new furniture and household gadgets once you're there, and so take only a few essentials and things of special value. On the other hand you may be too attached to the possessions accumulated over years to leave anything behind, and prefer to move lock, stock and barrel. Most people plump for a compromise between the two. When selecting what to take, bear in mind that many items can be bought cheaply in Spain, allowing you to save on removal costs and bother, and that many things that may have seemed essential in Britain – such as big, heavy carpets – will be a complete waste of space in a warmer climate.

One thing you do not have to worry about much these days is customs duties, as EU citizens do not need any special permission or have to pay duties on possessions that enter Spain. This is a one-off privilege and is only applicable to people who are taking up residency. You must, however, pay a deposit to the customs authorities, which will amount to approximately 50 per cent of the value of the goods. The deposit can be recovered within a year. Anyone importing furniture for a second or holiday home must also make a deposit, of a similar amount, but will have to wait for two years for it to be reimbursed. Go to your local Spanish consulate and ask for leaflet C16, where all the details are laid out. If you are shipping your effects from any non-EU country, though, you should check carefully on the current regulations with your nearest Spanish consulate (*see* 'Directory of Contacts', pp.321–5, for a list) and ask for leaflet C21.

If you decide to take just a few things with you to Spain, you will be able to do so yourself in a hired or borrowed self-drive van. If, though, you are moving a whole houseload or anything near that amount, it's better to use one of the many companies that specialise in international removals. When choosing a removal company, it's a good idea to ask around among other foreign residents in the part of Spain to which you're moving, to see which companies they have found most reliable. As with builders, get at least three written quotations before committing yourself to any company. Reputable companies should send an agent to look at your property and issue a detailed quote, not just give prices over the phone. An important thing to compare is the cost of packing, boxes and so on, and whether this is included in the overall price (this will normally be indicated in the quote). Check specifically on how they pack and carry any especially valuable or fragile items. Most international removal companies prefer to do all packing themselves – this is also to the advantage of the client, since it avoids any confusion over responsibility in the event of an insurance claim – but many will provide boxes for you to pack yourselves, for a lower fee.

Removals are charged by the cubic metre: moving the whole contents of a medium-sized, three-bedroom house from Britain to southern Spain may cost anywhere between £2,000 and £4,000, depending very much on what you have. If you do not want your things transported immediately after you move out of your old home, most companies will provide free storage for at least a month before shipping. In addition, if you want to save some money, can be flexible about when you need your effects in Spain and are not shipping enough things to fill a large truck – very few companies use smaller vehicles – you can book a 'part-load'. This means that your belongings are put into storage until there are enough other partial shipments going to the same area to make up a full truck-load. The price is naturally a lot lower than if you have a whole lorry to yourself and, if the part of Spain to which you are moving is quite well frequented, you should not have to wait too long. Whether you take a full- or part-load, when you make an agreement with a company the maximum time you can be required to wait should be stipulated in the contract.

Full insurance for the whole journey is essential. Most removal companies offer their own policies, or you can insure your things separately yourself, which some people prefer for fear of a conflict of interest if they ever have to claim on the remover's own insurance, although with reputable companies this should not be a problem. In either case, it's advisable to check the small print on any policy. Most 'all risks' policies will cover loss or breakage of any item on the basis of replacement value, but others will be conditional on packing being undertaken by the removers themselves (the most expensive option) and will require any claims to be made within a set time after delivery. Many also have an excess limit for small claims. Before your items are packed, it's a good idea to take photos of any valuable items to show in the event of a claim.

Another important thing to consider, but which is often forgotten, is whether the entry to your Spanish home is accessible to a full-size removal van. If it is a winding dirt driveway, you should let your removal company know in advance, and ask their opinion on how to deal with the problem. If the main van cannot get to your home, your belongings may have to be put into storage with a local company and then moved on by a smaller vehicle, which may cost more.

Removal Companies

Experienced international moving companies advertise frequently in the Spanish property press (*see* pp.127–9) and, of course, in your local *Yellow Pages*. Reliable companies should be members of the **British Association of Removers** (**www.bar.co.uk**) and either one of the two international associations, **FIDI** (**www.fidi.com**) or **OMNI** (**www.omnimoving.com**), all of which have bonded guarantee schemes that give you considerable comeback in case of any problems with any of their member companies, including completion of the move by another company if yours has failed to carry out the contract. Many British-based companies have very regular shipments to the Costa Blanca and Costa del Sol (often weekly), but travel much less frequently to other areas. For a list of removal companies, *see* **References**, p.325.

Dealing with Bureaucracy – Using a *Gestor*

When you first move to a new country, or even if you just buy a house there and stay for a month or so at a time, there are so many new things to come to terms with that, on a bad day, you can feel you've taken on a mountain to climb. In Spain, this is compounded by local officialdom's inordinate love of form-filling, certificates, official stamps and all forms of paperwork in general. Things are slowly changing in this regard, at least among local authorities in sophisticated areas like Catalonia, but in general, and especially in dealing with departments that are still the responsibility of central government, like vehicle registration, the days of user-friendly forms and streamlined, fast-track bureaucracy are a long way off. Apparently straightforward procedures require three or four different pieces of paper, all with lots of small print, and fees that have to be paid at separate counters – many bureaucratic procedures can only be done over the counter at the relevant department, not by phone, post or even less on-line. Many departments will only have one office in each province, in the capital, so if, for example, your new home is in Ronda, having to travel to Málaga to spend a whole morning waiting in line can be seriously annoying.

When they first arrive in Spain, many new home-buyers refer all their queries to their lawyer, but this will be expensive in the long run, and your lawyer may soon get tired of dealing with a string of 'petty' matters outside his true remit. Left to themselves to face the baffling demands of bureaucracy, foreign residents often wonder whether Spaniards go mad at having to deal with such a system all the time. The answer is, they don't. Instead, they turn to the very Spanish institution of the *gestor*, a word with no English translation since the job doesn't exist, although it could be rendered as 'administrative services'. The fundamental role of the *gestor* is to take away the burden of bureaucracy by handling things for you. You can go to *gestores* with anything and everything that might involve permits, licences, insurance or similar issues, and they will be able to explain what procedures you need to follow, and point out time- and money-saving shortcuts that you would never discover on your own. They will also have blank copies of many forms. Armed with a letter of authorisation signed by you, they can also go to present the papers at the relevant departments in your place. One standard procedure for which many foreign house-buyers use *gestores* is that of applying for Spanish residency (*see* pp.25–8). They can do many other useful things for you as well, such as acting as accountant, book-keeper and small business adviser. Many Spaniards routinely use a *gestor* in all small-scale dealings with the state – such as renewing a passport – in a way that would be completely unheard of in English-speaking countries.

A good *gestor* can be an invaluable asset, and is near-indispensable if you are working or, above all, setting up any kind of business in Spain. Regarding them as a luxury and insisting on doing everything yourself, as some expats do, is a recipe for spending much of your time feeling angry and frustrated rather than enjoying what brought you here in the first place. It is as worth building up a good, ongoing relationship with a *gestor*, to whom you can turn whenever you need a problem solving, as it is with a local lawyer for more substantial matters.

Gestores are much less qualified than full lawyers, but should still have an official licence; there will be a choice of small *gestorías* (the offices of *gestores*) in any town. In areas with significant foreign communities, there will probably be several who speak English. It's worth asking around for recommendations among the local foreign community, as this is a very personal way of doing business. *Gestores* are, of course, paid for their services, but fees are generally reasonable and, once you realise how much stress you've avoided, you won't begrudge the expense.

Retirement

If you are reading this book you may be thinking of retiring to Spain. If so, you are not a pioneer but are treading a well-worn path, for it is estimated that more than three-quarters of all expats living in Spain are retired. The reasons for taking this step are evident, and have already been discussed – relatively low living costs, affordable properties and, in most popular areas, better weather and a more relaxed lifestyle. If you are an EU citizen, retiring to Spain means not only these advantages but also being able to make use of the Spanish health system in just the same way a Spanish pensioner can.

Living in Retirement

Other chapters of this book stress the need to make the right choice of property type and area, and retired people are warned of the possible disadvantages of buying a home in a remote rural area some distance from essential facilities. While isolated living has many pluses when you are still robust, things may not seem so rosy when you are elderly and frail, more so if you end up alone. Driving for miles on bumpy back roads to do the shopping, see a doctor or socialise may become an uncomfortable chore. Moving to a place with a ready-made community, expat, Spanish or mixed, has many advantages, which explains why many older people plump for an *urbanización* near a town.

All reports show that the vast majority of retired residents are content with having made the move. Most point to the availability of practically year-round outdoor pursuits – swimming, sailing, tennis and golf to name but a few – as one of the major pluses. In most areas there are associations and clubs catering to just about every interest, with over 90 on the Costa del Sol alone. These range from bridge clubs through to amateur dramatics societies, and many retired people also end up doing voluntary work for charitable organisations. The climate, lifestyle and good, healthy food all help older people to remain fit and active in a way that is not possible in rain-soaked northern climes.

Despite all this, it does not work out for everyone and some retired people bitterly regret their move. This is usually because they have not sought proper advice on money issues, pensions, property or taxation and have gone into the venture 'blind'. Some end up being unable to afford to live on their pension as they move further into old age, perhaps accumulating health problems, and then realise that they have burned their bridges and cannot go back. Fortunately, this only applies to a tiny minority, but everyone should seek out expert advice before committing to the move.

If you retire to Spain, the question of the inheritance of your property, and making a will, will naturally loom larger than when you are younger. For more on this, *see* **Financial Implications**.

Pensions

UK (and other EU) state pensions can be paid into a Spanish bank account. The same applies to most company pensions, unless there are any stipulations to the contrary. If this is the case you can make arrangements for the money to be transferred from the receiving bank at home. Even as a non-EU citizen you can receive your pension in Spain; receiving funds from abroad, in fact, opens the door to obtaining residency. With sufficient means you can live – and spend your money – in the local economy, but will not compete with locals in the job market, and so you are welcomed.

If you receive a pension from abroad, look carefully into payment arrangements. Banks sometimes charge for transferring abroad and the receiving bank may also apply a commission (which is against EU regulations) so shop around. Monthly payments may be subject to proportionally higher transfer charges than quarterly ones so the latter option is often better, as long as you can spin the money out over a longer period. You may choose to make an annual arrangement with a currency dealer whereby they send you the money at an exchange rate that will apply for the whole year. This provides assured income but you may lose out because of exchange rate fluctuations. It could, of course, work the other way too.

Anybody residing for more than 183 days per year in Spain becomes liable to taxation there, on their worldwide income. Your UK state pension is no longer taxable in the UK but in Spain it is, because it is regarded as income. If you receive a UK government pension, however, you will be taxed in the UK. In order not to pay tax again in Spain, or to get it reimbursed if you do, contact: Inland Revenue, Inspector of Funds, Lynwood Road, Thames Ditton, Surrey, KT7 0DP, England. You can obtain forms from this office, in English and Spanish, to claim exemption from UK tax. Take (or get your *gestor* to take) both forms to the Agencia Tributaria (Spanish Inland Revenue) where one will be stamped for return to the Inland Revenue in the UK, showing that tax has been paid in Spain.

Since not everyone receives income solely from pensions, the problem of double taxation will arise anyway, especially during your first year's residency in Spain. To become exempt from paying tax in the UK you have to be absent for a full year, and there is an overlap period between the UK tax year (5 April–4 April) and the Spanish tax year, which coincides with the calendar year. Your income may be taxable – and taxed – in both countries. This problem is best solved by taking expert advice.

If you have not yet retired and you move to Spain, whether you intend to work or not, your UK pension entitlement is frozen. Depending on the number of years' contributions made, you may or may not become eligible for a UK pension on reaching the age of retirement. To make sure that you are entitled you can make additional payments from Spain. The decision as to whether to continue to make UK payments is an important one: information and advice is obtainable from: Inland Revenue, National Insurance Contributions Office, Benton Park View, Newcastle upon Tyne, NE98 1ZZ (**www.hmrc.gov.uk**). Also see **www.dwp.gov.uk** and **www.thepensionservice.gov.uk**.

Working in Spain

Employment

EU and EEA citizens enjoy full rights in the Spanish labour market and can seek work in their chosen field like anybody else, while non-EU citizens are subject to many more official restrictions. Legal rights aside, there are, though, practical difficulties that can still be encountered by anyone hoping to work in Spain – some of the most recurrent are high unemployment, a shortage of stable jobs and the growing reliance on ever more short-term contracts, the language barrier, and difficulties in getting qualifications recognised.

Looking for Work: Official Resources

Before going to Spain you could look at the **EURES** (European Employment Service) database, simply go to **http://europa.eu.int/jobs/eures** ('The European Job Mobility Portal'). In theory, vacancies throughout the EU are posted there, but in practice very few jobs are advertised for Spain. It is perhaps more useful for information on the Spanish labour market – nationally or by autonomous communities – and gives you an idea of what skills are in demand in any given place. In addition, you can place your CV on the site for potential employers to see.

Once in Spain go to the **INEM**, the Instituto Nacional de Empleo (Spain **t** 902 399 999, **www.inem.es**), or National Employment Institute. This is the equivalent of the British Department For Work and Pensions, and its Employment Offices, called *oficinas de empleo*, are both Jobcentres and benefit offices. To find your nearest office quickly, go to **www.inem.es** and click on *'Direcciones y Teléfonos'* where you can key your postcode into the space at the top of the page, and the address of your nearest office appears immediately.

To use their services you need to register as a job-seeker, or *demandante de empleo*, either on arrival or, if you have been working, after losing a job. EU citizens do not need to be officially resident in Spain to register, but it is advisable. Registration is simple, requiring only proof of identity, your professional profile and the type of work you are seeking. If you have already been working you may be entitled to unemployment benefit, which requires other documents that should be supplied by your former employer.

Non-EU citizens, in certain circumstances, can also register with the INEM. Broadly speaking, this right is afforded to those who have already been working and hold work and residence permits with at least 90 days' validity.

Once registered as a job-seeker, whether claiming benefits or not, you can use all the services available. These include information on vacancies, both locally and elsewhere in Spain; training courses; advice on 'selling' yourself effectively; help with becoming self-employed or setting up a business; and access to job-seeking resources.

You must be available for suitable employment and may refuse two offers, but not a third, otherwise you will incur penalties such as loss of benefit. You must also attend job interviews provided by the INEM and 'sign on' on the dates fixed by the INEM. Courses offered by INEM are not obligatory.

A final note: do not expect too much help from the INEM, however, especially if your Castilian (or Catalan, etc.) is ropey, as few INEM functionaries will be able to deal with you in English.

Private Employment Agencies

Two types of private employment agencies operate in Spain. One is the **private placement agency** (*agencia privada de colocación*), which plays an intermediary role in the job market and normally charges a fee for successfully placing a worker in a job. Alternatively, you might go to a **temporary work company** (*empresa de trabajo temporal* or ETT). These companies contract workers directly and then assign them to user companies via service contracts. ETTs tend to specialise in certain sectors, hiring for example catering, secretarial or construction personnel. Workers are usually hired out during times of exceptional demand or seasonal backlogs. Adecco, Manpower and Randstad are well-known operators in this field but there are many more in the *Yellow Pages*.

Internet Job Resources

The Internet is a powerful tool for job-seeking in Spain. There are many international sites but most have links to Spanish pages. While on the Internet you can sign up to any of the following websites:

- **www.infojobs.net**
- **www.trabajo.org**
- **www.overseasjobsexpress.com**
- **http://jobera.com**: This site gives tips on writing CVs and covering letters, interview techniques etc. in several languages. Beware, though, of the automatic translation software it uses; at best it will make your covering letter laughable, at worst it will guarantee your application is immediately binned!
- **www.monster.es**
- **www.abctodotrabajo.com**
- **www.anyworkanywhere.com/jobsearch.html**: Most jobs currently offered on this site are with tour operators in the Balearics and the Canaries.
- **www.jobs-in-europe.com**

Newspaper Classifieds

National and local dailies carry classified adverts in a job section called *'Ofertas de Trabajo'*, or 'Job Offers', although the offers are rarely interesting, concentrated as they are at the bottom end of the market. The major dailies have pull-out economics and finance sections on Sundays, with substantial jobs sections aimed at the higher end of the scale, where the well qualified may find something, especially in international companies. Alternatively, there are many English-language publications in Spain which have advertisements aimed more at the English-speaker (*see* **References**, pp.326–7).

Apart from the general press, if you are seeking work in a specific sector, check out trade magazines. In Spain itself there are other jobseekers' publications. The weekly *Mercado de Trabajo* has upwards of 1,200 job adverts, features on emerging markets for aspiring entrepreneurs, job fairs, training and work experience opportunities. Some people also recommend *Segundamano*, the thrice-weekly Spanish equivalent of *Exchange & Mart* which has a substantial classified jobs section. *Laboris* is another weekly tabloid-format publication with many job adverts.

Direct Contact With Potential Employers

Another tactic is to target potential companies in which you would like to work or where you think you might find a job. This is about selling yourself, and your target companies will most likely be British or North American multinationals operating in Spain. It may seem like a shot in the dark but remember that a good, well-presented CV that arrives on a personnel manager's desk unsolicited may attract more attention than one sent in reply to an advertised post (where it will be just one among many). Some companies actually prefer to recruit this way, and taking the initiative may stand you in good stead.

There are too many foreign companies operating in Spain to list here but chambers of commerce can be helpful. The British Chamber of Commerce in Spain is based at Calle Bruc 21, 1º 4ª, 08010 Barcelona (**t** 00 34 933 173 220, **f** 00 34 933 024 896. Alternatively, contact them via the website **www.british chamberspain.com**, **britchamber@britchamber.com**. For a fee you can also insert your profile on the site for 10 weeks. Once you have made a list of target companies, send a hard copy of your CV by post; alternatively most also have websites, usually with a 'work with us' button to click on, allowing you to send it electronically.

English-teaching

Teaching English as a foreign language (TEFL) is the longest-established standby for native English-speakers wanting to live and work in Spain. Spaniards today are more conscious than ever of the need to learn languages in order to operate in an increasingly global economy, and the state education system is still failing to provide them with the necessary linguistic competence. English teachers, therefore, remain in great demand. It is highly advisable to have some proper qualifications in the field, especially if you want to be decently paid, although it's still not absolutely necessary. Though there are various qualifications, the most internationally recognised is the Cambridge CELTA certificate, courses for which are offered at 286 centres in 54 countries. There are many in the UK and Ireland, check the website **www.celta.org.uk**. It is also offered in Spain through International House and other centres. It consists

TEFL-ing

Many centres in the UK and Spain run training courses in TEFL. A good starting point is International House, 106 Piccadilly, London W1J 7NL (**t** (020) 7518 6950 **www.ihworld.com**). If qualified, try the British Council's Teacher Vacancies department at 10 Spring Gardens, London SW1A 2BN (**www.britishcouncil.org**), or the *Guardian*'s education pages. There are also dozens of TEFL specialist sites with information about training and jobs. Try the following:

- **www.tefl.net**
- **www.developingteachers.com**
- **www.eflweb.com**
- **www.englishclub.com**
- **www.windsorinstitute.com**
- **www.tesol-spain.org**
- **www.bilc.co.uk**

of 109 hours of training which can either be completed through an intensive four-week course or part-time, spread over 12 weeks.

Language academies range from small schools to internationally established organisations such as International House, the British Council or Inlingua. Some only take on freelance teachers (*autónomos*), who have to pay their own social security contributions, while others contract teachers properly as full-time staff (*por cuenta ajena*) and pay social security contributions and at least partial holiday pay. Contracts are generally for a given number of hours, a term or the whole academic year, and many teachers supplement their income by giving private classes as well. Very few contracts available nowadays will carry you through the summer months, but at that time there is often work available on intensive summer courses. Academies may ask you to work in-house or send you outside to teach in local companies, in which case classes will often be scheduled from 7am to 9am, during the lunch hour or at the end of the working day. In-house classes can go on throughout the day, although the evening is the most common slot. Full-time, in-house annual contracts with paid holidays are currently very rare; the glut of young English teachers in Spain's larger cities has also dragged wages down in the last few years although, on the other hand, there is always lots of work around. Nowadays provincial capitals and smaller cities – industrial offshoot-towns like Sabadell or Móstoles rather than nearby Barcelona or Madrid, and prosperous Catalan country towns like Olot – will usually be much better for finding decently paid work than the fashionable cities themselves, with less travel time between classes, a lower cost of living, and yet higher rates per class.

There are several ways of searching for work. Language schools regularly offer jobs in newspapers, especially *El País*, in the classified *Enseñanza* (teaching) section. The Sunday edition, particularly, has many offers, especially at the beginning of the academic year. Job offers can also be found in publications aimed at expatriates. Often overlooked, but useful nevertheless, are the *Yellow Pages* (**www.PaginasAmarillas.es**), which list most language schools in any city. Simply look under *Academias de Idiomas* (language schools) and start phoning. As most have websites, a jobsearch can begin at home.

School-teaching

Holders of B.Ed degrees or PGCEs can find work in private international schools. These are found in most big cities and areas with large expatriate communities, particularly Andalucía, the Costa Blanca, Madrid, Barcelona, the Balearics and the Canaries. Over 45 are listed on the website of the National Association of British Schools in Spain (**www.nabss.org**) but that is by no means all of them. The pay is better than in TEFL academy work (though not as good as private ESL teaching). Not all schools offer full 12-month contracts; some opt to keep their teachers on 10-month contracts with pro-rata holiday payments, meaning you have to find alternative work for at least one summer month. The *Times Educational Supplement* carries job advertisements every Friday; alternatively look on its website: **www.tesjobs.co.uk**. To find out more about international schools, contact the **European Council of International Schools** at 21B Lavant Street, Petersfield, Hampshire GU32 3EW, UK, **t** (07302) 68244, **ecis@ecis.org**, **www.ecis.org**.

Qualified English-speaking teachers now also have the possibility of working in a Spanish public-sector school, though not under the same contractual conditions as Spanish staff, who have their jobs for life by virtue of having passed the arcane system of '*oposiciones*' (competitive public exams). This means they are functionaries of the educational authority run by the autonomous government in their region. Some autonomous communities have undertaken a commitment to making education bilingual from pre-school age, in co-operation with the British Council. Progress has been patchy; many Spanish teachers with a low level of English have been retrained to cover the English part of the curriculum but in some areas native speakers have been drafted in. It is worth checking with the British Council where there may be openings.

British students can spend a year working part-time as language assistants in schools or colleges. Applicants must have an A-level in Spanish. Contact the **British Council**'s Information Centre at Bridgewater House, 58 Whitworth Street, Manchester M1 6BB, **t** (0161) 957 7000, **f** (0161) 957 7111, or send an e-mail to **education.enquiries@britishcouncil.org**. The London offices are at 10 Spring Gardens, London SW1A 2B, **t** (020) 7389 4004, **f** (020) 7389 4426. All other UK addresses are to be found on the website **www.britishcouncil.org**.

Translating

Native English-speakers with good Spanish can earn extra money or make a career as translators (Spanish into English, rarely vice versa). There is always plenty of work, although it can be irregular and is more suitable for freelancers, since very few companies take on full-time translators. The work comes from endless sources – such as official institutions, businesses and websites – just about anywhere in Spain. The content can sometimes make the work practically impossible except for specialists, and becoming specialised is recommended in the long term: legal and financial translators, for example, command high fees. The *Yellow Pages* list translation agencies (under *Traducciones*). Knowing Spain's other co-official languages can also be very useful, as Catalan–English translators, for example, are not that common and their skills may useful for companies and institutions.

The London-based **Institute of Linguists** offers a qualification in translating. Contact them at Saxon House, 48 Southwark Street, London SE1 1UN, **t** (020) 7940 3100, **www.iol.org.uk**).

Seasonal Work

In tourist areas there are always jobs going during the summer season, and often for much of the rest of the year too. Bars, restaurants and clubs often need English-speakers. Knowledge of German can also be helpful, while Spanish is essential if you hope to get any of the less dreary jobs. Ideally, a job should include accommodation and board or at least access to cooking facilities. Tour companies are generally on the lookout for guides, couriers and holiday camp monitors, and the timeshare companies often need sales staff; sporty types may find work as tennis or ski instructors, or in one of the many marinas dotted around the coasts. All of these jobs, of course, involve a fair bit of ducking and diving, and they're roles that people go after for the adventure rather than as a career path. Forget, though, any romantic notions you may have about picking grapes or fruit, and getting a suntan while doing healthy field work. These jobs are nowadays done by poverty-driven immigrant labourers from Africa, Latin America and Eastern Europe, who work for about €3 per hour.

Word of Mouth

Many opportunities arise not so much as a result of who you are or what you can do but who you know. This is especially so in expat-dominated professions such as English-teaching, translation and so on, and in the expat *costa*-clusters of Málaga and Alicante. If you hope to work in these fields, contacts made socially can prove invaluable; in the expat world, a huge amount of business is done in bars. Networking, schmoozing, crawling – call it what you will, getting friendly with potentially useful people is extremely common in Spain. Business cards are frequently exchanged – get your own made, and give them out with abandon. The system of *enchufe* is not exclusive to locals; expats can take advantage of it too. Even if your aim is to get out of the Anglo 'ghetto', never shun other English-speakers.

Self-employment and Starting a Business

Recent years have seen big changes in the organisation of work, in Spain as everywhere, with corporations and companies downsizing and outsourcing tasks previously done by in-house employees. Consequently there are fewer stable jobs around, although the actual amount of work to be done has not lessened, hence the growth of the freelance and small business sector. Companies save on labour costs, social security payments and other overheads. The self-employed bear those costs themselves. In Spain the number of self-employed workers, or *trabajadores autónomos*, and small entrepreneurs is growing fast. There are also many government initiatives aimed at encouraging self-employment and the establishment of small businesses.

EU and EEA citizens can easily register as self-employed workers, while non-EU passport holders, as with other employment, face greater difficulties. In the case of the former, all you really need (as well as having a skill to offer) is to be able to deal with the necessary bureaucracy (for which the help of a good *gestor* is virtually indispensable, *see* pp.216–17) and then take your chances. You may register before or after obtaining your residence permit. Less fortunate non-EU citizens can only go it alone if they are already established and have acquired work and residence permits thanks to having been an employee, or if they arrive in Spain with substantial funds behind them. With this foot in the door they may then, after much paperwork, become officially self-employed.

Becoming Self-employed

Becoming an *autónomo*, or working *por cuenta propia*, as self-employed people are known, is an easy process. The good news is that, unless your annual turnover is in excess of €600,000, you no longer have to pay the *impuesto de actividades económicas* (business activities tax). The IAE was particularly irksome for the jack-of-all-trades as each activity carried its own tax; now you can exploit two or more skills without getting stung for it.

The first step is to go to the nearest office of the **Agencia Tributaria** (Spain **t** 901 553 355, **www. aeat.es**), the Spanish Inland Revenue, known by all under its older name of Hacienda. There you must acquire, for €1.50, 'Modelo 036' ('*modelo*' just means 'form') the '*Declaración Censal de alta, modificación o baja en el Censo de obligados tributarios*'. This is the form by which you register in the 'census' of self-employed taxpayers. You may find the form itself a little complicated so ask the functionary who deals with you to help with any difficulties.

You must also present your ID, which technically need not be a residence card (*see* pp.25–8), but do not bank on functionaries accepting just a passport. If you have applied for the card, the stamped copy of the application form given to you by the police should suffice. You will definitely need proof of your NIE (*see* p.25), which you should have applied for and obtained previously.

After the tax office, go to your local branch of Social Security – Tesorería de la Seguridad Social, **t** 900 616 200, **www.seg-social.es** – and register to pay your contributions as an *autónomo*. The amount you pay depends on the terms you choose, and this is an area where the advice of a good *gestor* can be especially useful, since you can pay very high contributions for no purpose. The basic question is whether you wish to invest more in a state pension, or put your money in a private scheme or investment that may, in the long-run, give you a better return. The current minimum that you are required to pay into the state scheme is a little over €205 per month, which gives you the right to sign up with the state health service and goes towards a very paltry pension. If at any point you will wish to claim illness or incapacity benefit you can make a further contribution of about €25 a month to a private mutual society which, by agreement with the Seguridad Social will pay you about 70 per cent of the minimum wage (itself only a little over €600 a month) during periods of sickness. Self-employed workers cannot claim unemployment benefit in any circumstances, under the rationale that they cannot make themselves unemployed.

Taxes for Freelancers

As an *autónomo*, or freelancer, you have to worry about two taxes: IRPF (*impuesto sobre la renta de las personas físicas* – income tax) and IVA (VAT). Everyone is liable for IRPF but you have the choice of having 7 per cent or 15 per cent withheld during your first 24 months as a signed-up freelancer. If you choose 7 per cent you will probably be looking at having to pay the difference when you file your return (which you may have to do when having 15 per cent withheld but, of course, it will be less). IRPF is withheld by those whom you invoice and it is their responsibility to pay it to the Agencia Tributaria.

The other tax you must be concerned about is IVA (VAT). Whether you must charge your clients this depends on what your activity is. It can be rather complicated and you will want to be very sure if the one that you are engaging in requires you to charge it. For example, if you are a translator, your liability to pay *IVA* depends on *which* type of translating you do. Texts to be published commercially, for example, usually carry IVA but an academic paper written for purposes of diffusion may not. You will want to consult the Agencia Tributaria (or a private *gestor*) to find out what your IVA obligations are. If you are liable for IVA, you charge it directly to your client and are then responsible for declaring and paying it directly to the Agencia Tributaria. IVA must be declared every three months, as opposed to IRPF, which you declare once a year. Language teaching is, fortunately, IVA-exempt.

Starting a Business

There are over 1,500,000 small businesses in Spain, employing over three-quarters of the population. As a foreign resident you have two choices: starting your own business from scratch or buying an existing one. In either case, you need to be careful. A combination of ill-conceived business plans and horrific red-tape, involving upwards of 70 documents, kills off around 80 per cent of small businesses in Spain before they ever get off the ground. Equally, many foreign residents buy existing businesses 'blind', something akin to buying a second-hand car from a man in a dodgy suit. Sadly, many are ripped off by their own countrymen. The golden rule is to trust no one whom you do not know well, and under no circumstances sink all of your savings or pension into a business until you are absolutely sure of what you are doing. If your Spanish is not up to scratch – and it will need to be if you're going to last the course – contract the services of a good English-speaking *gestor (see* pp.216–17) to deal with the red tape, plus a lawyer and an accountant.

EU citizens only need to fulfil the same bureaucratic requirements as any Spaniard. Non-EU citizens must obtain a visa and work permit to operate a business. To do so they will need a business plan and have upwards of €80,000 to finance it. Even then, they have to show that the business they wish to set up is likely to provide employment for Spanish or EU workers, and will not adversely affect (that is, compete with) already established companies in the same business sector or geographical area.

However, if you have a business idea and the necessary capital, do not let the above put you off. A great many foreigners establish and run successful businesses in Spain, which can be bars, clubs, restaurants, shops, language academies, riding schools, Internet cafés and more besides. But these people have done their homework, and taken only the necessary risks inherent in any business venture.

Things to Consider

• **Whether you are prepared to learn sufficient Spanish to deal with red tape. By all means use lawyers and *gestores* at the beginning, but their fees can prove to be a burden.**

• **Whether you have sufficient experience in the type of business you plan to operate. If not, are you prepared to work as an employee in that field in order to gain the experience?**

• **Whether you consider yourself a person with business acumen. If not – and be brutally honest with yourself – consider whether you might not be better off looking for paid employment.**

• **Whether you really have enough capital to invest. Seek advice, and over-estimate the potential costs.**

• **Whether you can afford to buy the premises (which can be sold if the business fails), or only rent them.**

- **Whether you are prepared to put in the long hours often necessary to get a business going.**

- **Whether you are prepared to eke out a living from your business. Not many get rich straight away, if ever.**

- **Whether there are any petty local regulations which may adversely affect your business – a vital point, and often overlooked.**

- **Whether there is much competition in the area. Bars and restaurants in tourist areas are notorious for failing, and competition is tremendous.**

- **If you are buying a business, find out why the owner is trying to sell it. Question their motives, and their book-keeping.**

Money and Banks

Whether you become a resident or not, it is necessary to have a Spanish bank account if you buy a property in Spain. As long as you are over 18 you can open an account and only need produce proof of your identity, your marital status (*estado civil*, see pp.170–71), your Spanish postal address, your NIE number (*see* p.25) and possibly some other particulars that a given bank may require. It is better to open the account in person rather than through your lawyer or *gestor*, as it helps to be known to the staff in the branch.

If you are not a resident you can open a *cuenta extranjera*, a 'foreigner's' account', which is subject to slightly different rules from residents' accounts but which for day-to-day purposes functions in practically the same way. If you are a resident then you can open an account under exactly the same conditions as a Spanish native.

Choosing a Bank

There are, basically, two types of bank in Spain: clearing banks, *bancos*, and savings banks, *cajas de ahorro* (or *caixes d'estalvis* in Catalan, *aurrezki kutxa* in Basque, *caixas d'aforros* in Galician). From the point of view of current account holders the differences between them are now fairly slim. Counter service can be a little slow, especially in small-town branches, but Spanish banks have an extensive and efficient system of ATM cashpoints, and many offer excellent Internet banking facilities, which are especially useful for non-residents.

Note that Spanish bank account numbers consist of 20 digits: the first four are the bank's code, the next four are that of the branch, the next two are the *dígito de control* (a random code number) and the last 10 are the account number proper. This is of some importance because some UK Internet accounts only offer the possibility of moving money to other UK accounts, since the form that

Banking Advice

Whichever bank you use and whatever type of account you open, some important things to know are:

• When writing a cheque in Spain you first state the amount in figures, and then in letters; the date is always written in full, in letters. **Learn to do this in Spanish**, and in figures use the continental 'crossed' 7 rather than the English 7.

• In Spain, numbers are punctuated differently from in Britain: €5,500.00 is written €5.500,00.

• Keep a close eye on your bank statements, and check them against the payments you have had sent to Spain and the items you paid out in Spain.

• Make sure you **never** write a cheque when there are insufficient funds in the account to cover it.

• Set up direct debits and standing orders from your Spanish account to cover all the regular payments needed to keep your house going – phone bills, utility bills, community charges – and make sure there is always enough in the account to cover these bills.

appears onscreen does not allow you to enter 20 digits. Check this when opening an account at home.

If you buy your property in or near a largish town or city you probably will have a plethora of *bancos* or *cajas* to choose from, but if you buy in a small town or village the choice will be far more limited. In tourist areas you may also notice many familiar names, those of British high street banks, but they often operate as separate Spanish companies, and do not offer any special facilities to UK account holders. In any case, it is best to bank locally. If your Spanish is weak, it is in your interest to find a branch with English-speaking staff; after that, if you still have a choice of banks, take a look at the finer details of accounts on offer. Check out particularly the bank's charging structure for transfers of money from abroad, and not just the alarm clock, coffee service or mountain bike offered as an incentive for opening an account. Most Spanish banks charge for just about everything, but some charge a lot more than others for the simple task of receiving money that you have sent from abroad. Confirm the potential charges before committing yourself to any bank or account type. Transfers from the UK or Ireland can take a long time, from several days to more than a week. This can be irritating, not only because of the delay but also because somebody, somewhere along the line, is sitting on your money and earning interest on it.

Types of Account

Everyone's banking needs differ. If you have a holiday home and visit only every few months, a simple **current account** (*cuenta corriente*) will suffice. This can be used to pay for utilities and standing charges by direct debit in your absence, and maybe to keep a 'float' of money available in Spain for whenever you visit. If you are living in Spain full-time, receive a pension from home or run a business then you will need a full and more sophisticated banking service. Spanish banks generally pay very little interest on current accounts, somewhere in the region of 0.1 per cent, so it is a good idea to have a **deposit account** as well. Most banks will arrange for the balance on the current account over a certain sum to be transferred automatically into an interest-bearing account. Interest rates in the euro zone are low at present so, if your needs are more complex than this, study carefully the various types of account available to you. These, and the terms of conditions of use, differ substantially from the accounts with which you may be familiar in the UK. In either case, there is no need to close existing accounts that you have at home, as it will be very useful to keep them open for whenever you want to move money into or out of Spain.

Not all Spanish accounts come with a **cheque book**, as many use a savings book system, and there are no cheque guarantee cards in Spain. Cheques are nevertheless widely accepted, if a little reluctantly (you may have to show your passport or residency card as a guarantee). This is because writing a 'bad' cheque, however unwittingly, is a criminal offence. Banks charge a lot for sorting out the mess, and you may jeopardise your chances of arranging a loan in the future.

Offshore and Gibraltar Accounts

Expat magazines are full of advertising offering offshore accounts in banks in various tax havens around the world, and in southern Spain, especially, the high-interest, tax-free (or all but) accounts offered by the dozens of local banks and branches of UK institutions based in Gibraltar have been taken up enthusiastically by UK residents, as the long queues of cars that build up at the Gibraltar border testify. Most such accounts require a fairly sizeable minimum deposit, such as £5,000. Many Costa del Sol expats, though, use them virtually as current accounts, driving over to 'the Rock' and returning with bags of cash, while a few accounts even give cash cards, so that you can withdraw money from a cashpoint in Marbella and yet still enjoy Gibraltar (that is, zero) tax rates.

Note, though, that many foreign residents in Spain also believe, quite erroneously, that offshore accounts, in Gibraltar or elsewhere, are exempt from Spanish tax in Spain. In fact, under a Spanish law specifically aimed at clamping down on tax evasion, all persons officially resident in Spain are liable for tax on their worldwide income, wherever the account is based and, whenever you 'patriate' any part of your offshore account into Spain to spend it, you could be held to account for unpaid tax. One aspect of the Gibraltar issue generally ignored in the UK is that the Spanish government's demanding attitude is in part due to their annoyance over the systematic and very deliberate way Gibraltar is used to avoid Spanish tax.

For all this, in practice, expats returning from Gibraltar are rarely disturbed; nevertheless, there is a certain risk that one day you might be the object of a spot check and, if a big wad of fresh euros is found, you might be used to set an example. Concealing the existence of an offshore account is a criminal offence. If you are taking up residence in Spain this is another reason why you should get detailed financial advice beforehand, and examine thoroughly the whole issue of the location of bank accounts; setting up an offshore account, in addition, gives relatively limited benefits unless you leave the bulk of the account to accumulate for a fairly long term. Also, you cannot pay direct debits in Spain from a Gibraltar account, so you will in any case still need a Spanish bank account.

Buying, Selling or Importing Cars

Importing a Car to Spain

Unless you are particularly attached to your vehicle, it is usually more trouble than it is worth for anyone moving permanently to Spain to bring their British car with them. Driving a right-hand-drive car on the right side of the road becomes increasingly tedious after a while, and can be hazardous on winding mountain roads. Right-hand-drive models are also manufactured differently in certain areas, so spare parts may be hard to come by. Cars with foreign registrations are also more likely to be broken into.

Legally, you are allowed to drive a foreign-registered car in Spain for up to six months in any one year. If you keep it there any longer, officially you should have it tested and re-registered as a Spanish car. Many foreign residents totally ignore this rule and carry on driving around in their UK-registered vehicles year after year. However, you need to be careful, as local police are cracking down on this, and are entitled to impound a foreign-registered car if they have good reason to believe it is used permanently in Spain (many people driving this way also have invalid insurance).

The relevant test, equivalent to the British MOT, is called the Inspección Técnica de Vehículos or ITV, and can be carried out by any authorised mechanic. Re-registering a car, however, can be an extremely bureaucratic process. If you plan to be in Spain for fewer than six months per year but want to keep the car there while away, you can choose to have the vehicle 'sealed' by Spanish customs each time you leave. This at least means customs know the car is being used for under six months a year and will not order its confiscation.

If you are officially resident in Spain and want to import a vehicle that you have bought and paid tax on in another EU country, you should be able to do so free of VAT. If you have owned it for more than six months then you should also be exempt from paying municipal registration tax. If, though, you bought the vehicle tax-free in another EU country, you have to pay the VAT, usually 16 per cent, on arrival in Spain. A customs certificate is issued to confirm that the vehicle is either free of VAT or that the tax has been paid. For cars bought tax-free in other EU countries, as well as the VAT you must pay the municipal registration tax, which is 6–12 per cent. Cars bought outside of the EU are liable to a further 10 per cent import tax. All of these taxes are based on the original price of the car, but are gradually scaled down so that, after a car is ten years old, tax will be calculated on only 20 per cent of its current value.

All these procedures can only be done in the **Jefatura Provincial de Tráfico** in the capital of the province in which you are resident. A full list of their addresses is on the website of the central Dirección General de Tráfico (**www.dgt.es**), which also has a lot of other information on vehicle and traffic laws in Spain, none of it in English. There are no branch offices outside provincial capitals. The papers cannot be sent in by post but must be presented at the office, although not necessarily by the owner of the car: hence, this is one of the bureaucratic operations that most Spanish people would automatically get a *gestor* (*see* pp.216–17) to do for them, and save themselves the trip.

If you do not want to drive your car all the way to Spain you can also have it shipped by truck from or to the UK, with Smart Rental in Màlaga (Spain **t** 952 817 233, **www.smartrental.es**). For general information on driving in Spain, renting a car and public transport, *see* 'Getting Around Spain', pp.84–9.

Buying a Car in Spain

Given all of the above, the option of selling your car at home and buying a new or used one in Spain becomes a good deal more attractive. Even for second-home-owners, who need a car while there but don't want to drive over every time, getting a Spanish car can be worth considering – although compare it with long-term rental, *see* 'Car Rental', p.89 – especially when you take into account that cars in Spain are cheaper than in the UK.

Generally, if you buy a new or used car from a Spanish dealer they will register it for you as part of the deal. The **registration certificate** is called the *permiso de circulación*, and is proof of the transfer of ownership. If you buy a second-hand car from a private individual, though, you will need to apply to register the car yourself within 10 days of its purchase. This is, again, a procedure for which many people prefer to use a *gestor*, especially if they don't have any other reason to go to the provincial capital. If you do it yourself, application forms are obtained from the Jefatura Provincial de Tráfico, at the *vehículos* counter. Ask for a *notificación de transferencia de vehículos*. Once you have completed this form you will also need to present the following:

- Registration document (*permiso de circulación*). The transfer of ownership should be stated on the back of the form, along with the seller's signature.

- Vehicle tax receipt, which must be up to date.

- Test certificate from an authorised ITV mechanic if the car is over four years old. This must be accompanied by a *ficha técnica*, or detailed breakdown of the tests carried out.

- A receipt showing that the transfer tax has been paid.

- Your residence card, or a photocopy of your property deeds (the *escritura*) if you are a non-resident home-owner. If you are living in rented accommodation, you should present a copy of your rental agreement.

- A receipt showing that the registration fee has been paid.

- A stamped, self-addressed envelope so that the traffic authorities can send you the new registration document.

Vehicle taxes are mostly paid at different counters in the same building. Hence, overall, it's much easier to use a *gestor*. You will also need to insure the car (*see* p.236).

Driving Licences

Whether you buy a car in Spain or bring your old one, you will have to decide what to do about your driving licence. Since the 1996 agreement on mutual recognition of driving licences within the EU, anyone from another EU country can drive in Spain with their original, home-country licence for as long as it is valid, with no obligation to take out a Spanish licence. It can, though, still be a good idea to obtain a Spanish driving licence. It can reduce problems and time spent at roadside checks, especially if you ever come on police officers who are not quite *au fait* with the law and may be suspicious of a Spanish resident driving with a foreign licence, and, in any event, you will be forced to do so if at any stage you pick up a penalty point under the Spanish traffic system. EU citizens can exchange their old licence for a Spanish one fairly easily, without the need for a fresh test, but will have to surrender the old licence.

In any case, if you are resident in Spain but do not obtain a Spanish driving licence you are still legally obliged to present your UK licence to the Jefatura Provincial de Tráfico for your details to be entered into their computer system. Citizens of non-EU countries who are resident in Spain are allowed to drive on their old licences for one year, after which they must get a Spanish licence. For this they will usually also have to take the Spanish driving test, which includes a brief medical examination and written and practical tests.

Insurance

Insuring your property, vehicle and health is not a matter to be taken lightly. Shop around widely, talk to as many people as possible and compare products before signing anything. The market for all types of insurance in Spain has expanded in recent years and many British companies have become well established, offering products that are tailored to the needs of foreign residents. With some you may be able to get a policy written in English, although in the case of disputes only the Spanish version is valid in a court of law. If you take out a policy in English, make sure it is a full and correct translation of the same policy written in Spanish. You are not obliged to buy cover from a company based in Spain, and may insure with a company registered in another EU country. The advantage here is that you can have your policy, and make any claims, in English. In general, the best plan is to get quotes from several solid, well-established, reputable firms, Spanish or not, and take your decisions after getting independent, professional advice.

General Insurance Companies

- **AXA, t** 902 212 123, **www.axa-seguros.es.**
- **Caser, t** 902 222 737, **www.caser.es.**
- **Direct Seguros (Axa & BBVA bank), t** 902 404 025, **www.directseguros.es.**
- **La Estrella, t** 902 212 123, **www.laestrella.es**. A subsidiary of Grupo Generali.
- **Liberty Seguros, t** 902 444 888, **www.libertyseguros-es.com.**
- **Pelayo, t** 902 352 235, **www.pelayo.com.**
- **Santa Lucía, t** 902 242 000, **www.santalucia.es.**

Insuring Your Home

Household insurance should cover the building, which will be described in Spanish policies as the *continente*, the contents, or *contenido* and third-party liability, *riesgo a terceros*. If you buy an apartment there may already be a separate buildings' insurance policy for the whole block, which will be paid for as part of your community charge, but this will often cover only certain specified parts of the building, and you will still need insurance for your own flat. The scope of any communal insurance policy needs to be clearly established by your lawyer, and explained to you during the process of buying the flat.

Look for a policy that covers damage caused by fire, smoke, storms, flooding, freezing, burglary, vandalism, terrorist acts (ETA is no longer the force it was, but may still leave bombs in waste bins in resort towns) and natural catastrophes. Many parts of Spain suffer sporadically from severe weather and flash floods, and the drier regions are prone to forest fires in the summer, so assess all possible sources of damage. External buildings and fittings such as satellite dishes, garden furniture, fences and garages should also be covered. A thorough inspection prior to purchase is recommended as you cannot later claim for damages that are demonstrably caused by structural faults or sub-standard construction. Contents should be insured against the same risks. Most policies pay for items such as bedding, furniture and clothing to be replaced. As well as this, contents insurance often covers accidental damage to plumbing, damages caused during a burglary, new locks being fitted after burglary or loss of keys, alternative accommodation if your house is rendered uninhabitable and property belonging to third persons that is in your home. Valuable items such as jewellery, computers, cameras, camcorders and porcelain must be duly documented and either photographed or recorded on video. The original receipts must be produced when making a claim. If your home is a villa or ground-floor apartment the insurance company will usually insist on iron bars over the windows, a reinforced door, alarms and other security devices.

Getting insurance for holiday homes is more complicated and involves a higher premium, usually based on the average number of days' occupancy and the length of time it is left empty. Getting a policy that specifies that the property is a holiday home and not a first residence is recommended. Check in the small print to see if you can make claims for thefts that happen while you are away.

The criteria for calculating your premium are the building's size, age, value of contents and security measures in place. Location also influences the calculation, and remote villas and properties in areas with high burglary rates are more expensive to insure. To make a claim, inform the company as soon as possible, and never later than seven days after the incident has occurred. If you are the victim of theft, report it immediately to the police, as no claim will be admitted by any company without a copy of the *denuncia*, or official police statement, which the police will give to you.

Insuring Your Car

Spanish law, like that in all other EU countries, demands that all vehicles be fully insured for third-party damage. Not everybody complies with the law, though, and there are many thousands of uninsured cars on Spanish roads. Uninsured drivers who have accidents, especially those involving injury, can face stiff fines or even imprisonment.

The basic types of car insurance available are similar to those in the UK. The minimum, obligatory level of third-party car insurance is called *responsabilidad civil*, and covers only third-party claims for injury and damage to property. The next step up is a third-party, fire and theft policy (*responsabilidad civil obligatoria, incendio y robo*), which also covers your vehicle for fire, natural hazards, theft, broken windscreens or windows and some legal costs. Theft of or damage to contents are not usually included. As elsewhere, though, the best plan is to have comprehensive insurance, *todo riesgo*, which covers all damages to your vehicle, however caused. There are, though, certain notable differences compared to the UK: in Spain some insurance companies will not provide *todo riesgo* insurance for vehicles more than a couple of years old; also, most importantly, comprehensive policies here generally cover only the car, not the driver and passengers, insurance for whom is usually offered as an optional extra for an added premium.

Car insurance is relatively cheap in Spain. Various criteria are taken into account for the purpose of calculating premiums – generally, the type of car, your age, your accident record, where you live, the number of kilometres you drive every year and any previous convictions for motoring offences, if you have them. All drivers under the age of 30 are considered to be 'young' and so pay higher premiums, as do residents of big cities. A middle-aged driver with a good safety record who lives in a small village will pay much less.

If you have an accident you must present a completed accident report form in order to claim. This will be amongst the insurance company's documents that you are obliged to carry by law. This form, along with police reports and reports from insurance company experts, will be used by the company to decide on the claim. As anywhere, you need to notify the insurance company as soon after the accident as possible. In the event of your car being stolen, report it to the police immediately and then claim from your insurance company, submitting a copy of the police statement or *denuncia*. Virtually all companies will hold on to the claim for at least 30 days before taking any action, and most will take a lot longer still before paying.

Car Insurance Companies

- **Línea Directa, t** 902 123 323. The Spanish subsidiary of Direct Line, offering the same kind of phone-only insurance service at low cost.
- **Maaf, t** 902 112 030, **www.maaf.es.**

Insuring Yourself

If you are not covered by Spanish Social Security (which EU citizens are for emergency purposes only) you will need private health insurance. In addition, a very large number of people in Spain have private insurance in addition to their state health service entitlement (for which, *see* pp.254–7), for the usual reasons: access to a wider choice of specialists and the prospect of being attended to more quickly. Throughout Spain, there are many private clinics serving private patients through insurance plans. As with home and car insurance, it pays to shop around among the various private health plans available and read the fine print carefully to see exactly what you are and are not entitled to. Particularly check for what services are available immediately after taking out a policy, as many do not cover certain types of treatment until six months have passed. You may find that foreign health insurance companies provide more comprehensive cover because they are aimed precisely at foreign residents, and usually include repatriation costs and treatment in countries other than Spain.

Spanish Health Insurance Companies

- **Adeslas, t** 902 200 200, **www.adeslas.es.**
- **Asisa, t** 901 101 010, **www.asisa.es.**
- **Sanitas, t** 902 102 400, **www.sanitas.es.** Large-scale Spanish specialist health insurance provider associated with BUPA.

UK Health Insurers

- **BUPA International, t** (01273) 208181, **www.bupa-intl.com.** Offers a range of health plans designed specifically for expatriates.
- **Exeter Friendly Society, t** 0808 055 6575, **www.exeterfriendly.co.uk.** Has health plans specifically for residents in Spain and Portugal.
- **PPP Healthcare, t** 0800 33 55 55, **www.ppphealthcare.com.** Like BUPA, PPP offers special health plans for expatriates, valid worldwide.

Utilities

Once you have bought your Spanish property, an essential first step will of course be to ensure that you are properly connected up to all the basic services – power, gas, water and so on.

Electricity

Since January 2003, Spain's energy market has been liberalised and consumers can choose which company bills them for their electricity, as can users of piped gas. Now, while you must still contract gas or electricity from the company that owns and operates the infrastructures in your area (the distributor), you can choose to be billed by another (the supplier), and therefore shop around for the best deal.

This will not necessarily mean lower electricity tariffs, as industry chiefs claim that they were artificially depressed for years, owing to regulation. Indeed, tariffs are actually expected to rise by about 1.5 per cent a year for the next few years but will still be subject to maximum 2 per cent raises until 2010. The main benefits to consumers will be better levels of service owing to competition. At present, the competing companies are all falling over themselves to design personalised supply and payment schemes to suit each customer, including incentive discounts to lure custom away from rival companies. They are offering other products, from installation of air-conditioning and heating systems to home insurance and even communications. It will certainly pay from now on to look at each and see how you can benefit.

Almost all property in Spain is now connected at 220 volts, in line with European standards; this current is entirely compatible with British 240v equipment. However, a few old properties in Spain are still wired for the 110 volts system that was used in many parts of the country until the 1970s. They can be converted, but at your expense, so this is something else that you should check for when buying a property of a certain age that has not been recently renovated. All Spanish plugs are of the standard European, two-round-pin type. If you are taking a lot of electrical appliances from the UK, with three-pin plugs, change the plugs or stock up on adaptors before you go, as they will be cheaper and much easier to find in the UK than in Spain.

The 'big four' competitors for business are:

- **Endesa, t** 900 848 384, **www.endesaonline.com.**

- **Gas Natural, t** 900 760 760, **www.gasnatural.com.**

- **Iberdrola, t** 901 202 020, **www.iberdrola.es.**

- **Unión Fenosa, t** 901 380 220, **www.unionfenosa.es.**

Newly built properties must be connected to the electricity supply. To do this, sign up with the electricity company stipulating the amount of electricity you want. This means the peak wattage you think you will need and therefore the tariff to which you will need to subscribe. To work this out, you will need to tell the company (or an electrician) the number of appliances that you might want to use all at once at any single time – they should be able to advise you on the wattage that you will need to cover this demand. Be careful not to underestimate the amount of power needed, especially during winter. If you contract too little, your supply will cut out at times of highest demand. On buying an established property you simply take over the existing supply and have the account transferred to your name. This is straightforward and involves a small fee. If you think the existing supply is going to be insufficient, ask for it to be upgraded, again for a small fee. For all dealings with the electricity company you will need to produce the usual documents, passport or residence card, bank details, etc. Before moving in, ask the company to make a special meter reading to avoid paying the previous occupant's bill. If your house is not already connected to the electricity supply, get a quotation for connection before committing yourself to the purchase – it may prove expensive.

Bills are two-monthly, with the standing charge paid in advance, the consumption in arrears. Pay by direct debit from your Spanish bank account, particularly if you are not there permanently. Make sure you have enough in the account to cover likely charges.

Blackouts are surprisingly common, especially in rural areas, though things are improving. Much of the problem stems from lack of preparation for rain. Substations and junction boxes are often built in stream beds, so get flooded and short out. Cuts may last a split second or many hours. Get a UPS (uninterruptible power supply) to protect computers and other vital equipment and a surge protector to guard sensitive devices.

Gas

Many Spanish homes still use bottled butane gas (*butano*). Mains gas is only generally available in larger cities and towns.

If your property is on the main gas network, connection and payment arrangements are similar to those for electricity. As with electricity, different companies operate regional monopolies: for a new or renovated property that has not previously been connected up to the mains system, contact your local gas company and make a contract for supply, but do look into other possibilities for payment (*see* above). The company will probably inspect your fittings before agreeing to supply gas. Payment is best done by direct debit, and bills are two-monthly.

If you are not on the mains network you will have to use butane, a cheap form of energy, which is delivered in big orange metal canisters from trucks that, in most areas, visit weekly (your neighbours will tell you the local routine), or you can go to a depot and get one yourself. The 12.5kg *bombona* (canister) costs around €9.81 at the present time, though this can fluctuate. It is slightly cheaper if you fetch them yourself. Repsol Butano has a near-monopoly on butane supply and you have to sign up with them to be supplied. The company usually orders a safety check first; old properties often need modifications, such as air vents, to meet safety standards. When signing the contract you pay a deposit of around €17 per bottle. Keep a spare – they unfailingly run out when you are showering or when your soufflé is about to rise; if you have two separate gas systems – such as a cooker and a water heater – you will need more than one canister at a time in any case. Ideally, ask a neighbour or the delivery man to show you how to change gas canisters. The snap-on regulator valve, known as an *alcachofa* (artichoke!) requires a certain knack to fit and, if incorrectly fitted, can be extremely dangerous.

Repsol also insists on five-yearly inspections and may send an authorized technician to carry them out, usually with advance warning. Be wary of 'cowboy' operators with the Repsol logo on their overalls. Their trick is to arrive unannounced, change tubing and *alcachofas* unnecessarily, charge the earth (on the spot) and then disappear without trace. The orange gas tubes that connect the canister to your appliance have the date printed on them, are sold in hardware stores and can be changed easily without the intervention of a technician.

As you will soon notice, delivering *butano* is very hard work. It is standard to give the delivery man a tip.

Water

A serious issue in Spain: water is a precious resource and not one to be wasted. Average rainfall provides sufficient water overall but some areas get too much, others not enough and at the time of writing Spain is suffering its worst drought for around 70 years. The south, most of the Mediterranean coast and the islands are often parched due to insufficient rain, these are precisely the areas with greatest demand, especially in the tourist season.

To offset this problem, various expensive engineering projects have been set up: desalination plants in the Canaries, pumped water in the Balearics and recycled waste water for irrigation and watering golf courses on the Costa del Sol. A hugely controversial (and expensive) national hydrological plan, designed to canalise water from north to south, was scrapped by the socialist government soon after coming into office. Instead, the idea now is to invest in desalination plants along the Mediterranean coast. Quite whether supplies will ever keep up with demand remains an open question.

Despite this, in many tourist areas water is used with irresponsible abandon. Many towns barely hold their own, and supplies may be restricted. One solution is to install an independent water tank, a *depósito*, filled by a tanker (*see* **Selecting a Property**, p.112). This system was used before piped water and is coming back into fashion as an emergency back-up.

Water supplies are generally metered in Spain. If your property does not have a meter, consider having one fitted, especially if you plan to let it to guests. The water company will fit one for a small charge. If the house you propose to buy is not connected to the water supply, check how much connection costs before committing yourself to the purchase – you may find it prohibitively expensive. Strangely, water prices in Spain are still low, as little as a thirtieth of prices elsewhere in Europe, according to *The Economist*, and families only dedicate 1 per cent of their income to water bills. It is felt that prices will have to be increased dramatically to force people to use water more carefully.

All Spanish tap water is drinkable, unless marked otherwise, though not all well-water is (*see* **Selecting a Property**, p.113). Not all the water that is drinkable tastes nice, though – so most people in the Mediterranean area still buy bottled water for drinking.

Heating and Hot Water

In the north and centre of Spain it can be as cold and wet as Britain. Even in southern Spain you should consider installing a decent heating system. It may be a lot warmer than it would have been in Manchester but, if you have been used to daily winter temperatures of 21°C (70°F), a drop to 16°C (60°F) will feel unpleasantly cold.

In many modern Spanish buildings heating (usually gas-fired) is under-floor rather than through radiators, and in apartment blocks there may be a central system for which you pay in part through your community charge and in part according to your own consumption. In Spain there are more types of water heater on the market than in the UK. Install a heater that can cope when the property is fully occupied by people who shower a lot. Many 'standard equipment' heaters and hot water tanks in older properties and holiday apartments are far too small for any long-term use.

The Language of Bills (Facturas)

Darse de alta – to sign up for supply.
Darse de baja – to terminate a supply contract.

Words and phrases frequently seen on bills:

General – Electricity/Gas/Water
Alquiler equipos de medida meter rental
Consumo consumption/use
Consumo medio average daily consumption
Domiciliar/domiciliación to order a direct debit/standing order
Electricidad electricity
Energía consumida energy consumed
Facturación billing
Forma de pago means of payment
Historial de consumo record of consumption, usually a graph with last 12 months' consumption
ImporteTotal (a pagar) amount payable
Impuesto sobre electricidad tax on electricity
Intereses de demora interests charged for late payment of previous bills
IVA VAT
Lectura (actual/anterior) (current/previous) reading
Potencia contratada wattage/power contracted
Servicio clientes – customer service

Specific – Telefónica
Detalle de consumo/llamadas, etc. breakdown of consumption/calls etc.
Línea básica basic line
Llamadas (metropólitanas/provinciales/interprovinciales/internacionales/automáticas/a móviles) (local/provincial/interprovincial/international/automatic, i.e. not via the operator/to mobiles) calls made

Air-conditioning

Air-conditioning is not an expensive, unnecessary luxury in southern Spain; consider installing at least a minimal system. If the 2am temperature is 30°C (86°F) you will not regret the outlay. Portable air-conditioning units can be bought in hypermarkets and electrical stores, and installers of larger, built-in systems advertise frequently in the local expat press, or can be found in the *Yellow Pages* under *Aire Acondicionado*.

Some systems combine a cooling and heating function, which is obviously more economical than having two separate systems. Individual air-conditioning units can be noisy, so always have them switched on and listen to them for a while before buying. Anyone with a record of asthma or any other respiratory problems should be doubly careful when buying any air-con system, and get independent advice on its health effects.

There are, on the market, alternatives to installed air-conditioning, for keeping individual rooms cool. The *pingüino* (penguin) is basically a fan that blows out air which has been passed through a tank for water and/or ice which is then pulverised. This system avoids the problems endemic to installed air-conditioning systems.

Communications

As in Britain and most other European countries, the communications scene in Spain has been transformed in the last few years by a combination of new technologies and the ending of state monopolies. Telephone services and electronic communications, once characterised by high prices and unreliability, are now of a much higher standard, even if the conventional mail service still has its problems.

Postal Services

There are main **post offices** (*oficinas de correos* or, more commonly, just *correos*) in all cities and large towns, and smaller offices in town districts, all towns, many villages, larger railway stations and airports. They are identified by yellow signs with a logo like an old-fashioned post horn. In larger post offices there are separate counters for all the different services, such as parcel post, fax, *poste restante* (*lista de correos* in Spanish) and so on. You can rent your own post office box (*apartado de correos*) in any post office. Main post offices are usually open from 8 or 9am to 9pm Monday to Saturday, and some also open 9am–2pm on Sundays; local offices, though, generally open Monday to Saturday (or sometimes just to Friday) only, 9am–2pm.

If all you want are **stamps** for a letter, you do not need to find a post office but can buy them from your local tobacconist, or *estanco*, identified by a brown and yellow sign with the word *tabacos*. As well as standard post you can also send letters and cards *urgente*, for an extra charge.

Normal **post boxes** are yellow, with two red stripes around them, and usually have two letter boxes, one for local mail and one for everywhere else. There are also a few red boxes specially for urgent mail, usually only found outside city post offices, in railway stations and in a few other prominent locations, collections from which are made every one or two hours. If you only want to buy stamps, you can go to the local tobacconists' shop, the *estanco*.

There are regular complaints about the unreliability of the Spanish **postal service**: when it works fine and a letter gets from Spain to the UK in three days or so you wonder what people are moaning about, but when it catches you out and your mail spends three weeks or more in transit it's very irritating. In the main cities, service is generally quite reliable, but it's more likely to be patchy in small towns and the countryside.

Businesses make great use of private **courier services** (*mensajeros*) when sending anything valuable or requiring guaranteed delivery. SEUR is the biggest Spanish courier company and has the largest network of depots throughout the country but, for international parcels, the big international players such as DHL or UPS will be quicker, if more expensive. All will be in the provincial *Yellow Pages* under *mensajeros* or *transportes*.

Well worth knowing about is the **Postal Exprés mail service**, the equivalent of Parcel Force in the UK (but actually better) which, although run by the post office, is reliable. Parcels sent within Spain are guaranteed delivery within 24 hours, to most EU countries within 48 hours. Postal Exprés is available at all post offices. It's naturally more expensive than standard post, but still a lot cheaper than private courier companies. Other information about mail services can be found at the official post office website (**www.correos.es**).

Telephones

The situation regarding phones and everything to do with them in Spain has noticeable similarities with that in Britain, only with a lot less flexibility. Historically, all phone services were operated by one company, **Telefónica**, which was owned by the state. Notorious for charging well above the European norm (especially for international calls) for mediocre service, for years it united the whole country against it in loathing, frustration and continual complaint. It was part-privatised in the 1980s and fully privatised in 1997, and over the last 20 years has considerably improved its performance. In 1998, Telefónica lost its statutory monopoly, in a move that, it was hoped, would rapidly open up the whole telecommunications market in Spain to competition and dynamic new

Phone Numbers and Codes

Since 1999, all Spanish landline numbers have had nine digits and include the former provincial area code as an integral part of the number, so that you need to dial it even if you're calling from the same town. Hence, all numbers in Málaga province will begin 95, all those in Alicante 96, all those in Tenerife 922 and so on (the full list is in the local phone book). After some confusion following the changeover from the older, separate-code system, numbers now tend to be written 333 333 333 (as in 952 787 878).

Numbers beginning 900 are freephone lines, although they are not widely used; there are also information and company lines that begin 902, 906 and so on that, in contrast, are more expensive than ordinary numbers – the higher the number after 90, the higher the rate).

All Spanish mobile numbers begin with 6.

To make an international call from Spain, first dial 00 and then the country code – Australia: 61; Canada: 1; Irish Republic: 353; United Kingdom: 44; USA: 1 – followed by the area code and number, omitting the first 0 in British area codes. To call Spain from abroad, the country code is 34.

companies. However, in the same way that more newly founded phone companies have failed to make huge inroads into the primacy of BT in the UK – only much more so – the new competitors have been unable to make more than a dent in the established position of Telefónica, amid dark accusations against the government of, contrary to its public posture, tilting the market in favour of the former state corporation and the big business investors that now control it. Telefónica continues to control over 85 per cent of all phone business in Spain, and is the only company from which you can get a landline telephone connection; the smaller companies only compete in supplying calls. Nevertheless, the arrival of competition in some areas has at least led to welcome reductions in many charges, and given a further spur to Telefónica to improve its services, which are now often quite efficient. Overall, though, phone costs in Spain remain significantly higher than in the UK.

The continuing niggling problems of fixed-line services are probably the main reason why Spaniards have taken to the arrival of mobile phones with huge enthusiasm. Spain is the fastest-expanding mobile phone market in the EU, and actually has more mobiles than fixed lines.

General Telefónica information is on the web (**www.telefonica.es**) but is presented in a very confusing, over-technical way and only a small (and not very useful) part is linked in English. More helpful is the company's general customer service and sales freephone number: **t** 1004. Operators sometimes speak English, or you can ask for one that does.

Getting a Phone Line and Making Calls

If your new Spanish home has no previous phone connection. to get a line installed you need to go to the nearest local office (*oficina commercial*) of Telefónica to take out your first contract. These are found in most towns but nowadays, as one sign of the organisation's new co-operativeness, this and other phone business can also be done at many of the company's high-street phone shops (*tiendas telefónicas*) and at independent shops that are authorised Telefónica agents, indicated by the company's blue and green logo. If you call t 1004, operators can tell you the location of the nearest one, or you can do some of the procedures over the phone. You will need to show your passport or residency card, proof of your new address, such as a recent utility bill, and a copy of the *escritura*, or property deed, to your new home. Charges for the initial connection currently begin at €79.50 for just the line or €112.55 for the line and a telephone (you may provide your own if you wish), followed by €17.87 per month line rental, both plus VAT at 16 per cent. Bills are sent every two months.

Operator and Emergency Numbers

The following information and emergency numbers are used throughout Spain. Phone directories (*guías telefónicas*) are published by province, except for the larger cities, which have their own. There are general directories and *Yellow Pages* (*Páginas Amarillas*). All have very useful opening sections with a wide variety of information – special numbers and addresses and so on – on many local services. Some cities – Barcelona and Madrid, especially, but also some smaller cities – operate an enormously useful citizens' information line, t 010, a great way of finding information that's otherwise hard to locate.

t 1002	breakdowns
t 1004	Telefónica customer service and sales
t 1005	international operator for most of the world
t 1008	international operator for Europe and North Africa
t 1009	operator for national calls
t 11825	international directory enquiries
t 091	national police line
t 092	municipal and local police (for whichever area you are in)
t 093	speaking clock (high-rate calls)
t 096	wake-up call
t 112	general emergency numbers (fire, police, ambulance)
t 012	general citizens' information line

Directory enquiries have now been opened up to competition. Telefónica has replaced its old 1003 service with 11818 (straight directory enquiries) and 11822 (offering a wider range of information. There is also a whole plethora of other 118xx information numbers belonging to the various competitors in this field.

If you are a tenant rather than the owner of the property, you will need to show your rental contract rather than the *escritura*. In towns and resort areas, new lines are generally installed within about four days of the contract being signed. In rural areas, though, you may not be able to get a phone installed at all, as Telefónica's new status as private company (as opposed to the – poor – public service it once was) means it is no longer obliged to provide everyone who wants one with a line.

If you are buying a property with an existing phone line, once the date of the sale is known, you or your lawyer should contact Telefónica to inform the company that the property is being sold on that date and instruct them to close the phone account, send a final bill to the previous owner and start your new account with the same number on the same day. Your lawyer should also formally remind the seller of the same thing. It is quite common for sellers – notably foreigners leaving Spain – to leave behind big bills to be picked up by new owners; you can fight having to pay them, but it's an aggravation best avoided. Transferring a phone line to a new subscriber costs around €30 plus VAT plus the usual line rental. You will usually keep the number but, in Spain, when you move house, for a small fee you can take your number with you as long as it is within the same province, otherwise you may be given a new one. Note that anyone over 65 is entitled to discounts on many Telefónica services. You can also buy a phone from the company as well as the line (or rent one, but this is generally a waste of money), or buy one from any of the independent phone shops that are now common in Spain. It's also possible to use a phone brought from Britain, although this is technically against the terms of your Telefónica contract. You will need to change the plug, and Spanish plugs are available from phone and electrical shops.

While you have to get your line from Telefónica, you are under no obligation to use it for calls, although with your line rental you get a certain amount of free call-time. Several national and regional landline providers operate in Spain, though many customers stay with Telefónica out of inertia or confusion about the complex tariff system. This is despite the potentially considerable savings that can be made by switching to an alternate provider. Competition has intensified recently; for the best deal, think where you will be calling and how often, then shop around. Some providers offer flat-rate charges (*tarifas planas*), which are useful if you will be calling a lot and some offer discounted indirect phone access via four-digit dialling prefixes (10xx). Dial the prefix before every call in order to get their rates. If you forget to dial it, you'll be billed at Telefónica rates. Some now offer automatic pre-dialling (*marcación automática*). Billing is as for other utilities, either by direct debit or by payment into a designated bank.

Main Providers

- **Auna, t** 935 020 000/902 500 060, **www.auna.es.**
- **Euskaltel,** information line **t** 1717, **www.euskaltel.es.**

- **Iberdrola, t** 901 20 20 20/901 220 230, **www.iberdrola.es.**
- **Jazztel, t** 912 917 178; information line **t** 1074, **www.jazztel.es.**
- **ONO, t** 902 929 000, information line **t** 1400, **www.ono.es.**
- **Retevisión, t** 935 020 000/902 500 060, **www.retevision.es.**
- **Telefónica,** customer attention **t** 1004, **www.telefonica.es.**
- **Uni2, t** 912 521 200/902 789 789, **www.uni2.es.**
- **Wanadoo, t** 902 011 412, information line **t** 1414, **www.wanadoo.es.**
- **Teltarifas, www.teltarifas.com/particulares.** Rate comparisons.

International Calls – Saving Money

Most providers make offers for cheaper international calls, which may be special rates to a certain number, or country, a certain amount of time for free, or cheaper weekend rates, etc. This is certainly an area where shopping around before contracting any provider's services is recommended.

Another option is to buy a prepaid **international calling card**. These offer huge reductions and can usually be used from any landline or mobile. Card providers can offer cheap rates because they buy large amounts of international minutes at discount prices. Here, the best thing is to try out several different cards over a period of time to see which is cheapest overall, as some include a connection charge, which can work out expensive if you make many, short calls. It is also worth checking how long the card remains 'alive', as most expire after 30, 60 or 90 days.

As well as this, many expats use a range of international phone services for their long-distance calls: **Telforce, t** 0800 900 321, **www.telforce.co.uk**, is one with competitive rates. Another alternative still is to use the **t** 902 999 007 service. All calls to 902 numbers are charged at the same national call rates. From fixed and public phones there is a connection charge of €0.08 then €0.04 per minute from Monday to Friday, 8pm to 8am and at weekends or €0.07 during the day time. From mobiles it is more expensive but still represents a saving: from 8pm to 8am during the week and at weekends calls cost €0.22 per minute, and it is €0.36 at other times, the connection charge is always €0.12. to use the system, dial **t** 902 999 007, after the recorded message dial 1 then the international code and the destination number. You can also preinstall the number on to mobile phones.

If you are going to be letting your property out for long periods of time, you need to think carefully whether you really want to have a fixed line, and if so, make clear to tenants how it is to be paid for. Many owners now prefer to rely on mobiles and leave tenants to do likewise rather than face any potential arguments over fixed-line bills.

Mobile Phones

There are three main mobile service providers in Spain, **Movistar** (owned by Telefónica, **www.movistar.com**), **Vodafone** (**www.vodafone.es**) and **Amena** (part of Retevisión, **www.amena.com**). Amena has recently been bought by Orange, itself part of France Telecom so users can expect changes (hopefully reduced rates) as from the autumn of 2005. Between them they cover most of the country, although there are still rural areas with no mobile service. All have plenty of shops and agents where you can sign up for a phone; rates have been fairly similar for all, and there have been price wars recently. Mobiles have become especially popular in Spain, in part because initial connection is much quicker, less bureaucratic and initially cheaper than getting a Telefónica landline. But note that if you make many calls, especially long-distance, their costs soon mount up, and it will still be cheaper in the long run to get a fixed line. You can pay for a mobile on a monthly account; all three operators have a wide range of contracts to suit different users' needs. Information is available on their respective websites, though Amena has to take credit for being the only one to provide all the information you need to know in English.

Pre-paid phones rarely use inserted cards these days, you simply buy credit and top it up when you are low. You do this by credit or debit card at many bank cashpoints: you key in your phone number, and however much you want to pay will be debited from your card. Alternatively, you can do it at the supermarket check-out.

Mobiles from the main UK networks work perfectly well in Spain provided they have a roaming facility, allowing you to connect via a Spanish network affiliated to your home provider. Calls are usually charged at the Spanish provider's local rate. While this is fine for holiday trips, if you are staying much longer it will be much cheaper to get a Spanish mobile.

Public Phones and Phone Centres

Most Telefónica **public phones** take coins and credit cards, but the most convenient way of using them is with a phone card, available to the value of €5, €10 and €15, from tobacconists and post offices, saving the need for fumbling with change. Most phones now in use have a digital display that lights up when you pick up the phone, and have a 'select language' (*selección de idioma*) button with which you can change the display into English. As you are speaking, the display will show how much time you have left for your coins or units left on your card. There are coin-only phones in most bars, but they are nearly always expensive, because the bar owner is entitled to charge extra for their use.

Still popular for international calls, and a bit cheaper, are **phone centres** (*locutorios*), offices where you are allotted a booth, make all your calls and then pay at the counter when you leave. They are often found at larger railway stations.

Internet and E-mail

Getting online in Spain is fairly painless these days. The options available, depending on your needs, are dial-up, ISDN (less in demand than previously), ADSL (more in demand than before) and cable. Wi-Fi is also increasingly being used. For straightforward dial-up connections, CD-ROMs with installation software are often given away by newspapers and computing magazines. In addition, many newly bought computers actually come with a pre-installed installation package enabling you to configure a dial-up connection to an ISP (Internet service provider) by yourself in just a few easy steps. Most dial-up ISPs offer three types of access: a pay-as-you-go service; a flat rate service (*tarifa plana*) for which you pay a fixed amount per month for unlimited access (starting from €20 a month or even less) or a combination of the two, which usually means a flat fee during off-peak hours and a charge per minute the rest of the time. If your needs are limited to checking and sending e-mail for an hour or so a day, one of these deals will suit you. Remember, of course, that your actual line must be provided by Telefónica whether you do a deal with another provider to take your call traffic or not.

If, on the other hand, you are going to use the Internet extensively, you will probably be interested in one of the many packages that give you an ADSL connection and cheap rate or flat rate telephone calls (local and national), all for one price. These services, if you contract them, will take a little while to set up. Telefónica has its own, which is slow to arrive, and other providers have to get authorisation from them to get their service installed since, after all, they are 'stealing' Telefónica's customers. Allow between 10 and 20 days – minimum – between the time you agree to contract a service and having it up and running. It might take longer. But once you have it and see the speed at which pages download – while you are chatting to your family – you will not regret having contracted the service. A basic ADSL line with a package including calls can cost as little as €30 a month, but prices are coming down all the time and providers are offering ever broader bandwidth for that price. Apart from the monthly fee, providers often charge for the sign-up (*cuota de alta*), for the installation and for the device itself (if one is needed). However, obliged by the amount of competition out there, operators are offering ever more for ever less, so look out for special offers. High-speed access is usually contracted for a minimum of one year, and if you terminate the contract early you may face stiff penalties or a lawsuit, so be sure to read the small print before you sign up.

Some Internet providers for getting connected are:

- **www.ya.com**
- **www.jazztel.com**
- **www.tiscali.es**
- **www.telefonica.es**
- **www.jazztel.es**

If you only need to access the Net occasionally, in most towns of any size you will find Internet cafés and work centres which will allow you to drop in and pay for anything from 15 minutes' connection upwards.

The revolutionary way of talking internationally, and cheaply, these days is by means of **Skype**. This is a programme for making free calls over the Internet to anyone else who also has Skype and the only cost involved is that which you already pay to your ISP. It is free and easy to download and use, and works with most computers. You need some additional hardware, namely a headset, speakers and/or a USB phone. Take a look at **www.skype.com** for more details.

Education

First Steps and Reasons for Buying (*see* pp.20–22) gives an overview of the educational options, state and private, available in Spain, and points out many of the questions you will have to ponder as you consider bringing your children to live in Spain. Here we look at schools in a little more depth and give practical advice on enrolment.

The State System

Infant Education

This is considered to run from ages three to six. Pre-school, *pre-escolar* or *educación infantil*, is, theoretically, universally available. It is not compulsory but recommended; children who have attended infant school are better socialised by age six. Pre-school education aims to favour the child's physical and personal development, encourage independence and personal hygiene and create awareness of self and others via play, and artistic, musical and corporal expression. Nursery schools or crèches (*guarderías*) for children from a very young age, both public and private, are widely available in cities and towns, although the best ones are often in strong demand.

Primary Education

Educación primaria, starting at age six, is compulsory. Over three two-year cycles, it aims to further the child's socialisation and independence. The broad subject areas are: the natural, social and cultural environment; art and music; sports; Spanish (or the co-official language where appropriate); mathematics and, from age eight, a foreign language, usually English (though in many regions they are now starting younger under the aegis of a bilingual scheme). Evaluation is continuous and global; under-achievers quite often have to repeat a year. Support teachers help integrate children with learning problems and disabilities, except in extreme cases. Classes have a maximum of 25 pupils.

There are five hour-long periods a day and 30 minutes' break. The school year runs from mid-September to late June, with two weeks' holiday at Christmas, a little more than a week at Easter, several public holidays throughout the year and some local holidays.

Secondary Education

Compulsory secondary education, *educación secundaria obligatoria* (ESO), comprises two two-year cycles from ages 12 to 16, and prepares students either for baccalaureate (*bachillerato*) or vocational training (*formación profesional*). Students cover a comprehensive range of subjects from the humanities, the natural and social sciences and the arts and can choose from several optional subjects according to their talents and interests. Evaluation is similar to that in primary education and insufficient progress can again mean repeating a year. The school year is basically the same as that in primary education but the day is shorter, from 8am until about 2pm.

Further Education

Those who do not pass ESO can either leave school or proceed to vocational training, *formación profesional*. Those that pass receive their secondary school graduation certificate (*graduado en educación secundaria*), and may go on to either specific vocational training or the more academic baccalaureate (*bachillerato*) programme. This two-year course prepares them for university entrance exams (*selectividad*), though they can also enter specific vocational training at this point. The university entry exam may be abolished in the future, what will replace it is at this point unknown.

Enrolment in Spanish State Schools

Enrolment in a Spanish school may require an interview and possibly an examination, though this is rare for foreign children. Schools have annual quotas and places are allocated on a first-come, first-served basis. Enrolment is usually during the spring term prior to the year the child is to enter school but may vary from one region to another. Check exact dates with any school in your area. If you hear good things about a particular school and want your child to attend, consider buying or renting in that area.

To enrol your child you will need:

- **the child's birth certificate or passport, plus a photocopy, and parents' passports, also photocopied.**
- **the child's immunisation records.**
- **proof of your residence .**
- **two passport-size photographs.**

For children who are of an age to enter the ESO third grade, at about 14 or 15, you need to produce your child's birth certificate, school record book and/or examination results. Contact the Ministerio de Educación, Cultura y Deportes, Calle Alcalá, 36, 28014 Madrid, **t** 917 018 500, **www.mec.es/educacion**). Alternatively, contact the ministry's representation at 20 Peel Street, London W8 7PD, **t** (020) 7727 2462. All necessary forms may be obtained and presented there. Try to complete the process before arrival in Spain – theoretically a child will not be admitted until the official papers have been received and stamped by the Department of Education. Allow between three and six months for this.

Private Schools

Of chief interest to foreign residents are international schools offering a British or American education. Some 46 British schools belong to **NABBS**, the **National Association of British Schools** in Spain (**www.nabbs.org**). Information about some of these and others too, particularly American schools, is also available on the website of the **European Council of International Schools** (**www. ecis.org**). They are to be found mainly in the big cities and, predictably, in areas with large expat populations, namely the *costas* and the islands.

Most take children aged from three to 18 and teach the national curriculum leading to GCSE and A-Levels, or their American equivalents. Preparation for Spanish ESO and *bachillerato* exams is often possible, too. These schools provide a good, across-the-board education – generally in line with a traditional British style, with compulsory uniforms – not only academically but also in extra-curricular terms. Membership of clubs and pupils' interests and hobbies are encouraged. Facilities vary but are often superb, including sports halls, playing fields, swimming pools, music rooms, auditoria and even stables, and skiing trips and other kinds of extra-curricular activities are also encouraged. Usually the staff is from Britain and other Anglophone countries plus some Spanish teachers. Students may be a mixture of Spaniards and other nationalities but foreigners are at times the overwhelming majority; most leave completely fluent in English and Spanish and perhaps another language or two. Most NABBS schools have a high academic reputation, and a very high percentage of pupils go on to university after leaving.

Predictably, though, they are not cheap. Do not be shocked at annual fees averaging around €3,000 for primary education and upwards of €5,000 for secondary. Some schools may be pricier still. Fees may or may not include the school bus and lunch but never include uniforms, school materials, extra-curricular activities or trips. The annual bill for, say, two children in secondary school could easily reach between €12,000 and €15,000. If cost is no problem for you, you're in the right area and you want a British or American education for your child, this is the option to choose.

Public versus Private

Much depends on where you live, your income and chosen lifestyle. If you cannot afford a private school, the only other option is public. If you live in an expat community and money is no option, the private school may be the better choice. If you only plan to live in Spain temporarily, a private school is probably advisable as your child will not then have to adapt to a different system. Your child's age at the time of moving, and his or her adaptability, are also crucial.

A child's knowledge of Spanish is usually tested before being admitted to a public school. As well as this, if entering the system at age 14 or older, his or her academic record has to be assessed and recognised – this can be a lengthy and costly process. Generally, the younger the child, the more adaptable – toddlers integrate easily, children over age 10 not so well. These issues are less important if you have an international school in mind.

Children attending Spanish public schools do not travel far – there should always be a public school within your catchment area – while international schools may be further away. Children will invariably make friends in the neighbourhood at a local school, while those at an international school may make friends who live a considerable distance away. Whichever option you choose, check the school before committing your child to it.

Health, Emergencies and Welfare Entitlements

See also **First Steps and Reasons for Buying**, pp.22–3.

Emergencies

The best way of dealing with emergencies is to be prepared for them, and then hope they never happen. Spanish emergency services can cope with most situations but availability depends on where you are. Away from the main towns, cities and tourist areas they may be a little slower in response time (because they have further to travel) and be less well-equipped. The **emergency number** to call in all cases is **t** 112; the operator will connect you to the service you require. In areas with large expatriate populations you may be attended to by an English-speaker, but do not rely on it.

If you do not speak the language you may have problems in summoning help. You should learn at least a few key phrases by heart. If you can at least say your address, explain where you are and what the problem is, you will increase your chances of getting help quickly – do not underestimate this. If you suffer from a specific condition, such as diabetes, learn to explain it, and rehearse your 'spiel' frequently. Also try to become familiar with the sort of questions you may be asked about your condition.

Taxi drivers in Spain must, by law, take all emergency cases to hospital and generally will if you can call one or flag one down – you still have to pay, though. You can also turn a private car into an ambulance by switching on the hazard lights and waving a white handkerchief out of the window. Do not abuse this privilege, however, or you will receive an on-the-spot fine. Ambulances summoned by means of the emergency number are free for those covered by social security. If you have private insurance the service may still be free, but you may have to pay first and claim later depending on the terms of your policy. Most ambulances carry oxygen and basic emergency kits, including ECG equipment, and standards are rising. Some private insurance schemes also offer a helicopter evacuation service, and this can be expensive, but if you live somewhere remote and the service is available it may be worth it.

On arrival in Spain, find out where your local emergency services are located. Keep a copy of the address and directions in a prominent place, and carry a copy with you. Remember, wherever you are, hospitals are obliged to treat you regardless of whether you are covered by insurance or not. Save your life first and haggle over payment later, if necessary.

Pharmacies (*Farmacias*)

Pharmacies or chemists are easily spotted from a distance by a flashing green cross. They have the same opening hours as shops and at night and on public holidays work a rotation system. Those open are known as *farmacias de guardia*. To find the nearest one, check the local section of any daily newspaper or look at the list displayed in the window. In the larger cities there are now some 24-hour pharmacies that supplement the *farmacias de guardia*.

Many people go to pharmacies instead of the doctor with minor ailments such as a cold or 'flu. Pharmacists are well trained (virtually paramedics) and are therefore able to recommend treatment on the spot. They may also sell you medicines over the counter that in other countries would only be available on prescription. Be careful, though: if your problem is more serious you really should see a doctor.

Social Security and Entitlements under EU Law

EU and EEA **visitors** to Spain, including UK residents, are entitled to emergency health treatment whilst on short-term visits to Spain, provided you can produce either a valid European Health Insurance Card (EHIC) each time you seek treatment from a Spanish National Health hospital or doctor. Dental care, other than emergency tooth extraction, is not covered. The EHIC has replaced the E111 and several other healthcare forms as of 1 September 2005. It is issued free of charge and can be obtained at UK post offices and online at **www.dh.gov.uk/travellers** or by calling **t** (0191) 203 5555. It does not cover you for attention or treatment from private hospitals or doctors.

The treatment UK residents receive on temporary visits to Spain is equivalent to that received by Spanish nationals, but may vary from that offered in the UK. Repatriation due to illness is not covered by reciprocal agreements, and private insurance (*see* pp.237–8) is strongly recommended to cover such costs or to provide a choice of clinics or doctors. If you forget to bring an EHIC, the *Convenios Internacionales* department of the Instituto Nacional de la Seguridad Social, Calle Padre Damian 4, Madrid, **t** 915 688 300, may, in exceptional circumstances, request the form from your country's authorities. Many frequent travellers assume that the EHIC will cover them indefinitely, but this is not the case. If you stay longer than 90 days and then become ill, you may have to foot some astronomical bills. This is another reason to consider taking out complementary private insurance. Travelling without either the EHIC card and with no private insurance is foolhardy, and could prove very expensive indeed.

If you **work and reside** in Spain, your employer should deduct social security contributions from your wages. These deductions should be shown on your pay slip. It is your employer's responsibility to register you with social security, deal with the bureaucracy, receive your **medical card** from them and pass it on to you (although some employers may give you time off to go and collect it yourself). This card entitles you to full medical cover from the Insituto Nacional de Salud (Insalud), or National Health Institute, to be presented at the health centre (*ambulatorio*) when seeking medical attention. The name of the GP (*médico de cabecera*) assigned to you appears on the card. You may later change to a doctor of your own choice if you wish. Medicines are free if prescribed to treat work-related accidents or illness, otherwise you must pay 40 per cent of the cost. If you are self-employed, get a residence card from the Policía Nacional then follow the steps described on pp.226–7. Entitlement to medical care for both employees and the self-employed is also extended to their legal dependants.

EU and EEA citizens who receive a **pension** in their own country and reside in Spain are entitled to receive free medical treatment under the same conditions as a qualified Spanish state pensioner. UK pensioners should obtain form E121 from the DSS in the UK and take it when registering with a local INSS office (Instituto Nacional de Seguridad Social), which will assign them to a health centre and a GP. You will have to present your passport as well as the E121, and possibly proof of residency or of application for residency (a *justificante*, or certificate). Prescribed medicines are free for pensioners and their dependants.

If you settle in Spain after early retirement – that is, before the normal pensionable age at home – you should consult your local UK social security office about medical cover. In normal cases you will be given form E106.

According to NI contributions made during your working life before moving to Spain, you may be entitled to free care for several months after your arrival.

Visitors from outside the EU and EEA are not, *a priori*, entitled to medical cover, although this will depend on whether there are reciprocal agreements between their home country and Spain. Those not entitled but who wish to become residents, for example pensioners, must take out private insurance in order to become eligible for residency.

All residents in Spain should check whether they are covered by Spanish social security and, if not, make private arrangements.

Security, Crime and the Police

It's a sad fact that since Spain's transition from police state to parliamentary democracy, and all the ensuing economic transformations, crime has risen, with a noticeable jump in the last decade or so. Very violent crime is not overly common, except among gangs of drug traffickers and *mafiosos*. Petty crime, though, is a problem and robberies at knife- or gunpoint are also increasing. Despite this, Spain remains one of Europe's 'safer' countries, one in which you can avoid a lot of problems by knowing what the main types of crime are and what precautions to take.

- **Pickpocketing, bag-snatching and mugging**. This generally happens in larger cities, shopping malls, airports, metro and train stations and other crowded places. Areas with a concentration of bars and nightclubs are also notorious. Thieves often target the newly arrived and unwary as well as those out enjoying themselves and overly relaxed.

- **Thieves working in pairs or teams**. One common method is to 'accidentally' spill something on you. The thief then apologises and proceeds to wipe the garment with a paper handkerchief while his partner is rifling your bag or pockets.

- **Thefts of – and from – cars**. These are rife, especially of those with foreign licence plates.

- **Stealing from cars at traffic lights**. Thieves on mopeds or bicycles draw alongside, snatch whatever is in sight and zoom off before the victim has time to react. Pedestrians can be also victims of this type of theft.

- **Modern-day 'highwaymen'**. These have been reported on major trunk roads. They either pretend their car has broken down, flag you down and rob you, or drive past you, point to indicate that you have some problem with your wheel or lights, and rob you when you stop to see.

- **Burglary, especially in resort areas**. Particularly when the new house owner is in the process of moving in, or shortly afterwards.

How to Avoid Being Robbed

The best ways of reducing your risk of being a crime victim are really common sense. It is, of course, much more necessary to be on your guard in big cities and busy areas than in smaller places.

Street and Beach Crime

• On arrival at airports or train stations, be alert, and never leave luggage unattended. Spread your money, credit cards and documents around in several inside pockets if possible.

• When you are sitting at a café, especially at an outside table, never leave bags or coats dangling over the back of your chair, or put them under the chair where you can't see them. Keep them in view, on your lap, on the chair beside you or on the table.

• Carry shoulder bags or small rucksacks across your chest or to the front of your body, or to the pavement side, away from the road. Keep a hand on top of your bag.

• When you are on a busy beach, be aware that there might be people around waiting to make off with bags. If you're in a group, try to have at least one of you stay with your things at all times while the others go in the sea.

• Only carry small amounts of cash with you, enough for your evening out or the shopping you plan to do. Use a moneybelt if you have one. Leave the rest in a safe place.

• Don't flash large denomination notes, or big wads of money, around. Ask for small denominations at the bank.

• Even if you do not know your way around, try to give the impression that you do. Body language encourages or deters thieves.

• Plan where you are going before setting out; in some areas, standing looking lost or consulting a map is asking for trouble.

• Be aware of thieves working in pairs or groups. If an unannounced stranger hassles you for money or asks for directions it might be a ruse. Walk on briskly and make for an area with lots of passers-by.

• If you are held up at knife- or gunpoint, hand over the goods and preserve your life. If you are only carrying small amounts of money the loss is trifling in comparison to what might happen.

Car Crime

• Never leave anything in your car, even the boot if leaving it overnight, especially if it has foreign registration plates.

• Park in a car park whenever possible. Many accept no responsibility for thefts of vehicles or their contents, but they are safer than the street.

• Keep your windows closed when stopping at traffic lights. Be wary of people trying to sell paper handkerchiefs and so on to drivers.

• Be very careful about stopping to help supposed breakdown victims; it is better to drive on and alert the police. If they are genuine they have nothing to worry about.

Burglary and Break-ins

• When moving house, do not leave jackets or coats containing wallets and purses unattended indoors while you are busy shifting furniture.

• On moving into a newly built property, change all external locks.

• Order a safe to be built into the wall if possible.

• Have bars (rejas) fitted on windows if your property is a villa or a ground-floor flat. You will need this for Spanish insurance policies in any case.

• Make sure your house is insured before you move in.

The Police

As in most parts of Europe, several different police forces operate in Spain, each with different responsibilities, although in practice these overlap a little. The new government has talked about uniting the Guardia Civil and the Policía Nacional into one force – basically to improve the gathering and processing of intelligence – but this does not yet seem an imminent prospect.

Policía Municipal

For practical purposes, these forces – called in some places by different names, such as Guàrdia Urbana or Policía Local – are the closest to citizens and generally the most amenable for dealing with day-to-day problems. Each city and town in Spain above a certain size has its own force; officers generally wear dark blue uniforms with either white or light blue shirts. They are responsible for traffic, parking regulations and minor offences in their areas, and in tourist areas generally have special units for helping foreign visitors, usually with English-speaking officers. You can also ask the Municipales for directions or the time, or complain to them about noisy neighbours. The phone number for the local force is t 092, anywhere in Spain.

Policía Nacional

The main state-run, central police force, with the primary responsibility for dealing with serious crime. If you are mugged, assaulted, raped, burgled or have your car stolen, report it to the nearest National Police *comisaría* (addresses of which will be in the phone book). An official statement (*denuncia*) is essential for insurance claims. National Police officers wear navy blue uniforms with white shirts except when on riot and public-order duty, when they wear an all-blue outfit with anti-riot gear. Residency matters are also dealt with at local National Police *comisaría*. Their central phone number is **t** 091; wherever you are you will be connected to your nearest station.

Guardia Civil

On entering the country and passing through customs you will see Spain's most famous security force, the green-clad Civil Guard, the ones who still occasionally wear their strange, shiny-black three-cornered hats, although nowadays they more usually go around in caps. Created in the 19th century to combat rural banditry, this is the most militarised of all of Spain's security forces. Today the corps' main responsibilities, apart from frontier controls, customs and certain anti-terrorist operations, concern rural areas without their own municipal police and highway policing on motorways and other roads outside the remit of local forces. If you have an accident on a main highway, report it to them. Officers have authority to fine traffic offenders on the spot for speeding or dangerous driving. The central phone number is **t** 062.

Regional Forces: Ertxaintxa and Mossos d'Escuadra

The Basque Country and Catalonia, the two regions with furthest-reaching autonomy, already have their own autonomous police forces, called the Ertxaintxa and the Mossos d'Escuadra respectively. Other regions may also have them in future. Eventually they may assume all the functions of the Policía Nacional and Guardia Civil in their respective communities but, for the time being, they co-exist with the national forces. The Mossos have already taken over rural and highway policing from the Guardia Civil in many parts of Catalonia – so that if you're speeding on the road south from the French border it may be them that stop you, not the men in green – while in the Basque Country the situation is (as in everything) more complex.

Pets

Until recently, taking a dog or cat to Spain involved a certain amount of soul-searching on the part of the owner. Britain's quarantine laws involved a level of expense for the owner and distress for the animal which discouraged anyone who thought they might wish to re-enter the UK at any time in the future.

Thankfully the introduction of the Pets Travel Scheme, PETS, more commonly referred to as the Pets Passport, has made the prospect of moving your animal between Britain and Spain much less painful, though not necessarily simpler. There are definite, and non-negotiable, steps which you must go through to get your animal permission to travel.

Firstly your dog or cat must be micro-chipped and then vaccinated against rabies. A vet must then take a blood sample which will be sent to a government-approved laboratory for testing. Six months must elapse between the date of your animal's blood test and the issuing of a valid PETS certificate. Between 24 and 48 hours before your animal is due to travel, a vet must administer a treatment for ticks and tapeworms and issue a certificate confirming the treatment. Finally, on the day of travel you must sign a declaration of residency (form PETS 3) confirming that your animal has not been in any country *not* covered by the PETS scheme during the previous six months. The PETS certificate is valid for a limited time depending on the date of your animal's rabies vaccination but can be renewed when a booster injection is administered.

It should be stressed that these steps are necessary to enter the UK rather than Spain, but it is highly recommended that you get your animal a PETS certificate on leaving the UK even if you have no intention of returning. If unforeseen circumstances mean that you have to bring your dog or cat back into Britain, then it is better to have the paperwork already in order.

If you acquire a pet while in Spain – and with the number of dogs and cats that are abandoned every year it can be hard for the animal-lover to resist – all the above steps can be performed in the country. However, it should be stressed that there is currently only one Spanish laboratory, in Granada, that carries out the requisite blood tests and results can be very slow in arriving. Stories of the lab subjecting the blood to the wrong tests also abound.

If you are in a major city or near one of the main expat communities there will probably be an English-speaking vet or animal organisation which can guide you through the process.

The PETS scheme only applies to dogs and cats and on certain approved routes, either air or sea. Visit the **DEFRA** website, **www.defra.gov.uk**, for up-to-date details. It should also be remembered that there are regulations which govern pet ownership, particularly with regard to dogs, inside Spain. These can vary from region to region but in most cases it is a legal requirement to have your animal micro-chipped and vaccinated against rabies. Consult a local vet for advice. In certain areas regular treatment for particular parasites, such as heart worm, may be advisable or even mandatory.

Food and Drink

The first thing to get used to about eating in Spain is the timing. Spanish people aim to get most of the important business of the day done in the morning, which goes on till about 2pm, when they traditionally stop for an unhurried lunch. They go back to work to do generally secondary things in the afternoon, around 4–5pm, and then have dinner from 9pm onwards. Timings get later, for perfectly understandable reasons, the further south you go and the hotter the weather gets, so that in Madrid or Andalucía in July it's not unusual for people to go out to eat at 11pm at weekends. This timetable is under pressure in large companies, many of which have adopted the *horario continuo* or *horario europeo*, 'continuous' or 'European' hours, working straight through from 9 till 6 with just a quick lunch, but dogged resistance is being maintained by most of the population, and whenever Spaniards are at their leisure nearly all revert to their traditional times. Hence, most restaurants will not be open for lunch before 1pm or sometimes 1.30pm, and certainly not for dinner before 8.30pm. In tourist areas, of course, a great many places have responded to demand by opening much earlier, but you cannot expect to get the best of local food if you insist on eating at these times.

There are now countless guides to Spanish food (and foods) available. For some recommended titles, *see* **References**, 'Further Reading', p.331.

Restaurants and Main Meals

In any town there will be a sizeable choice of restaurants, of different grades. Nearly all will offer local food, with only a few international options, although in any tourist area the choice will be larger and wider, with many restaurants catering to foreign tastes in different ways. Spaniards are used to eating casually in restaurants, especially for lunch, which is when they will be busiest. Far fewer people eat out regularly in the evenings, except on Fridays and Saturdays, so on weekday nights it will be much easier to get a table in popular places. Sunday lunchtime is another popular time for restaurant-going, while many restaurants will be closed completely on Sunday evenings and Mondays. Whether or not you need to book tends to depend on the popularity of the restaurant as much as any comfort-category, but some straightforward restaurants refuse to take bookings even though they're hugely popular. You can always tell which they are by the milling queues outside, which Spaniards, perversely, don't seem to mind.

Tipping Tips
Service is not often included in restaurant bills (if it is, it will say *servicio incluído*) but, even so, Spaniards are not big tippers). There is no obligation to tip, and no set percentage to calculate, but waiters always appreciate it (and often expect tips more from foreigners than locals). It's reasonable to leave 5 to 10 per cent, and to give more if service has been especially good rather than just apply a flat rate. Many locals also leave a bit of the change behind after paying in bars, even if they have not sat at a table.

Bar Food: Tapas and Bocadillos

Restaurants as such only make up part of the eating-out scene in Spain. *Tapas*, the little dishes served in bars, are among the Spanish culinary traditions most widely enjoyed by foreigners. At least one *tapa* used to come free whenever you ordered a drink, and this is still sometimes the case, but the complimentary *tapa* is increasingly small – a few olives, a couple of chunks of tortilla – compared with the separately ordered ones. However, this has not prevented *tapas* becoming more popular than ever. The most dazzling bar-top displays – stacks of prawns and crayfish, piles of spiced potatoes, salads or chorizo in red wine – are found in big city bars. The *tapas* range in small-town bars will tend to be more conventional, but still varied. Bar *tapas* divide between *tapas* themselves – very small, oval dishes – and slightly larger small platefuls called *raciones*. The most traditional way for Spaniards to have *tapas* is to order just a few with a drink as an aperitif while meeting up with a group of friends, before going on to sit down to a full meal; for foreigners, though, *tapas* can often take the place of the meal. *Tapa*-sampling is naturally a very easy, fun way of eating, because you can just point to anything you want. Take note, though, of the cost of *tapas* nowadays – if you try out five or six, for example, the price can easily be the same as that of a full meal.

Tapas may be more widely known, but an irreplaceable basic of Spanish bars is the *bocadillo*, or bread roll, generally consisting of a whole chunk of a crusty Spanish loaf sliced in two, and filled with a slab of Spanish omelette or slices of pork loin, Serrano ham, *chorizo*, other meats or cheese. Bar *bocadillos* are another of Spain's great bargains, and are always satisfying. Smaller sandwiches of sliced bread are usually called, yes, *sandwiches* or, if they're toasted, *bikinis*, and are not nearly such good value.

There are some particular types of restaurant serving different specialities, such as a *marisquería*, for fish and seafood, an *arrocería*, or rice restaurant, which will offer 20 or so variations on Valencian paellas and other rice dishes, or an *asador*, focusing on roast meat, typical of Castile. From their regional bases, these restaurants have spread all around the country. Restaurants are officially graded by the 'fork' system, with from one to five forks on their signs, but these classifications are often awarded on the basis of a bureaucratic checklist of facilities – size of toilets, air-conditioning – fairly useless as guides to food quality. Personal recommendations are a much better thing to go by.

As important a part as the actual eating of a traditional Spanish meal – whether lunch or dinner – is the *sobremesa*, the time spent at the end of the meal over coffees and brandies, talking and digesting (this is also the time when Spanish diners who have actually resisted smoking during the meal get to light up, and in upscale restaurants gentlemen will be offered a selection of Havana cigars, one sign of a really leisurely *sobremesa*). This is one of the reasons why people need three hours for lunch, and also why a good Spanish waiter should never bring you a bill at the end of a meal until you ask for it.

Breakfast (*Desayuno*)

Much the smallest meal of the day, usually taken quickly at home or in a café. As with most things there are regional variations: in Andalucía breakfast often consists of just a slice of toast with butter or olive oil (a *tostada*) with a white coffee (*café con leche*), or, for a full-on breakfast that's often given as a weekend treat to kids, *churros*, deep-fried sticks of batter dusted with sugar, *con chocolate*, with a cup of thick, real hot chocolate to dunk the *churros* in. Further north, breakfast more often features croissants or other pastries rather than *tostadas*. In response to contemporary demand, most hotels now offer mixed breakfast buffets as well as these limited offerings, including fruit juice, cereals, meats, cheeses and eggs, but the standard of Spanish hotel breakfasts still regularly disappoints. In the main tourist areas you will also have a choice of cafés that offer foreigners all the comforts of home for breakfast – full-English with tea for Brits; ham, eggs and milky coffee for Germans.

Lunch (*Almuerzo* or *La Comida*)

A great many Spanish people still have lunch regularly in restaurants near their work, rather than go home or take a sandwich, so virtually all restaurants offer a midday *menú del día*, usually consisting of three courses, with a choice for each one, plus bread and a drink, for a very reasonable set price. These *menús* are often a remarkable bargain, so lunchtime is the best time to eat cheaply in Spain, and to get the best value. Sunday lunch, in contrast, is a much more drawn-out affair. This is the best time to try one of the big, communal-eating dishes, such as a good *paella* or the great seafood stew of Menorca called *caldereta* (all best ordered ahead, to allow for cooking).

Dinner (*La Cena*)

Set-price menus are not normally available in the evenings, so eating in restaurants will be noticeably more expensive. If they're not going out for an occasion, most Spaniards now tend to eat less in the evening than at midday.

Spanish Cuisines

It's standard practice to talk about 'Spanish food' but, viewed from inside the country, this concept is not always easy to grasp. Spain's diversity is naturally reflected in its cooking, and each region has its own, sometimes radically distinctive, culinary traditions and specialities. Moreover, while there is a core of dishes that have spread all over the country, for the most part local restaurants still prefer to highlight their own local specialities, and you will not find menus the same from one region to another.

The dishes that can be found in every part of the country, and so can fairly truly be called 'Spanish food', are often simple things – the classic Spanish omelette (*tortilla española*) of potatoes, onion, garlic and eggs; hake (*merluza*) fried in batter; fried *calamares*; *chorizo* sausages; straightforward meats. One dish that has a clear regional origin – Valencia – but is now a universal and almost a global symbol of Spanish food is paella. The best, though, will still be found around Valencia or in specialist seafood restaurants elsewhere. Another feature of paella is that it is one of the original 'slow foods', best cooked with plenty of time and in one pan for a large number of people (which is why it's best to order it ahead). To order it straight off the menu on a Tuesday night in Seville is usually rather foolhardy.

Most of the more elaborate, individual dishes, meanwhile, tend to be regional rather than national. What follows is a brief introduction to some features of Spain's regional cuisines.

Andalucía

Andalucía is not a place known for sophisticated or innovative cooking, and the goodness of good Andaluz food tends to stem from the quality of fresh ingredients ahead of any subtlety in the recipes. The most famous Andaluz speciality of all, found in every single Andaluz restaurant, is *gazpacho*, the delicious cold tomato soup sprinkled with chopped peppers, onions, cucumbers and bread or croutons; a less common variant is *gazpacho blanco*, white gazpacho, made with garlic and almonds. Most other things are very simple: the main culinary attraction of the Andalusian coast is plainly prepared, very fresh fish and seafood, particularly *pescaíto frito* or *fritura mixta*, whitebait flash-fried in batter; inland, the greatest speciality is finest-quality, dry-cured Serrano ham.

Asturias

Great winter food for a chilly, often wet country facing the Atlantic Ocean: best-known specialities are *fabada*, a hearty casserole of *chorizo*, pork and haricot beans; *merluza a la sidra*, hake cooked in a cider sauce; and Cabrales cheese, one of the most wonderfully pungent blue goat's cheeses you will ever find.

The Balearics

A certain bog-standard touristy *calamares*-and-chips main menu has been dominant in the Balearics for years, but look again and you can find local specialities such as the Mallorcan *tumbet*, a vegetable and potato casserole rather like a more solid ratatouille, eaten on its own or with meat and fish, and, on Menorca, *caldereta*, a giant mixed stew of various fish, crayfish and small lobsters.

The Basque Country

The Basque Country has been traditionally considered the home of the most refined food in all Spain, with little in common with the rest of the country. There are any number of Basque specialities, the best-known of which feature fish and seafood, such as *bacalao al pil pil*, cod fried sizzling hot in a garlic sauce, and *marmitako*, a spicy tuna, tomato, and potato stew.

The Canaries

More simple fare: best-known speciality of all is *papas arrugadas*, new potatoes baked in rock salt served with *mojo picón*, a hot red sauce, and/or *mojo verde*, fish in a green herb sauce.

Castile

Another region, like Andalucía, that seems to prize an almost exaggerated simplicity in its cooking: fine meats, very few green vegetables, and classic dishes such as *cochinillo asado*, roast suckling pig, *cordero asado* (roast lamb) and *sopa castellana*, a garlic soup with chunks of ham and an egg poaching in it. Meat is served on its own, with no vegetables, in a way that many British people can never come to terms with.

Catalonia

A country/region that can rival the Basques as having the most refined food in Spain, and a complete cuisine of its own: if you feel afflicted by the 'sameness' sensation that sometimes comes over diners in Andalucía, you'll do far better here. Subtle fish dishes, varied rice offerings similar to those of Valencia, combinations of meat and fish and unusual, refreshing salads are among the Catalan hallmarks.

Galicia

Warming Atlantic food like that of Asturias, but with a much stronger emphasis on fish and seafood – Galicia is known for having the best in Spain, and many specialities feature mussels, octopus or hake. A hearty non-fish favourite is *caldo gallego*, a filling winter stew of greens, potatoes, bacon and sausage.

Valencia

So famous is paella that it tends to overshadow everything else here, but at least, in its homeland, it can be ordered with umpteen different combinations of ingredients.

Drinks

Spain has more acres of **vineyards** than any other European country, from which it can supply its own needs and send out huge quantities for export. This is one reason, together with a type of parochialism and belief-in-its-own that it shares with France and Italy, why you will not find many non-Spanish wines on sale in Spain, certainly not in conventional local shops. In fact, most regions tend to downplay the wines of other parts of Spain, let alone those from abroad, so that in Catalonia you will mainly find Catalan wines, in Andalucía wine lists will try to highlight Andaluz labels, and so on (although some wines, such as Rioja, are found everywhere). The lack of international wines is no loss, though, for the variety of Spanish wines, many of them rarely seen outside the country, is tremendous, and quality has increased continuously. Spain now has over 40 recognised wine-producing regions with a *denominación de orígen* (DO), indicating an official system of guaranteed quality control, like the French *appelation contrôlée*, or the still more demanding *denominación de orígen controlada* or DOC. As well as the well-marketed Rioja – the oldest DOC in the country – other major wine-growing areas are the Penedés in Catalonia, which produces both fine reds and whites and is the home of cava, Spanish sparkling wine, Valdepeñas in La Mancha, Valencia, and Jumilla in Murcia, known for powerful, almost sherry-like reds. Different regions are forever coming to the fore, such as, in recent years, Ribera del Duero in Castile, Toro, from Zamora, or Navarra.

The difference between shop and restaurant prices for the same wine is about the same as it would be in the UK – that is, a mark-up of about 100 per cent. Wines are on sale in every hyper- and supermarket and corner shop, but you are not likely to find a very enterprising range there. Many Spaniards still have a fairly utilitarian attitude to wine, as an everyday commodity rather than some-thing to be fussed over, and many expats buy on the principle of the cheaper the better, and both these influences are reflected in the big distributors' stocking habits. To find the best and most interesting Spanish labels, often from small-scale producers, you usually need to go to a shop that specialises in wines, which will most often be called a *bodega* (the most traditional name) but might also be a *vinacoteca* or a *celler*.

Andalucía, or rather just the southern part of Cádiz province around Jerez de la Frontera, is also the home of **sherry**, and visiting the historic sherry *bodegas* is one of the area's prime attractions. The kind of sherry most commonly drunk in Andalucía is dry, light *fino*, also known as *manzanilla*, which, served ice-cold with a small *tapa*, makes a deliciously refreshing aperitif. Heavier, sweeter sher-ries have more often been made for export. The Jerez area also produces large quantities of Spanish **brandies** (usually called *coñac*, thanks to their ultimately French origins), nuttier and more rounded than the French equivalents, and there are other sweet **dessert wines** from elsewhere in Andalucía and Valencia, such as *málaga* and moscatel.

The most popular tourist drink in Spain, though, is still *sangría*, which, as most veterans of teen *costa* holidays can testify, is often head-bangingly awful. However, if made with some care, and using something other than the cheapest possible wine as the base, it can also be very pleasant.

Most Spanish **beers** are fairly standard lagers, although there are variations, such as the dark, more ale-like and more satisfying Bock-Damm produced by the Damm brewery on the east coast. The most prominent brands vary by region: Cruzcampo in Andalucía, Mahou in Madrid and the centre, the Damm brewery's Estrella in Catalonia and Valencia. Draught beer is usually served in a small glass called a *caña*, or a larger mug or *jarra*. The name used for the standard 33cl beer bottle is yet another thing that changes by region, as it can be a *botella* in the south, a *tercio* in Madrid and a *mediana* (or *mitjana*, in Catalan) in Catalonia. Bottled beers are more expensive than draught, and often not as cold; imported beers such as Heineken or Guinness are pricier still, but this does not stop a legion of Irish and British theme pubs doing a roaring trade around Spain, with a mainly expat or local clientele depending on where they are located.

Coffee, Tea and Soft Drinks

Coffee can be ordered as a *café solo*, a small, black espresso, a *café con leche*, with plenty of milk and served in a glass or largish cup, or a *cortado*, an espresso with just a shot of milk. A *carajillo* is a solo with a shot of spirits, either brandy (a *carajillo de coñac*, the most common version), rum (*de ron*) or anything else you feel like trying.

If you order **tea** (*té*) in bars, even in many touristed areas, it will often arrive as just a teabag in a glass of hot water, clouded with a little milk; frankly, it's not worth bothering, although in these same places you can nearly always find British-run bars that make the real thing with imported tea. Better, in ordinary Spanish bars, are **herbal teas** (*infusiones*), such as *manzanilla* (camomile) or *menta* (mint).

Considering how many oranges Spain produces, it is a continuing mystery how rare it is to find decent **orange juice** in the country. If you ask for a juice (*zumo de naranja*) it will often come out of a packet, even in Valencia, unless you insist on *un zumo natural* (usually very expensive!). Another soft drink well worth trying, though, is *horchata* (or *orxata* in Catalan), another speciality of Valencia, which has a milky texture and is made by crushing a type of nut called a *chufa*. It curdles quickly once made, and so has to be bought fresh, from a specialist shop-café called an *horchatería* (*orxateria*), and is only available from Easter to November. Ignored by most foreigners in Spain, *horchata* is a bit of an acquired taste, but is wonderfully refreshing.

Water

The quality of mains water has improved everywhere in Spain in the last 30 years, and it is always safe to drink. However, it often has a quite strong taste and, for preference, most people drink bottled mineral water (*agua mineral*). This is what you will automatically be served if you ask for water in restaurants, unless you specify *agua del grifo* (tap water). Still water is *agua sin gas*, sparkling water *agua con gas*.

Shopping

Getting used to and enjoying shopping in Spain, especially if you're living some way from any of the busier towns, is a matter of accepting that there are some things you'll do without and valuing the real positives you gain in return. Anyone used to finding branches of the same major fashion chains in every town will have to get accustomed to making occasional trips to regional centres like Málaga or Alicante, or resorts like Marbella, for their major purchases. The great plus is in the personal, responsive service and fresh local produce still to be found in local shops and markets, which can make food shopping a true pleasure.

The small-shop economy may remain much stronger in Spain than it is in the UK nowadays, but it is nevertheless under serious pressure. Supermarkets (*supermercados*) and especially hypermarkets (*hipermercados*) are well established, and have made a big impact on the shopping habits of the urban population. Spanish *hipermercados* are vast, and really do sell everything under one roof – clothes, toys, sports goods, electrical appliances and many other things, as well as having a bakery, bars and giant food supermarkets. The main companies are Carrefour, Hipercor, Alcampo and Eroski, and there are a few on the highways outside all the main cities and in many resort areas. They are much appreciated for their convenience and cheapness by many foreign residents, who make weekly trips to stock up there as they would at home. They can be handy for packaged foods, but the fruit, vegetables and many other foods you find there will generally be of lower quality, and above all less fresh, than in smaller shops and markets. Elsewhere, there are smaller local supermarkets. Many modern developments have a small supermarket attached, but you're much better off if this is not the only shop that's easily reached from your home, and you have a choice of more traditional shops as well.

One thing that is worth buying in supermarkets, since it's not likely to be better anywhere else, is milk. Most sold in Spain is UHT or *leche esterilizada*; pasteurised milk (*leche pasteurizada*, or more casually *leche fresca*) is sometimes a little hard to find, and is kept separately in a cold cabinet.

The biggest gun in Spanish retailing is the Corte Inglés department store chain, which has branches in most provincial capitals and also owns the Hipercor hypermarkets as well as the OpenCor convenience shops, open from 7am to 11pm 365 days a year. Well known to British visitors, El Corte Inglés is established as a kind of universal standby in Spain, a place where you can always find anything you may not have been able to locate anywhere else, although its goods (especially clothes) are never exciting.

Much more stylish are the modern Spanish fashion chains like Mango, Zara and, for shoes, Camper, which also have branches in all larger cities. Increasingly sought-after abroad, their products are still cheaper on their home territory. A lot of mainstream Spanish furniture, on the other hand, tends to be heavy and traditional, with much use of French polishing; if, though, you prefer the IKEA style for furnishing your new home, there are currently seven stores in mainland Spain, two just outside Madrid, two close to Barcelona, and one apiece in Siero (Asturias), Barakaldo (Bilbao) and Castilleja de la Cuesta (Seville). A new branch is due to open in Murcia in spring 2006. Island-dwellers can go to the branches at La Laguna (Tenerife), Las Palmas (Gran Canaria) and Palma de Mallorca (Mallorca). The website with location information (in Spanish only) is **www.ikea.com/ms/es**.

You are missing out on one of the primary attractions of living in Spain, though – and one of the main routes to getting in touch with local life – if you do not get into the world of local shops and markets. Be clear that this is neither the quickest nor the cheapest way of shopping. Magazine features and TV and radio programmes in Britain have made a virtual cliché of the healthy qualities of the 'Mediterranean diet'. Its benefits, when they are real, are often due not to any specially healthy dishes – Spaniards in particular eat huge amounts of eggs and fatty meats – but to the fact that people in Spain, France and Italy are generally willing to spend more time and proportionately more money on their food than most Britons have got used to doing. If you want the cheapest price with the maximum convenience, and want to keep interactions with local people to a minimum, find your nearest *hiper*. It is also sadly the case nowadays that the produce in not all small shops will be as good or as locally sourced as in others. If you are in a fairly touristy village with just a couple of shops, you may find that the goods on offer are not much different from what you find in the supermarkets. In any town or place with more choice, it pays to look around the local shops, and find the ones that take most trouble with their produce – the best bread shop, the best for fruit and so on. Go to a shop a couple of times, make a decent effort to communicate and your face will begin to get known, and you will start to reap the rewards of personal attention. Apart from anything else, getting to know your local shopkeepers is one of the best, most real ways of building up practical language skills.

The best fresh foods will still be found in the local market (*mercado*), of which there will be one of varying size in virtually all towns, usually in a covered hall rather than an open market square. Again, it's good to get to know your nearest market, find out which stalls are better than others, and make yourself known to the stallholders.

A good way to divide up your shopping is to use super- or hypermarkets for long-term and packaged goods, markets for major shopping for fresh foods (fruit and, above all, fish and seafood) and local shops for top-ups and daily necessities. Stallholders will cut meat and gut and prepare fish exactly as you require. Don't hang back and be afraid to say what you want, and be choosy and demanding, in a friendly way: good stallholders will expect and respect it, and the more you work up a dialogue the more you'll build up your own confidence. Taking no interest in the food you buy is the sign of a dumb foreigner here, and an invitation to be served anonymously too.

Shopping Times, Holidays and Sales

Traditional Spanish **shopping hours**, as most people know, include the siesta. Most small shops still open from about 8.30–10am until 1.30–2pm and then have about a three-hour break, reopening from around 4.30–5 until 8–9pm, Monday to Friday. Most keep to the same hours on Saturdays too, although many do not reopen on Saturday afternoons, especially in summer. Markets tend to open earlier, at 8am, and are closed up for the day by 1–2pm, and smaller markets may only open on a few days each week. Larger stores, however – which include hypermarkets, department stores and a growing number of fashion stores – have introduced continual working, and are open through the day, generally 10am–9pm, Monday to Saturday. Opening times are a contentious issue in Spain, with the big retailers pushing to be allowed to open still more hours, and small shopkeepers complaining that this creates unfair competition.

Sunday opening is a still more controversial issue. Traditionally, the only traders allowed to open on Sundays were cake shops (so that everyone could buy a dessert for their Sunday lunch), some markets, news stands and a few others. The big retailers, though, have exerted huge pressure for Sunday opening. Sunday trading laws have been a regional responsibility and so the exact situation has varied from one region to another; the previous central government, enthusiasts for deregulation, introduced a uniform, much less restrictive law across Spain in 2001, although its application still varies from place to place. In most areas, the big stores are currently allowed to open one Sunday in each month and every Sunday in the four weeks before Christmas, but in general they are opening on more Sundays all the time. In response, the new law now allows small shops to open on Sundays too, although most still prefer to close. Public holidays – which also vary from one region to another – have been as sacrosanct as Sundays, but the big stores also now open on many of them too.

Real Shops

While you can do just about all of your shopping in super- and hypermarkets, if you do not like the bland, sterile atmosphere of '*las grandes superficies*' and want to practise the lingo, get along to your local shops where service is friendlier, the produce often better and the prices sometimes quite competitive.

Here are the main ones:

Carnicería: a butcher's where you can get the cuts of meat you want without polystyrene packaging.

Colmado: a general grocery store, stocking most types of food and drink, sometimes they display a sign saying *Alimentos*, *Alimentación* or *Ultramarinos*.

Droguería: not a drugstore but a shop selling cleaning products, shower gel and shampoo and paint, turpentine and other decorating materials.

Farmacia: a pharmacy or dispensing chemist's, usually indicated by a flashing green cross. Pharmacies, you'll be pleased to know, may often sort out your cold or flu with an over-the-counter product once you've explained the problem, thus avoiding the need to go to the doctor.

Ferretería – an ironmonger's and hardware store, often good for pots and pans.

Frutería: the best shops for fresh fruit and vegetables.

Librería: a bookshop.

Panadería: a baker's, you will sometimes see the words '*horno*' or '*forn de pa*' ('oven' in Castilian and Catalan, respectively), or '*tahona*'. Open daily in most places, baker's shops offer an ever-better range of fresh bread including the standard '*barra*' (like a thick French stick), the '*pistola*' (like a baguette) and the Italian-style '*chapata*'. Wholemeal bread is '*pan integral*'.

Papelería: stationer's, often sells books also.

Pastelería: a cake shop, sometimes combined with the *panadería*, always open on Sundays. It is customary, when being invited to a meal with a Spanish family, to take a selection of small cakes as a gift.

Pescadería: a fishmonger's, fresh fish is usually cheaper and fresher here than in the hypers. Usually they sell seafood (*mariscos*) too.

Tabacos: known to everybody as the *estanco*, the tobacconist's, apart from smoking materials also sells stamps, local transport tickets, phone cards, sweets, chewing gum, postcards and a range of official forms such as tax declarations.

Sales (*rebajas*) are held in most big stores, fashion shops, electrical stores and so on twice a year, in January–February and July–August. However, nowadays, as in Britain, many stores run offers (*ofertas*) all year round.

Queuing and Basic Etiquette

Preconceptions that Spaniards have no regard for queuing are based on an ill-informed assumption that to queue you necessarily have to stand in line. Actually, at small shops and market stalls a very precise queuing system operates. A group of ladies may not be standing in a row, but they will know exactly when their turn comes around, and anyone who muscles in can expect a sharp retort. When you arrive in a shop or at a stall, ask *¿Quién es el último/la última?* ('who's last?', for men/women) or *¿Quién da la vez?* ('whose turn is it?'); look to see who nods back at you, and go after them. Remember to nod or say *yo* ('me') to the next person who asks the same question. These problems are generally avoided in super- and hypermarkets these days by the use of numbered tickets at meat or charcuterie counters.

Another feature of shopping in Spain, large- or small-scale, is that you don't just walk up to an assistant and ask for what you want, or just plonk it on the counter, without any previous courtesies, as many would in British cities. When you enter a shop, say *buenos días* (or *bon dia* if you really want to get on in Catalan-speaking areas) and the shop person will say the same back to you. Polite formalities completed, you can begin your transaction.

Hard-to-obtain Items

Things you cannot get easily, or find of good quality, in ordinary Spanish shops, and for which you may pine, are, first of all, tea – Spanish teabags are below mediocre – and decent biscuits, jams and marmalades and interesting breakfast cereals. Many people stock up on these things whenever they're in Britain, but there are also now quite a few expat-orientated stores in places like the Costa del Sol and Costa Blanca to cater for these cravings.

Marmite is the centre of a strange cult among some expats, and all such stores have piles of the stuff.

Paying

Except in small family-run establishments, market stalls and shops in remoter villages, credit and debit cards are now more or less universally accepted in Spain. Cards issued by Spanish banks raise fewer eyebrows but any major card from abroad (Visa, American Express or Mastercard) will be accepted. Note that you may well be asked for some form of ID when paying by card. When shopping in smaller establishments, try to make sure you have small-denomination euro notes. Many shopkeepers may not have change for €50 notes or above.

VAT

Spain has differential rates of VAT, called IVA (*impuesto sobre el valor añadido*). For basic foodstuffs, some other essential items and cultural goods like books, the rate is just 4 per cent; for most other foods and hotel and restaurant bills it is 7 per cent. For most clothing, car hire, luxury-grade hotels (five-star) and restaurants and many other things it is 16 per cent.

In the Canaries, because of the islands' non-EU tax status, VAT does not apply, but instead there is a flat-rate local sales tax, the IGIC, at 4 per cent. This is why certain larger items in the Canaries are so cheap.

Media

A few years ago the range of English-speaking and international media of different sorts available in most parts of Spain was pretty limited. Today, with the Internet (*see* 'The Internet and E-mail', p.250), satellite and same-day paper deliveries, added to the continual expansion of local, Spanish media, there are few things in print or on TV that you have to go without.

Newspapers and Magazines

Spain has a great many newspapers, but the press has always been regional rather than nationally based. The only truly national paper is *El País*, which is based in Madrid but has a separate edition in Barcelona and regional supplements for other parts of the country. Serious-minded, liberal and learned, *El País*, founded in 1976, is synonymous with Spain's transition to democracy, and in general remains sympathetic to the Socialist party. It has the best international coverage of any Spanish paper, as well as wide-ranging comment columns and extensive arts coverage. If sometimes on the heavy side, *El País* is pretty much required reading for anyone wanting to keep up with events in Spain today, and carries many supplements, from a highly respected business section (in pink) to a trendy arts and music magazine on Fridays, a literary special on Saturdays and a glossy magazine on Sundays. If your Spanish is not up to the full paper, there is an eight-page *El País* English edition, published daily from Monday to Saturday (available as a pull-out with the *International Herald-Tribune*).

Second to *El País* in national coverage and circulation comes *El Mundo*, also based in Madrid and with separate editions in Barcelona and the Balearics, and regional supplements. In the early 1990s, *El Mundo* came to prominence by playing a big part in denouncing the sleaze and corruption that tarred the socialist governments in their last years, and so fomenting the climate of opinion that brought the Partido Popular to power (*see* 'The New Spain', pp.33–6). While it remained the PP government's favourite paper throughout much of its two terms of office, *El Mundo* did take an increasingly critical stance on certain issues, such as the handling of the *Prestige* crisis, or the military involvement in Iraq, where one of the paper's 'embedded' reporters was killed. With the Socialists back in power, *El Mundo* has again become anti-government, taking a particularly critical stance on issues such as gay marriage and adoption, and the process by which some autonomous regions are negotiating greater levels of autonomy via the reform of their statutes. It also has plenty of supplements, including the Friday *Metrópoli*, which, though mainly a Madrid arts and leisure magazine, also has informative features on things to do, travel restaurants and so on around the country.

The third paper with national projection is the arch-conservative *ABC*, which has a main edition in Madrid and two in Andalucía, *ABC Sevilla* and *ABC Córdoba*. Tabloid in size but extraordinarily old-fashioned in style, *ABC* also has heavyweight supplements, including a very high-quality (and surprisingly open-minded) arts weekly, *ABC Cultural*. Other than that, most regions have their own, also fairly solid-looking dailies that cover the same fields as the nationals – international, national and local news and sport – and remain the most-read papers in their home areas.

All newspapers carry large classified sections, but the best papers for useful small ads, flat rentals and the like are the locally based ones, like *La Vanguardia* in Barcelona, *Las Provincias* in Valencia and Alicante, *Sur* in Málaga and the Costa del Sol and *Diario de Mallorca* or *Diari de Balears* (in Catalan) in the Balearics. The largest small-ads supplements usually come with the Sunday editions.

There is no real tabloid or populist press in Spain – the nearest thing to it is the Barcelona *El Periódico*, published in Spanish and Catalan editions – in part because the potential market is taken by papers that dispense with the tedious necessity of carrying regular news at all, Spain's sports-only dailies, which actually outsell any conventional newspaper. Football is, naturally, the primary obsession, but recent Spanish successes in tennis, golf, motorsports and other fields have given them plenty to go on about when the football league is not in session. Their main topics reflect where they are based: Madrid's *Marca* and *As* are fixated above all on Real Madrid and to a lesser extent Atlético and other Madrid teams, while for Barcelona's *Sport* and *Mundo Deportivo* it has to be FC Barcelona. Other teams elsewhere can feel a bit hard done-by, but there are local sports papers in some parts of the country. For any football fan, reading the sports papers is an endlessly entertaining aid to learning Spanish, although in the process you'll pick up some dreadful puns and atrocious grammar.

Spain also has a great many magazines, among which the most permanent fixtures are its inimitable, never-changing gossip glossies. Gossip is an industry in which Spain leads the world, since *¡Hola!* is the parent of *Hello!* magazine in Britain. For anyone really wanting to get into the daily froth of Spanish life, keeping up with the mags and celebrity trivia is a must. You cannot expect to join in conversations in the *panadería* unless you can at least recognise who that girl is on page 23 and have an opinion on whether she should stay with or dump disreputable boyfriend number 42.

English-language Press

Those only interested in English-language newspapers have few problems nowadays, as most major British, North American and Irish papers are available at news kiosks in major cities and expat areas, arriving around midday, or earlier where there is an airport nearby. There is also a fair smattering of locally published, often free, English-language newspapers and magazines. Quality varies, and news coverage is at times superficial, but they do carry features of interest to expats. They can also be useful for finding accommodation or job offers. Look out for: *The Broadsheet* ('The Best of Spain in English'), published in Madrid but distributed in Barcelona and the *costas*; *Metropolitan*, Barcelona's monthly magazine in English; *Sur in English*, a weekly English edition of the Spanish-language newspaper *Sur*; *Absolute Marbella* and *Essential Marbella*, for Costa del Sol information, and *Costa del Sol News* and *Costa Blanca News*, which need no explaining. A full, if slightly outdated, list of English-language publications is to be found on **www.typicallyspanish.com**.

Television

Spanish people watch huge amounts of television, despite the fact that, as everyone complains, far too much Spanish TV is awful (although, in its defence, it has got better in the last few years). For years, most channels have chased the same mass-market audience, and often give the impression that the only way that occurred to them to do so was to head downmarket. Staples of programming are Latin-American soap operas (during the daytime), game shows, American series like *Ally McBeal*, reality shows, highly emotionalised, post-Oprah-style public confessional shows, and an ever-greater amount of celebrity chat, an offshoot of Spain's already giant in-print gossip industry.

Aside from some very Spanish peculiarities like bullfights, the biggest single mainstay of the TV schedules is football, and there are usually live games on one channel or other on most nights of the week. Live-broadcast rights to the Spanish first division have been the object of a huge bidding war between different TV channels and, in recent years, the LFP football league has incensed fans by preferring to place its wares on pay-per-view channels for vast pay-offs, although many games still turn up on other channels. As in the UK, the pay-per-view football phenomenon has greatly helped bar owners with the right system in place.

American and international shows are virtually always shown dubbed into Spanish (or Catalan, Basque or Galician on regional channels), but the more upmarket channels quite often show classic films in their original language with Spanish subtitles. Also, some channels – notably the Catalan TV3 – use the DUAL system with which, if you have the right set (with a NICAM stereo system) you can choose between a dubbed or an original-language soundtrack by flicking the stereo switch.

In most regions there are five or six open-access channels and one pay-per-view normally available, divided between the state broadcaster TVE, private channels and others owned by regional authorities. The main channels are:

- **TVE1**: The state-owned TVE's flagship channel, home to middle-of-the-road, mass-audience programming.

- **TVE2 (also called La 2)**: TVE's more 'worthy' channel, with a greater range of documentaries, arts and music, sports, kids' shows and less conventional films.

- **Antena 3**: Privately owned, commercial channel that's now the main competitor to TVE1, with a safe diet of family entertainment and big-audience game shows.

- **Tele 5**: Also privately owned: relentlessly tacky when it first opened in the early 1990s, recently Tele 5 has had the radical idea that it might also gain a bit of audience share by sometimes being more serious and original, and now hosts some innovative programmes and some of Spain's best TV news.

- **Regional channels**: Spain's regional governments support their own broadcasting services. The most 'solid' are the Catalan TV3 and Canal 33 – which often outdo the all-Spanish channels in local ratings – the Basque ETB-1 and 2, Telemadrid and Andalucía's Canal Sur. Others are more limited in their approach.

- **Canal+/Digital+**: The result of the merger of Canal+, Vía Digital and Digital+, this is not an open-access channel but viewable by subscribers only, even though via a terrestrial signal (the signal is encrypted, and subscribers are given a decoder box). With an audience prepared to pay extra, Canal Plus is the home of more sophisticated programming, especially of recent films and international series, with the option of seeing them undubbed. It has also gone determinedly after sports rights, paying an exaggerated price for the right to show a Spanish first division football game live each Sunday, and also often showing English Premiership matches on Saturdays. As well as this you can get CNN news in English via this network. Another element in the channel's eclectic schedule is porn, shown late-night. From late 2005, Canal+ will also broadcast on open-access, via the channel Cuatro. For more information, look at **www.plus.es**.

But it does not stop there. In the near future there will be a much wider choice of TV channels. The government recently approved the *Plan Técnico de la Televisión Digital Terrestre* (Technical Plan for Terrestrial Digital Televisión) which will allow more channels to broadcast by this means.

At some point in 2010 there will be an 'analogue blackout', after which all TV broadcasting will be digital.

One important thing to note about TV in Spain is that the standard transmission signal, called PAL-BG, is not exactly the same as the one used in the UK (PAL-1), so that if you bring a TV set to Spain from Britain it may not work properly, and will tend to pick up a picture but no sound. You can have your old TV modified for a small fee, but it may be easier just to buy a Spanish set. In any case, most recent-model TVs sold across Europe work on a Multi-PAL system, and adapt automatically, or via a switch button, to changes in signal standard.

Satellite TV

The form of TV of most interest to most foreign residents in Spain is satellite, which now allows you to receive all the UK TV channels (and a choice of others), just like at home. It has become a staple feature of expat bars, especially for English and Scottish football, and many *urbanización* developments now highlight built-in satellite TV as a selling point (take note, though, that not all these communal satellite systems are the same, and some may only give you a minimal choice of channels).

Satellite TV is now easy to obtain and set up in Spain. Sky TV in the UK will not actually take subscriptions from people living in Spain, but if you are already a Sky subscriber it is quite easy to take your Videocrypt decoder box with you to Spain and use it there, as a great many people now do. Do not take your mini-dish with you, but get a new, preferably motorised, dish in Spain of 1.2 to 1.5 metres diameter, which will also be able to pick up satellite radio. You should also take a British TV or a set with a modern Multi-PAL reception system, as an older Spanish set may not receive the Sky signal properly (*see* above). You will not be able to get new smart cards to re-activate your decoder direct from Sky if you 'officially' have a UK account but live in Spain, so may need to have them sent on to you by someone back in the UK. According to where you are this may not be necessary, as there are now quite a few satellite companies operating in the main tourist areas that can supply Sky cards, and which almost always advertise in the local expat press. Alternatively, if you don't have or don't want to bother with a UK satellite account, you can turn to local satellite providers – generally advertising in the same places – which, in response to expat demand, will connect you up to Sky as well as to the main Spanish packages.

A better option than the straight Sky package is Sky Digital, which gives you the UK terrestrial channels (BBC 1 and 2, Channel 4 and so on) as well as all the satellite or cable-only channels, and many more possibilities as well. Before setting up (and better still, before buying) a satellite dish you need to check whether this will be allowed under local bye-laws, or the community rules if you are in an apartment block or development. There may well be limitations on exactly where you can put it, and dish-location is becoming a recurrent source of argument among *urbanización*-dwellers. Satellite TV reception is good in most parts of the Spanish coast except on the Costa Blanca, particularly its southern stretch, where there is something of a 'hole' in the signal. Dishes here often have to be significantly larger (and uglier); local companies are well used to giving advice on how to get the best signal.

Radio

The Spanish radio scene consists of an extraordinary number of stations, some of them just serving one town, although the bigger ones tend to be part of four groups, the state-owned **RNE** and the private **SER**, **COPE** and the more youth-orientated **Onda Cero**. Within all this apparent diversity, programming tends to divide into just two kinds, continuous chat (phone-ins, rambling discussion-interviews) and continuous music, with few surprises in between. When you do find an interesting station, it is another excellent way of improving your Spanish.

To get the **BBC World Service** in Spain you need a short-wave radio. The best frequency to use can change slightly through the day; the World Service website (**www.bbc.co.uk/worldservice**) has a worldwide frequency guide, and an excellent information service to help listeners get the best signal. If you have satellite radio (see above), you can also get BBC Radios 1, 2, 3, 4 and 5 and some other UK stations.

There are also several local stations that broadcast in English for all or at least part of the day, such as **Central FM** (98.6 and 103.8), **Coastline Radio** (97.7), **Spectrum** (105.5) and **Radio Gibraltar** (91.3) on the Costa del Sol, or **Waves FM** (96.8) in the Canaries. Frequencies and even stations can change frequently, so check the current ones in the local English language press.

Learning the Language

First Steps and Reasons for Buying (*see* pp.17–20) looked briefly at the four languages of Spain and their importance for anyone seriously planning to live there. What follows here is information about learning any or all of them, with emphasis on Castilian, as this is the language that most people will use most frequently in Spain. Remember that it is not only useful to be able to get by in Castilian (or Catalan, Galician or Basque); it may be essential, above all if you plan to work or run a business, and in case of emergencies.

Courses

It is a good idea to make a start on learning the language long before you set off to buy in Spain. There are dozens of language academies throughout the UK and Ireland. Many local authority further education colleges run evening classes, and Castilian is a popular option these days. Courses in Catalan, Galician and Basque are not as common, but do exist. Many universities have Spanish language departments and some have courses for external students who are not enrolled on a degree course.

The **Instituto Cervantes** is a Spanish government-backed institution for the promotion of the Castilian language and culture abroad. The London centre is at 102 Eaton Square, London SW1W 9AN, **t** (020) 7235 0353, **f** (020) 7235 0329, **www.cervantes.es**. Other branches are in Manchester and Leeds and you can find their details on the website. Alternatively, contact the **Spanish Education Office** at 20 Peel Street London W8 7PD, **t** (020) 7727 2462, **f** (020) 7229 4965, **www.sgci.mec.es/uk** and **www.sgci.mec.es/ie**.

Also useful for London-based students is the **Hispanic and Luso-Brazilian Council**, at Canning House, 2 Belgrave Square, London SW1X 8PJ, **t** (020) 7235 2303, **f** (020) 7235 3587, **www.canninghouse.com**. This body runs classes organisation and provides extensive information about where to study Castilian both in London, other UK cities and in Spain itself.

Several large language-teaching organisations offer courses in Castilian in the UK. **Berlitz**, with six UK centres, is based at Paradise Forum, Birmingham B3 3HJ,, **t** (0121) 233 0974, **f** (0121) 233 1236, **www.berlitz.com/local/uk**. **Inlingua**, based at Rodney Lodge, Rodney Road, Cheltenham GL50 1HX, **t** (01242) 250493, **f** (01242) 250495, **www.inlingua-cheltenham.co.uk**, offers classes in the UK and organises courses in Spain. Also look at **www.cactuslanguage.com**, which lets you select courses by place, level and duration – most are in Brighton and London.

Self-study

The **BBC** has several on-line self-study courses. Check their website (**www.bbc.co.uk**), follow the links to education, then languages, and click on Spanish.

The online shop also has a series of materials available for sale, among them the following:

- *Talk Spanish*, a short course for absolute beginners consisting of a book accompanied by cassettes or CDs.

- *Get into Spanish*, an engaging and interactive introductory course, the full version of which includes a book, an audio CD and a CD-Rom.

- *España Viva*, a comprehensive introduction to everyday Spanish.

- *Sueños World Spanish 2*, which emphasises learning to speak and understand authentic Spanish at intermediate level, and building your reading and writing skills. A completely revised and updated edition is available.

Another two sites are **www.studyspanish.com** and **www.hola.org.uk**, both of which have tuition from beginner level upwards and provide online tutorials and assessment. There are many more courses on the market: *Spanish with*

Michel Thomas is a CD-only, bookless course that's currently very popular and some people find very helpful (although, as with all language courses, this is very much a matter of individual response).

If you cannot begin before moving to Spain, there are many options available once there. Information about schools and courses is available both from the Cervantes Institute and the Spanish Education Office (*see* above). Otherwise, look in the *Yellow Pages* under *Academias de Idiomas*. The **Escuela Oficial de Idiomas**, the Official Language School, run regionally by each of the autonomous communities, offers inexpensive classes throughout Spain; costs are much lower than at private language schools, but demand is very high, too, so you need to enrol well in advance. Contact the central school at Calle Jesús Maestro, s/n, 28003 Madrid, **t** 915 544 195, **www.eoidiomas.com**, for information about all regional schools. On the website, click on 'Otras EE.OO.II' then choose the region you want. Catalan, Galician and Basque, and more than a dozen other languages, may be studied at EOIs in the relevant regions, and their certificates issued on completion of a course are recognised as official qualifications in Spain. The UK-based **Open University** also offers structured courses in Castilian, either as part of a degree or just for personal satisfaction. Contact the OU co-ordinator in Madrid c/o King's Training, Edificio Serantes, Plaza Pablo Ruíz Picasso s/n 28020, Madrid, **t** 915 777 701.

Spain's Other Languages

While both Catalan and Galician have much in common with Castilian, they are languages in their own right, not dialects. Basque, unrelated to any other Indo-European language, is another story. No previous language-learning experience will help you – or interfere – here.

Catalan – *Català*

Catalan language and literature may be studied in many UK universities, generally in a sub-department of the Spanish or Hispanic Studies departments. Contact the relevant department at your nearest university, if not available there they will be able to put you in touch with a nearby department where Catalan is taught.

In Catalonia itself many are options available. The **Escuela Oficial de Idiomas** (*see* above) offers Catalan throughout the whole of Spain and in Catalonia is called (in Catalan, naturally) **La Escola Oficial d'Idiomes**. The main branch is at Avinguda Drassanes s/n, **t** 933 292 458. Alternatively, go to the **Centres de Normalització Lingüística**, central office, Carrer Pau Claris, 162, **t** 932 723 100. It is cheap, cover all levels and offer intensive summer courses.

Many private language schools also offer courses. An excellent series of Catalan-language resources and online courses may be found at **www.languages-on-the-web.com/links/link-catalan.htm**.

Galician – *Galego*

Possibilities for studying Galician outside Galicia are very thin on the ground. Some UK universities do have Galician lecturers within the Hispanic Studies departments. Contact the **Hispanic Studies Department** at the University of Birmingham, Edgbaston, Birmingham B15 2TT, **t** (0121) 414 6035, **www.bham. ac.uk/GalicianStudies**. It can also facilitate Galician links elsewhere.

Courses are offered at the **Escuela Oficial de Idiomas** all over Spain and in Galicia. The main branch there is at Calle Pepín Rivero, s/n, 15011, A Coruña, **t** 981 279 100, **www.arrakis.es~/eoi**.

At the **Universidade de Santiago de Compostela** is the Departamento de Filoloxía Galega, Avenida de Castelao s/n, 15705, Santiago de Compostela, **www. usc.es/fgsec/doc/xeral.html**.

Basque – *Euskera*

Basque is not taught widely outside of Euskadi but if you live in Erresuma Batua (Great Britain in Basque), however, contact the Institute of Basque Studies within the Department of Languages at **London Guildhall University**, Old Castle Street, London E1 7NT, **t** (020) 8374 5341, **ibs-queries@euskalerria.org**.

As well as this there is the **Basque Association Abroad (Euskal Elkartea)** at Oxford House, Derbyshire Street, Bethnal Green Town, London E2 6HD, **t** (020) 7739 7339, **f** (020) 7739 0435, **london@euskaledge.fsnet.co.uk**.

Courses in Basque are offered at **Escuelas Oficiales de Idiomas** throughout Spain; in Euskadi itself there is one in every province. In the Basque capital the address is Calle Nieves Cano, 18, 01006, Vitoria, **t** 945 138 760.

As well as this there are online Euskera resources to be found at **www.eirelink. com/alanking/introduc.htm**.

Sports and Recreation

Readership figures for the sports-only daily newspapers reveal just how enthusiastic the Spanish are about sport. Barcelona's staging of the 1992 Olympic Games gave a tremendous fillip, and Spanish sportsmen and women have achieved much over the last decade. During the same period, facilities have been built and improved throughout Spain. Non-participants are also well catered for. Televised sport is abundant and fans attend a considerable range of live competitions at all levels.

Participative Sport

Access to good sports facilities depends largely on where you are. As a rule, larger towns and cities as well as tourist areas are generally well-equipped. Many local councils offer inexpensive facilities, which can range from the slightly shabby to near Olympic standard. There is also a plethora of private gymnasiums and sports centres offering the whole gamut of activities, such as tennis, golf, riding, swimming, squash and more. If you join a club to play any competitive sport you must get the corresponding player's licence from the provincial or regional federation (usually obtained via the club or team that you join), which gives you some cover against accidents.

Spain's climate and geography also allows for outdoor types to take part in all manner of activities, such as fishing, hunting, hiking, trekking and rock-climbing, as well as more radical sports such as bungee-jumping, paragliding and hang-gliding. Cycling is a great favourite, too – mountain-bikers in particular find plenty of challenging, rugged terrain. Then, of course, there are watersports. The long coastline is a paradise for windsurfers, sailors and water-skiers. At the simplest level, in the sunnier spots a jog along the beach followed by a dip in the sea is available to all, practically year-round, for the price of a pair of trainers and a bathing suit!

Information about municipal and private sports facilities, clubs and regional federations is generally found in the telephone directory or the *Yellow Pages*. Alternatively ask at your local council for a list of sports centres and organisations. Here are some key sporting activities and contact points:

General

- The **Spanish Sports Council**, Consejo Superior de Deportes, is at Avenida de Martin Fierro s/n, 28040, Madrid, **t** 915 896 700. A full list of all national sports federations is available on its website, **www.csd.mec.es/ directorio/federaciones/federa2d.htm**.

Golf

- The **Spanish Golf Federation**, Capitán Haya, 9 5° 28020, Madrid, **t** 915 552 682, **www.golfspainfederacion.com**. Check **www.golfspain.com** for information in English about golf courses, clubs and green fees.

Cricket

- There are cricket clubs on the Costa del Sol, the Costa Blanca, Majorca, Ibiza and elsewhere. Information from **www.brittsabroad.co.uk** (follow links to the different areas) and **www.andalucia.com**.

Cycling

- The **Real Federación Española de Ciclismo**, Calle Ferraz, 16, 5°, 28008, Madrid, **t** 915 400 841, **www.rfec.com**.

Tennis

- The **Spanish Tennis Federation** is based in Barcelona at Avinguda Diagonal, 618, 08021 Barcelona, **t** 932 005 355, **www.fedetenis.es**. Alternatively, look at **www.playtennisspain.com** for independent information.

Sailing

- **Real Federación de Vela**, Calle Luis de Salazar, 9, 28002, Madrid, **t** 915 195 008, **www.rfev.es**). Some sailing clubs are listed, with links, on **www.sailing. org/sailingclubs/esp.asp**.

Windsurfing

- **www.windsurfspain.com**, information in Castilian only.

Water-skiing

- **Federación Española de Esquí Náutico**, Plaça Universitat, 4, 2°-1ª 08007, Barcelona, **t** 934 520 895, **feesqui@infonegocio.com**). Otherwise information is available in any resort town.

Winter Sports

- **Real Federación de Deportes de Invierno**, Calle Arroyofresno, 3, A, 28035, Madrid, **t** 913 769 930, **www.rfedi.es**.

Riding

- **Real Federación de Hípica Española**, Plaza Marqués de Salamanca, 2, 28006, Madrid, **t** 914 364 200, **www.rfhe.com**. Lots of information, in Castilian, also at **www.hipicalia.com**.

Spectator Sports

Known as *el deporte rey* (the king of sports), **football** is followed passionately throughout Spain, and La Liga is as competitive as the Premiership, the Bundesliga or the Calcio. Real Madrid (with 29 league titles) and Barcelona (with 17, the most recent conquered in 2005) have traditionally dominated. Only Atlético de Madrid, Athletic Bilbao and Valencia (with nine, eight and six titles respectively) have ever really managed to challenge that dominance. In the late 1990s and the first couple of years of this century, Spanish clubs did extremely well in the Champions' League, Real Madrid carrying off the 'Big Cup' in 1998, 2000 and 2002 (making nine in total) and Valencia were runners-up in 2000 and 2001. TV money had much to do with this, permitting Real Madrid to recruit so-called 'Galácticos' like Figo, Zidane, Beckham and Owen while Barcelona themselves captured the exciting Ronal dinho from Paris Saint-Germain.

Expat areas are fairly well served for teams if you're looking for top action. Andalucía has four first division teams: Seville's bitter city rivals Betis and Sevilla, Málaga and the recently promoted Cádiz, whose passionate supporters make every game a spectacle. Up the coast are Valencia and, a little further still, in Castellón, the plucky little upstarts Villarreal, nicknamed the 'Yellow Submarine', who are currently debuting in the Champions' League. Catalonia, of course, has 'El Barça' and the fabulous Nou Camp stadium, though city rivals

La Corrida

Along with flamenco, sun, Julio Iglesias and twanging guitars, bullfighting is of course one of the Spanish institutions of which everybody has heard, and on which many will have an opinion. In Spain, after a dip in interest in the 1980s, bullfighting bounced back in the '90s, and shows no sign of going away in the 21st century. For locals, star *toreros* are among the country's best-known faces, and staple fodder for the gossip industry (rising young bullfighters 'traditionally' go out with/eventually marry/break up with/have affairs with brash young singers and other names from Spain's entertainment world).

There are bullrings throughout the country, but *la corrida* is by no means equally popular in every part of Spain. In Catalonia there is a very low level of interest and the Catalan government, which actively disapproves of bullfighting, has subjected it to a series of legal restrictions so that, more than anywhere else, it survives only as a tourist attraction; Galicia, the Balearics and the Canaries, similarly, are areas with only a limited bullfighting tradition. Castile and Andalucía, on the other hand, are the great heartlands of bullfighting, and the most important bullrings of all, the twin meccas of the fiesta, are the Plaza de la Ventas in Madrid and the Real Maestranza in Seville. The bullrings in Valencia, Alicante, Málaga and indeed most cities in Andalucía also have a high reputation among aficionados.

The bullfighting season lasts from about March to October, varying from place to place, with *corridas* in each ring usually at 5pm or 7pm every Sunday. In addition, major events in the bullfighting year are the *ferias*, during which fights are held every day in their traditional locations, with all the most famous bullfighters present: the April *feria* in Seville; San Isidro in Madrid, which lasts virtually the whole of May; and San Fermín in Pamplona in July, which is accompanied by the famous bull-running through the streets, in which a steady stream of drunken foreigners are injured each year. There are also many smaller *ferias* around the country. If you do go to see a bullfight, and don't just want to be horrified, it's advisable to read at least a little of the abundant literature available on the subject, or maybe go with someone who can explain to you at least part of the sometimes complicated rituals that will be taking place.

Espanyol, based at the Olympic Stadium, are an alternative. The Balearics have the modest, occasionally successful Mallorca. Canary Island dwellers will have to put up with lower division football for the time being as Tenerife and Las Palmas now play in 'Segunda' and 'Segunda B', respectively. Check local TV listings for televised games – you will not have to look too far.

Another highly popular spectator sport is **basketball**, second only to football. Real Madrid and Barcelona are, predictably, the top teams but TAU Vitoria and Madrid-based Estudiantes are worthy rivals, too.

Motor sports fans can see Formula 1 racing at the circuits in Jerez de la Frontera (**www.circuitodejerez.com**) and Montmeló, close to Barcelona (**www.circuitcat.com**) and Spanish driver Fernando Alonso, recently crowned world champion, is something of a national hero. Rally driving is popular – look out for Madrid driver Carlos Saínz. Motorcycle racing also has a big following, and Spanish riders such as Carlos Checa, Alex Crivillé and Fonsi Nieto, nephew of the legendary Angel Nieto, have enjoyed international success.

If you like to watch **cycling**, La Vuelta de España, Spain's version of the Tour de France, takes place in September and has many exciting mountain stages before finishing in Madrid. Andalucía and Catalonia also have their own *vueltas*. Miguel Induraín, four-times Tour de France winner, has now long since retired but there are many top Spanish riders, such as Alejandro Valverde, whom Lance Armstrong has tipped as his successor.

Politics and Religion

Truly getting to know a country is an ongoing process, not something that you do from one day to the next, and one that has many different facets. Here is a brief taster-introduction to the sides of modern Spain with which you might like to start.

Politics

The parliamentary monarchy and constitutional system established after the end of the Franco dictatorship in 1975 (*see* 'The New Spain', pp.33–6) have now become so familiar a part of the scenery in Spain that it's often easy to forget that they are less than three decades old. The dictatorship and Spain's turbulent past still cast shadows over the country in subtle and often unnoticed ways, but most Spaniards, including politicians, are far more concerned with current problems and issues. Spain has been able to go through more than one political cycle and a whole generation of politicians since the country's remarkable 'transition' from authoritarian rule. Key points in this have been the election of the first modern Socialist government in 1982; their loss of power in 1996, after 14 years in office and the following eight years of centre-right rule by José María Aznar's **Partido Popular**; and the Socialists' return to office in 2004, in the dramatic wake of the 11 March bombings in Madrid.

The Socialist party (the Partido Socialista Obrero Español or **PSOE**), in power again since spring 2004, spent several years in the wilderness after losing power in 1996, and struggled to regain its former sense of direction. The PSOE could reasonably claim, though, that many PP voters aged 45 and under were its own ungrateful offspring. When the Socialists first came to power under the charismatic Felipe González in 1982 they inherited a ramshackle state suffering from years of neglect. They negotiated entry to the EU, from which Spain has benefited hugely, and undertook a far-reaching programme of reform and

The Monarchy

Possibly the least controversial political institution in Spain today is probably the monarchy, something which would have astonished anyone with a crystal ball in 1975. Gifted with charm and a natural warmth, King Juan Carlos and his family have worked hard to make contact with every part of the country, and become genuinely popular. They have also cultivated contacts with the minority nationalities, avoiding historic prejudices, and – except maybe among the worst Basque intransigents – do not attract any of the animosity in these regions that gets directed at tub-thumping Castilian politicians. Prince Felipe, the heir to the throne, put paid to speculation over the future of the monarchy by marrying Leitizia Ortiz, who until the announcement of the engagement was a journalist and newsreader on TV1, in May 2004. Doña Leitizia is at the time of writing expecting her first child.

renovation in areas such as transport, health and education, not through sweeping socialist measures but by using a combination of public and private money in a way that has since become a mantra for politicians elsewhere, such as Tony Blair. This essential modernisation helped set off an economic boom in Spain that, with ups and downs, has continued pretty much ever since. This boom has never solved all the country's problems – like rural unemployment – since booms never do, but it did provide a great deal more wealth and more opportunities for a new, younger middle class.

From the early 1990s, though, much of this same group transferred its allegiance to the PP and its promise of businesslike efficiency and tax cuts. The PP was helped by the fact that the PSOE, in its later years in power, became mired in a series of corruption scandals and that its policies of giving freedom to all and to everything had begun to sound vacuous.

The PSOE is flanked on its left by another parliamentary group, the **Izquierda Unida (IU)** or United Left, the core of which is made up of the remains of the old Spanish Communist Party, but most voters consider them to be out of touch with reality.

As the PP settled into office – and especially during its second term after 2000 when it had an absolute majority – a lot of the gloss wore off its promises of deregulation and modernity, and it tended to reveal itself as a more conventional right-wing party which, in turn, gave a bit of new life to the opposition. During the second term, the Aznar government begun actually to put into practice its more hard-hitting ideas by trying to cut back on social benefits introduced under González in the 1980s, which gave both the PSOE and IU a new, more everyday and very popular cause to rally around, through nationwide strikes and protest campaigns.

The PP's ups and downs are themselves illustrative of the changes Spain has gone through. The party began life in the late 1970s, as a regrouping (initially called Alianza Popular) of former supporters of the Franco regime, then in complete disarray in the face of an upsurge of left-wing support in reaction to the Franco years. From the late 1980s, though, and especially under Aznar, the PP managed very successfully to reinvent and repackage itself as a modern, dynamic, entirely constitutional right-wing party, which was free-market, pro-business, appealing to conservative voters but with no dogmatic attachments to the past. The latter is not entirely true, since belligerent undercurrents from the PP's authoritarian past have and do still occasionally bubble up from beneath its glossy public image, but not usually so much as to put too many voters off. The PP's massive success from the mid-1990s onwards was in part due to a reaction against some of the radical developments of the previous 20 years. In local and national elections between 1995 and 2000 it became pre-eminent in most of 'Spanish Spain' – that is, most of the country except the 'historic nationalities' of the Basque Country and Catalonia, and the Socialists' heartland of Andalucía – with an image combining a degree of social conservatism with modernity, managerial efficiency, pro-Europeanism, of being in touch with the global economy and, in practical terms, an agenda of economic deregulation, privatisation and lower taxes. The PP's fall in March 2004 came about as a result of an accumulation of factors, but principally its arrogant use and abuse of a parliamentary majority, and its mishandling of several major issues, most notably the Madrid bombings of 11 March that year (*see* p.35).

The left–right split is only one aspect of modern Spanish political life. Equally important are the argumentative relationships between the **central government and the regions**, and especially the main 'historic nationalities', the Basques and Catalans. Features of both these regions are that they have their own political 'maps', distinct from that of Spain as a whole: in Catalonia the two main parties are the moderate nationalist **Convergència i Unió**, which heads the regional government, and the **Catalan Socialist Party or PSC**, a semi-independent affiliate to the PSOE, with the PP some way behind; in the Basque Country the regional government is led by the **Basque Nationalist Party (PNV)**, and there are several other Basque parties. Other regions have their own local and nationalist parties too, but they are generally smaller, so that the central PP and PSOE can exert more influence. Part of the motivation behind the rise of the PP in the 1990s had been a vague Spanish-nationalist sentiment felt in central Spain (and especially in the corridors of power) that the powers of the Basques, Catalans and some other regions had gone too far, and needed reining in. From 1996 to 2000, lacking an overall majority, the Aznar government was dependent on deals with the Catalan nationalists to stay in office, and so had to proceed carefully, but, since it gained full power, a much more assertive attitude became evident. The Aznar government adopted a hard line on the Basque conflict – a difficult one to crack in any case, one in which the most obstreperous opponents, the ETA terrorist organisation and its supporters, seem incapable of backing off from their commitment to violence and all-or-nothing goals – and a gulf of distrust opened up between the central government and the PNV, which is accused of pandering to terrorism. The Basque government, on the other hand, argues that intransigence from Madrid only makes the extremists' case for them. In other regions, where terrorism is not an issue, such as Catalonia, Aznar's ministers were equally emphatic, albeit with less publicity, in demanding that the central government become involved in areas that, for the past 20 years, were under the control of local authorities. Under the current government, the question of taking autonomy a step further has arisen again and the Catalan Parliament recently approved a new statute, still to be approved by the central government congress, which has provoked criticism from the PP who claim it is the first step in the dismemberment of Spain as a unit, and will only lead to Balkanisation.

One area of modernisation in which Señor Aznar and his government could have won the eternal appreciation of a great many residents in Spain, native and foreign, is in the actual workings of the Spanish state itself, its intricate system of permits, forms, delays, sub-departments and provincial offices that only open a few hours a day. However, while the Aznar deregulation agenda hit out in some predictable directions – such as welfare cuts – it did little to simplify the state machinery and its strange ways. In fact, those public bodies in Spain that have notably streamlined their procedures – such as the Catalan Socialist-run Barcelona City Council, and some of the regional authorities – are more often controlled by other parties rather than the PP.

Religion

The Catholic Church has traditionally been a dominant force in Spanish society and politics. It is less so today but still claims that almost 94 per cent of all Spaniards are adherents. This figure is probably more nominal than real as an independent study in 2002 concluded that only about 82 per cent consider themselves 'believers', and as few as 19 per cent of them attend mass regularly. The same study also shows about 10 per cent of the population to be agnostic or non-believers and 4 per cent atheists. About 2 per cent follow other religions: including 350,000 Protestants, 450,000 Muslims, 50,000 Jews and 9,000 Buddhists. Hindus make up about 0.05 per cent of all believers.

The Catholic Church remains influential, despite the constitution, by which Spain became non-confessional with freedom of religion. Catholic baptisms, communions and marriages are still important family events, even for the most lukewarm. As well as this, popular fiestas, the majority of which celebrate some religious event or other, are the most visible manifestation of Catholicism's importance in Spanish culture, though many feel such evident religiosity is a mere excuse for partying.

A more illustrative example of the Catholic Church's continuing importance is that everybody must state on their tax returns if they do *not* want a percentage of their taxes to fund the Church but to be destined for other 'social ends'.

Failure to tick the relevant box is understood to mean tacit approval of the money going automatically to the Church. No other religious organisation, Protestant, Jewish, Muslim or otherwise, receives public funding.

The Catholic Church has been on the defensive since 1978, having to accept previously inconceivable social changes: divorce, contraception, abortion (not free and on demand but available nevertheless), a general relaxation of sexual customs and, now, legalised gay marriage and adoption. On top of that came the removal of obligatory religious education from the state school curriculum, leaving the choice up to parents.

The PP government, many of whom were traditionally minded, Opus Dei-educated Catholics, worked quietly to restore the Church's presence in the field of education. Grant-assisted private schools, mostly of a (Catholic) religious persuasion, had funding channelled their way to the detriment of purely state schools. More importantly, attempts were made to restore religious education as an evaluated subject to the state school curriculum. Many parents, products of the transition who valued the hard-won freedoms of the last quarter-century, were vehemently opposed to the move, which they, along with opposition political parties, saw as unconstitutional. Spain is also vastly more multi-racial and multicultural than it was even a decade or two ago and it is unclear how obligatory (Catholic) religious instruction, would square with a society that has a fast-growing number of non-Catholics. The PSOE, since coming into power, has, in any case, shelved these plans.

Letting Your Property

08

Around 70 per cent of British people who buy houses in Spain also let them at some time or another. They divide roughly into two groups. The first is people who see the property very significantly, or even exclusively, as an investment proposition, and want to let it seriously – that is, they want to make money by letting their property and will try to find the maximum number of tenants each year. The second group consists of people who are primarily buying a holiday home and are not so much looking to make a profit from renting as hoping to cover some or all of the costs of their new purchase through rental income, sometimes just by letting casually to family and friends.

There are fundamental differences in the way these two groups should approach the house-buying process. For the first group this is a business. Just as in any business, the decisions they take about where and what to buy, whether and how to restore the property and what facilities to provide will be governed by the wish to maximise profit. They should put themselves in the position of the person whom they want to rent their property, and consider which part of the market they expect to appeal to – whether, for example, it might be couples wanting to enjoy Spanish culture and cuisine or families wanting a cheap beach holiday – and anticipate what features clients like this would expect. They should choose an area, buy a property, convert it and equip it solely with their prospective tenants in mind.

The second group will have to bear in mind some or most of the same considerations, but overall can make far fewer concessions to their tenants. Theirs is first and foremost a holiday home for their own use, and they will be ready to compromise on the more 'businesslike' aspects of house-buying (and so reduce potential income) in order to maximise their own enjoyment of it. They will have to make some changes to accommodate visitors – extra bedding, setting aside some wardrobe space where they can lock away their own things while the house is let – but these should be as few as possible. Where they draw the line will be determined by just how much income they need to get out of the property.

This chapter relates mainly to the first group. If you identify more with the second category, you can pick and choose from the ideas within it, and there are also some points that are more directly relevant to your situation. And, whichever group that you feel you fall into, there is a very important point to remember: in either case, you are most unlikely to cover all of your expenses and both capital and interest repayments on a large mortgage from letting your property, however efficiently you do so.

Location , Choice of Property and Rental Potential

The Right Area

The choice of the area in which to buy your rental property is by far the most important decision that you will make. There are many parts of Spain in which it is fairly easy to let a property regularly enough to make it a commercially viable proposition. On the other hand, there are thousands of properties around the country that are, commercially speaking, almost impossible to let. A rustic house in a rural backwater may find a few tenants each year, but they will not be anywhere near enough to generate a real commercial return on your invest- ment. If you are interested in a house like this you will probably have taken this on board, and should view any rental income as a bonus that may help with some of your expenses, rather than any kind of nest-egg.

The factors to take into consideration when deciding on an area are slightly different from those you might look at when just thinking about buying a place for yourself. They will also vary depending on your target clientele and your preferred way of administering the property. Most are related, as one would expect, to the tourist traffic of an area, its attractions and services, and also to the practical services it has available that you can call on to help manage the letting.

If you advertise any property well, you will always get some tenants. You will only begin to get repeat customers and a spreading circle of recommendations from previous tenants – one of the best ways of building up your customer base, since it saves on repeat advertising – if the house or flat itself, the area around it and the things there are to do there really satisfy or, better still, exceed people's expectations of an enjoyable time.

Climate

Climate is, naturally, a major factor (*see* 'Climate', pp.93–6 and 332). Of course, anywhere around the Spanish Mediterranean coast and the islands can usually be relied on to have hot, sunny weather during the prime summer holiday season from July to September, but for letting purposes you will have much greater flexibility if you are in an area where you can also expect blue skies in April–June and October, and mild weather through the winter. For one thing, you may want to use the house yourself in summer, and so will need to let it at other times of the year (alternatively, if you want to maximise your rents, you will let it in summer, and use it yourselves in December–February). The resort areas with the greatest potential for summer, spring and winter lets are those south of Valencia – especially the southern Costa Blanca and, most of all, the Costa del Sol – and, in the islands, Ibiza and the Canaries; on the other hand, in more rural and mountain areas, where the beach is not the primary centre of activity, the weather may be a little less important a consideration.

Tourist Attractions

Of equal importance are the attractions of the area, both natural features such as spectacular landscape and 'tourist attractions' – a term that in itself covers a multitude of things. The most obvious of them on the *costus* is, of course, access to a good beach, but it helps if there are other things there such as sailing, diving and other watersports facilities. For some clients, proximity to a charming, historic town would be a major asset, while for others it might be being only a walk away from a nightlife scene. For families, it can be a big bonus to be within a short driving distance of the two big theme parks, Terra Mítica near Benidorm, whose future is unclear, and Universal Mediterrània near Tarragona, or, failing that, to be near one of the waterparks and similar child-orientated attractions found around the coast. Proximity to good golf courses and, to a much lesser extent, other sports facilities are major selling points (if not essentials) for a growing number of potential clients. On a far smaller scale, a local attraction might consist of a craft centre in the nearest village.

Local Facilities

Added to these 'activities' are the more everyday attractions of an area which, for most people, loom as large as the more spectacular features in their enjoyment of a holiday let. Most people who rent self-catering accommodation will want to be able to stock up on food, drink and other necessities without too much trouble, and, since they won't want to cook all the time, will also want to be able to eat out. They will appreciate it greatly – and your property will be much easier to let – if your villa is within easy distance (preferably walking distance) of at least a few shops, and a choice of bars and restaurants.

Access

As important as climate and the charms of the locality is the ability of tenants to get to your property. The area where your flat or villa is located must be reasonably accessible from the places where your prospective tenants live, and the property itself must be easy to find.

For most British visitors, convenient access means how easy it is to get there from a local airport with direct flights from a UK airport reasonably close to where they live (for details of airports and routes to Spain, *see* 'Travelling to Spain', pp.68–81). It is worth repeating here the travel industry figures that show that 25 per cent of all potential visitors will not come if it involves travelling for more than one hour from a local airport at either end of their journey, and that if the travelling time rises to 1½ hours, this will deter around 50 per cent. Of course, this does not mean that if your home is over an hour's drive from an airport you will never let it – with characterful rural houses, for example, a different set of rules applies, and their very remoteness can be an attraction. For more conventional apartments and coastal villas, though, there is no doubt that finding interested tenants will be simpler if you are within the magic hour's distance of an airport.

Owners should not underestimate, either, the importance of being able to find the property easily. Navigation in the depths of rural Spain can be trying: there are few people to ask for directions (especially if you don't speak Spanish) and few signposts of much help in locating a single villa or farm. The situation is not much better among the *urbanizaciones* of the *costas*. Giving tenants decent maps and guidance notes on getting there is essential.

Letting Agencies

Strange as it may seem, the decision as to how you are going to let your property is one of the first that you are going to have to take, before you actually buy it. This is because if you decide to use a professional management or letting agency it will alter your target market and therefore the area in which you ought to be buying (*see* 'Management Agencies', pp.302–4). If you are going to let your property through a professional agency, then it is worth contacting a few before you make a final choice of location, to see what they believe they can offer in the way of rental returns. They will also be able to advise you on what type of property is likely to be most successful as rented property in that area.

If, on the other hand, you expect to find tenants yourself, then you need to decide on your primary market. Most British people who let their property themselves in Spain do so mainly to other British people or other foreigners, chiefly because of a lack of language skills.

The Right Property

Picking the right property is just behind choosing the right area in terms of letting potential. Not all properties let to the same extent – villas and flats that most potential clients find attractive let up to five times more frequently than others that do not stand out for any reason. New properties are generally cheaper to maintain than older ones; however, they are not likely to be as attractive to potential tenants. Most people going on holiday to rural Spain are looking for a character property, while most going to coastal Spain are looking for proximity to facilities and a pool. Even in *costa* villas, people usually like to see 'traditional' features – balconies, terraces, window boxes – rather than purely plain modern styles.

It's very useful, therefore, to pick a home that's pretty (if it isn't one of those big enough to count as spectacular) if you intend to let it out. Most people will decide whether to rent a holiday home after they have seen only a brief description and a photograph, and of these two the photograph is by far the more important. When buying a house for rental purposes, make sure that it 'takes a good picture'.

The number of bedrooms is also important. In cities, you will generally get a better return on your investment in properties with fewer (one or two) bedrooms – a good deal cheaper to buy – than on bigger apartments. On the coast or in the countryside, where the majority of your guests may well be families, a three-bedroom property is probably the most popular.

The Right Price

When buying a property as a business you will be concerned to pay as little as possible for the property consistent with getting the right level of rental return. If you are only buying the property as a business proposition this price/rental balance (or return on investment), together with your judgement of the extent to which the property will rise in value over the years, are the main criteria on which you should decide which property to buy.

If you are going to use the property not just as a rental property but also as a holiday home there is an additional factor to take into account: the amount of time that you will be able to use the property yourself consistent with getting a certain level of rental return. For example, if you bought a one-bedroom beachfront flat in Tenerife for €140,000, that property might be let for 45 weeks a year and produce a return after expenses of, say, 7.5 per cent; however, if you bought a two-bedroom apartment in a small town in Almería for, say, €95,000 and let that for just 20 weeks per year you might also generate 7.5 per cent on your (smaller) investment. Both would be performing equally well, but the Almería flat would allow you and your family to use the property for 30 weeks in each year, whereas the Tenerife one would only give you five weeks' use. This and the fact that it had a second bedroom could make the old town property a more attractive proposition. These figures are simply examples, rather than indications as to what will be actually obtainable at any particular moment. Whichever way you look at it, though, paying the minimum necessary for the property is the key to maximising investment performance.

Legal Restrictions

If you intend to let a property you must also make sure, before you buy it, that there are no legal restrictions that could inhibit your ability to do so. The main situation in which this might arise is in a certain number of developments or apartment blocks where the *comunidad* (see 'Comunidad de Propietarios', pp.115–17 and 171–2) has specific rules against letting. Your lawyer should always check for this whenever you buy into a *comunidad*.

In order to let property legally you should also be registered with the tourist authorities, although many people ignore this. Additional restrictions apply in the Balearics and the Canaries so, if you want to let in these areas, check your plans carefully with your lawyer.

Equipping the Property

After selecting an area and a property, you then have to think about fitting-out the villa or flat with all the features that tenants will expect. It should, of course, be well maintained at all times, and the external decoration and garden and/or pool area should be kept in good condition – apart from anything else, these are the parts that create the first impression as your guests arrive. Other than that, the facilities required will depend to some extent on the target audience that you are trying to attract – if, for example, you are trying to attract mountain walkers, sailors or scuba-divers, they will appreciate somewhere to dry their clothes quickly so that they can be ready to get wet again the following day.

The following is a quick checklist of the main points to be taken care of when preparing any property for holiday tenants:

• **Documents**: Make sure that all guests are sent a pre-visit pack. This should include notes about the area and local attractions and a map of the immediate area (all usually available free from your local tourist office), notes explaining how to get to the house, emergency contact numbers and instructions as to what to do if they are for any reason delayed.

Inside the property there should also be a house book. This should give much more information and recommendations about local attractions, restaurants and so on – collect as many local leaflets as you can – and a comprehensive list of contact numbers for use in the case of any conceivable emergency. The more personal recommendations you can give (best bakery, best café, etc.), the more people will appreciate it. Provide some space in it too, or in a separate book, to be used as a visitors' book. As well as being a useful vehicle for obtaining feedback, this builds up positive feelings about your home, and can also be a means of making future direct contact with visitors who might have been supplied by an agency.

• **Welcome**: It is best if someone is present, either at the property or at a nearby house, to welcome your guests when they arrive. They can sort out any minor problems or any particular requirements of the guests. You should also consider leaving a **welcome pack**: make sure that basic groceries such as bread, milk, teabags, coffee, sugar and a bowl of fruit are left in the house to welcome your guests on arrival. A bottle of wine always goes down well, too!

• **Cleanliness**: The property must be spotlessly clean, above all in the kitchen and bathroom. You will probably employ a local cleaner, to whom you may well need to give some training and/or a detailed schedule, as people's expectations of rented accommodation are often higher than their expectations in an ordinary home.

• **Kitchen**: This must be modern, even if traditional in style, and everything should (of course) work. The fridge should be as large as you can manage since, in hot weather, your tenants will need to keep a wide range of things chilled. The kitchen should have a microwave, and you should check regularly that there is sufficient cutlery and cooking equipment and that it is all in good condition. A cookbook giving local recipes is a nice extra touch.

• **Bathroom**: Or, these days, more usually bathrooms – en-suite bathrooms for each bedroom are the ideal. Spanish bathrooms will usually have a bidet. Make sure there is soap in the bathrooms, and guests will also much prefer it if you provide towels as part of the service.

• **Laundry facilities**: A washing machine and drier are now fairly standard.

• **Bedrooms**: These should have adequate storage space. Most importantly, they should also have clean and comfortable beds, as nothing except dirtiness produces more complaints than uncomfortable beds. If you can afford it, it is a very good idea to bring good-quality, high-strength mattresses from Britain, where they are much easier to find, rather than buy locally and get the cheaper mattresses most widely available in Spain, which, as anyone who has stayed regularly in Spanish hotels below four-star level knows, tend to be uncomfortably soft. Your tenants will appreciate it, and the mattresses will need replacing much less frequently. Beds should be protected from obvious soiling by the use of removable mattress covers, which should be changed with each change of tenant. All clients will much prefer it if you supply bedding as part of your service rather than expecting them to bring their own.

• **Living areas**: Furniture and upholstery should be comfortable and in good condition; the style is a matter of personal preference, but a 'local' style is often attractive. Also make sure that sofa covers, etc. are fairly hard wearing and easily washable. There should be adequate means of cleaning, including a working and regluarly emptied vacuum cleaner.

• **Heating**: An effective heating system, covering the whole house, is essential even in warmer regions – weather is unpredictable, and you may well want to get winter lets.

• **Air-conditioning**: While it is a substantial asset, air-conditioning is not yet considered obligatory except in the most expensive lettings, and can be expensive both to run and maintain. In more basic lets it's probably best avoided.

• **Swimming pool**: A pool is always highly desirable, and in just about any area it will significantly increase your letting potential. A pool should be of reasonable size and well maintained, but need not be heated.

Marketing the Property

Properties do not let themselves, and anyone wishing to let their Spanish home at all regularly will have to do some marketing. In the early years you will have to do more than later on, because you will have no existing client base. As in any other business, the cheapest type of marketing is catching repeat clients, so a bit of money spent on making sure the property lives up to, or exceeds, their expectations (and so brings them or their friends back next year) is probably the best spend that you will make. Otherwise, there seems to be no correlation between the amount spent on marketing and the results achieved, and this is a field in which much money spent is often wasted.

The key points are to choose the method of marketing most appropriate to your property and circumstances and to follow up all leads generated at once. Contact them again after a couple of weeks to see if they have made their minds up. Send them your details again next year at about the same time, as they are likely to be taking another holiday. Remember that your marketing is only as good as the quality of the response you give to people making enquiries. You will probably do better spending less money on advertising and paying more attention to following up the leads that you have actually generated than anything else.

If you have decided to let your property yourselves, there are several well-tried means of publicising your property in the UK and Irish market, which are outlined below. If you also wish to tap into the Spanish market, you can advertise it in local papers, and especially in advertising magazines and websites like **www.segundamano.es** (*see* pp.130–31). However, your Spanish must be good enough for you to handle all enquiries, and many people in this situation prefer to use a letting agency (*see* 'Management Agencies', pp.302–4).

Directories and Web Directories

If your property is pretty then you are likely to get good results from the various directories and joint information and booking services that deal with self-catering properties to let in Spain. Most have moved over partly – or, increasingly, completely – from producing brochures and magazines to being website-based. Some provide a full booking service and take part in managing lettings while others, which are cheaper to use and give owners more freedom of manoeuvre, just give you space for photographs and a presentation of your property.

The travel industry directory websites **www.travelgate.co.uk** and **www.uk-villasabroaddirectory.co.uk** have lists of the many such companies now operating. Some of the most useful are the monthly magazine *Private Villas*, **t** (020) 8329 0120, **www.privatevillas.co.uk**, though advertising is handled via the sister site **www.daltonsholidays.com**; **Owners Direct, t** (01372) 722708, **www. ownersdirect.co.uk**; and the **Owners' Syndicate, t** (020) 7801 9804, **www. owners syndicate.co.uk**, all joint 'noticeboard' services for independent owners looking for tenants.

Private owners with private homes in Spain and France can also let properties through **Brittany Ferries Holidays** at **www.brittanyferries.co.uk**. Click first on 'Property Owners Travel Club', then on the 'Letting Your Property' button and finally on 'Holiday Homes, Our Managed Letting Service', where you find information about their service. More simply, send an e-mail enquiry to **holidayhomes@brittany-ferries.com**. Advertisers will also get special discounts on Plymouth–Santander ferries.

Advertising in this way only really works if the services are inexpensive, because a private owner with only one property to let has only one opportunity of letting each week, and so a directory that produces, say, 50 enquiries for the first week in July is not particularly helpful. Six months' web space on the Owners Direct site currently costs £65 plus three extra months free for first-time private advertisers; a full year, with three extra months, is £100.

Press Advertising

The problem with traditional advertising is its scattergun approach and, usually, its cost. As mentioned above, if you have just one property you only need a very small number of responses, and you cannot afford to pay a large amount in advertising fees for each week's let. Except for very upscale properties, advertising in the magazines that specialise in Spanish properties (see 'Press Sources', pp.127–9) is too expensive, and is mainly used by property companies and agencies. For individual owners, better places to advertise are, in the UK, the small-ad pages in newspaper travel sections such as the Sunday Times and, in Spain, the expat-orientated free magazines like 123 Property News. According to your target market, apparently unconnected special-interest magazines – literary, historical, Private Eye – can be a good idea, because your ad doesn't get swamped by 20 others.

On the other hand, you can also get very good results very cheaply by putting a card on your local supermarket notice board.

Personal Website and E-mail

The Internet offers tremendous opportunities for bringing a specialist niche product – such as an isolated villa – to the attention of a vast audience at very little cost. For no extra effort, it can allow people to find out about your Spanish home not just in the UK and Spain but in Scandinavia, Germany, the USA and other places that will surprise you. For independent owners offering property for holiday lets, it is strongly recommended that they set up their own website. For many, it quickly becomes their primary means of finding new tenants.

Your website will be your principal brochure, with space to show lots of pictures and other information about the house and the area around it. It is much cheaper to have someone print off a copy of this brochure from their own computer than it is for you to have it printed and sent by post.

If you don't know enough about the web to design a site yourself, it is now quite easy to find web designers around Spain, as it is everywhere else, who will create the site for you at low cost. It is very important be listed on some of the many Spanish property websites that can be found around the internet, links to which are either free or quite cheap, otherwise a small, private site will be just lost among the thousands of search results that come up when somebody looks for rental properties via, say, Google. You will soon find out which ones work for you and which ones don't; some of the best are those that are region- ally based, since people find it easy to get to what they want with fewer irrelevancies.

As well as a publicity medium, the website can also be a means of taking book- ings. You will have to decide how sophisticated an electronic booking system you want, or whether you are happy just to use the Internet to make contacts. Actually taking money through the web by credit card is far too expensive an option for most independent property-owners, so you will have to receive payments by more traditional means. Your website will, of course, have your e-mail address on it. Even if you do not set up a website, anyone letting out property with any consistency really should have e-mail, which is more and more people's favourite means of making such bookings. And remember to check it at least once a day.

Doing Deals

There are two kinds of 'mutual aid' deals that can be helpful to independent owners, both of which work best in slightly out-of-the-way areas. If your prop- erty, for example, is in a rural area where there is somebody offering a very local tourist service, it can be a good idea to make contact with them and to try to arrange for the people starting their hikes or attending their cookery or craft or courses to stay over in your property. This can significantly increase your lettings, particularly off-peak. If you agree to pay the tour organisers a commis- sion of around 20 per cent you will still be well ahead.

The second type of 'deal' involves co-operating with other people in the area who let properties, assuming there are any. One of the frustrations of marketing your property is when you have four lots of people who all want to rent it for the same week. Getting together with others in a mutual assistance group will allow you to pass excess lettings to each other.

Your Own Contacts

All these methods aside, personal, direct contacts are still among the best means you have of marketing a property in Spain. If you want to use a second home for a fair amount of time yourself, you will perhaps only want to let it for, say, 25 weeks each year. Given that many people will take it for two weeks or more, you will probably therefore only be looking for around 10 to 15 lettings, and if you put the word out, these should not be hard to put together from friends and from friends of friends.

Among the people who have an advantage in 'marketing' a holiday home in this way are those who work for large organisations, and can publicise it internally. Even without people from work, most owners will be able to find enough friends, neighbours and relatives to let a nice property in Spain for 10 weeks each year, which will leave only a relatively small number of tenants to be found by other means. With most of your lettings you will also have the additional advantage of knowing the people who are going to rent the property, which reduces the risk that they will damage it or fail to pay you.

When letting to family and friends, or indeed work colleagues, you will have to learn how to raise the delicate issue of payment. Given that you are not going to be running up any marketing costs and, probably, not much in the way of property management costs, you should be able to offer them a bargain price and still generate as much income as you would have done by letting through an agency. Make sure that you address this issue when you accept the booking, as doing so later can be very embarrassing.

Management Agencies

On the whole, the people who are most successful over time in letting their second homes are those who find their tenants themselves. This, however, requires a level of commitment that many people simply cannot afford. For non-resident owners who cannot dedicate much time to keeping track of their property, it is far simpler to use a local letting agency. Agencies – or at least good ones – will be able to attract local, Spanish clients as well as foreigners of different nationalities. You will have to pay them a sizeable commission (typically 17.5 to 20 per cent of your letting income, plus VAT at 7 per cent of the commission), but they will argue that this will be recovered by the extra lettings that they make during the holiday season. This may or may not be true. Larger agencies, who publish glossy brochures, are best contacted well in advance, such as early autumn in the previous year, if you want a property to be advertised for the summer; smaller agencies will take on properties at any time.

In all the resort areas there are many agencies that manage and let holiday properties, many of them local estate agencies, and there are also many that operate from Britain. If you decide to use one of them, the choice of agency is critical. Some are excellent, both in Spain and in the UK, and some are crooks, and between the two there are some that are just bumbling and inefficient. At worst, agencies may hold on to rents for long periods of time, or let your house while telling you it is empty and pocket the rent themselves; others may just charge a 'signing-on fee' to agree to put your property on your books and then do nothing to let it. In the past, many have assumed that foreign owners a thousand miles away will never find out about anything they do. This is a field where it is important for owners to be cautious and demanding.

Selecting an Agency

When selecting a letting agency, there are various checks to make.

- **If it is a Spanish agency, find out whether staff are professionally qualified and experienced. Many such services are offered as an adjunct to estate agencies, who should have qualified staff.**

- **Check the premises, and make an initial judgement on whether they seem welcoming and efficient, and if there's evidence of significant letting activity.**

- **Check on how capable staff seem to be, especially if you're making contact before actually buying your property. Ask what type of property they think would be best for letting purposes in this area, how many weeks' rental they think you will be able to obtain, and how much they think they would generate for you after deduction of expenses and their own fees.**

- **Ask for references, preferably from other overseas clients, and follow them up. Phone other owners if you can, and ask whether they are happy with the overall performance of the agency and whether the financial projections given to them have been met.**

- **Take a look at what marketing they do. If they are reliant only on passing trade then, except in the most exceptional areas, they will not get good results.**

- **Ask to see a sample information pack sent to a potential client. You will be able to judge a lot from this; think about whether this is the image you want to give of your property.**

- **Ask to inspect two or three properties that they are already managing. If they are dirty or badly cared-for, then so will yours be, and it will not let.**

- **Check carefully what kind of contract they offer you; unless you are familiar with Spanish law it is sensible also to get it checked by your lawyer before you sign, as some give you far more rights than others (many also include restrictive conditions, such as insisting that you let the property in July and August, which you may not wish to accept). Make sure that the** contract entitles you to full reports showing when the property was let and for what money; these must give a breakdown week by week, not by quarter- or half-year. You should also insist on a full breakdown of all expenses incurred in connection with the property, and ensure the contract gives you the right to dismiss the agency at fairly short notice.

Controlling the Agency

After you have appointed a letting agency, you need to keep a check on what they are doing; you may not wish to seem so suspicious, but there are too many horror stories around to allow anyone to be complacent.

- **Check the reports you receive from the agency and check that the money you receive corresponds to the amounts shown in them.**
- **Let the agency know, in the nicest possible way, that you and all of your friends in the area check each other's properties every time you are there, and compare notes about which are occupied and the performance of your letting agencies. If they believe you, this is a good deterrent to unauthorised lettings.**
- **Phone the property every week. If someone answers the phone make a note, and make sure that there is income shown for the week of the phone call.**
- **From time to time, have a friend pose as a prospective customer and send for an enquiry pack.**
- **If you get the chance, call to see the property without warning to check its condition.**

Formalising the Letting

If you let through an agency, they will draw up fairly standardised rental contracts for you and your tenants to sign. If you handle all your lettings yourself, unless you let only to family and close friends, it is still advisable for you to give tenants a written contract in line with Spanish law, the 'model' for which should preferably be drawn up, with the advice of your lawyer, when you first begin letting.

For the basics of rental agreements in Spain, *see* 'Renting Before, or Instead of, Buying', pp.142–4. From the point of view of landlords, the safest type of letting is a short holiday let of furnished property, or *contrato por temporada* or *arrienda de temporada*. To be classified as furnished the property must have all the basic items required to live in a home, such as, at least, a bed, a cooker, a table, a refrigerator, some chairs and so on. A place without these things could be treated as an unfurnished property, in which case, from the legal point of view, the tenant could claim that there was a *de vivienda*, or permanent, rental contract, potentially giving them the right to an extension after the contract's first term. Otherwise, a holiday letting is one that takes place in a recognised holiday season, which obviously means something different in a ski resort than in Marbella.

The Letting Agreement

A properly drafted tenancy agreement will take into account all these factors and protect you in the event of a dispute with your tenants and, in particular, if any of them wish to stay on at the end of the tenancy. If your property forms part of a *comunidad de propietarios* (*see* pp.115–17 and 171–2) your tenants will also have to agree to abide by the rules of the community, and this should be indicated in the rental agreement. Tenants should be supplied with a copy of these rules, or at least of the part of them that is relevant. In the rental contract you should also stipulate what things are going to be covered by your insurance and what are not – typically, for example, tenants' personal possessions would not be covered under your policy.

For information on taxation of rental income, *see* **Financial Implications**, 'Taxation', pp.190–207.

References

Dictionary of Useful and Technical Terms

A plazo corto	(In the) short term
Abogado	Lawyer or solicitor
Abono de transportes (semanal/ mensual/anual)	(Weekly/monthly/annual) travel pass
Acequia	Water channel; ditch
Acristalado	Glassed over, glazed
Acueducto	Aqueduct, or state-supplied water
Administrador de fincas	Administrator of an apartment building or communal property
Adosado	Semi-detached, usually in modern suburban developments
Aduana	Customs
Agencia Estatal de Administración Tributaria	Tax authorities, usually called 'Hacienda'
Agencia inmobiliaria	Estate agency
Agente de propiedad inmobiliaria	Estate agent – if qualified s/he should have a title of API
Agricultor/granjero	Farmer
Agua	Water
Aire acondicionado	Air-conditioning
Albañil	Bricklayer, handyman or mason
Albergue	Hostel
Alcalde	Mayor
Aldea	Hamlet or small town
Alfombra	Carpet
Alicatado	Tiling (in a bathroom or kitchen)
Alimentos	Food shop selling cheese, cold meats and canned goods
Alojamiento	Lodging
Alojar(se)	To take a room/lodge
Alquilar	To rent
Amortizar	Reducing debts, like a mortgage, in smaller payments
Amueblado	Furnished
Anexos	Attachments or building extensions
Antiguo/a	Old or antique
Aparcamiento/Parking	Car park
Aparejador	Architectural engineer
Apartamento de vacaciones	Holiday apartment
Apartamento/piso	Apartment or flat
Apartamento/piso amueblado	Furnished apartment/flat
Apartamento/piso de lujo	Exclusive apartment/flat
Apartamento/piso dúplex	Duplex apartment/flat
Apartamento/piso en alquiler	Apartment/flat for rent
Aparthotel	A room or flat within a hotel complex for rent weekly or monthly
Árboles	Trees

Archivo municipal	Municipal archives
Archivo	Archive/filing cabinet
Arco	Archway
Armario	Cupboard/wardrobe/closet
Armarios empotrados	Fitted or built-in wardrobe
Arquitecto	Architect
Arras	Deposit paid when making a pre-purchase contract (*contrato de opción de compra*). If the buyer backs out, the deposit is lost; if the seller backs out, he must pay the buyer double
Arroyo	Stream
Artesano	Artisan, craftsman
Ascensor	Lift/elevator
Asegurar	To insure
Asesor fiscal	Tax consultant
Ático	Top-floor apartment with terrace; penthouse
Autobús	Public bus
Autopista	Motorway, highway
Ayuntamiento	Municipality or town hall
Ayuntamiento/Consistorio	Town hall
Azotea	Flat roof, especially on top of an apartment block, often used as a drying area or for sunbathing
Azulejos	Tiles
Balcón	Balcony
Banco	Bank
Bañera	Bath
Baño/cuarto de baño	Bathroom or toilet
Barbacoa	Barbecue
Barrio	Neighbourhood
Barro cocido	Terracotta
Basura	Rubbish, trash, garbage
Biblioteca	Library
Bien situado/comunicado	Good location
Billete(s)	Ticket(s)
Bodega/enoteca	Wine merchant or shop
Bodega	Storage cellar or wine cellar; can also be a bar/wine shop
BOE (Boletín Oficial del Estado)	State publication with all new legislation; most *comunidades autónomas* now publish their own at regional level
Bombilla	Light bulb
Bombona	Butane gas canister/bottle
Bosque	Woods/forest
Buen estado	Good condition
Buena presencia	Something that gives off a good impression
Buhardilla	Top-floor apartment under eaves, sloping ceilings
Cabina telefónica	Telephone box/booth
Caja	Cash register/till

Cajero automático	Bank card or automatic teller machine (ATM)
Calcio	Limescale
Caldera	Water heater; boiler
Calefacción	Heating
Calefacción general	One main boiler heats a building and the apartment owner does not decide when it is turned on or off. Cost is divided between all inhabitants
Calefacción individual	Means a house has its own boiler and the owner can turn the heat off or on as desired. Owner pays for his/her individual use
Calle	Street, often written as C/ followed by street name
Calle mayor	Main street
Callejón	Narrow street
Cámara de comercio	Chamber of Commerce
Carnet de conducir	Driver's permit, licence
Carnicería	Butcher's shop
Carpintero/carpintería	Carpenter/carpenter's/carpentry/woodwork
Carretera	Highway, main road
Carretera de circunvalación	Ring road around a major city, such as Madrid or Barcelona
Casa	House; home
Casa de época	Old house; period home
Casa de huéspedes	Guest house
Casa rural	Rural house
Casa señorial	Exclusive house or property
Casa urbana	Urban property
Caserío	Country house
Casero/a	Landlord/landlady (slang)
Castillo	Castle
Catastro	Land registry
Censo	Census/electoral roll
Centro	Centre of a city
Centro histórico	Historic centre, the most expensive area
Cerámica	Ceramics
Cerrajero	Locksmith
Certificado	Certificate
Certificado de defunción	Death certificate
Certificado de empadronamiento	Certificate proving that a person resides or owns property in a given district, town or city
Certificado de fin de obra	Certificate issued by builder or architect on completion of work according to the plans
Certificado de matrimonio	Marriage certificate
Césped	Lawn
Chalet	Detached house; villa
Chalet semi-adosado	Semi-detached house, often modern
Ciclomotor	Moped
Circunscripción	Electoral district
Ciudad	Town or city
Ciudadanía	Citizenship
Cláusula condicional	Conditional clause

Coche/automóvil	Car
Cocina	Cooker; kitchen; cuisine
Cocina a gas	Gas cooker
Cocina americana	American-style fitted kitchen
Cocina-comedor	Kitchen-diner
Columna	Column
Comedor	Dining room
Comisaría (de la Policía Nacional)	Police station where you apply for a residency permit
Complejo residencial	Residential or housing complex
Compra	Purchase
Comprar al contado	To pay cash
Comprar sobre plano	Purchase of a property before it has been built, based on blueprints ('off plan')
Compraventa	Buying and selling
Comunidad	Community
Comunidad Autónoma	Autonomous community (Andalucía, Catalonia, etc.)
Condición	Condition
Construcción	Building
Constructor(a)	Builder; building company
Contable	Accountant
Contactos	Contacts
Contador	Meter for utilities
Contrato	Contract
Contrato de arrendamiento/ alquiler	Rental or lease agreement
Contrato de compraventa	Sales contract
Contrato de opción de compra	Option contract showing intention to purchase
Contrayente	Contracting party
Convivir	Living together, sharing an apartment
Corrala	Tenement apartments that look on to an interior courtyard
Correos	Post office; postal service in general
Cortijo	Country estate/country house/farmhouse
Cristal	Glass (window pane)
Cuadro	Painting
Cuarto	Room
Cuarto de baño	Bathroom
Cuenta	Bill
Cuenta corriente	Current account
Cuenta en divisas	A bank account in foreign currency
Cúpula	Dome
Declaración de obra nueva	Declaration of a new property development made before a notary
Declaración de renta	Annual or quarterly tax declaration
Decorador	Interior decorator
Demanda	Lawsuit
Demanda de desahucio	Eviction order

Demandar (a alguien)	To sue (someone)
Denuncia	Police report
Departamento de extranjeros	Foreign residents' department, often in a town hall
Dependencia	Outbuildings
Depósito (de agua)	Water storage tank
Desalajo/desahucio	Eviction
Descuento	Discount
Desván/altillo	Attic/loft
Día	Day
Día de descanso/asueto	Rest day; day off
Dirección	Address
Disponible	Available
Divisas	Foreign currency
DNI (Documento Nacional de Identidad)	National Identity Document; Spanish citizens must always carry theirs with them
Doble cristal	Double glazing
DOC (Denominación de Origen Controlada)	Official level of quality for a regional wine that is governed by geographic origin
Documento de identidad	Identity documents
Domiciliación (de pagos)	Standing order used for paying bills from a bank account
Domicilio	Address; official residency as registered at the local council
Dormitorio	Bedroom
Dormitorio principal	Master bedroom
Ducha	Shower
Dúplex	Duplex/maisonette
Edificio	Building
EFE	Spain's news or information agency
Electricista	Electrician
Electrodomésticos	Appliances
El Mundo	Daily newspaper, with the second-highest circulation in Spain
El País	Spain's leading daily newspaper
Empadronarse	To register on the Padrón Municipal (*see* Padrón)
Empapelado	Wallpaper (existing)
Empapelar	To wallpaper
(En) primera línea de playa	Facing the sea directly, on the beachfront
Enchufado	Plugged in, but also meaning having friends in high places
Enchufe	Plug
Entrada	Entrance; down payment on a property, not returnable if the buyer backs out; ticket for cinema, theatre, bull-ring, football stadium, etc.
Equipado	Equipped
Ertxaintxa (Euskadi)	Autonomous Police Force in the Basque Country
Escaleras	Stairs
Escalinata	Stairway
Escrituras	Notarised deeds of sale

Establo	Stable (for animals)
Estación de autobuses	Bus/coach station
Estación de ferrocarril	Train station
Estado	Condition, state
Estancia	Room
Estanco	State-licensed tobacco store where you buy cigarettes, bus tickets, phone cards and postage stamps, and obtain tax forms
Estatutos	Statutes, rules or bye-laws governing the internal running of a company/community development
Estructura	Structure
Estructuralmente	Structurally
Estudio	One-room apartment/studio apartment
Euro	Spain's currency (€)
Explotación agrícola	Working farm
Extrarradio	Suburbs/surrounding areas
Fachada	Façade
Factura	Invoice, bill
Farmacia	Pharmacy
Ferretería	Hardware store
Ferry	Ferry boat
Fianza	Deposit paid on renting a flat
Finca	Estate or farm – refers to any property and the area it occupies
Finca urbana	Urban estate; land apartment blocks are built on
Fonda	Inn
Fontanería	Plumbing
Fontanero	Plumber
Fosa séptica	Septic tank
Frigorífico	Refrigerator
Fuente	Fountain or spring
Galería	Covered walkway, or arcade
Garaje	Garage
Garaje doble	Double garage
Garantía	Guarantee
Garantizar	To guarantee
Gasolinera	Petrol station
Gastos	Expenses
Gastos de comunidad	Community fees paid for common services and maintenance
Gastos excluidos	Expenses, such as utilities, not included
Gestor	Go-between used for accounting purposes, tax declarations and all types of red tape
Gestoría	*Gestor*'s office
Grande	Large
Granero	Barn (for crops)
Granja	Farm
Guardia Civil	Civil Guard, customs/highway patrol

Habitable	Habitable
Habitación	Room
Habitación doble	Double room (twin beds)
Habitación sencilla	Single room
Habitación/suite matrimonial	Room with queen-size bed
Hágalo-usted-mismo/bricolage	Do-it-yourself
Hall de entrada	Entrance way
Hectárea	Hectare
Herrero	Blacksmith
Hipoteca	Mortgage
Hogar/chimenea	Fireplace
Honorarios	Fees paid to a *gestor*, lawyer, estate agent, etc.
Horario	Business hours, schedule
Horario continuo	Non-stop business hours, no lunch break
Horno	Oven
Horno de leña	Wood-burning oven
Hospital	Hospital
Huerta	Vegetable garden or orchard
Huerto	Vegetable garden
Humedad	Humidity/damp, a common problem in old homes
Impuesto	Tax
Impuesto sobre Actividades Económicas	Business tax as paid by entrepreneurs and self-employed persons (now only payable with turnover in excess of €600,000 p.a.)
Impuesto sobre Actos Jurídicos Documentados	Broadly speaking, stamp duty, paid on all property transfers
Impuesto sobre Bienes Inmuebles (IBI)	Property tax paid annually
Impuesto sobre el Patrimonio	Wealth tax
Impuesto sobre el Patrimonio y la Renta de no Residentes	Tax on property owned by non-residents
Impuesto sobre el Valor Añadido (IVA)	Value added tax/VAT (varies according to item)
Impuesto sobre la Renta de las Personas Físicas (IRPF)	Personal income tax
Impuesto sobre Sociedades	Company tax
Impuesto sobre Transmisiones Patrimoniales (ITP)	Transfer tax, paid when buying a resale property
Independiente	Detached
Ingeniero	Engineer
Inmobiliaria	Estate agent's office
Inquilino	Tenant
Inspección	Inspection or survey of a property
Interior	Hinterland; also the inside of a house
Jardín	Garden
Jardinero	Gardener
Jornada	Working day
Juzgados	Courthouse

Ladrillo	Brick
Lago	Lake
Lavabo	Washbasin
Lavadora	Washing machine
Lavandería	Launderette
Lavavajillas	Dishwasher
Lechería	Dairy shop
Leña	Firewood
Ley	Law
Ley de arrendamientos urbanos	Law covering property rentals
Ley de costas	Law that covers construction in coastal areas
Libre	Unoccupied (e.g. a taxi, parking space, hotel room)
Librería	Bookshop
Libro de familia	Document (in book form) issued on registering the birth of a first child, consecutive births are noted on following pages
Licencia	Licence; can also mean a university degree
Licencia de apertura	Licence permitting a business to open and start operating
Licenciarse	To graduate
Llave	Key
Llave en mano	Ready to occupy, building that is finished
Lujo	Luxury
Luz	Light, often refers to electricity
Madera	Timber/wood
Manantial/fuente	Spring source of water
Mantenimiento	Maintenance
Mar	Sea
Mármol	Marble
Masía	A type of farmhouse found in Catalonia
Matricular	To register a car
Media pensión	Half-board, just room and breakfast
Médico	Doctor
Medidas	Size, measure, also means measures as in government action
Mensual	Monthly
Mensualidad	Monthly payment
Mercado	Market
Metro	Metro or underground service; ruler (measure)
Metros cuadrados	Square metres
Mobiliario	Fixed furnishings
Moqueta	Fitted carpet
Mossos d'Escuadra	Autonomous Police Force in Catalonia
Motocicleta	Motorbike
Mudanza	Removal
Mudar(se)	To move house
Muebles	Furniture
Multa	Fine (penalty)

Multipropiedad	Timeshare
Muro	Wall, surrounding a city or a property
NIE (Número de Identificación de Extranjero)	Foreigner's Identification Number (used for tax and banking purposes)
NIF (Número de Identificación Fiscal)	Personal taxpayer's number
Negociable	Negotiable
No residente	Non-resident of Spain
Notario	Notary public. Very important when buying property because s/he must oversee the signing and exchange of documents
Nuevo/a	New
Número de póliza	Insurance policy number
Obra	Work or construction. Can mean a building site
Ocasión/ganga	Bargain
Oferta de compra	Initial offer made on a property
Olivar	Olive grove
Olivo	Olive tree
Padrón Municipal	List of inhabitants in a district or town. Also used to make the electoral roll
Pagar a plazos	To pay in instalments
Pago	Payment
Palacio	Palace
Panadería	Bread shop
Panadería/Tahona/Horno de pan	Bakery
Papel del estado	Tax stamps, used for making any offical payments to the government, sold in '*estancos*'
Papelería	Stationery supplier
Para entrar	Ready to be lived in, or moved into
Parabólica	Satellite dish
Pared	Wall (internal)
Pared de carga	Supporting wall
Parque	Park
Partida de nacimiento	Birth certificate
Pasillo	Corridor or hallway
Pasos	Phone units or segments of time used to calculate phone bills
Pastelería	Pastry or cake shop
Patio	Courtyard
Pensión	Small hotel
Pequeño	Small
Permiso de obra	Planning permission
Permiso de trabajo	Work permit
Persianas	Blinds
Piedra	Stone
Pinar	Pine forest
Pintor (de brocha gorda)	Painter and decorator

Pintoresco	Picturesque, quaint, charming
Pintura	Painting
Piscina	Swimming pool
Placas de matrículu	Licence plates for a car
Plano/carta catastral	Zoning maps showing land ownership and use
Planta	Floor/storey of a building
Planta baja	Ground floor (first floor in the USA)
Playa	Beach
Playa particular	Private beach
Playa pública	Public beach
Plaza	Square
Plaza Mayor	Town square, usually where the *ayuntamiento* is situated
Plazos	Instalments, as when paying bills
Poder	Power of attorney, note attesting to the same
Policía Municipal/Local	Local or Municipal Police, responsible for traffic, parking and petty offences
Policía Nacional	National Police, responsible for crime prevention, public order and foreigners' questions
Portal	The main door of a communal building
Portería	The porter's quarters at the entrance of a building
Portero/Conserje	Porter, caretaker, doorman or woman
Pórtico	Portico, porch, arcade
Potencia	Electricity supply rating, measured in watts
Pozo	Well
Pozo negro	Cesspit
Prado	Meadow
Precio	Price
Préstamo	Loan
Presupuesto	Estimate of work costs, quotation
Prima	Insurance premium (also means female cousin)
Primera planta	First floor (second floor in USA)
Promotor	Developer (of a block of flats or housing complex)
Propiedad	Property
Proyecto	Project
Pueblo	Village or town
Pueblo blanco	Whitewashed village, typical of parts of Andalucía
Puente	Bridge (can also mean a long bank holiday weekend)
Puerta	Door
Puerta blindada	Armoured door with steel beams that extend onto the wall
Puerto	Port (sea port; local port on a computer)
Quiosco de prensa	Newspaper kiosk
RACE (Real Automóvil Club de España)	Spain's driving association, equivalent of the AA or the RAC
Radiadores	Radiators
Rascacielos	Skyscraper

Rebajas	Sales (end of season)
Recargo	Surcharge, extra charge
Recaudación Municipal	Local property tax office (for rates, etc.)
Recibo	Receipt
Reconstruir	To be reconstructed, re-built
Red Nacional de Ferrocarriles de España (RENFE)	Railway system
Reforma	Modernisation, renovation
Reformado	Modernised, 'done up'
Reformar	Refurbish, restore
Registro de Propiedad	Property registry
Rejas	Bars commonly fitted on ground-floor windows
Renta	Income
Renta antigua	Controlled rent on an old building, flat or house, often ridiculously low (new legislation is making these ever rarer)
Reparación/Arreglo	Repair
Reservación	Reservation, such as for a train or in a restaurant
Residencia	Residency permit or card
Residente	Resident of Spain
Responsabilidad civil a terceros	Third-party insurance
Restauración	Restoration
Restaurado	Restored
Restaurante	Restaurant
Restaurar	To restore
Río	River
Ruinas	Ruins
Rústico	Rustic
Sala	Room
Sala (de estar)	Sitting room
Salón	Living room
Se alquila	For rent
Se alquila/en alquiler	To rent/to let
Se alquilan habitaciones	Rooms to let
Se vende/en venta	For sale
Segunda residencia	Second home
Seguridad Social	Social Security
Seguro(s)	Insurance
Seguro de hogar	Home insurance
Seguro de viaje	Travel insurance
Seguros de coche	Car rental
Sello	Stamp (for letters)
Semi-adosado	Semi-detached house
Semi-amueblado	Partially furnished
Señal	Deposit, small amount of money paid to secure a transaction
Sociedad	Company
Solar	Empty plot of land (for building on)
Sótano	Basement

Subasta	Auction
Suelo de barro cocido	Terracotta floor
Suelo	Ground/floor (or building land)
Supermercado	Supermarket
Tabique	Non-supporting wall
Taller	Workshop
Taller del constructor	Builder's yard
Tarjeta de residencia	Residence permit
Tasa	Fee
Techo	Ceiling
Techo abovedado	Vaulted ceiling
Tejado	Roof
Telefónica	Previously the state-owned telephone company, now privatised and facing competition from other companies
Teléfono fijo	Landline phone
Teléfono móvil	Mobile phone
Terraza	Terrace
Terreno	Land (plot)
Testamento	Will, or last testament
Tierra cultivada	Cultivated land
Tintorería	Dry cleaners
Tipo de interés	Interest rate
Título de propiedad	Deed of property
Torre	Tower
Trabajo	Work
Trabajo negro	Illegal (black market) work
Transferencia de propiedad	Ownership change, such as when you sell a car
Traspaso	Lease or transfer of property or business
Trastero	Storage room, or broom cupboard
Trienios	Wage increase based on length of employment (three-year periods)
Turismo rural	Rural tourism, often involving staying in restored farm houses and with access to good walking, bird-watching or fishing areas
Último piso	Top floor
Urbanización	Purpose-built community housing development
Usufructo	A life interest (for example, in a property)
Valla	Fence
Vallado	Fenced in/off
Valor	Value
Valor catastral	Value of property for official and tax purposes
Vaso	Glass (for drinking)
Vecindad	Neighbourhood; neighbourliness
Vecino	Neighbour
Ventana	Window
Verdulería	Greengrocer's shop

Vespa/Escúter	Scooter
Vía	Wide street/throughfare
Vidrio	Glass (material)
Viejo	Old
Viga de madera	Wooden ceiling-beam
Viñedo	Vineyard
Visado	Visa for travel to Spain for non-EU citizens, for purposes of studying, working or living
Vista	View
Vistas a la montaña	Mountain views
Vistas al mar	Sea views
Vistas de la costa	Coastal views
Vivienda de protección official (VPO)	Low-income/subsidised housing
Vivienda(s)	Housing
Wáter/WC	Toilet
Zona tranquila	Quiet area
Zona verde	Green belt area where no building is allowed, park areas

Internet Vocabulary

Apagar el equipo	Shut down
Arroba	@
Barra	/ (forward slash)
Barra barra; doble barra	// (double forward slash)
Base de datos	Database
Borrar/Cancelar	Delete
Descifrar	Decode
Dirección de correo electrónico	E-mail address
Dos puntos	: (colon)
En línea	Online
Explorar	To browse
Guión	– (hyphen)
Guión bajo	_ (underline)
Punto	. (dot)
Red	Network
Reiniciar	Re-start
Seleccionar	To select
Usuario	User
Uve doble, uve doble, uve doble/tres uve dobles	www

Directory of Contacts

Major Resources in Britain and the Irish Republic

Spanish Embassy in the UK
39 Chesham Place, London SW1X 8SB
t (020) 7235 5555
f (020) 7259 5392
embespuk@mail.mae.es

Spanish Consulate General
20 Draycott Place, London SW3 2RZ
t (020) 7589 8989
f (020) 7581 7888
conspalon@mail.mae.es

Other Spanish Consulates in the UK
Manchester
Suite 1A, Brookhouse, 70 Spring Gardens, Manchester M2 2BQ
t (0161) 236 1262
f (0161) 228 7467
conspmanchester@mail.mae.es

Edinburgh
63 North Castle Street, Edinburgh EH2 3LJ
t (0131) 220 1843/220 1439/220 1442
f (0131) 226 4568
cgspedimburgo@mail.mae.es

Spanish Embassy In Ireland
17 Merlyn Park, Ballsbridge, Dublin 4, Republic of Ireland
t (01) 269 1640/269 2597/283 8827/283 9900,
f (01) 269 1854/269 2705
www.mae.es/embajadas/dublin

British Resources in Spain

British Chamber of Commerce Spain
Calle Bruc 21-1°-4ª, 08010 Barcelona
t 933 173 220
f 933 024 896
www.britchamberspain.com

British Embassy in Madrid
C/Fernando el Santo 16, 28010 Madrid
t 917 008 200
f 917 008 272
General enquiries: **presslibrary@ukinspain.com**
Public office hours: winter 9–1.30 and 3–6; summer 8.30–3

British Consulates, Vice-Consulates and Honorary Consuls in Spain

British Consulate in Alicante
Plaza de Calvo Sotelo 1-2°, Apdo. de Correos 564, 03001 Alicante
t 965 216 190/965 216 022
f 965 140 528
enquiries@alicante.fco.gov.uk
Public office hours: summer 8–2; winter 9–2

British Consulate-General in Barcelona
Avenida Diagonal 477-13°, 08036 Barcelona
t 933 666 200
f 933 666 221
bcon@cyberbcn.com; barcelonaconsulate@ukinspain.com
Public office hours: winter 9.30–2 and 4–5; summer 8.30–1.30

British Consulate in Benidorm (Honorary Vice-Consul)
(to be contacted through British Consulate in Alicante, *see* above)

British Consulate-General in Bilbao
Alameda de Urquijo 2-8°, 48008 Bilbao
t 944 157 600/944 157 711/944 157 722
f 944 167 632
mailto:bilbaoconsulate@ukinspain.com
Public office hours: winter 9–2 Mon–Thu; 9–1.30 Fri; summer 8.30–1.30

British Consulate in Cádiz (Honorary)
Unión Marítima Española S.A., Avda Ramón de Carranza 27,
11006 Cádiz
t 956 264 479
f 956 286 909
(initial enquiries to be directed to British Consulate, Málaga, *see* below)

British Vice-Consulate in Ibiza
Avda de Isidoro Macabich 45-1°, 07800 Ibiza
t 971 301 818/971 303 816
f 971 301 972
Public office hours: winter 9–3; summer 9–2

British Consulate in Gran Canaria
Edificio Cataluña, C/Luis Morote 6-3°, 35007 Las Palmas
t 928 262 508/928 262 658
f 928 267 774
Videoconference: t 928 490 150
laspalmasconsulate@ukinspain.com
Commercial Information, Canary Islands: **www.tradepartners.gov.uk/canary_islands**
Public office hours: 8–1.30

British Consulate-General in Madrid
Paseo de Recoletos, 7/9, 28004 Madrid
t 915 249 700
f 915 249 730
madridconsulate@ukinspain.com

British Consulate in Málaga
Edificio Eurocom, Bloque Sur, C/Mauricio Moro Pareto 2-2°,
29006 Málaga
Postal address: Apartado Correos 360, 29080 Málaga
t 952 352 300
f 952 359 211
malaga@fco.gov.uk
Public office hours: 8.30–1.30

British Vice-Consulate in Menorca
Sa Casa Nova – Cami de Biniatap 30
07720 Es Castell
t 971 363 373
f 971 354 690

British Consulate in Mallorca
Plaza Mayor, 3, D, 07002 Palma de Mallorca
t 971 712 445/971 716 048
f 971 717 520
consulate@palma.mail.fco.gov.uk
Public office hours: winter 9–2; summer 8.30–2

British Consulate in Tenerife
Plaza Weyler, 8-1°, 38003 Santa Cruz de Tenerife
t 922 286 863
f 922 289 903
tenerife.enquiries@fco.gov.uk
Commercial Information, Canary Islands: **www.tradepartners.gov.uk/canary_islands**
Public office hours: winter 8.30–3 and 3–6; summer Mon–Thurs 8–1.30, Fri 8–1

British Consulate in Seville (Honorary)
Apartado de Correos/P.O. Box 143, 41940 Tomares (Sevilla)
f 954 155 018
(initial enquiries to be directed to British Consulate, Málaga, *see* above)

British Consulate in Vigo (Honorary)
Plaza Compostela 23-6 Izq, 36201 Vigo
t 986 437 133
f 986 437 133
(initial enquiries to be directed to the consulate in Madrid)

Foreign Embassies in Spain

Australia
Australian Embassy
Plaza del Descubridor Diego de Ordas 3, 28003 Madrid
t 914 416 025
f 914 425 362
www.spain.embassy.gov.au

Australian Consulate, Barcelona
Gran Via Carlos III 98-9°, 08028 Barcelona
t 934 909 013
f 934 110 904
mailto:habitat@habitat-sa.es

Australian Consulate, Sevilla
C/Federico Rubio 14, 41004 Seville
t 954 220 971
f 954 211 145

Canada
Embassy of Canada
C/Núñez de Balboa 35, 28001 Madrid
t 914 233 250
f 914 233 251
www.canada-es.org

Republic of Ireland
Embassy of Ireland
Ireland House, Paseo de la Castellana, 46-4°, 28046 Madrid
t 915 763 500
f 914 351 677
embajadairlanda@terra.es

Honorary Vice-Consul, Barcelona
Gran Vía Carlos III 94, 08028 Barcelona
t 934 519 021
f 934 112 921

Honorary Consul, Málaga
Galerías Santa Mónica, Avenida Los Boliches 15, 29640 Fuengirola, Málaga
t 952 466 783
f 952 466 783

New Zealand
Embassy of New Zealand
Plaza de la Lealtad 2-3°, 28014 Madrid
t 915 230 226

United States of America
Embassy of the United States of America
C/Serrano 75, 28006 Madrid
t 915 872 200
f 915 872 303
www.embusa.es

United States Consulate in Barcelona
Paseo Reina Elisenda de Montcada 23, 08034 Barcelona
t 932 802 227
f 932 806 175
www.embusa.es

Removal Companies

Bishop's Move: Large company with nationwide coverage in Britain.
t (020) 7498 0300
www.bishopsmove.com

Bradshaw International: Manchester-based company.
t (0161) 877 5555
www.bradshawinternational.com

Burke Brothers: Wolverhampton;
t (01902) 714555
www.burkebros.co.uk

International Removals SC
t 00 34 952 235 054
www.internationalremovals-sc.com

Moving Solutions: London-based, and offering particularly personal service.
t (020) 8871 4466
www.moving-solutions.com

Roy Trevor: Cheshire-based company.
t (01925) 630441
www.roy-trevor.com

Union Jack Removals
t 0800 036 1011
www.union-jack-removals.co.uk

Resources and Reference

English-language Resources
English-language Press and Magazines

Absolute Marbella
Office 21, Edificio Tembo, C/Rotary Internacional s/n, 29660 Puerto Banús, Marbella
t 952 908 617
f 952 908 743

Madrid office: Palacio de Miraflores, Carrera de San Jerónimo 15-2°, 28014 Madrid
t 914 547 268
f 914 547 001

info@absolute-marbella.com
www.absolute-marbella.com

Costa del Sol News
Apartado 102, 29630 Benalmádena Costa, Málaga
t 952 449 250
f 952 568 712
costasol@dragonet.es

Costa Blanca News
Apartado 95, 03500 Benidorm, Alicante
t 966 812 841
www.costablanca-news.com

Costa Golf
Martínez Campos,16-2°D, 29001 Málaga
t 952 224 931
webmaster@servicios-gi.es

Diario Sur (English version)
Avenida Doctor Maraiton 48, 29009 Malaga
t 952 649 600
www.surinenglish.com

The Entertainer
Avda de la Constitucion, Edificio Fiesta, Planta Primera, Locales 32 & 33,
Arroyo de la Miel, 29630 Benalmadena, Malaga
t 952 561 245
www.theentertainer.net

The *Island Gazette*
C/Iriarte 43-2°, Puerto de la Santa Cruz, Tenerife

Lookout
Urb. Molino de Viento, C/Rio Darro, Portal 1, 29650 Mijas Costa
t 952 473 090
lookout@jet.es

The *Mallorca Daily Bulletin*
San Feliu, 25, Palma de Mallorca, Mallorca

The Reporter
Avenida Alcalde Clemente Dia Ruiz 37, Pueblo Lopez, 29640 Fuengirola
t 952 468 545
thereporter@alsur.es

A full list of all English-language publications in Spain can be found on the website www.spainview.com, which has many resources for journalists and editors, also.

Bookmark These

This list includes some of the many internet sites dedicated to property in Spain. It is by no means exhaustive as there are literally hundreds of them.

www.123propertynews.com	Website of the free *Costa del Sol* magazine.
www.4seasonsestates.com	Apart from property searches, this site also has information on legal questions, and more.
www.andalucia.com	Property information and much more, focused, as the name suggests, on Andalucía.
www.apartmentspain.co.uk	This site looks more to the cheaper end of the market.
www.buyspanish.co.uk	Much more than just property, this is a one-stop site for buying all things Spanish, including yachts and accessories, books, music and exclusive photographic work.
www.buyaspanishhome.com	Run in association with Fincas Corral, a Spanish estate agent, so has access to lots of local agents.
www.christianhenche-properties.com	This site specialises in country properties in the Costa del Sol area.
www.countrylife.co.uk	An offshoot of the well-known magazine which focuses on the upper end of the market.
www.expatfocus.com	This site does not have property advertising but offers lots of advice for expats worldwide, including those living in Spain.
www.findahomeinspain.com	Based on the Costa del Sol but with an office in Dublin, this site offers search facilities and lots of useful information about living in southern Spain.
www.headlands.co.uk	International property consultants specialising in Spain, Portugal and Cyprus.
www.hiddenspain.co.uk	This site goes beyond the well-trodden areas and helps buyers who are looking for out-of-the-way properties.
www.holiday-villa-spain.com	Information about rentals, purchases and legal aspects.
www.homesspain.co.uk/links.html	Mainly focused on Torrevieja, this site has many links to other useful sites.

www.idealspain.com	Legal and financial advice plus lots of links to property companies.
www.johntaylorspain.com	An upmarket property company with top-of-the-range properties, especially in Catalonia.
www.marbella-lawyers.com	A very useful site covering all aspects of law affecting the foreign resident in Spain, from conveyancing to drink-driving.
www.medbars.com	Residential and commercial properties on the Costa del Sol.
www.propertyfile.net/ international.htm	Information about renting and buying in the Canary Islands, the Costa del Sol, the Costa Blanca and many links to other sites.
www.propertyfinance4less. com/spain.html	Information on mortgages for those intending to buy in Spain, Portugal, France and Italy.
www.property-in-spain.com	The website of Harringtons International, property consultants specialising in all the *costas*.
www.property-spain.com	Costa del Sol specialists with information on apartments, townhouses and villas.
www.selectspain.com	Aimed at those looking for a villa or apartment close to golf facilities.
www.spain-info.com	General tourist information and property links for most of Spain.
www.spainrealestate.co.uk	Costa Blanca specialists; in order to view properties it is necessary to register.
www.spanish-living.com	Property and much, much more including information about shopping, sport, children, schools, and health and beauty.
www.spanishpropertyco.com	Lots of useful information about many aspects of living in Spain.
www.spanish-villas-for-sale.com	From two offices in Spain, in Marbella and Torrevieja, this company uses well-informed, locally based British agents.
www.vivendum.com	A joint site of thousands of local estate agents, in Spanish.
www.worldclasshomes.co.uk	A full range of services including inspection visits, advice on mortgages and more besides.

Miscellaneous

http://spanish.about.com/
www.spainexchange.com/
www.spain.info/Tourspain/?language=en
www.in-spain.info/index.htm

Spanish Holidays and Celebrations

Days celebrated nationwide are asterisked; others are celebrated almost everywhere.

1 January*	New Year's Day (*Año Nuevo*)
6 January	Epiphany or Kings' Day (*Reyes Magos*)
19 March	San José (*Día de San José*)
March/April*	Good Friday (*Viernes Santo*)
Easter (Holy Week)*	Semana Santa
Easter Monday	
1 May*	International Labour Day (*Fiesta del Trabajo*)
May/June	Corpus Christi, on the second Thursday after Whitsun
	Ascension Day (*Ascensión*) 40 days after Easter
15 August*	Assumption of the Virgin (*Asunción*)
12 October*	Virgin of Pilar, National Day (*Día de la Virgen del Pilar*)
8 December*	Immaculate Conception (*Inmaculada Concepción*)
25 December*	Christmas (*Navidad*)

Spain's fiestas are rightly famous all over the world. Every city, town and village has fiestas in honour of its patron saint, while many others are national events.

1 January	New Year's Day is quite quiet, but it is a public holiday.
5 January	In most parts of Spain there are processions to celebrate the coming of the Reyes Magos, the Three Kings, who will bring children presents the next morning. In Barcelona they come into the old port from the sea; in Alicante they arrive by helicopter; Madrid has a big, televised, procession with many floats.
6 January	*Reyes* or *Epifanía*. More important than Christmas for many families, this is when children receive their 'big' presents. Children who have not been good receive a piece of 'coal', usually made of sugar, though few really go without presents.
January– February	Carnival, *Carnaval* in Spanish, is an occasion for much dressing up and wild behaviour throughout Spain though the celebrations are most visually impressive in Cádiz and Tenerife, the latter said to be second only to Rio de Janeiro's.
March or April	Easter, *Semana Santa*, is a major fiesta throughout Spain though the most spectacular processions are to be found in the south, especially in Andalucía. Those thinking of attending the festivities in Sevilla are advised to book accommodation well ahead; similarly, Córdoba attracts many visitors at this time of year.
19 March	During the week leading up to San José, papier-mâché statues representing celebrities, usually caricatured none-too flatteringly, adorn the streets of Valencia. These are the famous *fallas* (fires in the local dialect). The statues are then burnt and there are impressive fireworks displays.
April	*Feria de Abril*, Seville. Coming a couple of weeks after the Easter festivities, the April Fair was originally a cattle market but is now a week-long party. Practically all of Seville's womenfolk wear the traditional flamenco dresses and the singing, dancing and sherry-drinking goes on well into the night.

23 April	*Sant Jordi*, the Catalan name for Saint George. On this day the tradition is for men to give their loved one a rose, and she should respond with a book. The tradition has spread to the rest of Spain nowadays, and bookshops do a roaring trade.
Whitsuntide	Every year, 50 days after Easter Sunday, there is a pilgrimage to the shrine of El Rocío in the village of Almonte, Huelva province. This colourful event attracts thousands of pilgrims, most dressed up in traditional Andalucían garb, who travel on foot, horseback or in horsedrawn carts – motor vehicles are not allowed. They camp in the nearby Doñana park, with merry-making for two days.
1 May	International Labour Day has lost much of its political significance nowadays, but the main trades union organisations CCOO and UGT hold large marches throughout Spain.
May/June	Corpus Christi is celebrated nationally but the processions and other festivities are especially colourful in Andalucia, Salamanca, Toledo and Barcelona.
24 June	San Juan, the shortest night of the year, is celebrated all over Spain, most spectacularly in Alicante where hundreds of bonfires are lit all over town. Jumping over the bonfire three times is an act of purification.
6 July	On this day the week-long San Fermín fiestas are declared open in Pamplona. The next day the fun and games begin, the main attraction being the bull-running, *encierros* – an exciting, if dangerous, spectacle. Many tourists get injured every year.
July–August	During the summer practically every village in Spain celebrates its local fiesta with concerts and dances held in the main square. In Buñol, Valencia, during the last week of August there is the famous Tomatina, a huge tomato-throwing battle.
15 August	The Assumption of the Virgin, *Asunción*, is celebrated nationally.
12 October	This is a national fiesta, sometimes called *El Día de la Raza* (Day of the Race) or *El Día de la Hispanidad* (Day of the Hispanic World) and the Virgin of Pilar is venerated, particularly in Zaragoza.
1 November	All Saints' Day, *Día de Todos los Santos*.
2 November	All Souls' Day, when people take flowers to the tombs of their dead relatives.
8 December	Immaculate Conception, *La Inmaculada Concepción*.
25 December	Christmas is celebrated with gifts and, more recently, a tree, but tradition calls for a *Belén*, a Nativity scene with handmade figurines. The big family meal usually takes place on Christmas Eve, *Noche Buena*; roast lamb is preferred to turkey and the festive sweet *par excellence* is turrón. Boxing Day is not a holiday.
31 December	New Year's Eve is celebrated with a large dinner with family and friends. As midnight approaches, the custom is to eat a grape with each chime of the clock, it is hard to eat all 12 but those who manage are assured good luck for the coming year.

Further Reading

This brief selection of the vast literature available on Spain in no way claims to be definitive. Some of the best books on travel, food, outdoor pursuits and general living in Spain, mainly written by long-term expat resident travel writers, are published by Santana Books (**www.santanabooks.com**). A good place to search for titles covering all things Spanish is **www.amazon.co.uk**.

Guides and Travel Literature

David Baird, *Excursions in Southern Spain*, Santana.
George Borrow, *The Bible in Spain*, Century (Travellers Series).
Gerald Brenan, *South From Granada*, Penguin Books.
Dana Facaros and Michael Pauls, *Spain*, Cadogan Guides.
Nick Inman and Clara Villanueva, *Excursions in Eastern Spain*, Santana.
Michael Jacobs, *Between Hopes and Memories*, Picador.
Juan Lalaguna, *Traveller's History of Spain*, Interlink Publishing Group.
Laurie Lee, *As I Walked Out one Midsummer Morning*, Penguin Books.
Cees Noteboom, *Roads to Santiago: Detours and Riddles in the Lands and History of Spain*, Harcourt Brace.
George Sands, *A Winter in Majorca*.
Alastair Sawday, *Special Places to Stay: Spain*, Alastair Sawday Publishing.
Hugh Thomas (ed), *Spain: The Best Travel Writing from the New York Times*.

Food and Wine

Pepita Aris, *Spanish Cooking*, Apple Press.
Pepita Aris, *The Spanish Kitchen*, Ward Lock.
Penelope Casas, *Tapas, The Little Dishes of Spain*, Alfred A. Knopf.
Keith Floyd, *Floyd on Spain*, Penguin Books.
Elisabeth Luard, *The 'La Ina' Book of Tapas*, Schuster.
Janet Mendel, *The Best of Spanish Cooking*, Santana.
Janet Mendel, *Cooking in Spain*, Santana.
Jan Read, *Spanish Wines*, Mitchell Beazley.
Jan Read and Maite Manjón, *The Wine and Food of Spain*, Wedenfeld & Nicholson.

History

Gerald Brenan, *The Spanish Labyrinth*, CUP.
Raymond Carr, *The Spanish Tragedy*, Weidenfeld.
Richard Fletcher, *Moorish Spain*, Phoenix.
Ian Gibson, *Federico García Lorca: A Life*, Faber & Faber.
George Orwell, *Homage to Catalonia*, Penguin.
Paul Preston, *Franco, a Biography*, Harper-Collins.
Hugh Thomas, *The Spanish Civil War*, Penguin.
Pierre Vilar, *Spain, a Brief History*.

Modern Spain

Raymond Carr, *Modern Spain*, Opus.
Robert Elms, *Spain, A Portrait After the General*, Mandarin.
John Hooper, *The New Spaniards*, Penguin Books.
Robert Hughes, *Barcelona*, Harvill.
Paul Preston, *The Triumph of Democracy in Spain*, Routledge.

Bullfighting

Carrie Douglas, *Bulls, Bullfighting and Spanish Identities*, University of Arizona Press.
A. L. Kennedy, *On Bullfighting*, Anchor Books/Doubleday.
Gary Marvin, *Bullfight*, Illinois University Press.
Adrian Shubert, *Death and Money in the Afternoon: A History of the Spanish Bullfight*, Oxford University Press.

Miscellaneous

Phil Ball, *Morbo, The Story of Spanish Football*, WSC Books.
Miguel de Cervantes (translation: John Rutherford), *Don Quixote*, Penguin Classics.
Lucía Graves, *A Woman Unknown*.
Chris Stewart, *Driving Over Lemons, A Parrot in the Pepper Tree*, Sort of Books.

Climate Chart

Average Monthly Temperatures °Centigrade (daily maximum and minimum) and Rainfall (monthly mm)

(Source: USA Today/US Met Office)

	Jan	Feb	Mar	Apr	May	Jun	Jul	Aug	Sep	Oct	Nov	Dec
Málaga												
max	17	15	18	20	24	27	30	30	28	23	20	17
min	11	7	12	11	14	17	20	20	18	16	13	10
rainfall	8	8	7	9	6	3	1	1	3	8	9	9
Alicante												
max	18	19	22	26	28	31	34	31	24	24	18	17
min	7	8	13	15	19	20	21	22	18	14	12	8
rainfall	9	6	9	9	6	6	3	5	7	8	10	7
Mallorca												
max	17	10	17	18	23	25	31	32	29	22	19	17
min	4	0	7	7	8	14	16	18	18	13	8	7
rainfall	13	11	9	11	5	5	3	4	9	11	11	10

	Jan	Feb	Mar	Apr	May	Jun	Jul	Aug	Sep	Oct	Nov	Dec
Madrid												
max	9	11	15	18	21	27	31	30	25	19	13	9
min	2	2	5	7	10	15	17	17	14	10	5	2
rainfall	8	8	10	9	7	6	3	3	4	7	8	9
Las Palmas												
max	13	14	16	18	21	25	28	28	25	21	16	13
min	6	7	9	11	14	18	21	21	19	15	11	8
rainfall	7	7	9	8	6	6	4	5	7	8	6	6
Tenerife												
max	21	22	23	22	23	24	27	28	27	26	24	22
min	16	16	16	16	17	19	21	22	22	21	19	17
rainfall	3	3	4	3	2	1	0	1	2	2	5	4

Regional Calling Codes

To call Spain from abroad, dial 00 34 and then the 9-digit number of the subscriber. The subscriber's number incorporates the regional code so is the same wherever you are dialling from in Spain, even from within that province. Thus all numbers in Madrid (and its surrounding province) begin with 91, followed by seven more digits. In the list that follows you will notice that some provinces' codes comprise three digits. This is because they actually coincide in the first two with a larger or more important province and the third digit is a 'sub-code' of that one. Thus 95 is the code for both Málaga and Seville, in Andalucía, but other Andalucian provinces take 95, then another number, plus six digits. Almería is, by this logic, 950, etc.

To call Gibraltar from within Spain, dial 9567 and the subscriber's number.

A Coruña	981 (may be referred to as La Coruña in some publications)
Álava/Araba	945 (includes the city of Vitoria, Gasteiz in Basque and capital of the Basque Autonomous Region, Euskadi)
Albacete	967
Alicante	96 (the city is also called Alacant by Catalan speakers. Note that the code is the same as that for Valencia)
Almería	950
Asturias	98 (includes both the cities of Gijón and Oviedo)
Ávila	920
Badajóz	924
Barcelona	93
Burgos	947
Cáceres	927
Cádiz	956
Cantabria	942
Castellón de la Plana	964
Ceuta	956 (North African enclave)
Ciudad Real	926

Córdoba	957
Cuenca	969
Girona	972
Granada	958
Guadalajara	949
Guipúzcoa/Guipuzkoa	943 (includes the city of San Sebastián, Donostia in Basque)
Huelva	959
Huesca	974
Illes Balears	971 (the name of the Balearic Isles in Catalan, which is spoken there)
Jaén	953
La Rioja	941 (includes the city of Logroño)
Las Palmas	928
León	987
Lleida	973 (this city is referred to as Lérida by Castilian speakers)
Lugo	982
Madrid	91
Málaga	95
Melilla	95 (North African enclave)
Murcia	968
Navarra	948
Ourense	988 (may be spelt 'Orense' in some publications)
Palencia	979
Pontevedra	986
Salamanca	923
Santa Cruz de Tenerife	922
Segovia	921
Seville	95 (note it is the same as Málaga)
Soria	975
Tarragona	977
Teruel	978
Toledo	925
Valencia	96 (note it is the same as Alicante)
Valladolid	983
Vizcaya/Bizkaia	94 (includes the city of Bilbao, Bilbo in Basque)
Zamora	980
Zaragoza	976

Post Codes

All Spanish post codes consist of five digits. The first two of those are present in practically all codes in a given province and are then followed by three more digits. Thus, all Madrid postcodes begin with 28 (+ three more digits), all Barcelona codes begin with 08 (+ three more digits) etc. In larger cities and provincial capitals, a code in which the first two digits are followed by a zero usually indicates an address within the provincial capital, the first two followed by a number greater than one onwards usually indicates locations outside the provincial capital. Some provinces, for reasons of proximity, have a few outlying villages with a code corresponding to the neighbouring province.

In the following table, the first two digits only are given and the more important exceptions are indicated. Names in co-official languages are indicated in italics.

Province	Provincial Capital (*where different from the province name*) and other main cities	First two digits in provincial code:
A Coruña	This province also includes the city of **Santiago de Compostela** which is the capital of the Galician Autonomous Community.	15---
Álava/*Araba*	Vitoria/*Gasteiz*	01---
Albacete		02---
Alicante/*Alacant*		03---
Almería		04---
Asturias	Oviedo/Gijón/Avilés	33---
Ávila		05---
Province	Provincial Capital (*where different from the province name*) and other main cities	First two digits in provincial code:
Badajoz	This province also includes the city of **Mérida** which is the capital of the Autonomous Community of Exremadura.	06---
Barcelona		08---
Burgos		09--- (Plus some beginning with **26---, 34---, 39--- 42---,** villages bordering on the provinces of La Rioja, Palencia, Cantabria and Soria respectively).
Cáceres		10---
Cádiz		11---
Cantabria	Santander	39---
Castellón de la Plana/ *Castelló de la Plana*		12---
Ceuta (North African enclave)		51---
Ciudad Real		13---
Córdoba		14---
Cuenca		16---
Gerona/*Girona*		17---
Granada		18---
Guadalajara		19--- (plus one, 28190, bordering on Madrid province)
Guipúzcoa/*Guipuzkoa*	San Sebastián/*Donostia*	20---
Huelva		21---

Province	Provincial Capital (*where different from the province name*) and other main cities	First two digits in provincial code:
Huesca	Jaca	22---
Islas Baleares/*Illes Balears*	Palma de Mallorca/Mahón (*Maó*)/Ibiza (*Eivissa*)	07--- (*Maó*) 077---
Jaén		23---
La Rioja	Logroño	26---
Las Palmas de Gran Canaria		35---
León		24---
Lérida/*Lleida*		25--- (except several villages bordering on Barcelona province, beginning 08---).
Lugo		27---
Madrid		28---
Málaga		29---
Melilla		52---
Murcia	Murcia/Cartagena	30---
Navarra	Pamplona	31--- (plus one, **50686**, a village bordering on Zaragoza province).
Orense/*Ourense*		32---
Palencia		34---
Pontevedra	Pontevedra Vigo	36---
Salamanca		37---
Santa Cruz de Tenerife		38---
Segovia		40---
Sevilla		41---
Soria		42---
Tarragona		43---
Teruel		44---
Toledo		45---
Valencia		46---
Valladolid		47---
Vizcaya/*Bizkaia*	Bilbao/*Bilbo*	48---
Zamora		49---
Zaragoza		50--- (Plus some beginning with **22---, 42--- and 44---**, villages bordering on Huesca, Soria and Teruel provinces respectively).

Appendices

Appendix 1

Checklist – Do-it-yourself Inspection of Property

Task   ✓

Title – check that the property corresponds with its description:
    Number of rooms
    Plot size

Plot
    Identify the physical boundaries of the plot
    Is there any dispute with anyone over these boundaries?
    Are there any obvious foreign elements on your plot such as pipes,
        cables, drainage ditches, water tanks, etc.?
    Are there any signs of anyone else having rights over the property –
        footpaths, access ways, cartridges from hunting, etc.?

Garden/Terrace
    Are any plants, ornaments, etc. on site not being sold with the property?

Pool – is there a pool? If so:
    What size is it?
    Is it clean and algae-free?
    Do the pumps work?
    How old is the machinery?
    Who maintains it?
    What is the annual cost of maintenance?
    Does it appear to be in good condition?

Walls – stand back from property and inspect from outside:
    Any signs of subsidence?
    Walls vertical?
    Any obvious cracks in walls?
    Are walls well pointed?
    Any obvious damp patches?
    Any new repairs to walls or repointing?

Roof – inspect from outside property:
    Does roof sag?
    Are there missing/slipped tiles?
    Do all faces of roof join squarely?
    Lead present and in good order?

Guttering and Downpipes – inspect from outside property:
    All present?
    Securely attached?
    Fall of guttering constant?
    Any obvious leaks?
    Any recent repairs?

Checklist – Do-it-yourself Inspection of Property (*cont.*)

Task   ✓

Enter Property
Does it smell of damp?
Does it smell musty?
Does it smell of dry rot?
Any other strange smells?

Doors
Signs of rot?
Close properly – without catching?
Provide proper seal?
Locks work?

Windows
Signs of rot?
Close properly – without catching?
Provide proper seal?
Locks work?
Excessive condensation?

Floor
Can you see it all?
Does it appear in good condition?
Any sign of cracked or rotten boards?

Under floor
Can you get access under the floor?
If so, is it ventilated?
Is there any sign of rot?
How close are joists?
Are joist ends in good condition where they go into walls?
What is maximum unsupported length of joist run?
Is there any sign of damp or standing water?

Roof Void
Is it accessible?
Is there sign of water entry?
Can you see daylight through the roof?
Is there an underlining between the tiles and the void?
Is there any sign of rot in timbers?
Horizontal distance between roof timbers
Size of roof timbers (section)
Maximum unsupported length of roof timbers
Is roof insulated – if so, what depth and type of insulation?

Checklist – Do-it-yourself Inspection of Property (*cont.*)

Task ✓

Woodwork

    Any sign of rot?

    Any sign of wood-boring insects?

    Is it dry?

Interior walls

    Any significant cracks?

    Any obvious damp problems?

    Any sign of recent repair/redecoration?

Electricity

    Check electricity meter:

        How old is it?

        What is its rated capacity?

    Check all visible wiring:

        What type is it?

        Does it appear in good physical condition?

    Check all plugs:

        Is there power to plug?

        Does plug tester show good earth and show 'OK'?

        Are there enough plugs?

    Lighting:

        Do all lights work?

        Which light fittings are included in sale?

Water

    Do all hot and cold taps work?

    Is flow adequate?

    Do taps drip?

    Is there a security cut-off on all taps between mains and tap?

    Do they seem in good condition?

    Hot water:

        Is hot water 'on'? If so, does it work at all taps, showers, etc.?

        What type of hot water system is fitted?

        Age?

Gas

    Is the property fitted with city (piped) gas? If so:

        Age of meter?

        Does installation appear in good order?

        Is there any smell of gas?

    Is the property fitted with bottled gas? If so:

        Where are bottles stored?

        Is it ventilated to outside of premises?

Checklist – Do-it-yourself Inspection of Property (*cont.*)

Task   ✓

Central Heating – is the property filled with central heating? If so:
   Is it on?
   Will it turn on?
   What type is it?
   Is there heat at all radiators/outlets?
   Do any thermostats appear to work?
   Are there any signs of leaks?

Fireplaces – is the property fitted with any solid fuel heaters? If so:
   Any sign of blow-back from chimneys?
   Do chimneys (outside) show stains from leakage?
   Do chimneys seem in good order?

Air-conditioning
   Which rooms are air-conditioned?
   Are units included in the sale?
   Do the units work (deliver cold air)?
   What type of air-conditioning is it?
   How old is it?

Phone
   Does it work?
   Number?

Satellite TV
   Does it work?
   Is it included in the sale?

Drainage
   What type of drainage does property have?
   If septic tank, how old?
   Who maintains it?
   When was it last serviced?
   Any smell of drainage problems in bathrooms and toilets?
   Does water drain away rapidly from all sinks, showers and toilets?
   Is there any inspection access through which you can see
      drainage taking place?
   Is there any sign of plant ingress to drains?
   Do drains appear to be in good condition and well pointed?

Checklist – Do-it-yourself Inspection of Property (*cont.*)

Task ✓

Kitchen

Do all cupboards open/close properly?
Any sign of rot?
Tiling secure and in good order?
Enough plugs?
What appliances are included in sale?
Do they work?
Age of appliances included?

Bathroom

Security and condition of tiling?
Ventilation?

Appliances

What appliances generally are included in sale?
What is *not* included in sale?

Furniture

What furniture is included in sale?
What is *not* included in sale?

Repairs/Improvements/Additions

What repairs have been carried out in last two years?
What improvements have been carried out in last two years/
    ten years?
What additions have been made to the property in last
    two years/ten years?
Are there builders' receipts'/guarantees?
Is there building consent/planning permission for any
    additions or alterations?

Defects

Is seller aware of any defects in the property?

Appendix 2

Checklist – What Are You Worth?

	Value €	Value £s
Current Assets		
Main home		
Holiday home		
Contents of main home		
Contents of holiday home		
Car		
Boat		
Bank accounts		
Other cash-type investments		
Bonds, etc.		
Stocks and shares		
PEPs		
Tessas		
ISAs		
SIPS		
Other		
Value of your business		
Value of share options		
Future Assets		
Value of share options		
Personal/company pension – likely lump sum		
Potential inheritances or other accretions		
Value of endowment mortgages on maturity		
Other		

Index

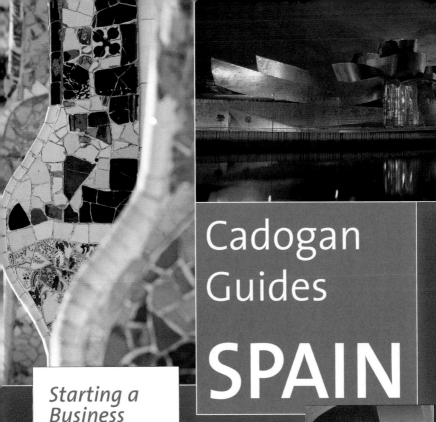

Cadogan
Guides

SPAIN

Starting a Business SPAIN

John Howell

CADOGANguides

flying visits
SPAIN
*great getaways
by budget airline & ferry*

CADOGANguides

BARCELONA

Dana Facaros & Michael Pauls

CADOGANguides

Also Available
Andalucía, Bilbao & the Basque Lands, Granada Seville Cordoba, Madrid,
Northern Spain, Pick Your Brains Spain, Working and Living Spain

CADOGANguides

*well travelled **well read***

Also available
Amsterdam
Bruges
Brussels
Edinburgh
Florence
London
Madrid
Milan
Paris
Rome

Cadogan City Guides...
the life and soul
of the city

CADOGANguides
well travelled well read

Spain touring atlas

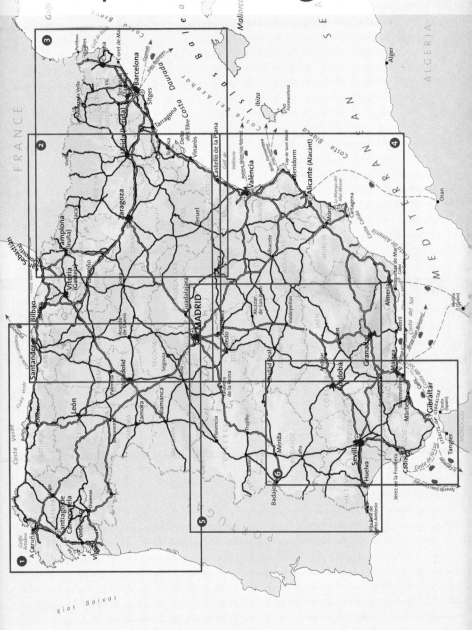

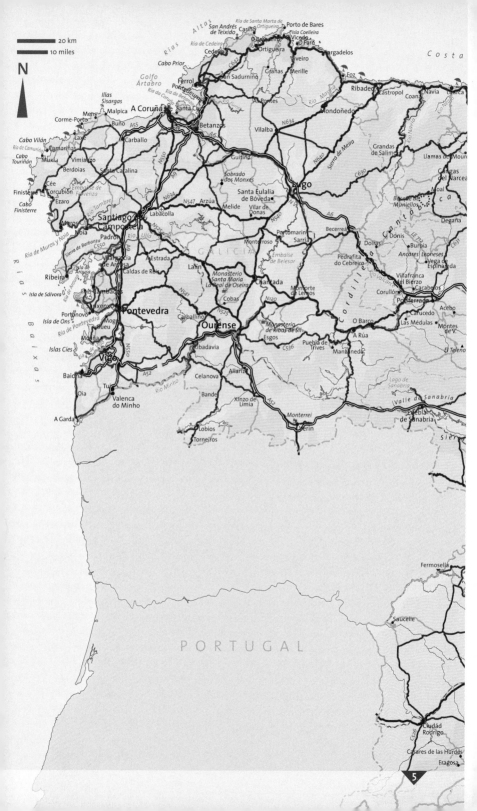

Rías Altas
Río de Santa Marta de Ortigueira
San Andrés de Teixido
Carino
Porto de Bares
Ría de Cedeira
O Barqueiro
Isla Coelleira
Vicedo
Cedeira
Ortigueira
Faro
Bargadelos
Cabo Prior
C642
Riveiro
Merille
Costa
Ría de Santa Marta
San Sadurniño
Grañas
Ferrol
Pontedeume
Ría da Coruña
Santa Cla
San Sadurniño
N634
Ría de Betanzos
A Pontes
Río Masma
Ribadeo
Castropol
Coaña
Navia
Luarca
Illas Sisargas
Golfo Ártabro
A Coruña
Betanzos
Vilalba
Mondoñedo
Monte
Corme-Porto
Mens
Malpica
Buño
AG55
Río Navia
Cabo Vilán
Laxe
Carballo
N550
Guitiriz
N634
Sierra de Meira
Lugo
Grandas de Salime
Llamas del Mouro
Ría de Camariñas
Camariñas
Vimianzo
Berdoias
Santa Catalina
A6
Sobrado dos Monxes
Santa Eulalia de Bóveda
N540
Cangas del Narcea
Moal
Cabo Touriñán
Muxía
N634
N547
Arzúa
Melide
Vilar de Donas
Becerreá
Bosque de Muniellos
Degaña
Cée
Corcubión
Embalse de Fervenza
N634
Labacolla
Santiago de Compostela
Padrón
N525
Portomarín
Sarria
Dolras
Donis
Burbia
Ancares Leoneses
Finisterre
Ezaro
Río Tambre
C550
Santiago de Compostela
G A L I C I A
Monterroso
Embalse de Belesar
Pedrafita do Cebreiro
Vega de Espinareda
Cabo Finisterre
Muros
Noia
Sierra de Barbanza
Estrada
Latín
Monasterio Santa María La Real de Oseira
Chantada
Monforte de Lemos
Villafranca del Bierzo
Corullón
Cacabelos
Ponferrada
Ría de Muros y Noia
Vilagarcía de Arousa
Caldas de Reis
N547
Cobas
N120
O Barco
Carucedo
Acebo
Ribeira
Isla de Arousa
N525
Carballino
Ourense
Monasterio de Ribas de Sil
Puebla de Trives
Manzaneda
Las Médulas
Montes de V.
Isla de Sálvora
Cambados
Sanxenxo
Pontevedra
Carballino
Esgos
C536
A Rúa
El Teleno
Isla de Ons
Portonovo
Mogor
Bueu
N550
Ribadavia
Allariz
Puebla de Trives
Islas Cíes
Moaña
Río Miño
Celanova
Bande
Xinzo de Limia
A52
Monterrei
Lago de Sanabria
Valle de Sanabria
Vigo
A52
Tui
Río Miño
Xinzo de Limia
A52
Verín
Puebla de Sanabria
Sierra
Baiona
Oia
Valença do Minho
Lobios
Torneiros
A Garda

P O R T U G A L

Fermoselle

Saucelle

Ciudad Rodrigo

C526

Casares de las Hurdes
Eragosa

20 km
10 miles

N

5

Verde

Costa Verde

Costa de Cantabria

Playa de Salinas
Capo Vidio
Cudillero
Cabo de Peñas
Luanco
Gijón
Tazones
Lastres
Villaviciosa
Cudillera
Avilés
Salas
Grado
Trubia
Oviedo
Nava
Cangas de Onis
Cueva del Buxu
Covadonga
Arenas de Cabrales
Tresviso
Llanes
Poo
Ribadesella
Peña-Tú
Cueva del Pindal
San Vicente de la Barquera
Comillas
Cuevas de Altamira
Santillana del Mar
Suances
plymouth
Cabo de Ajo
Noja
Santoña
Santander
Tieno
Langreo
Pola de Laviana
Mieres
Tuñón
Proaza
Caranga de Abajo
La Plaza
Pola de Somiedo
Reserva Nacional de Somiedo
Peña Ubiña
Tuiza
Pajares
Busdongo
Puerto de San Isidro
Puerto de Tarna
Soto de Sajambre
Picos de Europa
Posada de Valdeón
Espinama
Potes
Lebeña
Reserva Nacional de Saja
CANTABRIA
Cordillera Cantábrica
Unquera
Caberzón de la Sal
Torrelavega
Puente Viesgo
Liérganes
Puerto de Pajares
Valporquero de Torío
Mora
Riaño
Reserva Nacional de Fuentes Carrionas
Cordillera
Cantábrica
Cistierna
Alto Campoo
Cotibre
Bárcena Mayor
Embalse del Ebro
Corconte
Espinosa de los Monteros
La Parte de Sotoscueva
Soncillo
Villarcayo
C6318
Cordillera
Abano
León
San Miguel de Escalada
Almanza
Moarves
Branosera
Cervera
San Cebrián
Santa María de Mave
Alar del Rey
Aguilar de Campoo
S.Medio
Retortillo
Cervatos
Barruelo de Santullán
Cillamayor
Reinosa
Ruesga de Bistones
Ruerrero
Orbaneja del Castillo
Mata
Foncebadón
Castillo de los Polvazares
Astorga
Hospital de Órbigo
La Bañeza
N120
Valencia de Don Juan
Mansilla de las Mulas
Sahagún
Villacázar de Sirga
Pedrosa de la Vega
Renedo de la Vega
Saldaña
Carrión de los Condes
Frómista
Boadilla del Camino
Castrojeriz
Hornillos del Camino
Tardajes
Burgos
Sasamón
BURGOS
Hontoria de la Cantera
Benavente
Paredes de Nava
Becerril de Campos
E80
Palencia
Venta de Baños
Medina de Rioseco
Baños de Cerrato
Quintanilla de las Viñas
Covarrubias
Lerma
Santo Domingo de Silos
Caleruega
Gumiel de Hizán
Aranda de Duero
Peñaranda de Duero
El Campillo
Zamora
Toro
Tordesillas
Valladolid
Río Duero
Peñafiel
Plaza
La Fundía
Parque
Medina del Campo
SEGOVIA
Ledesma
Embalse de Almendra
Río Tormes
Madrigal de las Altas Torres
Arévalo
Pedraza de la Sierra
Collado Hermoso
Torrecaballeros
Segovia
San Ildefonso La Granja
Rascafría
Nacional de Caza
de Somsi
Salamanca
Alba de Tormes
Zamarramala
Ríofrío
Valsaín
Valcotos
Valdesquí
Miraflores de la Señora
La Cabre
SALAMANCA
Villacastín
Cercedilla
Navacerrada
Collado-Villa
San Agustín del Guadalix
Béjar
Sierra de la Peña de Francia
El Cabaco
La Alberca
Las Batuecas
Nuñomoral
Candelario
Las Cogotas
Ávila
AVILA
Sierra de Gredos
San Lorenzo de El Escorial
Valle de los Caídos
MADRID
Torrejón
Navarredonda de Gredos
El Tiemblo
San Martín Valdeiglesias
Toros de Guisando
Gredos

2

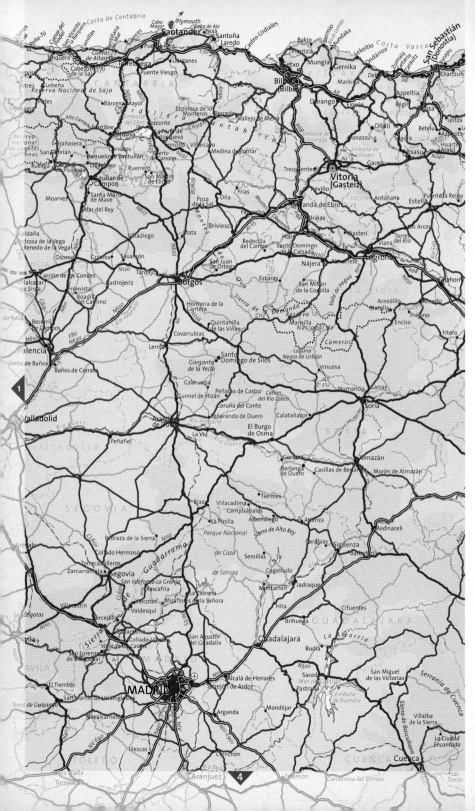

20 km
10 miles

N

FRANCE

Cabo Higuer
Fuenterrabia
Vera (Bera)
Irún
Zubieta
Lesaka
Parque Natural
Señorío de Bertiz
Urdazubi
Puerto de Izpegui
Zubieta
Elizondo
Valcarlos
Orhí
Pic d'Anie
Roncesvalles
Burguete
Ochagavía
Auñamendi
Pamplona (Iruña)
Agoitz
Noam
Roncal
Saba
Zuriza
Candanchú
Puerto de Somport
Sallent de Gállego
Balneario de Panticosa
El Formigal
Panticosa
Anso
Siresa
Echo
Canfranc
Biescas
Valle de Ordesa
Torla
Ordesa
Bielsa
Benasque
Cerler
Erill la Vall
Caldes de Boí
Espot
Parc Nacional d'Aigüestortes
Taüll
Vall d'Aran
Vielha
Túnel de Vielha
Artíes
Baqueira
Valle d'Aneu
Hoz de Arbayún
Navascués
Burgui
Berdún
Yesa
Embalse de Yesa
Javier
Jaca
Santa Cruz de la Serós
Ainsa
Graus
La Pobla de Segur
Tremp
Sangüesa
Ujué
Sos del Rey Católico
Uncastillo
Loarre
Ayerbe
Esquedas
Sierra de Guara
Alquézar
Torreciudad
Barbastro
Embalse de El Grado
Monasterio de Nuevo
Monzón
Sádaba
Villas
Ejea de los Caballeros
Huesca
HUESCA
Tafalla
Olite
Artajona
Obanos
Lumbier
Cinco Villas
Bárdenas Reales
Los
Cinca
Tudela
Sancho Abarca
Tauste
Tarazona
Borja
N122
Aragón
Zaragoza
ZARAGOZA
Río Ebro
Los Monegros
Lleida (Lérida)
Fraga
Bellpuig
CATALUÑA
La Almunia de Doña Godina
Quinto
Mequinenza
Monestir de Poblet
Cornudella
Prades
Scala Dei
Siurana
Falset
Ateca
Calatayud
Cariñena
Belchite
Embalse de Mequinenza
Hijar
Móra la Nova
Castillo Miravet
Cambrils
Miami Platja
Monasterio de Piedra
Daroca
Caspe
Alcañiz
El Pinell de Brai
Gandesa
L'Ametlla de Mar
Valderrobres
Tortosa
Delta de L'Ebre
Parc Natural de l'Ebre
Deltebre
Els Alfacs
Montalbán
Monreal del Campo
N211
Soriva
Villarluengo
Forcall
La Iglesuela del Cid
Mirambel
Morella
Vallibona
Traiguera
St Carles de la Ràpita
Reserva Nacional de los Montes Universales
La Puebla de Valverde
Cantavieja
Castellfort
Cati
Ares del Maestrat
Sant Mateu
Vinaròs
Benicarló
Teruel
TERUEL
Albarracín
Sierra de Gúdar
Valdelinares
La Virgen de la Vega
Vilafranca
Benassal
Albocàsser
Les Coves de Vinromà
Alcalà de Xivert
Peñíscola
Castillo de Xivert
Castielfabib
Ademuz
Montes Universales
Rubielos de Mora
Montanejos
Arc de Cabanes
Vilafamés
Cabanes
Benicàssim
Orpesa del Mar
Castelló de la Plana
El Grau de Castelló
Onda

3
4

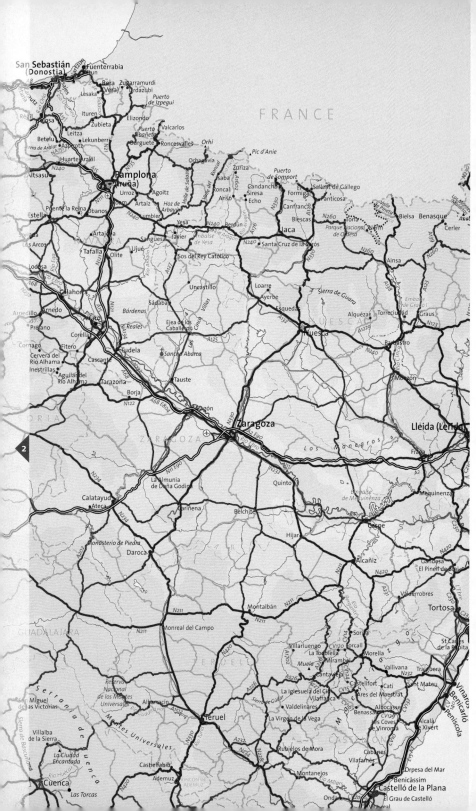

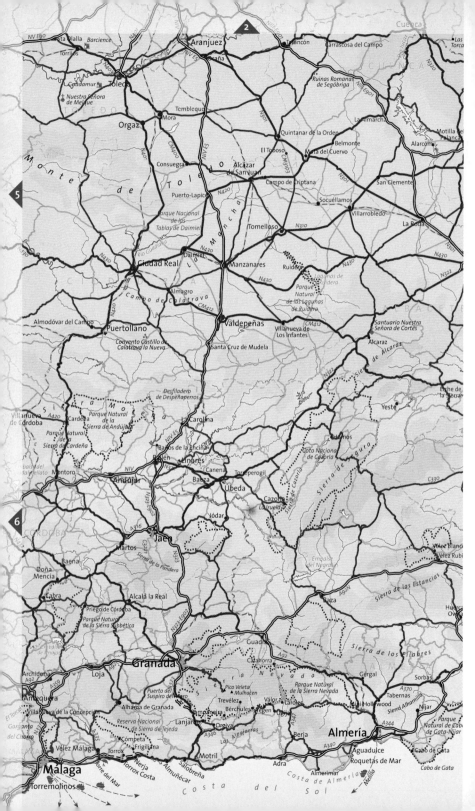

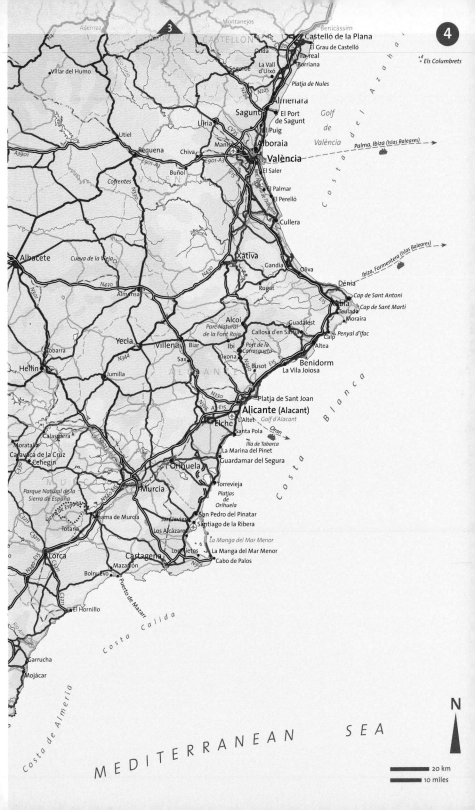

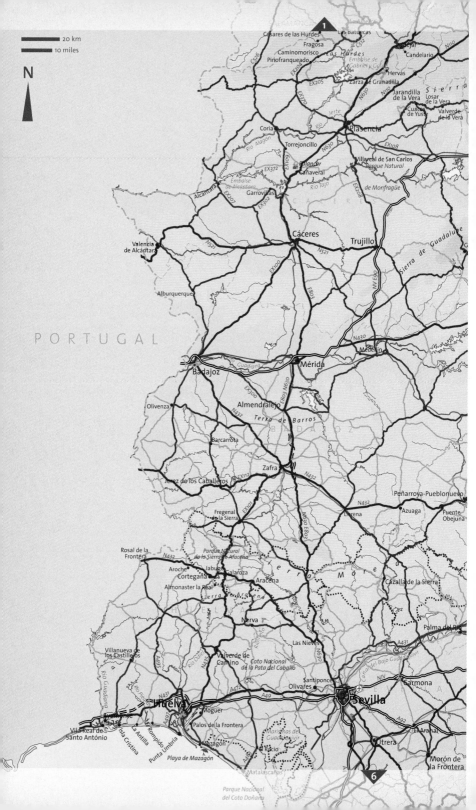

N

20 km
10 miles

Cesares de las Hurdes
Las Batuecas
Fragosa
Caminomorisco
Pinofranqueado
Las Hurdes
Embalse de Gabriel y Galán
Béjar
Candelario
Hervás
Sierra
Zarza de Granadilla
Jarandilla de la Vera
Losar de la Vera
Coria
Torrejoncillo
Plasencia
Cuacos de Yuste
Valverde de la Vera
Galisteo
Cañaveral
Villareal de San Carlos
Parque Natural
Alcántara
Garrovillas
de Monfragüe
Embalse de Alcántara
Río Tajo
Cáceres
Trujillo
Sierra de Guadalupe
Valencia de Alcántara
PORTUGAL
Alburquerque
Medellín
Badajoz
Mérida
Olivenza
Almendralejo
Tierra de Barros
Barcarrota
BADAJOZ
Zafra
Peñarroya-Pueblonuevo
Jerez de los Caballeros
Llerena
Azuaga
Fuente Obejuna
Fregenal de la Sierra
Rosal de la Frontera
Parque Natural de la Sierra de Aracena
Sierra
Morena
Cazalla de la Sierra
Aroche
Jabugo
Galaroza
Cortegana
Aracena
Almonaster la Real
Palma del Río
Nerva
A431
Villanueva de los Castillejos
Las Nieves
Valverde del Camino
Coto Nacional de la Pata del Caballo
Santiponce
Carmona
Olivares
Huelva
Sevilla
Moguer
Palos de la Frontera
Vila Real de Santo António
Isla Cristina
La Antilla
Rompido
Punta Umbría
Mazagón
Utrera
El Arahal
Playa de Mazagón
Marismas del Guadalquivir
Morón de la Frontera
Matalascañas
Parque Nacional del Coto Doñana

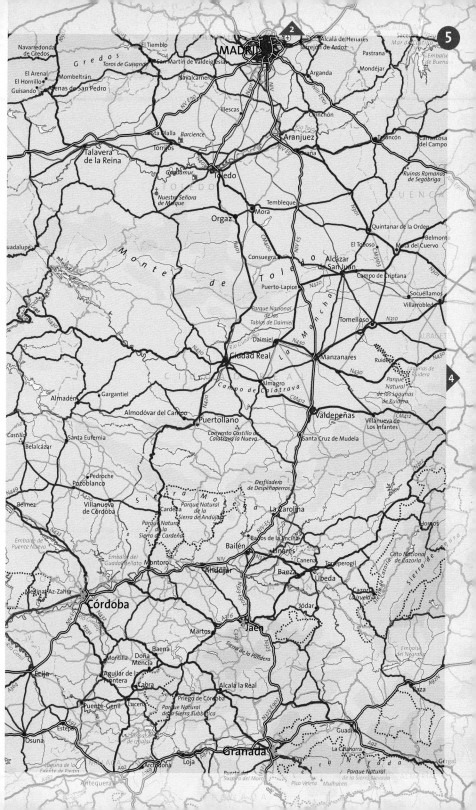

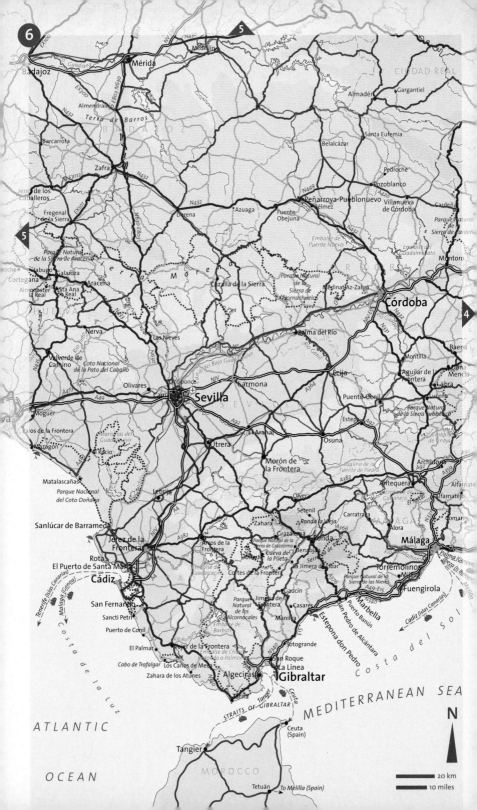

Titles available in the *Buying a Property* series

Buying a Property: France
Buying a Property: Italy
Buying a Property: Portugal
Buying a Property: Ireland
Buying a Property: Florida
Buying a Property: Greece
Buying a Property: Turkey
Buying a Property: Cyprus
Buying a Property: Eastern Europe
Buying a Property: Abroad
Buying a Property: Retiring Abroad

Related titles: *Working and Living*

Working and Living: France
Working and Living: Spain
Working and Living: Italy
Working and Living: Portugal
Working and Living: Australia
Working and Living: New Zealand
Working and Living: Canada
Working and Living: USA

Related titles: *Starting a Business*

Starting a Business: France
Starting a Business: Spain